THE NEW INTERNATIONAL
GREEK TESTAMENT COMMENTARY

Editors
I. Howard Marshall
and
W. Ward Gasque

The Epistle of
JAMES

The Epistle of
JAMES

A Commentary on the
Greek Text

by

Peter H. Davids

WILLIAM B. EERDMANS PUBLISHING COMPANY
GRAND RAPIDS, MICHIGAN / CAMBRIDGE, U.K.

THE PATERNOSTER PRESS
CARLISLE

Published jointly in the United States of America by
Wm. B. Eerdmans Publishing Co.
255 Jefferson Ave. S.E., Grand Rapids, Michigan 49503
and in the U.K. by
Paternoster Press
P.O. Box 300, Carlisle, Cumbria CA3 0QS

Printed in the United States of America

04 03 02 01 00 99   7 6 5 4 3

Library of Congress Cataloging-in-Publication Data

Davids, Peter H.
The epistle of James.
Bibliography: p. xiii.
1. Bible. N.T. James — Commentaries.   I. Title.
BS2785.3.D38   227′.91077   82-1498
ISBN 0-8028-2388-2   AACR2

British Library Cataloguing-in-Publication Data

A catalogue record for this book is available from the British Library.

ISBN 0-85364-334-2

TO
JUDITH
Beloved wife
True Helpmeet
Dearest Friend
Trusted Advisor

CONTENTS

CONTENTS

FOREWORD

While there have been many series of commentaries on the English text of
the New Testament in recent years, it is a long time since any attempt has
been made to cater particularly to the needs of students of the Greek text.
It is true that at the present time there is something of a decline in the study
of Greek in many traditional theological institutions, but there has been a
welcome growth in the study of the New Testament in its original language
in the newer evangelical schools, especially in North America and the
Third World. It is hoped that *The New International Greek Testament
Commentary* will demonstrate the value of studying the Greek New Testament and help towards the revival of such study.

The purpose of the series is to cater to the needs of students who want
something less technical than a full-scale critical commentary. At the same
time, the commentaries are intended to interact with modern scholarship
and to make their own scholarly contribution to the study of the New Testament. There has been a wealth of detailed study of the New Testament in
articles and monographs in recent years, and the series is meant to harvest
the results of this research in a more easily accessible form. The commentaries will thus include adequate, but not exhaustive, bibliographies. They
will attempt to treat all important problems of history and exegesis and
interpretation which may arise.

One of the gains of recent scholarship has been the recognition of the
primarily theological character of the books of the New Testament. This
series will, therefore, attempt to provide a theological understanding of the
text, based on historical-critical-linguistic exegesis. It will not, however,
attempt to apply and expound the text for modern readers, although it is
hoped that the exegesis will give some indication of the way in which the
text should be expounded.

Within the limits set by the use of the English language, the series aims
to be international in character; the contributors, however, have been
chosen not primarily in order to achieve a spread between different countries but above all because of their specialized qualifications for their
particular tasks. This publication is a joint venture of The Paternoster Press,
Exeter, England, and Wm. B. Eerdmans Publishing Company, Grand
Rapids, USA.

The supreme aim of this series is to serve those who are engaged in the ministry of the Word of God and thus to glorify his name. Our prayer is that it may be found helpful in this task.

I. Howard Marshall
W. Ward Gasque

PREFACE

IN the spring of 1971 Dr. Richard N. Longenecker suggested to his students at Trinity Evangelical Divinity School that "Communal Concern in the Epistle of James" would be an appropriate research topic. Little did I know that I would still be working on James in 1980. That initial research project was only partially successful, for at that time I lacked both Souček's article and R. B. Ward's thesis, but the paucity of research on James was still impressive. Later that year at the University of Manchester that observation and my interest in NT ethics interacted with a comment by Dan O. Via: "Although redaction criticism has been most closely associated with the Gospels, there is no reason why it could not be used—and actually it is being used—to illuminate the relationship between tradition and interpretation in other New Testament books" (Perrin, viii). The result of this interaction was my Ph.D. thesis, completed in 1974, "Themes in the Epistle of James that are Judaistic in Character." In this thesis I tried to show how Jewish traditions were changed when they met in the Epistle of James. It was during this writing process that I became convinced that there was a dearth of scholarly commentaries in the English language on James. The works of Mussner and Cantinat have no counterparts in English. The translation of Dibelius was helpful, but his work was basically a retouched product of 1921; neither the Qumran material nor the gains of redaction criticism are fully considered. Ropes and Mayor are over 65 years old; Mitton and Adamson are limited by their readership (particularly in their discussion of Greek). Thus when Dr. W. Ward Gasque first suggested to me in 1975 in Marburg that I might do such a project as this one, I readily agreed. I have set as my goal, however, not the replacement of the earlier works (their massive scholarship need not be simply reproduced) but (1) a clear exposition of the text of James, (2) a making available in English of the best insights of modern German and French scholarship, and (3) a supplementation of this scholarship with my own research and that of the scholarly community over the past 10 to 16 years. Thus this work will freely refer the reader to Mayor or Dibelius for useful charts, references, and other data: the attempt in this work is not to reproduce, but to collect and digest.

It is obvious that this work was not done alone. I am grateful to Dr.

Longenecker for the original inspiration and the encouragement he has given along the way, and to Dr. Paul E. Leonard for his friendship and help, particularly while in Manchester. Rev. Canon S. S. Smalley was longsuffering in his guidance of my thesis research, while Prof. F. F. Bruce offered constructive criticism at many points. Prof. Birger Gerhardsson of Lund and Mr. Lanney Mayer stimulated and advised me on the testing and *yēṣer* traditions respectively. Ms. Susan Sheldon typed the original thesis manuscript (parts of which are in this work) and Dr. James R. Moore has offered support and constructive advice through the production of this work. Dr. Timothy R. Friberg supplied to me (and allowed me to take part in the production of) a computer-generated analysis of the text of James that has been very useful in discovering grammatical patterns. At various ups and downs in the process I have been helped by Dr. W. W. Wessel and Ms. S. S. Laws with advice, good wishes, and copies of their work.

I am also grateful to those who have assisted in the physical publication of this work: Dr. W. Ward Gasque and Prof. I. Howard Marshall for their initial invitation and editorial guidance, to Mr. Peter Cousins of Paternoster Press and Mr. Marlin VanElderen of William B. Eerdmans Publishing Company and their staff for their patience, prodding, encouragement, and production efforts, to Ms. Maryanne Grafmueller, one of my students, and Ms. Gretchen Bailey for their patient typing of the manuscript (a work of supererogation to be sure!), and to my colleagues at Trinity Episcopal School for Ministry for giving me the time and other necessities for writing, especially to Dr. Stephen Noll for proofreading.

Finally I am grateful to my wife Judith, who has continually supported me in this project from America to England to Germany and back to America, through the births of three children and the death of one, and through an array of ecclesiastical and teaching situations. Without her support, not to say proofreading and suggestions, this work would never have seen the light of day. She has also continually reminded me that all of the scholarship which goes into such a work is worthless unless one takes its doctrine to heart and lives the teaching of James in the world.

                                              Ambridge, PA
                                              June 3, 1980

ABBREVIATIONS AND BIBLIOGRAPHY

1. BOOKS OF THE BIBLE

Gn., Ex., Lv., Nu., Dt., Jos., Jdg., Ru., 1, 2 Sa., 1, 2 Ki., 1, 2 Ch., Ezr., Ne., Est.,
Jb., Ps., Pr., Ec., Ct., Is., Je., La., Ezk., Dn., Ho., Joel, Am., Ob., Jon., Mi.,
Na., Hab., Zp., Hg., Zc., Mal.
Mt., Mk., Lk., Jn., Acts, Rom., 1, 2 Cor., Gal., Eph., Phil., Col., 1, 2 Thes., 1, 2
Tim., Tit., Phm., Heb., Jas., 1, 2 Pet., 1, 2, 3 Jn., Jude, Rev.

References to the OT are to the chapter and verse division in English usage;
where necessary, references to the LXX (especially in the Psalms) are added in
parentheses or brackets; references to the Hebrew text are indicated by MT.

2. OTHER ANCIENT SOURCES

Apocrypha:

Bar., 1 Esd., Jud., 1, 2 Macc., Sir., Sus., Tob., Wis.

Pseudepigrapha:

Apoc. Abr.	Apocalypse of Abraham
Apoc. Mos.	Apocalypse of Moses
Aristeas	Letter of Aristeas
Ass. Mos.	Assumption of Moses
Asc. Isa.	Ascension of Isaiah
2 Esd.	2 Esdras or 4 Ezra
Eth. Enoch	Ethiopic Enoch or 1 Enoch
Gr. Enoch	Greek Book of Enoch
Heb. Enoch	Hebrew Book of Enoch or 3 Enoch
Jub.	Book of Jubilees
Life of Adam	Life of Adam and Eve
3 Macc.	3 Maccabees
4 Macc.	4 Maccabees
Mart. Isa.	Martyrdom of Isaiah
Par. Jer.	Paralipomena Jeremias
Pss. Sol.	Psalms of Solomon
Sib.	Sibylline Oracles
Sl. Enoch	Slavonic Book of Enoch or 2 Enoch
Syr. Bar.	Syriac Apocalypse of Baruch or 2 Baruch
Test. Abr.	Testament of Abraham, cited from *The Testament of Abraham* (trans. Michael E. Stone, SBLTT 2), Missoula, Montana, 1972

Test. Job	Testament of Job, cited from *The Testament of Job* (trans. Robert A. Kraft, SBLTT 5), Missoula, Montana, 1974
Test. XII	Testaments of the Twelve Patriarchs
Test. Ash.	Testament of Asher
Test. Ben.	Testament of Benjamin
Test. Dan	Testament of Dan
Test. Gad	Testament of Gad
Test. Iss.	Testament of Issachar
Test. Jos.	Testament of Joseph
Test. Jud.	Testament of Judah
Test. Lev.	Testament of Levi
Test. Naph.	Testament of Naphtali
Test. Reub.	Testament of Reuben
Test. Sim.	Testament of Simeon
Test. Zeb.	Testament of Zebulun

Dead Sea Scrolls and Related Texts

CD	Cairo Damascus Document
1QapGen	*Genesis Apocryphon* from Qumran Cave 1
1QH	*Hodayot* (Thanksgiving Hymns) from Qumran Cave 1
1QpHab	*Pesher on Habakkuk* from Qumran Cave 1
1QM	*Milhamah* (*War Scroll*) from Qumran Cave 1
1QMyst	*Mysterion* from Qumran Cave 1
1QS	*Serek hayyahad* (*Rule of the Community* or *Manual of Discipline*) from Qumran Cave 1
1QSa	Appendix A to 1QS (*Rule of the Congregation*)
1QSb	Appendix B to 1QS (*Blessings*)
4QpPs	*Pesher on Psalms* from Qumran Cave 4
11QPs[a]	Psalms Scroll from Qumran Cave 11

Other conventional sigla may also be used.

Rabbinic Writings

Frg. Tg.   *Fragmentary Targum*
Tg. Ps.-J.   *Targum Pseudo-Jonathan*

Tractates of the Mishna:

		R. Sh.	Rosh ha-Shanah
Ab.	Aboth	Sanh.	Sanhedrin
A. Zar.	Abodah Zarah	Shab.	Shabbath
Arak.	Arakhin		
B.B.	Baba Bathra	Shebu.	Shebuoth
Ber.	Berakhoth	Sukk.	Sukkah
B. K.	Baba Kamma		
B. M.	Baba Metzia	Taan.	Taanith
Hag.	Hagigah		
Kidd.	Kiddushin		
Meg.	Megillah	Yeb.	Yebamoth
Men.	Menahoth	Yom.	Yoma
Ned.	Nedarim		

Pes. Pesahim
m. = Mishna
b. = Babylonian Talmud
Bar. = Baraita
j. = Jerusalem Talmud
t. = Tosephta

Other Conventional Sigla and Notations

Abot R. Nat.	*Abot de Rabbi Nathan*
Mek.	*Mekilta*
Midr.	*Midrash*, cited with usual abbreviation for the biblical book
Pesiq. R.	*Pesiqta Rabbati*
Pirqe R. El.	*Pirqe Rabbi Eliezer*
Rab.	*Rabbah*, cited with usual abbreviation for the biblical book.
Sipra	*Sipra*
Sipre	*Sipre*

Classical and Hellenistic Writers and Sources

Aelian	Aelian, *De Natura Animalium*
Antigonus	Antigonus Carystius, *Mirabilia*
Antiphanes	Antiphanes, *Comicus*
Aristotle	Aristotle
Eth. Eud.	*Ethica Eudemia*
Pol.	*Politica*
Q. Mech.	*Quaestiones Mechanica*
Cicero	Marcus Tullius Cicero
Nat. D.	*De Natura Deorum*
Parad.	*Paradoxa Stoicorum*
Dem.	Demosthenes
De Cor.	*De Corona*
Dio Chrys.	Dio Cocceianus, also called Chrysostomos
Diod. Sic.	Diodorus Siculus
Diog. Laert.	Diogenes Laertius
Diog. Oin.	Diogenes of Oinoanda
Dion. Hal.	Dionysius of Halicarnassus
Epict.	Epictetus (*Discourses*)
Ench.	*Enchiridon*
Galen	Galen, *De Simplicitate medicamamentum temperatum et facile*
Hdt.	Herodotus
Heracl.	Heraclitus
Homer	Homer
Od.	*Odyssey*
Isid. *Epis.*	Isidore of Pelusium, *Epistles*
Jos.	Flavius Josephus
Ant.	*Jewish Antiquities*
Ap.	*Against Apion*
War	*The Jewish War*
Lucian	Lucian
Amores	*Amores*

Bis. Accus.	*Bis Accusatus*
Dem.	*Demonax*
Herm.	*Hermotimus*
Jup. Trag.	*Juppiter Tragoedus*
Lucretius	Lucretius
M. Ant.	Marcus Aurelius Antoninus
Musonius	Musonius Rufus, *Reliquiae*
Ovid	Ovid, *Ex Ponto*
Philo	Philo of Alexandria
Abr.	*De Abrahamo*
Cher.	*De Cherubim*
Decal.	*De Decalogo*
Det. Pot. Ins.	*Quod Deterius Potiori Insidiari Soleat*
Deus Imm.	*Quod Deus Sit Immutabilis*
Ebr.	*De Ebrietate*
Exsec.	*De Exsecrationibus*
Flacc.	*In Flaccum*
Fug.	*De Fuga et Inventione*
Gig.	*De Gigantibus*
Jos.	*De Josepho*
Leg. All.	*Legum Allegoriae*
Migr. Abr.	*De Migratione Abrahami*
Mut Nom.	*De Mutatione Nominum*
Omn. Prob. Lib.	*Quod Omnis Probus Liber Sit*
Op. Mund.	*De Opificio Mundi*
Plant.	*De Plantatione*
Post. C.	*De Posteritate Caini*
Praem.	*De Praemiis et Poenis*
Prov.	*De Providentia*
Sacr.	*De Sacrificiis Abelis et Caini*
Som.	*De Somniis*
Spec. Leg.	*De Specialibus Legibus*
Virt.	*De Virtutibus*
Philostr.	Philostratus
VA	*Vita Apollonii*
Phocyl.	Phocylides
Poema Admon.	*Poema Admonitionis*
Plato	Plato
Alc.	*Alcibiades*
Menex.	*Menexenus*
Phdr.	*Phaedrus*
Rep.	*Respublica*
Symp.	*Symposium*
Pliny	Pliny the Elder
Nat. Hist.	*Naturalis Historia* (*Natural History*)
Plut.	Plutarch
Co. Ir.	*De Cohibenda Ira*
Gar.	*De Garrulitate*

Lyc.	*Lycurgus*
Mor.	*Moralia*
Per.	*Pericles*
Q. Adol.	*Quomodo Adolescens Poetas Audire Debeat*
Thes.	*Theseus*
Tranq.	*De Tranquillitate Animi*
Polyb.	Polybius
Procl.	Proclus
In Tim.	*In Platonis Timaeum Commentari*
Ps.-Cal.	Pseudo-Callisthenes
Ps.-Isocrates	Pseudo-Isocrates, *Ad Demonicum*
Ps.-Menander	Pseudo-Menander
Ps.-Phocyl.	Pseudo-Phocylides
Seneca	L. Annaeus Seneca
Benef.	*De Beneficiis*
De Clem.	*De Clementia*
Ep.	*Epistulae*
Ira	*De Ira*
Vit.	*De Vita Beata*
Simplicius	Simplicius, *In Aristotelis de Caelo Commentaria*
Soph.	Sophocles
Ant.	*Antigone*
Stob.	Iohannis Stobaeus
Ecl.	*Eclogues* (*Eklogai*)
Teles	Teles Philosophus
Thuc.	Thucydides
Hist.	*History of the Peloponnesian War*
Xen.	Xenophon
Ap.	*Apologia Socratis*
Cyr.	*Cyropaedia*
Mem.	*Memorabilia*

New Testament Apocrypha and Early Christian Writers

Act. Jn.	Acts of John
Act. Phil.	Acts of Philip
Act. Thom.	Acts of Thomas
Barn.	Epistle of Barnabas
1, 2 Clem.	1 and 2 Clement
Clem. Alex.	Clement of Alexandria
Paed.	*Paedagogus*
Strom.	*Stromateis*
Clem. *Hom.*	Pseudo-Clementine *Homilies*
Did.	Didache
Epiph.	Epiphanius
Haer.	*Haereses* (*Refutation of All Heresies*)
Euseb.	Eusebius of Caesarea
HE	*Historia Ecclesiastica*
Praep. Ev.	*Praeparatio Evangelica*

Hermas	The Shepherd of Hermas
Man.	*Mandates*
Sim.	*Similitudes*
Vis.	*Visions*
Ign.	Ignatius of Antioch
Eph.	*Letter to the Ephesians*
Mag.	*Letter to the Magnesians*
Phil.	*Letter to the Philadelphians*
Pol.	*Letter to Polycarp*
Trall.	*Letter to the Trallians*
Iren.	Irenaeus
Haer.	*Adversus Haereses*
John Dam.	John of Damascus, *De Fide Orthodoxa*
Justin	Justin Martyr
Apol.	*Apology*
Dial.	*Dialogue with Trypho*
Maximus	S. Maximus Confessor, *Quaestiones ad Thalassium* (*PG* 90)
Od. Sol.	Odes of Solomon
Origen	Origen
Hom.	*Homilies*
Polycarp	Polycarp, *Letter to the Philippians*
Ps.-Ign.	Pseudo-Ignatius, *Letter to the Ephesians*

All classical, Hellenistic, and early Christian works are cited according to standard editions (cf. LSJ) with conventional notations and sigla unless otherwise noted.

3. TEXTUAL AND OTHER SYMBOLS

The text cited in the commentary is that of *The Greek New Testament* (London, 1975³). The textual symbols employed are those used in the apparatus of this edition of the text.

4. REFERENCE WORKS, PERIODICALS, AND SERIALS

AB	Anchor Bible
AnBib	Analecta biblica
ANET	J. B. Pritchard (ed.), *Ancient Near Eastern Texts*, Princeton, 1969³
APOT	R. H. Charles (ed.), *Apocrypha and Pseudepigrapha of the Old Testament*
ASNU	*Acta seminarii neotestamentici upsaliensis*
ATANT	Abhandlungen zur Theologie des Alten und Neuen Testaments
ATR	*Anglican Theological Review*
BAG	W. Bauer, W. F. Arndt, and F. W. Gingrich, *A Greek-English Lexicon of the New Testament*, Chicago, 1957
BDF	F. Blass, A. Debrunner, and R. W. Funk, *A Greek Grammar of the New Testament*, Chicago, 1961
BeO	*Bibbia e Oriente*

BHT	Beiträge zur historischen Theologie
Bib	*Biblica*
BJRL	*Bulletin of the John Rylands University, Library of Manchester*
BWANT	Beiträge zur Wissenschaft vom Alten und Neuen Testament
BZ	*Biblische Zeitschrift*
BZNW	Beihefte zur *ZNW*
Cath	*Catholica*
CBQ	*Catholic Biblical Quarterly*
ConB	Coniectanea biblica
ConNT	*Coniectanea neotestamentica*
DAGR	*Dictionaire des Antiquités Grecques et Romaines*
DNTT	C. Brown (ed.), *Dictionary of New Testament Theology*, Exeter/Grand Rapids, I, 1975, II, 1976, III, 1978
DTT	*Dansk teologisk tidsskrift*
EBib	Etudes bibliques
EKKNT	Evangelisch-katholischer Kommentar zum Neuen Testament
ETL	*Ephemerides theologicae lovanienses*
ETR	*Etudes theologiques et religieuses*
EvQ	*Evangelical Quarterly*
EvT	*Evangelische Theologie*
Ex	*Expositor*
ExpTim	*Expository Times*
HNT	Handbuch zum Neuen Testament
HNTC	Harper's New Testament Commentaries
HTKNT	Herders theologischer Kommentar zum Neuen Testament
HTR	*Harvard Theological Review*
HUCA	*Hebrew Union College Annual*
IB	*Interpreter's Bible*
ICC	International Critical Commentary
IEJ	*Israel Exploration Journal*
Int	*Interpretation*
JAAR	*Journal of the American Academy of Religion*
JB	A. Jones (ed.), *Jerusalem Bible*
JBL	*Journal of Biblical Literature*
JQR	*Jewish Quarterly Review*
JR	*Journal of Religion*
JSS	*Journal of Semitic Studies*
JTS	*Journal of Theological Studies*
Judaica	*Judaica: Beiträge zum Verständnis*
KD	*Kerygma und Dogma*
LCL	Loeb Classical Library
LPGL	G. W. H. Lampe, *Patristic Greek Lexicon*, Oxford, 1961
LSJ	H. G. Liddell, R. Scott, and H. S. Jones, *A Greek-English Lexicon*, Oxford, 1968
LUÅ	Lunds universitets årsskrift

MeyerK	H. A. W. Meyer, *Kritisch-exegetischer Kommentar über das Neue Testament*
MHT	J. H. Moulton, W. F. Howard, and N. Turner, *Grammar of New Testament Greek*, Edinburgh, I, 1908, II, 1929, III, 1963, IV, 1976
MM	J. H. Moulton and G. Milligan, *The Vocabulary of the Greek New Testament*, London, 1930
MNTC	Moffatt New Testament Commentary
NEB	*New English Bible*
NedTTs	*Nederlands theologisch tijdschrift*
Nestle	E. Nestle (*et al.*), *Novum Testamentum Graece*, Stuttgart, 1963²⁵, 1979²⁶
NIV	*New International Version*
NICNT	New International Commentary on the New Testament (also called the New London Commentary on the New Testament)
NovT	*Novum Testamentum*
NovTSup	Novum Testamentum, Supplements
NTD	Das Neue Testament Deutsch
NTS	*New Testament Studies*
NTTS	New Testament Tools and Studies
OTS	*Oudtestamentische Studiën*
PG	J. Migne, *Patrologia graeca*
RB	*Revue biblique*
RevExp	*Review and Expositor*
RevistB	*Revista biblica*
RevQ	*Revue de Qumran*
RHPR	*Revue d'histoire et de philosophie religieuses*
RHR	*Revue de l'histoire des religions*
RNT	Regensburger Neues Testament
RSV	*Revised Standard Version*
RTQR	*Revue de théologie et de questions religieuses*
SB	Sources bibliques
SBLTT	Society of Biblical Literature Texts and Translations
SBT	Studies in Biblical Theology
SE	*Studia Evangelica* I, II, III (=TU 73 [1959], 87 [1964], 88 [1964])
SGV	Sammlung gemeinverständlicher Vorträge und Schriften
SJT	*Scottish Journal of Theology*
SP	*Studia patristica*
ST	*Studia theologica*
StB	*Studia biblica*
StBTh	Studia Biblica et Theologica
Str-B	H. Strack and P. Billerbeck, *Kommentar zum Neuen Testament*
SWJT	*Southwestern Journal of Theology*
TDNT	G. Kittel and G. Friedrich (eds.), *Theological Dictionary of the New Testament*, Grand Rapids, I–X, 1964–1976

TGl	*Theologie und Glaube*
Th	*Themelios*
THAT	E. Jenni and C. Westermann (eds.), *Theologisches Hand-wörterbuch zum Alten Testament*, München, I, 1971, II, 1976
TLb	*Theologisches Literaturblatt*
TLZ	*Theologische Literaturzeitung*
TNTC	Tyndale New Testament Commentaries
TQ	*Theologische Quartalschrift*
TRE	*Theologische Realenzyklopädie*
TRu	*Theologische Rundschau*
TU	Texte und Untersuchungen
TynB	*Tyndale Bulletin*
TZ	*Theologische Zeitschrift*
UBS³	K. Aland (*et al.*), *The Greek New Testament*, United Bible Societies, 1975³
UUÅ	Uppsala universitetsårskrift
VD	*Verbum domini*
VE	*Vox Evangelica*
Vermes	G. Vermes, *The Dead Sea Scrolls in English*, Harmonds-worth, Middlesex, 1968
VTSup	Vetus Testamentum, Supplements
WH	B. F. Westcott and F. J. A. Hort, *The New Testament in Greek*, London, 1881
WUNT	Wissenschaftliche Untersuchungen zum Neuen Testament
ZKT	*Zeitschrift für katholische Theologie*
ZNW	*Zeitschrift für neutestamentliche Wissenschaft*
ZRGG	*Zeitschrift für Religions- und Geistesgeschichte*
ZTK	*Zeitschrift für Theologie und Kirche*
Zürcher	*Zürcher Bibel*

5. COMMENTARIES AND OTHER WORKS

Adamson	J. B. Adamson, *The Epistle of James* (NICNT), Grand Rapids, 1976.
Adamson, "Inductive"	J. B. Adamson, "An Inductive Approach to the Epistle of James," Ph.D. diss., Cambridge, 1954.
Aland	K. Aland, "Der Herrnbruder Jakobus und der Jakobus-brief," *TLZ* 69 (1944) 97–104.
Alford	H. Alford, *The Greek Testament*, London, I–IV, 1857–1861.
Allen	E. L. Allen, "Controversy in the New Testament," *NTS* 1 (1954–1955) 143–149.
Althaus	P. Althaus, "'Bekenne eurer dem anderen seine Sünden': zur Geschichte von Jak 5, 16 seit Augustin," in *Festgabe für Theodor Zahn*, Leipzig, 1928, 165–194.
Amphoux	C.-B. Amphoux, "À propos de Jacques 1, 17," *RHPR* 50 (1970) 127–136.

Amphoux,   C.-B. Amphoux, "Vers une description linguistique de
"description"   l'Épître de Jacques," *NTS* 25 (1978) 58–92.
Argyle   A. W. Argyle, "Greek Among Palestinian Jews in New
                    Testament Times," *NTS* 20 (1973) 87–89.
Bacon   B. W. Bacon, "James, Epistle of," *Encyclopaedia Britan-
                    nica*[11] XV, 145–146.
Baird   W. R. Baird, Jr., "Among the Mature," *Int* 13 (1959)
                    425–432.
Baly   D. Baly, *The Geography of the Bible*, London, 1957.
Bardenhewer   O. Bardenhewer, *Der Brief des heiligen Jakobus*, Freiburg,
                    1928.
Baron   S. W. Baron, *A Social and Religious History of the Jews*,
                    New York, I–XVI, 1952–1976.
Barrett   C. K. Barrett, *A Commentary on the First Epistle to the
                    Corinthians* (HNTC), London, 1968.
Batley   J. Y. Batley, *The Problem of Suffering in the Old Testa-
                    ment*, Cambridge, 1916.
Bauer   J. B. Bauer, "Sermo Peccati," *BZ* nf 4 (1960) 122–128.
Belser   J. E. Belser, *Die Epistel des heiligen Jakobus*, Freiburg,
                    1909.
Belser,   J. E. Belser, "Die Vulgata und der griechische Text im
"Vulgata"   Jakobusbrief," *TQ* 90 (1908) 329–339.
Bennett   W. H. Bennett, *The General Epistles* (Century Bible),
                    Edinburgh, 1901.
Berger   K. Berger, "Abraham II. Im Frühjudentum und Neuen
                    Testament," *TRE* I, 372–382.
Berger,   K. Berger, *Exegese des Neuen Testaments*, Heidelberg,
Exegese   1977.
Betz   H. D. Betz, *Lukian von Samosata und das neue Testament*
                    (TU 76), Berlin, 1961.
Beyer   K. Beyer, *Semitische Syntax im Neuen Testament*, Göt-
                    tingen, 1962.
Bieder   W. Bieder, "Christliche Existenz nach dem Zeugnis der
                    Jakobusbrief," *TZ* 5 (1949) 93–113.
Birkeland   H. Birkeland, *'Ānî und 'Ānāw in den Psalmen*, Oslo,
                    1933.
Bischoff   A. Bischoff, "Tò τέλος κυρίου," *ZNW* 7 (1906) 274–
                    279.
Bishop   E. F. F. Bishop, *Apostles of Palestine*, London, 1958.
Björck   G. Björck, "Quelques cas de ἓν διὰ δυοῖν dans le Nou-
                    veau Testament et ailleurs," *ConNT* 4 (1940) 1–4.
Blackman   E. C. Blackman, *The Epistle of James* (Torch Bible Com-
                    mentaries), London, 1957.
Boismard   M.-E. Boismard, "Une Liturgie Baptismale dans la Prima
                    Petri II.—son Influence sur l'Épître de Jacques," *RB* 64
                    (1957) 161–183.
Bolkestein   H. Bolkestein, *Wohltätigkeit und Armenpflege in vor-
                    christlichen Altertum*, Utrecht, 1939.
Bonhöffer   A. F. Bonhöffer, *Epiktet und das Neue Testament*, Gies-

sen, 1911, 1964.

Bord　　　　　　J. B. Bord, *L'Extrême Onction d'après l'Épître de S. Jacques examinée dans la tradition*, Brussels, 1923.

Bornkamm　　　G. Bornkamm, *Jesus of Nazareth*, London, 1960.

Bornkamm,　　　G. Bornkamm, G. Barth, and H. J. Held, *Tradition and*
Tradition　　　*Interpretation in Matthew*, London, 1963.

Bousset　　　　W. Bousset, *Kyrios Christos*, Nashville, 1970.

Bowker　　　　J. Bowker, *The Targums and Rabbinic Literature*, Cambridge, 1969.

Bowman　　　　J. W. Bowman, *The Letter of James* (Layman's Bible Commentary 24), Richmond, 1962.

Brandt　　　　W. Brandt, "Der Spruch von lumen internum," *ZNW* 14 (1913) 177–201.

Braun　　　　　H. Braun, "Qumran und das Neue Testament," *TRu* 28 (1962) 97–234; 29 (1963) 142–176; 189–260; 30 (1964) 89–137.

Brinktrine　　　J. Brinktrine, "Zu Jak 2, 1," *Bib* 35 (1954) 40–42.

Brockington　　L. H. Brockington, "The Septuagintal Background to the New Testament Use of δόξα," in D. E. Nineham (ed.), *Studies in the Gospels* (for R. H. Lightfoot), Oxford, 1955, 1–8.

Brooks　　　　J. A. Brooks, "The Place of James in the New Testament," *SWJT* 12 (1969) 41–55.

Brown　　　　　S. Brown, *Apostasy and Perseverance in the Theology of Luke* (AnBib 36), Rome, 1969.

Bruce　　　　　F. F. Bruce, "The General Letters," in G. C. D. Howley (ed.), *A New Testament Commentary*, London, 1969.

Brushton　　　C. Brushton, "Une 'crux interpretum' Jacq. 4.5," *RTQR* 4 (1907) 368–377.

Büchler　　　　A. Büchler, *The Economic Conditions in Judea after the Destruction of the Second Temple*, London, 1912.

Bultmann　　　R. Bultmann, *Der Stil der paulinischen Predigt und die kynisch-stoische Diatribe*, Göttingen, 1910.

Bultmann,　　　R. Bultmann, *Theology of the New Testament*, London, I,
Theology　　　1952, II, 1955.

Burchard　　　C. Burchard, "Gemeinde in der strohernen Epistel," in D. Lührmann and G. Strecker (eds.), *Kirche* (für G. Bornkamm), Tübingen, 1980.

Burchard,　　　C. Burchard, "Zu Jakobus 2, 14–66," *ZNW* 71 (1980) 27–
"Jakobus"　　　45.

Burge　　　　　G. M. Burge, "'And Threw Them Thus on Paper': Recovering the Poetic Form of James 2:14–26," *StBTh* 7 (1977) 31–45.

Burkitt　　　　F. C. Burkitt, *Christian Beginnings*, London, 1924.

Burkitt,　　　　F. C. Burkitt, "The Hebrew Papyrus of the Ten Com-
"Papyrus"　　　mandments," *JQR* 15 (1903) 392–408.

Burton　　　　E. D. Burton, *Spirit, Soul, and Flesh*, Chicago, 1918.

Cadbury　　　　H. J. Cadbury, "The Single Eye," *HTR* 47 (1954) 69–74.

Cadoux　　　　A. T. Cadoux, *The Thought of St. James*, London, 1944.

Cantinat   J. Cantinat, *Les Épîtres de Saint Jacques et de Saint Jude* (SB), Paris, 1973.

Carmignac   J. Carmignac, *Recherches sur le "Notre Pere,"* Paris, 1969.

Carmignac,   J. Carmignac, "La théologie de la souffrance dans les
"théologie"   Hymnes de Qumrân," *RevQ* 3 (1961) 365–386.

Carpenter   W. B. Carpenter, *The Wisdom of James the Just*, London, 1903.

Carr   A. Carr, *The General Epistle of St. James* (Cambridge Greek Testament for Schools and Colleges), Cambridge, 1896.

Carr,   A. Carr, "The Meaning of Ο ΚΟΣΜΟΣ in James iii, 6,"
"Meaning"   *Ex* ser. 7, 8 (1909) 318–325.

Carroll   K. L. Carroll, "The Place of James in the Early Church," *BJRL* 44 (1961) 49–67.

Causse   A. Causse, *Les "Pauvres" d'Israël*, Strasbourg, 1922.

Chadwick   H. Chadwick, "Justification by Faith and Hospitality," *SP* 4/2 = TU 79 (1961) 281.

Chaine   J. Chaine, *L'Épître de Saint Jacques* (EBib), Paris, 1927.

Cirillo   L. Cirillo, "La christologie pneumatique de la cinquième parabole du Pasteur d'Hermas," *RHR* 184 (1973) 25–48.

Clark   K. W. Clark, "The Meaning of ΕΝΕΡΓΕΩ and ΚΑΤΑΡΓΕΩ in the New Testament," *JBL* 54 (1935) 93–101.

Conzelmann   H. Conzelmann, "Paulus und die Weisheit," *NTS* 12 (1966) 231–244.

Cooper   R. M. Cooper, "Prayer: a Study in Matthew and James," *Encounter* 29 (1968) 268–277.

Coppieters   H. Coppieters, "La Signification et la Provenance de la citation Jac. IV, 5," *RB* 12 (1915) 35–58.

Cranfield   C. E. B. Cranfield, "The Message of James," *SJT* 18 (1965) 182–193, 338–345.

Crenshaw   J. L. Crenshaw, "Popular Questioning of the Justice of God in Ancient Israel," *ZAW* 82 (1970) 380–395.

Cronbach   A. Cronbach, "The Social Ideas of the Apocrypha and the Pseudepigrapha," *HUCA* 18 (1944) 119–156.

Cullmann   O. Cullmann, *Christ and Time*, London, 1951.

Culter   C. R. Culter, "The Aktionsart of the Verb in the Epistle of James," Ph.D. diss., Southwestern Baptist Theological Seminary, 1959.

Dale   R. W. Dale, *The Epistle of James*, London, 1895.

Dalman   G. Dalman, *Arbeit und Sitte in Palästina*, Gütersloh, I–VII, 1928–1942.

Dalman,   G. Dalman, *Jesus-Jeshua*, London, 1929.
Jesus

Dalman,   G. Dalman, *Die Worte Jesu*, Darmstadt, 1965.
Worte

Daniélou   J. Daniélou, *The Theology of Jewish Christianity*, London, 1964.

Daube   D. Daube, *The New Testament and Rabbinic Judaism*,

London, 1956.

Davids	P. H. Davids, "Themes in the Epistle of James that are Judaistic in Character," Ph.D. diss., Manchester,1974
Davids, "Meaning"	P. H. Davids, "The Meaning of 'Απείραστος in James 1. 13," *NTS* 24 (1978) 386–392.
Davids, "Poor"	P. H. Davids, "The Poor Man's Gospel," *Th* 1 (1976) 37–41.
Davids, "Tradition"	P. H. Davids, "Tradition and Citation in the Epistle of James," in W. W. Gasque and W. S. LaSor (eds.), *Scripture, Tradition, and Interpretation* (for E. F. Harrison), Grand Rapids, 1978, 113–126.
Davies	W. D. Davies, "'Knowledge' in the Dead Sea Scrolls and Matthew 11:25–30," *HTR* 46 (1953) 113–139.
Davies, *Paul*	W. D. Davies, *Paul and Rabbinic Judaism*, London, 1962
Davies, *Setting*	W. D. Davies, *The Setting of the Sermon on the Mount*, Cambridge, 1964.
Davies, *Torah*	W. D. Davies, *Torah in the Messianic Age and/or the the Age to Come*, Philadelphia, 1952.
Deasley	A. R. G. Deasley, "The Idea of Perfection in the Qumran Texts," Ph.D. diss., Manchester, 1972.
Degenhardt	H.-J. Degenhardt, *Lukas—Evangelist der Armen*, Stuttgart, 1965.
Deissmann	A. Deissmann, *Light from the Ancient East*, London, 1927, repr. 1978.
Delling	G. Delling, "Partizipiale Gottesprädikationen in den Briefen des Neuen Testaments," *ST* 17 (1963) 1–59.
de Vaux	R. de Vaux, *Ancient Israel: Its Life and Institutions*, London, I–II, 1961.
DeWette	W. M. L. DeWette, *Kurzgefasstes exegetisches Handbuch zum Neuen Testament*, Leipzig, I–III, 1965[3].
Dibelius	M. Dibelius, *Der Brief des Jakobus* (revised by H. Greeven, MeyerK), Göttingen, 1964[11] = *James* (Hermeneia), Philadelphia, 1976 (English page numbers referred to).
Dibelius, "Motiv"	M. Dibelius, "Das soziale Motiv im Neuen Testament," in *Botschaft und Geschichte* I, Tübingen, 1953.
Drane	J. W. Drane, *Paul: Libertine or Legalist?*, London, 1975.
Drummond	J. Drummond, *The New Testament in the Apostolic Fathers*, Oxford, 1905.
Du Plessis	P. J. Du Plessis, ΤΕΛΕΙΟΣ. *The Idea of Perfection in the New Testament*, Kampen, 1959.
Dupont	J. Dupont, "Les pauvres en esprit," in *À la rencontre de Dieu* (au A. Gelin), Le Puy, 1961, 265–272.
Easton	B. S. Easton, *The Epistle of James* (*IB* 12), New York, 1957.
Easton, "Lists"	B. S. Easton, "New Testament Ethical Lists," *JBL* 51 (1932) 1–12.
Eckart	K.-G. Eckart, "Zur Terminologie des Jakobusbriefes," *TLZ* 89 (1964) 521–526.

Edlund   C. A. E. Edlund, *Das Auge der Einfalt* (*ASNU* 19), Lund, 1952.

Edsman   C.-M. Edsman, "Schöpferwille und Geburt. Jac. 1, 18," *ZNW* 38 (1939) 11–44.

Eichholz   G. Eichholz, *Glaube und Werk bei Paulus und Jakobus*, Munich, 1961.

Eichholz, *Jakobus*   G. Eichholz, *Jakobus und Paulus*, Munich, 1953.

Eichrodt   W. Eichrodt, *Theology of the Old Testament*, London, I, 1964, II, 1967.

Eichrodt, "Vorsehungsglaube"   W. Eichrodt, "Vorsehungsglaube und Theodizee im Alten Testament," in A. Alt (ed.), *Festschrift Otto Procksch*, Leipzig, 1934, 45–70.

Ekstrom   J. O. Ekstrom, "The Discourse Structure of the Book of James," International Linguistics Center, Dallas, Texas, n.d.

Eleder   F. Eleder, "Jakobusbrief und Bergpredigt," Ph.D. diss., Vienna, 1966.

Elliott-Binns   L. E. Elliott-Binns, *Galilean Christianity* (SBT 1/16), London, 1956.

Eliott-Binns, "James I. 18"   L. E. Elliott-Binns, "James I. 18: Creation or Redemption?", *NTS* 3 (1956) 148–161.

Elliott-Binns, "James i. 21"   L. E. Elliott-Binns, "James i. 21 and Ezekiel xvi. 36: An Odd Coincidence," *ExpTim* 66 (1955) 273.

Elliott-Binns, "Meaning"   L. E. Elliott-Binns, "The Meaning of ὕλη in Jas. III. 5," *NTS* 2 (1955) 48–50.

Ellis   E. E. Ellis, "Wisdom and Knowledge in 1 Corinthians," in *Prophecy and Hermeneutic in Early Christianity*, Tübingen, 1978, 45–62 = *TynB* 25 (1974) 82–98.

Exler   F. X. J. Exler, *The Form of the Ancient Greek Letter*, Washington, 1923.

Fabris   R. Fabris, "La 'Legge' della Libertà in Giac. 1:25, 2:12," Ph.D. diss., Pontifical Biblical Institute, Rome, 1972.

Feuillet   A. Feuillet, "Jésus et le sagesse divine d'après les Évangiles synoptiques," *RB* 62 (1955) 161–196.

Feuillet, "sens"   A. Feuillet, "Le sens du mot Parousie dans l'Évangile de Matthieu," in W. D. Davies and D. Daube (eds.), *The Background of the New Testament and its Eschatology* (for C. H. Dodd), Cambridge, 1956.

Findlay   J. A. Findlay, "James iv. 5, 6," *ExpTim* 37 (1926) 381–382.

Flusser   D. Flusser, "Qumran and Jewish 'Apotropaic' Prayers," *IEJ* 16 (1966) 194–205.

Fonjallaz   O. Fonjallaz, "Le probleme de l'Épître de Jacques," Ph.D. diss., Lausanne, 1965.

Forbes   P. B. R. Forbes, "The Structure of the Epistle of James," *EvQ* 44 (1972) 147–153.

Francis   F. O. Francis, "The Form and Function of the Opening and Closing Paragraphs of James and I John," *ZNW* 61 (1970) 110–126.

Friesenhahn   H. Friesenhahn, "Zur Geschichte der Überlieferung Exegese des Textes bei Jak V, 14f," *BZ* 24 (1938) 185–190.

Furnish   V. P. Furnish, *The Love Command in the New Testament*, Nashville, 1972.

Geffcken   J. Geffcken, *Kynika und Verwandtes*, Heidelberg, 1909.

Gelin   A. Gelin, *Les Pauvres de Yahvé*, Paris, 1953.

Gerhardsson   B. Gerhardsson, *The Testing of God's Son* (ConB 2), Lund, 1966.

Gerhardsson,   B. Gerhardsson, "The Parable of the Sower and Its Interpretation," *NTS* 14 (1968) 165–193.
"Parable"

Gertner   M. Gertner, "Midrashic Terms and Techniques in the New Testament: the Epistle of James, a Midrash on a Psalm," *SE* 3 (1964) 463 = TU 88.

Gertner,   M. Gertner, "Midrashim in the New Testament," *JSS* 7 (1962) 267–292.
"Midrashim"

Ginzberg   L. Ginzberg, *The Legends of the Jews*, Philadelphia, I–IX, 1909–1938.

Gnilka   J. Gnilka, "Die Kirche des Matthäus und die Gemeinde von Qumrân," *BZ* nf 7 (1963) 43–63.

Godet   F. Godet, *Studies in the New Testament*, London, 1876.

Goodenough   E. R. Goodenough, *Jewish Symbols in the Greco-Roman Period*, New York, I–XII, 1953–1965.

Goodspeed   E. J. Goodspeed, *An Introduction to the New Testament*, Chicago, 1937.

Gordon   R. P. Gordon, "καὶ τὸ τέλος τοῦ κυρίου εἴδετε (Jas. 5, 11)," *JTS* 26 (1975) 91–95.

Gotaas   D. Gotaas, "The Old Testament in the Epistle to the Hebrews, the Epistle of James, and the Epistle of Peter," Ph.D. diss., Northern Baptist Theological Seminary, Chicago, 1958.

Gowan   D. E. Gowan, "Wisdom and Endurance in James," paper read at the Eastern Great Lakes Biblical Society, Pittsburgh, 1980.

Grant   F. C. Grant, *The Economic Background of the Gospels*, Oxford, 1926.

Graves   A. W. Graves, "The Judaism of James," Ph.D. diss., Southern Baptist Theological Seminary, Louisville, 1942.

Greeven   H. Greeven, "Jede Gabe is gut, Jak 1, 17," *TZ* 14 (1958) 1–13.

Grill   S. Grill, "Der Schlachttag Jahwes," *BZ* nf 2 (1958) 278–283.

Guillaume   A. Guillaume, "The Midrash in the Gospels," *ExpTim* 37 (1926) 394.

Guthrie   D. Guthrie, "The Development of the Idea of Canonical Pseudepigrapha in New Testament Criticism," *VE* 1 (1962) 4–59.

Guthrie,   D. Guthrie, *New Testament Introduction*, Downers Grove, Illinois, 1970³.
Introduction

Hadidian   D. Y. Hadidian, "Palestinian Pictures in the Epistle of James," *ExpTim* 63 (1952) 227–228.

Hadorn   F. Hadorn, *Christus will den ganzen Menschen*, Zurich,
                  1953.
Hadot   J. Hadot, *Penchant mauvais et volenté libre dans la sagesse
                  de Ben Sira*, Brussels, 1970.
Halston   B. R. Halston, "The Epistle of James: 'Christian Wis-
                  dom?'", *SE* 4 (1968) 308–314 = TU 102.
Hamann   H. P. Hamann, "Faith and Works in Paul and James,"
                  Lutheran Theological Journal 9 (1975) 33–41.
Hamman   A. Hamman, "Prière et culte dans la lettre de St. Jacques,"
                  ETL 34 (1958) 35–47.
Hatch   W. H. P. Hatch, "Note on the Hexameter in James 1:17,"
                  JBL 28 (1909) 149–151.
Hauck   F. Hauck, *Die Briefe des Jakobus, Petrus, Judas und
                  Jakobus* (NTD 3), Göttingen, 1937.
Heichelheim   F. M. Heichelheim, "Roman Syria," in T. Frank (ed.),
                  An Economic Survey of Ancient Rome, Baltimore, IV,
                  1938, 121–257.
Henderlite   R. Henderlite, "The Epistle of James," *Int* 3 (1949) 460–476.
Hengel   M. Hengel, *Property and Riches in the Early Church*,
                  London, 1974.
Hiers   R. H. Hiers, "Friends by Unrighteous Mammon," *JAAR*
                  38 (1970) 30–36.
Hill   R. Hill, "An Analysis of James 3–5 to the Paragraph Con-
                  stituent Level," International Linguistics Center, Dallas,
                  Texas, 1978.
Hoppe   R. Hoppe, *Der theologische Hintergrund des Jakobus-
                  briefes* (Forschung zur Bibel 28), Würzburg, 1977.
Hort   F. J. A. Hort, *The Epistle of St. James*, London, 1909.
Humbert   P. Humbert, "Le mot biblique *'ebyôn*," *RHPR* 32 (1952) 1–6.
Huther   J. E. Huther, *Critical and Exegetical Handbook to the
                  General Epistles of James and John* (MeyerK), Edinburgh,
                  1882.
Jacob   I. Jacob, "The Midrashic Background for James II, 21–23,"
                  NTS 22 (1975) 457–464.
Jeremias   J. Jeremias, "Jac 4, 5: epipothei," *ZNW* 50 (1959)
                  137–138.
Jeremias,   J. Jeremias, *Jerusalem in the Time of Jesus*, London,
    Jerusalem   1969.
Jeremias,   J. Jeremias, *Neutestamentliche Theologie*, Gütersloh,
    Theologie   1973².
Jeremias,   J. Jeremias, "Paul and James," *ExpTim* 66 (1954–1955)
    "Paul"   368–371.
Jeremias,   J. Jeremias, *The Prayers of Jesus* (SBT 2/6), London,
    Prayers   1967.
Jocelyn   H. D. Jocelyn, "*Horace*, Epistles 1," *Liverpool Classical
                  Monthly* 4 (1979) 145–146.
Jocz   J. Jocz, "God's 'Poor' People," *Judaica* 28 (1972) 7–29.
Johanson   B. C. Johanson, "The Definition of 'Pure Religion' in

James 1:27 Reconsidered," *ExpTim* 84 (1973) 118–119.

Jones, P.   P. R. Jones, "Approaches to the Study of the Book of James," *RevExp* 66 (1969) 425–434.

Jones, R.   R. B. Jones, *The Epistles of James, John, and Jude*, Grand Rapids, 1961.

Judge   E. A. Judge, *The Social Pattern of Christian Groups in the First Century*, London, 1960.

Kamlah   E. Kamlah, *Die Form der katalogischen Paränese im Testament* (WUNT 7), Tübingen, 1964.

Keck   L. E. Keck, "The Poor Among the Saints in the New Testament," *ZNW* 56 (1965) 100–129.

Kelsey   M. Kelsey, *Healing and Christianity*, London, 1973.

Kennedy   H. A. A. Kennedy, "The Hellenistic Atmosphere of the Epistle of James," *Ex* ser. 8, 2 (1911) 37–52.

Kidd   B. J. Kidd, *Documents Illustrative of the History of the Church*, London, I–III, 1923.

Kilpatrick   G. D. Kilpatrick, "Übertreter des Gesetzes, Jak 2:11," *TZ* 23 (1967) 433.

King   G. H. King, *A Belief that Behaves*, Fort Washington, Pennsylvania, 1941.

Kirk   J. A. Kirk, "The Meaning of Wisdom in James," *NTS* 16 (1969) 24–38.

Kittel   G. Kittel, "Der geschichtliche Ort des Jakobusbriefes," *ZNW* 41 (1942) 71–105.

Kittel, "Jakobusbrief"   G. Kittel, "Der Jakobusbrief und die apostolischen Väter," *ZNW* 43 (1950) 54–112.

Kittel, Probleme   G. Kittel, *Die Probleme des palästinensischen Spätjudentums*, Stuttgart, 1926.

Kittel, "Stellung"   G. Kittel, "Die Stellung des Jakobus zu Judentum und Heidenchristentum," *ZNW* 30 (1931) 145–157.

Kittel, "τροχόν"   G. Kittel, "τὸν τροχὸν τῆς γενέσεως," *TLb* Beilege I, 141ff.

Klausner   J. Klausner, *Jesus of Nazareth*, London, 1925.

Klostermann   E. Klostermann, "Zum Texte des Jakobusbriefes," in W. Foerster (ed.), *Verbum Dei* (für O. Schmitz), Witten, 1953.

Knowling   R. J. Knowling, *The Epistle of St. James*, London, 1904.

Knox   W. L. Knox, "The Epistle of St. James," *JTS* 46 (1945) 10–17.

Koch   R. Koch, "Die Wertung des Besitzes im Lukasevangelium," *Bib* 38 (1957) 151–169.

Korn   J. H. Korn, ΠΕΙΡΑΣΜΟΣ. *Die Versuchung des Gläubigen in der griechischen Bibel* (BWANT), Stuttgart, 1937.

Krauss   S. Krauss, *Talmudische Archäologie*, Leipzig, I–III, 1910–1912.

Kromrei   G. Kromrei, *Sozialismus aus Glauben*, Stuttgart, 1948.

Kugelman   R. Kugelman, *James and Jude*, Wilmington, Delaware, 1980.

Kümmel	W. G. Kümmel, *Introduction to the New Testament*, London, 1966.
Kürzdorfer	K. Kürzdorfer, "Der Charakter des Jakobusbriefes," Ph.D. diss., Tübingen, 1966.
Kuschke	A. Kuschke, "Arm und reich im Alten Testament," *ZAW* 57 = nf 16 (1939) 31–57.
Kutsch	E. Kutsch, "Eure Rede aber sei ja ja, nein nein," *EvT 20* 20 (1960) 206–218.
Laws	S. Laws, *A Commentary on the Epistle of James*, London, 1980.
Laws, "Ethics"	S. S. Laws, "The Doctrinal Basis for the Ethics of James," *SE* (forthcoming).
Laws, "Scripture"	S. S. Laws, "Does Scripture Speak in Vain?" *NTS* 20 (1974) 210–215 (cf. S. S. C. Marshall).
Leaney	A. R. C. Leaney, "Eschatological Significance of Human Suffering in the Old Testament and the Dead Sea Scrolls," *SJT* 16 (1963) 286–296.
Légasse	S. Légasse, "Les pauvres en esprit et les 'volontaires' de Qumran," *NTS* 8 (1962) 336–345.
Lightfoot	J. B. Lightfoot, *Saint Paul's Epistle to the Galatians*, London, 1896.
Lindblom	J. Lindblom, "Wisdom in the Old Testament Prophets," in M. Noth and D. W. Thomas (eds.), *Wisdom in Israel and in the Ancient Near East* (for H. H. Rowley) (VTSup 3), Leiden, 1955, 192–204.
Lindemann	A. Lindemann, *Paulus im ältesten Christentum* (BHT 58), Tübingen, 1979.
Lohmeyer	E. Lohmeyer, *The Lord's Prayer*, London, 1965.
Lohse	E. Lohse, "Glaube und Werke — zur Theologie des Jakobus," *ZNW* 48 (1957) 1–22.
Longenecker	R. N. Longenecker, *The Christology of Early Jewish Christianity* (SBT 2/17), London, 1970.
Longenecker, *Exegesis*	R. Longenecker, *Biblical Exegesis in the Apostolic Period*, Grand Rapids, 1975.
Longenecker, *Paul*	R. N. Longenecker, *Paul, Apostle of Liberty*, Grand Rapids, 1976.
Luck	U. Luck, "Der Jakobusbrief und die Theologie des Paulus," *TGl* 61 (1971) 161–179.
Luck, "Weisheit"	"Weisheit" und Leiden; zum Problem Paulus und Jakobus," *TLZ* 92 (1967) 253–258.
Luff	S. G. A. Luff, "The Sacrament of the Sick," *Clergy Review* 52 (1967) 56–60.
Lührmann	D. Lührmann, *Glaube im frühen Christentum*, Gütersloh, 1976.
Lys	D. Lys, *L'Onction dans la Bible* (ETR), Montpellier, 1954.
MacGorman	J. W. MacGorman, "Introducing the Book of James," *SWJT* 12 (1969) 9–22.
McNeile	A. H. McNeile, *Introduction to the Study of the New*

Testament, Oxford, 1953².

Malina
B. J. Malina, "Some Observations on the Origin of Sin in Judaism and St. Paul," *CBQ* 31 (1969) 18–34.

Manson
T. W. Manson, "The Lord's Prayer," *BJRL* 38 (1955) 99–113, 436–448.

Marmorstein
A. Marmorstein, "The Background of the Haggadah," *HUCA* 6 (1926) 141–204 = *Studies in Jewish Theology*, Oxford, 1950, 1–71.

Marmorstein, *Doctrine*
A. Marmorstein, *The Doctrine of Merits in Old Rabbinic Literature*, London, 1920.

Marshall
S. S. C. Marshall, "The Character, Setting, and Purpose of the Epistle of St. James," Ph.D. diss., Oxford, 1968.

Marshall, "Δίψυχος"
S. S. C. Marshall, "Δίψυχος: A Local Term?", *SE* 6 (1969) 348–351 = TU 112 (1973).

Martin
R. P. Martin, "The Life-Setting of the Epistle of James in the Light of Jewish History," in G. A. Tuttle (ed.), *Biblical and Near Eastern Studies* (for W. S. LaSor), Grand Rapids, 1978, 97–103.

Martin, *Foundations*
R. P. Martin, *New Testament Foundations*, Grand Rapids, I, 1975, II, 1978.

Martin-Achard
R. Martin-Achard, "Yahwé et les 'ᵃnāwīm," *TZ* 21 (1965) 349–357 = *Approche des Psaumes*, Neuchâtel, 1969, 18–25.

Marty
J. Marty, *L'Épître de Jacques*, Paris, 1935.

Maston
T. B. Maston, "Ethical Dimensions of James," *SWJT* 12 (1969) 23–39.

Mayor
J. B. Mayor, *The Epistle of St. James*, London, 1913³.

Meecham
H. G. Meecham, "The Epistle of James," *ExpTim* 49 (1937) 181–183.

Meinertz
M. Meinertz, *Der Jakobusbrief*, Bonn, 1921.

Meinertz, "Krankensalbung"
M. Meinertz, "Die Krankensalbung Jak 5, 14f," *BZ* 20 (1932) 23–36.

Metzger
B. M. Metzger, *A Textual Commentary on the Greek New Testament*, London, 1971.

Meyer
A. Meyer, *Das Rätsel des Jakobusbriefes*, Giessen, 1930.

Michaelis
W. Michaelis, *Das Ältestenamt*, Bern, 1953.

Michl
J. Michl, *Die Katholischen Briefe* (RNT 8), Regensburg, 1968².

Michl, "Spruch"
J. Michl, "Der Spruch Jakobusbrief 4, 5," in J. Blinzler (*et al.*, eds.), *Neutestamentliche Aufsätze* (für J. Schmid), Regensburg, 1963, 167–174.

Minear
P. S. Minear, "Yes or No, The Demand for Honesty in the Early Church," *NovT* 13 (1971) 1–13.

Miranda
J. Miranda, *Marx and the Bible*, Maryknoll, New York, 1974.

Mitton
C. L. Mitton, *The Epistle of James*, London, 1966.

Moffatt
J. Moffatt, *The General Epistles* (MNTC), London, 1928.

Molin
G. Molin, "Der Prophet und sein Weiterleben in den Hoff-

nungen des Judentums und der Christenheit," *Judaica* 8 (1952) 65–94.

Moore, A.   A. L. Moore, *The Parousia in the New Testament*, Leiden, 1966.

Moore, G.   G. F. Moore, *Judaism in the First Centuries of the Christian Era,* Cambridge, Massachusetts, I–III, 1927–1930.

Motyer   J. A. Motyer, *The Tests of Faith,* London, 1970.

Moule   C. F. D. Moule, *An Idiom Book of New Testament Greek,* Cambridge, 1968.

Moulton   J. H. Moulton, "The Epistle of James and the Sayings of Jesus," *Ex* ser. 7, 4 (1907) 45–55.

Murphy   R. E. Murphy, "*Yēṣer* in the Qumran Literature," *Bib* 39 (1958) 334–344.

Mussner   F. Mussner, *Der Jakobusbrief* (HTKNT 13/1), Freiburg, 1967².

Mussner, "Christologie"   F. Mussner, "'Direkte' und 'indirekte' Christologie im Jakobusbrief," *Cath* 24 (1970) 111–117.

Mussner, "Tauflehre"   F. Mussner, "Die Tauflehre des Jakobusbriefes," in H. auf der Maur and B. Kleinheyer (eds.), *Zeichen des Glaubens* (für B. Fischer), Zurich, 1972, 61–67.

Nauck   W. Nauck, "Freude im Leiden," *ZNW* 46 (1955) 68–80.

Nauck, "Lex"   W. Nauck, "Lex inculpta in der Sektenschrift," *ZNW* 46 (1955) 138–140.

Navone   J. Navone, *Themes of St. Luke,* Rome, 1970.

Noack   B. Noack, "Jacobsbrevet sem Kanonisk skrift," *DTT* 27 (1964) 163–173.

Noack, "Jakobus"   B. Noack, "Jakobus wider die Reichen," *ST* 18 (1964) 10–25.

Noret   J. Noret, "Une Scholie de l'Epître de Jacques tirée de Syméon Métaphraste," *Bib* 55 (1974) 74–75.

Nötscher   F. Nötscher, "'Gesetz der Freiheit' im NT und in der Mönchsgemeinde am Toten Meer," *Bib* 34 (1953) 193–194.

Nötscher, *Terminologie*   F. Nötscher, *Zur theologischen Terminologie der Qumrantexte,* Bonn, 1956.

Obermüller   R. Obermüller, "¿ Contaminacion? En torno a una definicion de la religion (Sant. 1, 27)," *RevistB* 34 (1972) 13–19.

Obermüller, "Themen"   R. Obermüller, "Hermeneutische Themen im Jakobusbrief," *Bib* 53 (1972) 234–244.

O'Callaghan   J. O'Callaghan, "New Testament Papyri in Qumrān Cave 7?" sup. to *JBL* 91 (1972) 1–14 = *Bib* 53 (1972) 91–100 (Spanish).

Oesterley   W. E. Oesterley, *The General Epistle of James* (Expositor's Greek Testament 4), London, 1910.

Orbiso   T. A. Orbiso, "Zelus pro errantium conversione," *VD* 32 (1954) 193–208.

Osborn   E. Osborn, *Ethical Patterns in Early Christian Thought,* Cambridge, 1976.

Parry   R. St. J. Parry, *A Discussion of the General Epistle of*

St. James, London, 1903.

Peake   A. S. Peake, The Problem of Suffering in the Old Testament, London, 1904.

Pearson   B. A. Pearson, The Pneumatikos-Psychikos Terminology in 1 Corinthians, Missoula, Montana, 1973.

Percy   E. Percy, Die Botschaft Jesu (LUÅ I Avd. 49, 5), Lund, 1953.

Perrin   N. Perrin, What is Redaction Criticism? London, 1970.

Peterson   E. Peterson, ΕΙΣ ΘΕΟΣ, Göttingen, 1926.

Pichar   C. Pichar, "'Is anyone sick among you?'", CBQ 7 (1945) 165–174.

Plummer   A. Plummer, The General Epistles of St. James and St. Jude (Expositor's Bible), London, 1891.

Plumptre   E. H. Plumptre, The General Epistle of St. James (Cambridge Bible for Schools and Colleges), Cambridge, 1876.

Polhill   J. B. Polhill, "The Life-Situation of the Book of James," RevExp 66 (1969) 369–378.

Porter   F. C. Porter, The Yeçer Hara: A Study in the Jewish Doctrine of Sin (Biblical and Semitic Studies), New York, 1902, 93–156.

Powell   C. H. Powell, "'Faith' in James and its Bearing on the Problem of the Date of the Epistle," ExpTim 62 (1950) 311–314.

Prentice   W. K. Prentice, "James, the Brother of the Lord," in P. R. Coleman-Norton (ed.), Studies in Roman Economic and Social History (for A. C. Johnson), Princeton, 1951, 144–151.

Preuschen E. Preuschen, "Jac 5, 11," ZNW 17 (1916) 79.

Radermacher L. Radermacher, "Der erste Petrusbrief und Silvanus," ZNW 25 (1926) 287–299.

Rahlfs   A. Rahlfs, ʿĀnî und ʿĀnāw in den Psalmen, Göttingen, 1892.

Rankin   O. S. Rankin, Israel's Wisdom Literature, Edinburgh, 1936.

Reicke   B. I. Reicke, The Epistles of James, Peter and Jude (AB), Garden City, New York, 1964.

Reicke,   B. I. Reicke, Diakonie, Festfreude und Zelos (UUÅ, 1951),
Diakonie   Uppsala, 1951.

Reicke,   B. I. Reicke, "Traces of Gnosticism in the Dead Sea
"Gnosticism" Scrolls?", NTS 1 (1964) 137–141.

Rendall   G. H. Rendall, The Epistle of St. James and Judaic Christianity, Cambridge, 1927.

Rendtorff H. Rendtorff, Hörer und Täter, Hamburg, 1953.

Resch   A. Resch, "Agrapha," TU 14/2 (1896) 253.

Riesenfeld H. Riesenfeld, "Von Schätzesammeln und Sorgen," in H. Baltensweiler (ed.), Neotestamentica et Patristica (für O. Cullmann), Leiden, 1962, 47–58.

Rigaux   B. Rigaux, "Révélation des mystères et perfection à Qumran et dans le Nouveau Testament," NTS 4 (1959) 237–262.

Roberts   D. J. Roberts, "The Definition of 'Pure Religion' in James
                 1:27," *ExpTim* 83 (1972) 215–216.
Robertson   A. T. Robertson, *A Grammar of the Greek New Testa-
                 ment in the Light of Historical Research,* Nashville, 1934.
Robinson   J. A. T. Robinson, *Redating the New Testament,* Lon-
                 don, 1976.
Ropes   J. H. Ropes, *A Critical and Exegetical Commentary on the
                 Epistle of St. James* (ICC), Edinburgh, 1916.
Ross   A. Ross, *The Epistles of James and John* (NICNT), Grand
                 Rapids, 1967.
Rost   L. Rost, "Archäologische Bemerkungen zu einer Stelle
                 des Jakobusbriefes (Jak. 2, 2f.)," *Palästinajahrbuch* 29
                 (1933) 53–66.
Rountree   C. Rountree, "Further Thoughts on the Discourse Struc-
                 ture of James," International Linguistics Center, Dallas,
                 Texas, 1976.
Rusche   H. Rusche, *L'Épître de Saint Jacques (Lumières Bib-
                 liques),* Le Puy, n.d.
Rustler   K. Rustler, "Thema und Disposition des Jakobusbriefes,"
                 Ph.D. diss., Vienna, 1952.
Rylaarsdam   J. C. Rylaarsdam, *Revelation in Jewish Wisdom Literature,*
                 Chicago, 1946.
Salmon   G. Salmon, *A Historical Introduction to the Study of the
                 Books of the New Testament,* London, 1894[7].
Sanday   W. Sanday, "Some Further Remarks on the Corbey St.
                 James (*ff*)," *StB* 1 (1885) 233–263.
Sanders, E.   E. P. Sanders, *Paul and Palestinian Judaism,* Philadelphia,
                 1977.
Sanders, J. A.   J. A. Sanders, *Suffering as Divine Discipline in the Old
                 Testament and Post-Biblical Judaism,* Rochester, New
                 York, 1955.
Sanders, J. T.   J. T. Sanders, *Ethics in the New Testament,* Philadelphia,
                 1975.
Schammberger   H. Schammberger, *Die Einheitlichkeit des Jakobusbriefes
                 im antignostischen Kampf,* Gotha, 1936.
Scharbert   J. Scharbert, *Der Schmerz im Alten Testament,* Bonn, 1955.
Schechter   S. Schechter, *Some Aspects of Rabbinic Theology,* London,
                 1909.
Schlatter   A. Schlatter, *Der Brief des Jakobus,* Stuttgart, 1932.
Schmithals   W. Schmithals, *Paul and James* (SBT 1/46), London, 1965.
Schnackenburg   R. Schnackenburg, *The Moral Teaching of the New Testa-
                 ment,* London, 1965.
Schneider   J. Schneider, *Die Briefe des Jakobus, Petrus, Judas und
                 Johannes* (NTD 10), Göttingen, 1961.
Schökel   L. A. Schökel, "James 5, 2 [sic] and 4, 6," *Bib* 54 (1973)
                 73–76.
Schoeps   H. J. Schoeps, *Theologie und Geschichte des Judenchris-
                 tentums,* Tübingen, 1949.

Schrage   W. Schrage, *Der Jakobusbrief*, in H. Balz and W. Schrage
                   (eds.), *Die Katholischen Briefe* (NTD 10), Göttingen, 1973[11].
Schürer   E. Schürer, *The History of the Jewish People in the Age of
                   Jesus Christ* (revised and edited by G. Vermes and F. Mil-
                   lar), Edinburgh, I, 1973, II, 1979.
Schürmann   H. Schürmann, *Das Gebet des Herrn*, Leipzig, 1957.
Schwarz   G. Schwarz, "'Ihnen gehört das Himmenreich?' (Matthäus
                   v. 3)," *NTS* 23 (1977) 341–343.
Seitz   O. J. F. Seitz, "Afterthoughts on the Term 'Dipsychos,'"
                   NTS 4 (1958) 327–334.
Seitz,   O. J. F. Seitz, "Antecedents and Significance of the Term
"Antecedents"   ΔΙΨΥΧΟΣ," *JBL* 66 (1947) 211–219.
Seitz,   O. J. F. Seitz, "James and the Law," *SE* 2 (1964) 472–486
"James"   = TU 87 (1964).
Seitz,   O. J. F. Seitz, "The Relationship of the Shepherd of
"Relationship"   Hermas to the Epistle of James," *JBL* 63 (1944) 131–140.
Seitz,   O. J. F. Seitz, "Two Spirits in Man: An Essay in Biblical
"Spirits"   Exegesis," *NTS* 6 (1959) 82–95.
Selwyn   E. G. Selwyn, *The First Epistle of St. Peter*, London, 1947.
Sevenster   J. N. Sevenster, *Do You Know Greek?* (NovTSup 19), Lei-
                   den, 1968.
Shepherd   M. H. Shepherd, "The Epistle of James and the Gospel of
                   Matthew," *JBL* 75 (1956) 40–51.
Sidebottom   E. M. Sidebottom, *James, Jude and 2 Peter* (Century
                   Bible), London, 1967.
Sisti   A. Sisti, "La parola e le opere (Giac. 1, 22–27)," *BibOr* 6
                   (1964) 78–85.
Smalley   S. S. Smalley, "The Delay of the Parousia," *JBL* 83 (1964)
                   41–54.
Smith, C.   C. R. Smith, *The Bible Doctrine of Salvation*, London, 1946.
Smith, G.   G. A. Smith, *Jerusalem*, London, I, 1907, II, 1908.
Smith, H.   H. M. Smith, *The Epistle of S. James*, Oxford, 1914.
Smith, M.   M. L. Smith, "James 2:8," *ExpTim* 21 (1910) 329.
Smyth   H. W. Smyth, *Greek Grammar*, Cambridge, Massachu-
                   setts, 1956.
Souček   J. B. Souček, "Zu den Problemen des Jakobusbriefes,"
                   EvT 18 (1958) 460–468.
Souter   A. Souter, *The Text and Canon of the New Testament*,
                   London, 1913.
Spicq   C. Spicq, "ΑΜΕΤΑΜΕΛΗΤΟΣ dans *Rom.*, XI, 29," *RB*
                   67 (1960) 210–219.
Spitta   F. Spitta, *Der Brief des Jakobus untersucht*, Göttingen, 1896.
Spitta,   F. Spitta, "Das Testaments Hiobs und das Neue Testament,"
"Testaments"   in *Zur Geschichte und Literatur des Urchristentums*, Göt-
                   tingen, 1907, III/2, 139–206.
Stacey   W. D. Stacey, *The Pauline View of Man in Relation to its
                   Judaic and Hellenistic Background*, London, 1956.
Stählin   G. Stählin, "Zum Gebrauch von Beteuerungsformeln im Neu-

en Testament," *NovT* 5 (1962) 115–143.

Stamm   J. J. Stamm, *Das Leiden des Unschuldigen in Babylon und Israel* (ATANT 10), Zürich, 1946.

Stauffer   E. Stauffer, "Zum Kalifat des Jakobus," *ZRGG* 4 (1952) 193–214.

Stauffer, "Gesetz"   E. Stauffer, "Das 'Gesetz der Freiheit' in der Ordensregel von Jericho," *TLZ* 77 (1952) 527–532.

Stendahl   K. Stendahl, *Paul Among Jews and Gentiles*, Philadelphia, 1976.

Stiglmayr   P. J. Stiglmayr, "Zu Jak. 3,6: Rota nativitatis nostrae inflammata," *BZ* 2 (1913) 49–52.

Strauss   L. Strauss, *James Your Brother*, Neptune, New Jersey, 1956.

Strobel   A. Strobel, *Untersuchungen zum eschatologischen Verzögerungsproblem* (NovTSup 2), Leiden, 1961.

Stuhlmacher   P. Stuhlmacher, *Der Brief an Philemon* (EKKNT), Neukirchen, 1975.

Sumner   J. B. Sumner, *Practical Exposition of the General Epistles of James, Peter, John, and Jude*, London, 1840.

Sutcliffe   E. F. Sutcliffe, *Providence and Suffering in the Old and New Testaments*, London, 1955.

Tasker   R. V. G. Tasker, *The General Epistle of James* (TNTC), London, 1956.

Taylor   C. Taylor, "St. James and Hermas," *ExpTim* 16 (1905) 334.

Tennant   F. R. Tennant, *The Sources of the Doctrine of the Fall and of Original Sin*, Cambridge, 1903.

Thomas   J. Thomas, "Anfechtung und Vorfreude," *KD* 14 (1968) 183–206.

Thrall   M. E. Thrall, *Greek Particles in the New Testament* (NTTS 3), Grand Rapids, 1962.

Thyen   H. Thyen, *Der Stil der Jüdisch-Hellenistischen Homile*, Göttingen, 1935.

Torakawa   K. Torakawa, "Literary-Semantic Analysis of James 1–2," International Linguistics Center, Dallas, Texas, 1978.

Townsend   M. J. Townsend, "James 4:1–4," *ExpTim* 87 (1975) 211–213.

Trench   R. C. Trench, *Synonyms of the New Testament*, London, 1876[8].

Trocmé   E. Trocmé, "Les Eglises pauliniennes vue du dehors: Jacques 2, 1 à 3, 12," *SE* II (1964) 660–669.

Urbach   E. E. Urbach, *The Sages*, Jerusalem, 1975.

van der Ploeg   J. van der Ploeg, "Les pauvres d'Israël et leur piété," *OTS* 7 (1950) 236–270.

van Eysinga   G. A. van den Bergh van Eysinga, "De Tong . . . en Erger! Proeve van Verklarung van Jakobus 3, vs. 6," *NedTTs* 20 (1931) 303–320.

van Unnik   W. C. van Unnik, "The Teaching of Good Works in I Peter," *NTS* 1 (1954) 92–110.

Vermes	G. Vermes, *Jesus the Jew*, London, 1973.
Via	D. O. Via, "The Right Strawy Epistle Reconsidered," *JR* 49 (1969) 261–262.
Völter	D. Völter, "Zwei neue Wörter für das Lexicon des griechischen Neuen Testaments?", *ZNW* 10 (1909) 326–329.
von Campen-hausen	H. von Campenhausen, *Die Askese im Urchristentum* (SGV 192), Tübingen, 1949.
von Campen-hausen, "Nachfolge"	H. von Campenhausen, "Die Nachfolge des Jakobus zur Frage eine urchristlichen 'Kalifats,'" *ZKT* 63 (1950) 133–144.
von Rad	G. von Rad, *Old Testament Theology*, London, I, 1962, II, 1965.
von Waldow	H. E. von Waldow, "Social Responsibility and Social Structure in Early Israel," *CBQ* 32 (1970) 182–204.
Walker	R. Walker, "Allein aus Werken. Zur Auslegung von Jakobus 2, 14–26," *ZTK* 61 (1965) 155–192.
Ward	R. B. Ward, "The Communal Concern of the Epistle of James," Ph.D. diss., Harvard, 1966.
Ward, "Partiality"	R. B. Ward, "Partiality in the Assembly: James 2:2–4," *HTR* 62 (1969) 87–97.
Ward, "Works"	R. B. Ward, "The Works of Abraham: James 2:14–26," *HTR* 61 (1968) 283–290.
Wessel	W. W. Wessel, "An Inquiry into the Origin, Literary Character, Historical and Religious Significance of the Epistle of James," Ph.D. diss., Edinburgh, 1953.
Wibbing	S. Wibbing, *Die Tugend- und Lasterkataloge im Neuen Testament* (BZNW 25), Berlin, 1959.
Wichmann	W. Wichmann, *Die Leidenstheologie: eine Form der Leidensdeutung im Spätjudentum* (BWANT 4/2), Stuttgart, 1930.
Wifstrand	A. Wifstrand, "Stylistic Problems in the Epistles of James and Peter," *ST* 1 (1948) 170–182.
Williams, N.	N. P. Williams, *The Ideas of the Fall and of Original Sin*, London, 1927.
Williams, R.	R. R. Williams, *The Letters of John and James* (Cambridge Bible Commentary), Cambridge, 1965.
Windisch	H. Windisch, *Die Katholischen Briefe* (HNT 15), Tübingen, 1951.
Wolverton	W. I. Wolverton, "The Double-minded Man in the Light of the Essene Psychology," *ATR* 38 (1956) 166–175.
Wordsworth	J. Wordsworth, "The Corbey St. James (ff) and its Relation to Other Latin Versions and to the Original Language of the Epistle," *StB* 1 (1885) 113–123.
Yadin	Y. Yadin, *The Scroll of the War of the Sons of Light against the Sons of Darkness*, Oxford, 1962.
Yoder	J. H. Yoder, *The Politics of Jesus*, Grand Rapids, 1972.
Young	F. W. Young, "The Relation of I Clement to the Epistle of James," *JBL* 67 (1948) 339–345.

Zahn	T. Zahn, *Introduction to the New Testament*, Edinburgh, I–III, 1909.
Ziegler	J. Ziegler, *Die Liebe Gottes bei den Propheten*, Münster, 1930.
Ziener	G. Ziener, *Die theologische Begriffssprache im Buche der Weisheit*, Bonn, 1956.
Ziesler	J. A. Ziesler, *The Meaning of Righteousness in Paul*, Cambridge, 1972.

INTRODUCTION

T HE Epistle of James has long languished in comparative neglect while its more famous sister-letters in the Pauline corpus (not to say the synoptic gospels) enjoyed the limelight of NT research. Perhaps Luther's overrated disparaging remarks were the cause of this, turning German Lutheran scholarship aside and directing it to the more christological Pauline literature, or perhaps its small size, obscure position (tucked in as it is behind the mighty book of Hebrews), and apparent disjointedness produced the effect without Luther's assistance, but the fact stands that the mainstreams of scholarly interest have flowed in other directions.

Now, however, there are signs that this pall of obscurity is coming to an end. New interest in the work has been sparked by the appearance of several commentaries over the last decade. In 1964 two major commentaries appeared, H. Greeven's updating of M. Dibelius's work and F. Mussner's own fine work. Since then there have been significant updates of most of the series aimed at the pastor: J. Michl, C. L. Mitton, R. R. Williams, B. Reicke, W. Schrage, and J. B. Adamson are a few examples. More recently J. Cantinat has produced a major French work replacing J. Marty's now dated masterpiece, and S. S. Laws has added an original work in English. All of this interest has been matched by an upsurge in journal articles and theses on the epistle.

But this activity has only reopened questions that have been hovering over this work ever since the turn of the century, questions of author and provenance, certainly, but more especially questions of structure, purpose, and theology. It is toward these questions that this introduction aims, attempting to make some contribution by using tradition-critical and (to the extent possible) redaction-critical methodology to apply the insights which in many cases others have discovered. In doing this it pays little attention to the questions others have thoroughly answered: their works are available for consultation. This essay wishes rather to point up some of the still-to-be-answered questions and to make an approach toward answering them on the basis of the following commentary on the text.

1

I. AUTHORSHIP AND DATE

One cannot discuss the background of a book unless he has a good idea of its date in history. Thus, the debate over the dating of James[1] leaves some of the conclusions concerning its background open to question. Conversely, discoveries concerning the Jewish background of the book support some theories about its date more strongly than others. In the case of this epistle, authorship is related to its date, for if one must date it in its present form within the lifetime of James the Just, the Lord's brother, then this James probably wrote the work, or at least provided its major source.[2] Therefore one cannot separate the discussion of date and authorship of James into two discussions—it is properly a single issue.

1. The Major Historic Positions

The traditional position on the authorship and date of James definitely appeared by AD 253 (the death of Origen) and established itself firmly by the end of the fourth century (Jerome, Augustine, and the Council of Carthage). From then until the sixteenth century James was generally accepted as coming from the hand of James the Just while he presided over the church in Jerusalem (roughly AD 40–62, the lower limit being the less clear). Luther, like Erasmus,[3] attributed the work to another pious Christian named James due to internal evidence, but criticism of the epistle remained muted in the church until the rise of its modern criticism with DeWette in 1826.[4] Three new major lines of thought appeared after him.[5]

The first major new line of thought, chronologically as well as in order of presentation, dates the epistle later than the lifetime of James the

1. In this commentary "James" and "the epistle" will refer to the Epistle of James. The author of the work will be referred to as "the author" or "James" without implying either unitary authorship or a particular person as author. The term "James the Just" will refer to James the brother of Jesus, popularly known as the first bishop of Jerusalem.

2. Elliott-Binns, 43–52, is the one major exception. He believes one must date the work early, but he holds to a Galilean, non-Jacobean authorship, arguing that 1:1 is an interpolation. Kennedy, 37–52, could argue for a similar date with Hellenistic authorship, but does not state a clear preference. Spitta dates the epistle earlier than James the Just; Meyer and Easton date it later, although their positions do not require this.

3. Ropes, 45. Erasmus, according to Ropes, had doubts, but only Luther definitely denied apostolic authorship (including James the Just as an apostle).

4. Hort, xii, claims that Kern in 1835 was the first modern scholar to deal with the criticism of James, but Ropes, 46, is correct in claiming that DeWette preceded Kern in his *Einleitung* of 1826. Cf. DeWette, III, 192–193, who there confirms the position he took 39 years earlier in his *Einleitung*.

5. Table 1 (p. 4) gives a summary of the positions held by the various scholars; it is not a complete list, but does give a large number of the scholars of this present century who have taken clear positions. Schammberger, 7–32, presents in a long essay data on the interpretation of James between Kern (1835) and Schlatter (1932). The main weakness in this article is that it ignores English scholarship completely (e.g. Ropes, Hort, Mayor, Knowling) and misses one or two important Germans (e.g. DeWette).

Just. Harnack, Jülicher, and the Tübingen School, who dated the epistle late in the second century because of its apparent synthesis of Jewish Christian and Pauline concepts, represent the more radical form of this position.[6] Recent scholars holding this general position usually date the book in the last quarter of the first century or very early in the second century, assigning the work to a pseudonymous author.[7] Scholars holding this general position stress the epistle's late attestation, its good Greek, its Greek rather than Jewish thought and form, and its dependence upon some version of Paulinism (usually a Paulinism dependent upon Romans and Galatians, if not these letters themselves).

The second and more recent new line of thought believes that the epistle depends upon material coming from James the Just, either in oral or written form, but that in its final form the epistle represents a reworking of and adding to this material. Burkitt holds this position, but on unsubstantial evidence, claiming the epistle is a free translation of an Aramaic original.[8] On the other hand, W. L. Knox has elaborated a more easily defended form of this position, carefully separating the various layers of material he believes are present.[9] The arguments for a Hellenistic origin of this epistle put forward by the first group impress these scholars, but they also accept those arguments which point toward a primitive Jewish Christian or Palestinian Jewish origin for much of the material. Thus this position is a compromise attempting to solve a difficult dilemma.

The third new line of thought argues for a purely Jewish origin for James with later Christian reworking or interpolations. In its simplest form, F. Spitta and L. Massebieau independently originated this theory, arguing that James represents a pre-Christian Jewish work taken over into Christianity by the simple addition of two interpolations, one at 1:1 and one at 2:1.[10] Arnold Meyer, followed by Easton and Thyen, intrigues the reader by arguing that James is an address of the patriarch Jacob to the twelve tribal fathers, his sons, each represented allegorically by a characteristic virtue, vice, or action. On first examination this theory sounds very plausible and exciting, for it explains some of the difficulties of the

6. This extreme position is virtually abandoned today. Cf. Mayor, clxxviii–cxcii.

7. Except for Moffatt, 2, who believes a James wrote it, but not James the Just. Windisch, 3, does not directly attribute any of the tradition to James the Just, but his theory allows for a core of it to come from him. For an evaluation of the question of pseudonymity and a history of the development of these theories, cf. Guthrie.

8. Burkitt, 69–70. "The original was no doubt in Aramaic; what we have is a rendering, not very literal, into Greek." His evidence is one place where he claims there is a mistranslation: in 3:6 ὁ κόσμος is an error where '*lm*' was read for *m'ln'*, "entrance."

9. Knox, 10–17. He claims that the epistle consists of a text, probably from James the Just, divided between sections of Hellenistic commentary. Chap. 2 is a complete, additional Hellenistic diatribe. In some places in chaps. 4 and 5 he is not certain about the source of the material.

10. Spitta wrote the more famous work in 1896, but Massebieau preceded him by a year. Of the two passages, 2:1 shows the most evidence in favor of an interpolation theory, as even Mayor, cxciii–cxciv, admits.

TABLE 1

REPRESENTATIVE POSITIONS ON THE DATING OF JAMES

JEWISH ORIGIN	JAMES THE JUST	POST-JACOBEAN
pre-James the Just	early (AD 40–50)	partial authorship
L. Massebieau 1895	R. J. Knowling 1904	W. O. E. Oesterley 1910
F. Spitta 1896	T. Zahn 1909	F. C. Burkitt 1924
	J. B. Mayor 1910	W. L. Knox 1945
post-James the Just	G. H. Rendall 1927	H. Windisch 1951?
A. Meyer 1930	G. Kittel 1942	E. C. Blackman 1957
H. Thyen 1955	W. W. Wessel 1953	
R. Bultmann 1955?	A. Ross 1954	pseudonymous
B. S. Easton 1957	D. Guthrie 1964	authorship (AD 70–130)
	J. A. T. Robinson 1976	B. W. Bacon 1911
non-Jacobean, but early		J. H. Ropes 1916
L. E. Elliott-Binns 1956	no preference (AD 40–62)	J. Moffatt 1928
	J. H. Moulton 1907	B. H. Streeter 1928
	A. Schlatter 1932	J. Marty 1935
	J. Schneider 1961	E. J. Goodspeed 1937
	F. Mussner 1964	F. Hauck 1937
	J. Michl 1968	F. Young 1948
	J. Adamson 1976	H.-J. Schoeps 1949
		H. Windisch 1951?
	late (AD 51–62)	A. H. McNeile 1953
	W. H. Bennett 1901	R. Bultmann 1955
	R. St. J. Parry 1903	M. H. Shepherd, Jr. 1956
	F. J. A. Hort 1909	M. Dibelius 1964, 1976
	J. Chaine 1927	B. Reicke 1964
	R. V. G. Tasker 1956	W. G. Kümmel 1966
	C. L. Mitton 1966	S. S. C. Marshall
	E. M. Sidebottom 1967	(Laws) 1968
	F. F. Bruce 1969	W. Schrage 1973
		J. Cantinat 1973
		S. Laws 1980

Notes: 1. This selection includes only works of this century: the following older commentators favor the early date: H. Alford (1859), E. H. Plumptre (1878), J. Huther (1882), A. Plummer (1891), G. Salmon (1894), A. Carr (1899). F. Godet (1876) favored the later date.

2. The dates listed after the names are normally those of the latest edition of the work in which the author states a preference.

work, especially the address in 1:1. But Meyer disappoints us in his identifications of the tribes, for most of his identifications are very weak and the better ones are for Isaac, Rebecca, and several non-Israelite nations— none of them sons of Jacob.[11] Both Meyer and Spitta, however, have a strong case for the essentially Jewish nature of the epistle, explaining away the evidence for a Hellenistic origin.

The traditional position has not lacked defenders, but it has split into two distinct positions. Parry and Tasker exemplify one position, which argues that James the Just wrote the work, but that he did it late in his life, c. AD 60–62.[12] These men believe that the settled and widespread nature of the church indicates a later date. But their belief that Jas. 2:14– 26 argues against a distorted form of Paulinism and is thereby probably later than Galatians and Romans decides the question. This position is, therefore, a conservative version of the first new line of thought mentioned above.

On the other hand, Mayor and Kittel argue that James the Just wrote the work early in his leadership of the Jerusalem church. A probable date would be just prior to the Jeusalem Council.[13] This group of scholars believes that the evidence points to a primitive stage of church development and doctrine before the rise of Paulinism and before the controversy over the admission of gentile converts into the church. Jewish practices are not defended—they are assumed.

One wishes he could brush aside one or more of these positions and so come up with a firm solution, but this is not the case. Strong evidence and careful argumentation support each of these positions in its best form. Therefore, only a careful review of the evidence will produce even the possibility of selecting a working hypothesis for this commentary.

2. Direct Claims

The best type of evidence would be the testimony of a reliable contemporary of the author, identifying the author and the work clearly (e.g. with quotations from the work). Lacking this, as is so obviously the case, one must scan the work itself for its own claim to a date of composition. Not even this evidence appears, but 1:1 does assert that the epistle is written by one called James, and this name could be a clue to the date of the work.

11. Meyer. Both Easton, 10–11, and Thyen, 16, follow Meyer and see some analogy with Test. XII. Thyen's teacher, Bultmann, *Theology*, II, 143, allows that the epistle is very likely a Jewish work taken over by Christians, but he does not favor any particular Jewish theory: "Every shred of understanding for the Christian's position as that of 'betweenness' is lacking here. The moralism of the synagogue tradition has made its entry, and it is possible that James not merely stands in the general context of this tradition but that its author took over a Jewish document and only lightly retouched it."

12. Parry, 99–100; Tasker, 20, 31.

13. Mayor, cxix–cli; Kittel. Kittel expands his ideas in two other articles, the last answering criticisms by K. Aland.

The identification of this James, however, constitutes an interpretative problem. At this point one does not need to consider the authenticity of the self-designation, but only its meaning, to have an interpretative task. If one could accept A. Meyer's thesis stated above, then 1:1 has little significance for the dating of the epistle. But despite its initial attractiveness, we must dispense with Meyer's hypothesis as improbable because of the weakness of his identifications.[14] Moffatt believes that 1:1 designates some otherwise unknown teacher of the church named James as the author.[15] This is certainly possible, but not probable, for what teacher of so little significance that he is now unknown would take it upon himself to address such a significant portion of the church (i.e. the twelve tribes), let alone in such weighty tones? One can also rule out some well-known Jameses: James the son of Zebedee probably died too early to leave any literary remains,[16] and James the son of Alphaeus drops from sight so completely that he (and James the Little, if he is other than the son of Alphaeus) faces the same problems that Moffatt's unknown James does—he was too unimportant to have been able to get away with such a simple self-designation. Mitton, in arguing against identifying the name in 1:1 with a poorly known James, states four reasons for preferring James the Just: (1) tradition must have had some good reason for assigning the letter to James the Just, not to one of the apostolic Jameses, (2) the letter fits what is known about James the Just, (3) only James the Just had the authority this letter claims, and (4) the letter corresponds in some respects to Luke's record of James the Just.[17] One may question Mitton's second and fourth reasons, but Kümmel still gives a good summary of the overall value of the evidence: "Indeed, in primitive Christianity there was only one James who was so well known and who assumed such a transcending position that his mere name would identify him sufficiently, James the brother of the Lord. Without doubt, James purports to be written by him."[18]

But one immediately asks if 1:1 is original. Could it not be a gloss resulting from the later tradition?[19] In answer to this one can point to a

---

14. See above, pp. 3–5. Meyer includes a chart containing his identifications that is helpful in grasping his thesis. If one could construct a form of his hypothesis that lacked the detailed identifications with their apparent improbability (i.e. which made the epistle a general address of Jacob to his sons), he would have a better hypothesis (in essence Spitta's theory). But all theories of Jewish origin founder on the amount of Christian material in this epistle; cf. below, pp. 14–16.

15. Moffatt, 2. Luther's position (p. 2 above) also fits here.

16. Acts 12 indicates that he died before AD 44, ruling out the probability, although not the possibility, of his writing the epistle.

17. Mitton, 229–231. Most supporters of James the Just's authorship state similar reasons; Mitton's are simply the most concise, even if stated in too concrete terms.

18. Kümmel, 290.

19. Elliott-Binns, 47–48. Blackman, 25, gives qualified approval to a form of this thesis.

firm textual tradition and the probability that part of 1:2 requires 1:1,[20] but these considerations do not rule out the possibility of 1:1 being a gloss. Even if it is not a gloss, does it necessarily indicate authorship? On the one hand, it might be just a pseudonym, or, on the other hand, it might be the designation of the patron of this parenesis.[21] This last suggestion gives more meaning to the name than a purely pseudonymous use does. Therefore, it is the more probable theory. But one must decide between these theories and actual authorship, and he must do this on the basis of the arguments for and against authenticity and those supporting one date-authorship combination over against another.

3. External Evidence

Lacking convenient direct support for any certain date, we turn to the external evidence for the date and authorship of James. This external evidence itself presents a problem, for direct attestation is both weak and late. Origen made the first clear reference to James as both being written by James the Just and being scripture.[22] The Western church did not completely accept the epistle until the end of the following century (the Synod of Hippo, AD 393 and the Third Council of Carthage, AD 397), although Jerome (with some reservations) and Augustine accepted it prior to the Council. While the Catechism of Cyril, Gregory of Nazianzus, and Athanasius cite it as canonical, Theodore of Mopsuestia rejected it, the pre-Peshitta Syriac did not include it, and Eusebius, although using it himself as scripture, cites it among the ἀντιλεγόμενα.[23]

This evidence is negative. The epistle lacks early attestation; the East accepted it before the West. By its very nature the evidence cannot ex-

20. Some scholars point out that in 1:2 πᾶσαν χαρὰν ἡγήσασθε, ἀδελφοί μου seems to require 1:1 to identify to whom he is writing; cf. Windisch, 3.

21. Dibelius, 24–30. Windisch, 3, claims that the full title is Διδαχὴ Ἰακώβου ταῖς δώδεκα φυλαῖς ταῖς ἐν τῇ διασπορᾷ. He adds that "Diese 'Lehre des Jakobus' besteht aus zwölf-lose zusammengefügten Spruchreihen" similar to Jewish wisdom books and Hellenistic parenetic material.

22. The exact date of the reference is unknown. It must have been before his death in AD 253. Mayor, lxvi–lxxxiv, offers the best compilation of citations of and allusions to James before AD 397.

23. Mayor, lxvi–lxix. Cf. Kidd, II, 130; Guthrie, *Introduction*, 737; and Souter, 220–226, who points out that (1) the Roman Canon, the Peshitta, the Council of Carthage, Augustine, Jerome (*Letter to Paulinus*), and Athanasius's Festal Letter 39 all accepted or listed James (AD 367–435); and (2) the Syriac Canon, the African Canon of 360, and the Doctrine of Addai all omit James. The last work mentioned is very exclusive: "The Law and the Prophets and the Gospel . . . and the Epistles of Paul . . . and the Acts of the Twelve Apostles . . . these books read ye in the church of God and with these read not others." This evidence shows acceptance beginning in Egypt and spreading north and west. Theories which claim a limited circulation for the epistle would have an easier time if the early Syriac evidence were more favorable. Only theories claiming an Egyptian provenance find this evidence easy to deal with. The Nag Hammadi Codices also witness to the prevalence of Jacobean traditions in Egypt.

plain the reason for this silence. While the evidence certainly allows for theories which entail late, nonapostolic authorship, a theory of limited interest in and circulation of the epistle would also explain the evidence.[24] Carr points out how this evidence has disturbed more than just modern minds: "The [early] doubt as to the authenticity of the Epistle seems to have arisen not from any improbability of the alleged authorship, or from erroneous doctrine contained in it, but from the absence of citation by succeeding writers."[25] No one directly cites the book for one hundred to one hundred twenty-five years after it was completed.[26] Any theory finds it hard to explain this fact. It forces one to look carefully for evidence to disprove that it accurately represents the early use of James.

Perhaps, then, indirect external evidence exists for James that would help to fill in this curious gap. J. B. Mayor claims to find such indirect evidence and fills fourteen pages with allusions to James by the early church fathers, the clearest being those in 1 Clement and the Shepherd of Hermas.[27] The allusions in Hermas are strong enough that both Moffatt and Laws use them to establish a *terminus ad quem* for the book of AD 90.[28] Yet the allusions have a problem: they consist of the common use of rare vocabulary, the common treatment of similar themes, or the common use of similar ideas. They do not consist of the common use of syntactical units large enough to absolutely prove dependence of the one on the other. Even if such quotations were present, the direction of borrowing could be either way, or both James and the work with which it is compared could be borrowing from some third work.[29] An overall comparison of the way James treats themes with the way they are treated in the Apostolic Fathers, however, reveals that probability is on the side of James's being the earlier work. Yet, such an argument must necessarily

24. Guthrie, *Introduction*, 737–739, argues for such a theory of disinterest in the epistle resulting from its noncontroversial nature, which would have been of little use in the antignostic battle. At the same time its Jewishness would have repelled the gnostics. Of course to accept this contention one must reject Schammberger's assertions that the letter is in fact antignostic.

25. Carr, ix.

26. One does not find a date later than the mid-second century proposed by post-Tübingen writers. Thus the latest possible date would be 100 years before Origen, the earliest one 200 years before him, who gives the first undisputed citation of the work.

27. Mayor, lxix–lxxxiv.

28. Moffatt, 1; Laws, 22–23. Marshall, 230–231, claims after examining Hermas *Man.* 5, 9, and 12, "The number of echoes of James to be found in the comparatively small context of these three Mandates leads us to think that Hermas did in fact know and use the epistle." She argues that James was composed in Rome in a different section of the church shortly before Hermas.

29. Seitz, "Relationship," 131–140, argues that for parts of his work James has a common source with Hermas and 1 and 2 Clement. This relationship is the best explanation of the similarities. Shepherd, 40–51, accepts this source hypothesis and claims it is the one Origen (Sermon on Mt. 27:9) asserts is quoted in 1 Cor. 2:9, the Secrets of Elijah. Young, 339–345, supports Seitz's argument for an apocryphal source document, but believes that James received the material secondhand through Clement. The evidence from this common material is not unequivocal.

remain subjective: Hermas, for example, probably knew James, but the case cannot be made ironclad.[30]

The external evidence, then, does not produce a definitive conclusion about the date of the epistle. It is consistent with either a late date or a limited circulation of the epistle, e.g. circulation in the contracting group of Jewish Christian churches. Indeed, a comparison with the Apostolic Fathers indicates that James is probably earlier than any of them and may have been known by several of them. Yet this evidence is inferential and thus uncertain. This uncertainty means that one must turn to the internal evidence, comparing each theory with the data contained in the book.

4. Internal Evidence

An examination of the internal evidence for the date and authorship of James leads straight back to the claim of authorship in 1:1. The question now is: would James the Just or some other (later) author be more likely to construct this type of greeting? Against a theory of pseudonymous authorship stands the simplicity of the greeting, the lack of exalted titles ("brother of the Lord," "elder in Jerusalem," or "apostle of Christ"); for a pseudonymous author would most likely identify his "James" better and would stress his authority. This simplicity likewise affects theories of partial authorship, unless one holds that this self-designation is itself a part of the tradition from James the Just, a memory of his normal self-designation. The greeting, therefore, supports best a theory of authorship by James the Just, although some scholars dispute this point.[31] The open-

---

30. The present writer has offered evidence to this effect in two restricted areas when he compared James with Hermas on the piety-poverty link and the meaning of δίψυχος (Davids, 472–473, 63–66). One should observe that James 5 presents a more vivid, present, and immediate eschatology than, for example, Did. 16 or 10:6, Ign. *Eph.* 11:1, Barn. 4, or Hermas *Sim.* 9. James's use of the synoptic tradition is also different. When James uses it, he never cites it as Jesus' words (unlike Didache or Clement); yet he has more allusions to these sayings per line of text than any of the Apostolic Fathers. He lives in a period when the sayings are "in the air," but quotation is not necessary. Kittel, "Jakobusbrief," 54–112, examines both this evidence and the position of James and the Apostolic Fathers on the faith and works issue, supporting the conclusion above that James appears more "primitive." Cf. Kittel, 83–84, 93–94, and Spitta, 230–236 (on James and 1 Clement).

31. Some who feel that the greeting supports authorship by James the Just are Kümmel, 290, who cites the "simplicity of the majestic self-designation" as one of two pieces of evidence for his authorship, and Windisch, 3, who places it in favor of James the Just's authorship because of "die Berechtigung des Herrenbruders, an die 12 Stämme in der Zerstreuung zu schreiben." Meyer, 110–111, however, argues that since the greeting lacks "seinem Titel Herrenbruder" it stands against authenticity. Kittel, 73–75, counters Meyer by pointing out that the failure to mention James the Just's relationship to Jesus rules out pseudonymous authorship *after* the death of James, for that relationship was stressed after and only after his death. "Erstens, das gegen Ende des 1. und im 2. Jh. die Verwandtschaft mit dem Herrn wichtig genommen und, wo sie vorlag, betont wurde; zweitens aber, dass in der frühapostolischen Zeit aus dieser selben Herrnverwandtschaft noch keinerlei spezielle Tongebungen und Authoritätsansprüche abgeleitet worden sind." One will observe the evidence for the importance placed on physical relationship to Jesus and the leading position it gave his relatives in the church in Euseb. *HE* 1.7.14; 3.19–20; and 4.22.4–5; cf. Epiph. *Haer.* 29.7. Kittel argues his case convincingly, for the evidence demonstrates increasing stress on relationship to Jesus only *after* the death of James the Just.

ing verse suggests an answer, but one must compare its evidence with that provided by a careful examination of other aspects of the letter: (1) the Hellenistic culture of the epistle, (2) the Jewish Christian culture of the epistle, (3) the historical-doctrinal position of the epistle, and (4) the "James-Paul debate" of the epistle.

a. The Hellenistic Culture of the Epistle

Within the area of Hellenistic culture the problem of the language of the epistle ranks first. It has presented the most difficult problem to those who believe that James the Just, a Galilean Jew, wrote the book, for the Greek, it is claimed, is among the best in the NT. This claim is partially justified.[32] Those who are impressed with the Hellenistic culture of James add to the problem of language the further claim that James apparently quotes the LXX, not the MT, although this is far from certain,[33] and that James is close to the thought of Philo and other Hellenistic Jews. Therefore, Kennedy remarks, "It seems difficult for any unprejudiced enquirer to evade the conclusion that the Jewish writer of this Epistle moved with more than ordinary freedom in the region of Hellenistic culture."[34]

The first issue, then, is the Greek ability of James the Just. On the question of the Greek ability of a Galilean, Moulton claims: "That Jesus and his disciples regularly used Aramaic is beyond question, but that

32. Mayor, ccxliv, claims that the Greek is closer to the standard of classical purity than any other NT book except, perhaps, Hebrews. Zahn, I, 112, modifies this claim, for while free of gross errors, James's grasp of Greek is limited: his short, simple sentences are not beautiful periodic sentences. The Greek quality does rule out theories which claim that James is a translation of an Aramaic original, for not only is the Greek not rough translation Greek, but the frequent examples of paronomasia and other figures of speech could not have been present in a translation (cf. below, pp. 57–61).

33. Kennedy, 39, states, "The quotations from the OT in the Epistle agree with the text of the LXX, even when that differs from the Hebrew." This statement is true, but it is based on very limited evidence. (1) Jas. 2:11 quotes Ex. 20:13–14 (15 LXX) in reverse order as B and Philo do, but this may be a reversing of the order of effect as much as the use of a source with the reversed order. (2) Jas. 2:23 quotes Gn. 15:6 only adding δέ to the LXX for grammatical connection, but the LXX does not diverge from the MT in this passage. (3) Jas. 4:6 quotes Pr. 3:34. James diverges from the LXX in substituting θεός for κύριος; he follows the LXX in that both he and it do not pick up the wordplay in the MT. This is the only clear evidence for James's use of the LXX, but in this case the form of the citation was obviously traditional in Christian parenesis. (4) Jas. 2:8 quotes Lv. 19:18, but the LXX and MT do not diverge. (5) Jas. 3:9 may allude to Gn. 1:26–27, for James uses καθ' ὁμοίωσιν θεοῦ while the LXX uses both εἰκόνα and ὁμοίωσιν without modifiers in Gn. 1:26 and κατ' εἰκόνα θεοῦ in Gn. 1:27. Thus the data show no clear dependence upon the LXX. Laws, "Scripture," 211–212, claims that when James quotes scripture he quotes the LXX *exactly*, not knowing the Hebrew text, but this claim goes far beyond the evidence. Ward, 25–26, sums up the evidence well: "On the basis of the scripture quotations and strong allusions to scripture, it is not at all certain that EpJas is directly dependent on the LXX. Of the OT passages in question, only Prov. 3:34 differs markedly in the LXX as compared with the M.T. But since EpJas, 1 Pet, and 1 Clem all cite this passage in the same form, it is more than likely that this quotation comes to the author by way of the paraenetic tradition in which the LXX form of Prov. 3:34 is associated with the themes of subjection and humility."

34. Kennedy, 51; Laws, 4–6. But cf. Davids, 33–36, and below, pp. 57–61.

Greek was also at command is almost equally certain. There is not the slightest presumption against the use of Greek in writings purporting to emanate from the circle of the first believers." He adds that they would use Greek as those having used it from childhood, varying in quality according to education, neither having to translate into it nor using it as "foreigners painfully expressing themselves in an imperfectly known idiom."[35] Other competent scholars see the epistle's quality of Greek as the chief factor against James the Just's having written it.[36] The real issue must be one of education, for since Galilee was a region with many Greek cities and non-Jews and since there is extensive evidence of the use of Greek by Jews throughout Palestine, there is no reason to suppose that James could not speak Greek fluently.[37] But one might question whether he had access to the education necessary to enable him to write using the style observed in the letter.

Closely related to the above is the issue of Hellenistic influence in Palestine. Would James the Just use the form of a Hellenistic letter and would he use phrases and scriptures current in the more Hellenized Jewish communities? This is not improbable: first, Galilee certainly contained many Hellenized Jews, and, according to Acts 6, the Jerusalem church included Hellenized Jewish Christians. When one adds to this the evidence for Hellenism among the Jews of Jerusalem and Palestine in general, he will not find it surprising if James the Just should use such materials.[38] But second, it is highly debatable whether the epistle does indeed show a significant dependence upon distinctively Hellenistic materials. We have argued above[39] that James may use the LXX but he is not limited to this version. Both Jas. 2:11 and Jas. 4:6 may actually follow common church usage (especially since both 1 Peter and 1 Clement quote a similar version of Pr. 3:34) rather than depend directly on the LXX. Jas.

35. MHT I, 8. In II, 26–27, W. F. Howard claims that Peter's Greek may have been better than his Aramaic and that there is evidence for a Semitic mother tongue and therefore Semitic thought patterns underlying the Greek in James. Dalman, *Jesus*, 1–7, argues for the wide use of Greek in Galilee and Judea despite the normal use of the Aramaic mother tongue among Jews in Palestine, but he does not discuss the quality of their Greek knowledge. Cf. Argyle, 87–89.

36. Ropes, 50; Windisch, 3; Kümmel, 290, and Blackman, 26, are a few examples. The reasons for this determination, however, must be carefully examined. For example, Burkitt, 66, states, "it is written in better, more literary Greek than we should expect from the unshaven devotee who haunted the Temple Colonnades." Thus Burkitt's reason why James could not have written good Greek shows a great dependence on Hegesippus's legends concerning James.

37. After an examination of the evidence for Greek culture in Palestine Sevenster, 190–191, concludes that James the Just certainly could speak Greek and that one cannot preclude the possibility that he could have written good Greek. Cf. Goodenough, V, 13, 51, 56, 184–198.

38. Ibid. Since Goodenough even finds extensive evidence of the adoption of pagan symbols in synagogue decoration, the penetration of literary terminology must have been extensive.

39. See n. 35.

3:9 points against James's exclusive use of the LXX. Furthermore, in the author's larger study of the themes in James (e.g. Davids, 529) it was argued that James is not especially dependent upon the wisdom literature or Philo (whom he may never have read). Likewise, the commentary will show that none of the Hellenistic formulas commonly cited would have been strange in Palestine. In fact, several (e.g. 3:6) show evidence that their original meaning has been forgotten and they have received a new sense in the Jewish milieu. Formally, of course, the epistle could be "Hellenistic." It will be argued below (22–28) that James uses a definite form which appears in some Hellenistic letters as well as in 1 John. On the other hand, Adamson, "Inductive," 245–256, and Wessel, 73–89, argue that the work shows signs of being a synagogue sermon. Wessel in particular points out (and this is certainly the major contribution of his thesis) that the features of the Hellenistic diatribe or the features Dibelius finds in parenesis are either lacking in James ("lack of real coherence," "lack of a definite situation to which the exhortations are addressed") or they are found in the synagogue homily as well ("dialogue," "method of address," "variability of subject matter," "alliteration"). In fact, some classical scholars now question whether a distinct literary form of diatribe ever existed.[40] Rather, certain features are found wherever discursive oral discourse is reduced to writing. There is no reason to suppose that the form of such discourse would be different in a Palestinian Jewish setting from that of a Greek setting. The presentation in epistolary form of that which was originally a sermon, however, is of note.

If one wishes to explain the apparent contradiction of forms, it will be necessary to come to some type of a two-level hypothesis for the composition of the work. This same hypothesis may also explain some of the curious divergences in vocabulary (e.g. ἐπιθυμία in 1:13ff. and ἡδονή in 4:1ff.), some of the conflict between the very good Greek in places and Semitisms in others, and some of the apparent disjointedness between topics in the epistle (even though the epistle does appear in the end to be a unitary work). The hypothesis is quite simple: the epistle is very likely a two-stage work. The first stage is a series of Jewish Christian homilies, sayings, and maxims, many of which would have been composed in Greek by a person who spoke Aramaic as his mother tongue, while others may have been translations. The second stage is the compilation of an epistle by editing these pieces together into a whole. As will be shown in the commentary, there are many places in which such a two-stage theory will enable the student to discover the redactional unity missed by such scholars as Dibelius, while recognizing the diversity of the materials and forms which he and others found.

40. Cf. Jocelyn, 145–146: "The term [diatribe] should disappear from scholarly discourse along with all other bogus antiquities which moderns use to adorn their essays on classical literature." Wifstrand, 177–178.

James the Just could well be the author of the first set of materials (the homilies) or the author of both stages (i.e. he put several of his own homilies together into an epistolary form). Then an amanuensis with considerable ability in literary Greek may have assisted the author in writing this work. This concept has commended itself in the past to those who are convinced that the work is early and carries the authority of James the Just but who are not convinced that James the Just could write this quality of Greek. Thus Mussner, although arguing that James the Just *could* have written the Greek, suggests, "Vielleicht stammt das sprachliche und stilistische Kleid des Briefes von einem griechisch sprechenden Mitarbeiter."[41] Other scholars place more stress than Mussner on the Hellenistic scribe, some suggesting that he was a pilgrim who abstracted samples of James the Just's teaching (perhaps with his approval and supervision) for the benefit of his home congregation.[42] Finally, the editor may have been quite unknown to the author, simply a reviser and compiler of his material, either before or after the author's death. In such a case the ascription to James the Just is certainly warranted even though James may never have known the epistle was sent. The epistle would also have two dates: the date of the original homilies and the date of the redacted composition.[43]

The evidence from the Hellenistic culture of James, then, is inconclusive. While it has traditionally been the strongest evidence for a non-Palestinian background and late date for the epistle, one can no longer say that this is the case. A Palestinian could have written this epistle. The valid issue is whether James the Just was educated well enough to have written the letter. This question favors those who claim that the final version was not by James, for one is inclined to doubt the educational level of a carpenter's son. But since we lack evidence proving the quality of Greek that James the Just could have produced and since we do not know if he would use a Greek secretary, we cannot conclusively argue from the Hellenistic culture of the epistle that James the Just could not have produced either the epistle itself or the homilies on which it is based.

b. The Jewish Christian Culture of the Epistle

The question of Hellenistic culture introduces the question of Jewish Christian culture, for Judaism forms a bridge between the two. The indications of Jewish culture are widespread, from the frequent use of ἰδού to theological ideas, such as the stress on the unity of God (2:19). Jewish culture forms the ideological background of the epistle, and scholars do

41. Mussner, 8.
42. Mitton, 232; Schneider, 4.
43. Bruce, 127, presents a variation of this theory: "The Greek of the letter may be the result of careful literary revision."

not normally dispute its presence,[44] but one particularly Palestinian example needs attention. Jas. 5:7 mentions ἕως λάβῃ πρόϊμον καὶ ὄψιμον.[45] These autumn and spring rains are characteristic of the Palestinian climate, not of Egypt, Italy, or most of Asia Minor (all candidates for the origin of this epistle). One concludes from this reference that the author was familiar with Palestine; he was either so familiar that he referred to the rains unconsciously (and perhaps to non-Palestinian readers, whom he failed to realize might not understand his accustomed climate) or familiar enough to cite correctly local weather conditions known to his Palestinian audience.[46]

But, while few dispute the Jewishness of the work, several scholars, notably Spitta and Meyer, claim that nothing Christian exists in this work other than minor Christian editing. We must firmly reject this claim for three reasons: (1) James contains some individual ideas embedded in the work which are not Jewish, but Christian, (2) James has close affinities with some NT literature, and (3) James probably alludes to the words of Jesus.[47]

Few specifically Christian statements exist in James, but those that do are important. Of course 1:1 and 2:1 are Christian, but since their Christian sections could easily be interpolations, one cannot use them as evidence. Yet if one agrees that the epistle has other Christian material, these verses should also be accepted as genuine. Some of the Christian material which does exist and cannot be interpolations are: (1) τοὺς πρεσβυτέρους τῆς ἐκκλησίας (5:14), (2) the concept of being an ἀπαρχή and being saved through the word (1:18ff.),[48] and (3) the references to

44. Spitta builds his whole presentation on establishing this fact. Cf. Guthrie, *Introduction,* 741; Ropes, 29–31. Marshall, 248, claims that James is Jewish only "in a derived sense." The Judaism is that of a gentile who one time listened to the teaching in the synagogue (cf. Laws, 4). The commentary will show that such can hardly be the case, for Jewish traditions are too important in explaining James's teaching for them to have been only a tangential part of his thought.

45. Since the context is that of farming, this expression refers to the early and late rains (October and April). Cf. Je. 5:24.

46. Oesterley, 392ff., 401, sees this point as does Kittel, 81. On the climatic condition cf. Baly, 47–52. These climatic conditions are most important in Palestine proper, which has less rainfall than the northern areas of the eastern Mediterranean coast, but the cycle extends over the whole eastern coast, including the southeastern end of Asia Minor. Therefore, although Palestine is the most likely area of reference, Phoenicia, Syria, and Cilicia would be possible.

Marshall, 106, claims that this reference to climatic phenomena is simply a use of a stylized illustration from the LXX (cf. Laws, 212). She has no evidence, however, that the phrase in Je. 5:24 was ever so used; it is not even used to illustrate patient waiting in Jeremiah. Thus we doubt that this expression is stock language.

47. Ropes, 32–33, gives a good summary of these arguments. Cf. Guthrie, *Introduction,* 743–744, 756.

48. Mayor, cc–cci.

Jesus' using the terms "judge," "Lord," and "the name."[49] Only with great difficulty can one fit these examples—and the larger whole of which they are examples—into a purely Jewish context.

But beyond these specific statements James shows affinities with NT literature. Mayor presents pages of references illustrating these affinities; they show close contact in thought, although no literary relationships, with the bulk of the NT.[50] Nevertheless, one possible literary relationship may exist with 1 Peter.[51] The contact between these two works is much greater than that between James and the noncanonical works previously discussed (e.g. Hermas). Still, no claimed allusion is close enough to prove that one author used the other's work, although the evidence does prove that the two works at least depend upon the same tradition, which might mean that the authors lived in the same location for some significant part of their lives (although not necessarily while the other author was in that place) or that they were in the same part of the church, e.g. Jewish Christian congregations. If anything, James is the more "primitive" of the two works and therefore the earlier, but judgments of primitiveness are necessarily subjective and therefore uncertain.[52]

Allusions to Jesus and his teaching make up the final area of evidence of James's Christianity. Some scholars feel that the lack of any reference to Jesus' life, resurrection, or relationship to the claimed author is a decisive argument against authorship by James the Just (or any other personal follower of Jesus during his lifetime).[53] Several considerations, on the other hand, weaken the effect of this argument: (1) according to the information preserved in the gospels, James the Just was not a follower of Jesus before Jesus' crucifixion; (2) the greater familiarity of the audience with the OT than with the life of Jesus (if the epistle preceded the written gospels) might occasion the author's use of the OT rather than

---

49. Ropes, 32. "Judge" (4:12; 5:9) is the least likely to refer to Christ. On "Lord" cf. 5:7–8; on "the name" cf. 2:7 and 5:14. For contrary arguments see Spitta and Marshall, 188–193.

50. Mayor, lxxxv–cix.

51. Mayor, cvi–cvii.

52. Parry, 99–100, argues that James was used by the author of 1 Peter; cf. Mayor, clxix, who states: "Where it is agreed that there is a direct literary connexion between two writers, A and B, treating of the same subject from apparently opposite points of view, and using the same illustrations, if it shall appear that the argument of B meets in all respects the argument of A, while the argument of A has no direct reference to that of B, the priority lies with A. Again where it is agreed that there is a connexion between two writers, treating of the same subject on the same scale from the same point of view, and using the same quotations, it is probable that the writer who gives the thought in its most terse and rugged form, and takes the least trouble to be precise in the wording of his quotations, is the earlier writer." But if one rejects any direct literary connection between James and 1 Peter (or Paul's letters) and since the second argument only establishes probability, Mayor's argument is not as conclusive as he believes.

53. Parry, 4, cites this as a major problem; cf. Oesterley, 397, and Kümmel, 290.

Jesus' life as examples of conduct; (3) James the Just might deliberately play down his physical relationship to Jesus; and (4) even if the above considerations are not accepted, allusions to the teaching of Jesus in James mitigate the effect of the argument.[54]

These allusions are a clear and important piece of information about the background of the book. First, the references to the ethical teaching of Jesus are very numerous; indeed, the whole book exudes the Sermon on the Mount.[55] Second, these allusions are often practical applications of Jesus' general principles (as Jas. 5:2–3 applies Mt. 6:19). Third, the material comes from the preliterary synoptic tradition, not from the written gospels.[56] Collectively, these allusions argue that the author was someone saturated with the teaching of Jesus and that the work was written before its author contacted written gospel traditions.[57] They may point toward a similar source of tradition as that which produced Matthew's gospel. The noncitation of Jesus even when dependent upon his thought is fully characteristic of the NT epistles. Paul, for instance, only cites Jesus a couple of times, yet in many places draws on the tradition. James is much closer in his allusions due to the nature of his topics, but he simply follows the NT practice of allusion rather than citation, a practice that may have been necessary in an age of oral tradition without gospel books. This evidence favors a theory demanding an early date and authorship by James the Just, but it does not establish such a theory. One can conceive of a later author who had yet to contact the written gospels or who would not change the form of the traditions received from James, perhaps considering them more sacred than the gospels.

c. The Historical-Doctrinal Position of the Epistle

But granting this Christian substratum to the epistle, the historical-doctrinal position of the epistle raises other problems. Here the most important problems are: (1) Christology, (2) ecclesiology and the church situation, and (3) missionary concern.

James's christological problem is his apparent lack of explicit Christology! Only 1:1 and 2:1 contain explicit Christology. Windisch and others feel this is too little to prove that the author had any messianic belief.[58]

---

54. Moulton, 45–55, produces another reason: the book was written by a Christian to Jews, mixing the teaching of Jesus with other ethical material. The object was to attract the Jews and thus pave the way for the gospel. All direct references to Jesus are later glosses. We reject Moulton's theory, however; only he sees evangelistic intent in James. On the allusions to the teaching of Jesus in James, see below, pp. 47–50.

55. Mayor, lxxxv–xc.

56. One must reject Shepherd's argument, 50–51, that these allusions come from inaccurate memory quotations of the gospels the author had heard read in church. Elliott-Binns, 47, and others have clearly shown the preliterary character of the material. Some allusions may even be agrapha; cf. Resch.

57. Windisch, 3, and Kümmel, 290. Kittel, "Jakobusbrief," 92–93, points out that the form of these allusions is unlike that in the Apostolic Fathers.

58. Windisch, 3; Oesterley, 399.

But, even if Tasker is wrong in asserting that Jesus' brothers would not stress Christology,[59] the apparent lack of Christology is not a fault in a letter which neither needs much Christology nor lacks an implicit one. First, the accusation of a lack of Christology posits a need for it. This letter appears to assume a sharing of dogmatic beliefs with its readers (at the least, the acceptance of Jesus' teaching) and to argue for ethical, not dogmatic, results. Such an aim does not require the presentation of a detailed Christology.[60]

Second, James does contain an implicit Christology, assuming one accepts the letter as Christian.[61] If the letter is Christian, then 1:1 and 2:1 are genuine references to ὁ κύριος Ἰησοῦς Χριστός; this certainly constitutes messianic belief. Besides these references James refers to Jesus as ὁ κύριος several times, believes he now lives in glory, and looks to him to come as judge.[62] This Christology may be primitive, pointing to an early date for the epistle,[63] but it might also be the unexpanded christological sentiments of one who believed much more.

Ecclesiology and the church situation present a problem equal in importance to that of Christology. The first feature of this problem is the terminology which the author uses for the church. The author uses a Jewish-sounding expression, unique in the NT, when he speaks of a man coming εἰς συναγωγὴν ὑμῶν (2:2). This could be a primitive Jewish Christian expression.[64] At the same time the author writes of τοὺς πρεσβυτέρους τῆς ἐκκλησίας (5:14), which is common Christian terminology, although the phrase dates the passage before the rise of the bishopric.[65] Thus the terminology rules out a Tübingen-type date and may indicate a rather early date.

The next feature of the church situation is that the readers are ἐν τῇ διασπορᾷ (1:1) and have ποικίλοι πειρασμοί (1:2), some of which rich men cause (2:6–8). Despite the fact that the author does not mention official involvement in the persecution by the government, the description does

59. Tasker, 28.
60. There is nothing in this epistle that should make one believe that it is a full presentation of the faith of its author. Cf. Mitton, 9: "It was written for the benefit of Jewish-Christian visitors to Jerusalem who wished to have some record of James' characteristic teachings to take back with them for the benefit of christians in their home towns." But even if this was the reason for the epistle, such a sample might be far from representative, showing more the problems of the Jerusalem congregation at the time of composition than the full teaching of James.
61. Cf. Ropes, 32.
62. Jas. 5:7–8, 14; 2:1; 4:12; and 5:9 are the respective references.
63. The "lack" of Christology in actuality means a relatively "primitive" Christology, which points not to a late date when gnostic and other christological controversies were in the air, but to an early date before the development of the later detailed christological formulae. Cf. Kittel, "Jakobusbrief," 83–109.
64. This is an expression which is probably used for the judicial assemblies of the church; cf. Ward, "Partiality," and the commentary.
65. Moffatt, 1, adjusts his date according to this evidence.

not rule out the mid-first century. The "scattering" of the church must have been very early, if the early believers represented a cross section of the group mentioned in Acts 2:9–11. The church at Jerusalem, at any rate, surely saw the διασπείρων of Acts 8:1–4 as producing a διασπορά, despite the fact that later history makes it look limited. This forced scattering resulted from persecution by men whom the church would have described as "the rich."[66] Thus it is probable that during the pre-AD 70 period the Jerusalem church (and the Palestinian church in general) suffered sporadic persecution from rich Jews (because the rich often oppress the poor, if for no other reason). Thus, while this description could envision official persecution by Romans against a widespread church, it also fits the situation of sporadic persecution of Christians in the vicinity of Palestine by wealthy Jews.[67]

A third feature of the church situation is the moral problems found within the church (e.g. 4:1ff.; 2:1ff.); some scholars claim that these problems indicate a church whose first zeal has died away and whose vices show a settled, late situation.[68] On the other hand, the problems are not described clearly by the author, and what he does say could surely occur within a few years of the genesis of any church; they might even be the faults of recently converted Jews who needed to realize the implications of their new faith. This would explain the application of the teachings of Jesus to the practical problems. While the severity of James's condemnation may favor a late date, the church situation as a whole favors an earlier date for the epistle.

Unlike the church situation, the problem of the lack of missionary concern contains little indication of date. No evidence exists to indicate a premissionary period in the church and thus an early date. But likewise it does not indicate a late date, for at what date was the church so settled as to forget missionary activity? And if the date is so late, why does the epistle not contain indications of the doctrinal controversies of the period?[69] It is safer to assume that ethical problems had to be dealt with at every period of church history and that at no period did an author have the requirement of mentioning his missionary concern every time he wrote. One needs a great deal of information about an author, his main activities,

66. See Introduction, 41–47, and the commentary on 1:9–11; 2:5–6; and 5:1–6.

67. Acts 8:1–4 and 9:1ff. assert that persecution occurred early in Jerusalem and spread from there to the centers to which the Christians had fled. This may not have been a major or total persecution to modern historiography, but to those running from the high priest's agents it must have seemed important and widespread indeed. Also by AD 56 Paul had been persecuted over a wide area (2 Cor. 11:23ff.), some of which displeasure must also have fallen upon Jewish Christian groups. Of course Jas. 2:6–8 might not indicate religious persecution at all, but rich men taking advantage of a poor, unprotected, and unpopular minority group.

68. Cf. Parry, 4.

69. Tasker, 32, seems to rely upon this argument to establish the date of AD 62. Cf. McNeile, 203, and Bultmann, *Theology*, II, 162f.

his general church situation, and his specific needs in writing to determine from a work's content whether or not a certain piece of writing could have been produced by him at a certain time. In the case of James one does not have that information.

d. The "James-Paul Debate" of the Epistle

The issue of the "James-Paul debate" supplements the material already gathered with the final pieces of information. Here the following create major issues: (1) James the Just's "legalism," (2) the reception of the gentiles, and (3) the "anti-Pauline polemic" of 2:14ff.

The question of James the Just's legalism stands as one of the major deciding points in the investigation of the date and authorship of this epistle. The epistle does not mention circumcision and certainly does not stress the observance of ritual and cultic piety; indeed, the reference to the "law of freedom" (2:12) seems to imply just the opposite. Those scholars who couple these facts with the assumption that James the Just was a strict ritualist of Pharisaical piety argue that these facts mean that the epistle was not produced by James the Just; it is later than he.[70] But we must challenge the assumption that James the Just was legalistic. Too often a dependence on Hegesippus's account, one which is certainly exaggerated by an Ebionite glorification of James the Just and may be largely false,[71] produces a picture of an ascetic, legalistic James who certainly did not write this epistle.[72] Acts presents James the Just as a mediating personality who tried to keep peace between the extreme Jewish legalistic segment of the church and the supporters of the Pauline mission. He appears as a Jew who kept the law (as Paul also probably did), who was dedicated to the mission to the Jewish community (a mission Paul certainly supported despite his separate calling), and who also agreed with Paul's position over against the legalists.[73] One would hardly expect such

---

70. E.g. Kümmel, 290; Windisch, 3.

71. Hegesippus's account portrays James the Just as a strict legalist (a Pharisee of the Pharisees, a Nazirite held in high repute by all the Jews), but it also has him entering the holy place of the temple (among other improbabilities), and it has Jews setting him up as a witness against the Christians. James might possibly have been a Nazirite (but not from birth!), but the improbabilities of the account are so great that one cannot rely upon any of its statements about James. Cf. Kittel, "Stellung," 145; Lightfoot, 367.

72. Burkitt, 66, is an example of the acceptance of Hegesippus, as is Martin (see also Martin, Foundations, II, 360). Plumptre tries to redeem the account by explaining some of the improbabilities away, but he only succeeds in showing how untrustworthy the narrative is.

73. The position attributed to James the Just in Acts 15:13–21 is a mediating position, for he resisted the demands of those who wished to make the gentile converts proselytes while restraining the gentile church from offending the most important scruples of the Jews. Acts 21:18–26 presents him among those who wish Paul to placate the fears of Jewish Christians, but the picture is certainly not that of an extremist or a legalist, for he totally accepts the Pauline mission to the gentiles. Gal. 2:1–10 claims that James recognized Paul's ministry and doctrine; Paul received no legalistic additions to his gospel. The "some from James" of Gal. 2:12 were certainly a delegation from him, but (1) their mission may have had nothing to do with the legalistic ideas they pressed once in Antioch, and (2) they

a person to stress legal piety in his letter, although he might use illustrations from it, if needed. But even if James the Just were a legalist, one would not expect him to stress this form of piety when writing to Jewish Christians who held the same position, especially if he were writing before the Jerusalem Council and its legal controversy arose.

The controversy over the reception of the gentiles presented itself above in relation to James the Just's legalism. On this point we note that, with the possible exception of Galatians 2, James the Just in NT records never resists the reception of the gentiles, but rather takes a mediating position acceptable to Paul in both Acts 15 and Acts 21. The issue was important enough that, despite the fact that James might be writing to Jewish Christians who might only be irritated by his position and despite the fact that the issue does not fit the subject of his letter, one might expect him to have mentioned it, if it had arisen by the time he wrote. The nonmention of this controversy indicates that the letter (or at least its sources) was probably written either before the Jerusalem Council or long enough after AD 70 that the controversy had ceased to be an issue, if arguments from silence are of any value.

But one who agreed with Paul could not have penned 2:14–26 as a strong "anti-Pauline polemic." One's decision on the intention of this passage is another important turning point as one moves toward a conclusion concerning the date and authorship of James. If James depends upon or refutes Galatians or Romans, then one must date the epistle later, perhaps much later (to allow time for the circulation of Paul's works) than these works. But scholars today generally do not believe that James tried to refute these Pauline works or Paul himself directly. Ropes states:

> While James and Paul thus stand in this sharp contrast, no hint appears in James of controversy with Pauline Christianity over the validity of the Jewish law, nor of attack on Paul personally. In 2:14–26 James is not engaged in doctrinal controversy, but is repelling the practical misuse which was made, or might be made, of Paul's doctrine of justification by faith alone in order to excuse moral laxity. James shows no comprehension of what Paul actually meant by his formula; but the formula itself is foreign to him and he heartily dislikes it.[74]

themselves may not have raised the problem of legal observance for the gentiles, but only noted the effect Peter's behavior might have on the mission to the Jews (with pointed references to the persecution which arose when Stephen tried to set aside the law). The data are too meager to discover whether James would have agreed with their opinions at all. The overall picture of James, then, is not one of a legalist, but one of a man who personally kept the law, who accepted Paul's position, and who tried to keep the peace between Paul's mission and the more legalistic factions in the church. Cf. Kittel, "Stellung"; Carroll; and Schmithals.

74. Ropes, 35.

Indeed, to argue that James directly attacks Paul is to argue that James is a consummate blunderer, for he fails to meet Paul's arguments at all and instead produces a work with which Paul would have agreed! The real issue, then, is whether the author intended to attack a misunderstood Paulinism, requiring a date either late in the life of James the Just or one later than he,[75] or something like a rigid Jewish Christian orthodoxy.[76]

If one chooses a misunderstood Paulinism, a date later than Paul's early missionary work in Syria and earlier than either the wide circulation of Paul's letters (which would provide material for effective quotations to aim at a corruption of Paul's position) or Paul's meeting James the Just (if he is the source of the tradition) is easiest to defend. Although such a misunderstood Paulinism is a good assumption, there is no evidence other than this epistle that such a position ever actually existed in the shape found here. If it did exist, it could have existed very early. Therefore, it does not demand a late date for the original tradition.

The alternative assumption of a doctrine with its roots in Judaism, not Paulinism, is as likely. For instance, in light of the connection between Gn. 15:6 and Gn. 22:1 in 1 Macc. 2:52 and of James's use of the testing tradition, it is unlikely that James depends upon Paulinism at all for the example of Abraham. Further, since Jas. 2:14–26 at its heart demands charity, its subject is not similar to Paul's concern with legalism, and, as shall be noted in the commentary, James uses every significant term πίστις, ἔργα, and δικαιοσύνη, with a differing and more "primitive" meaning than Paul. Finally, this passage amplifies Jas. 1:22–25, and those who see the Paulinism in James 2 normally do not see any in James 1. It seems best to understand James to be refuting a Jewish Christian attempt to minimize the demands of the gospel rather than a misunderstood Paulinism.[77]

e. Conclusions

From the evidence presented above one can draw some limited conclusions. First, the evidence of Christian material deeply embedded in the text of James makes those theories claiming a purely Jewish origin for the book unlikely. Second, some of the material favors an early date for the traditions behind the epistle and the probability of their authorship by James the Just: (1) the indirect external evidence, (2) the self-designation of the author, (3) the strong Jewish influence, (4) the use of a preliterary tradition of the words of Jesus, (5) the situation of the churches he addresses, and (6) the lack of reference to the issue of the reception of the gentiles. Several of these arguments point only weakly to an early

---

75. Ropes, 35, supports the post-AD 70 date from this evidence. Tasker, 32, however, believes it simply justifies a date late in the life of James the Just. Cf. Laws, 15–18; Burchard, "Jakobus," 44–45.

76. Kittel, "Jakobusbrief," 56–68.

77. Cf. below, pp. 47–51 and the relevant commentary passages.

date, but some are fairly strong. If one assumes that these traditions come from a period within the lifetime of James the Just, an early date, the period between AD 40 and the Jerusalem Council, has the best claim to being the period during which they originated, because the book does not mention the problem of the reception of the gentiles, a burning issue for some time after this period. The lack of explicit Christology might also support an earlier date. Third, some material weakly favors a later date for the epistle: (1) the direct external evidence, (2) the Greek idiom, (3) the similarity to the Apostolic Fathers, and (4) the possibility that the epistle interacts with Paulinism. Obviously one's decisions about the ability of James the Just to produce idiomatic Greek and the presence of an "anti-Pauline polemic" are key issues. But these features may be easily explained if we assume that the final redaction of the book took place during the period AD 55–65 or possibly AD 75–85 (assuming the redactor had no access to Paul's epistles as yet). The redaction was probably made in a Jewish Christian context and thus limited the circulation of the epistle; the destruction of Jewish Christianity with the fall of Jerusalem would also have tended to limit the circulation.

This brief discussion has certainly not settled the complex problem of the date and provenance of the Epistle of James. The evidence examined does point toward a supportable conclusion. G. Kittel appears to be correct in arguing for an early date for the book, in that the source material probably was early, and this means that this material is probably by James the Just. In the light of the Greek idiom used in the work, it is likely that either James received assistance in the editing of the work or that his teaching was edited at a later date (perhaps after his death) as the church spread beyond Jerusalem and began to use Greek more exclusively. This conclusion fits the possible *Sitz im Leben* which will be proposed for James's teaching on poverty and wealth; it also appears to explain most satisfactorily the phenomena observed in the epistle, such as the Greek idiom. It forms a viable working hypothesis to use in examining the epistle.

II. FORM AND STRUCTURE

The preceding section has argued that James is a two-stage work, an initial series of sermons and sayings, which ostensibly come from James the Just (i.e. we assume the redactor believed that all the material came from James, but we cannot be sure that all of the smaller units belonged to the same stream of tradition: some of the proverbs, for example, may have been favorites of the redactor), and a later redaction of these units into an epistle by either James or a member of the church. The signs which lead to this conclusion are the same that have led many to throw up their hands in despair over finding any unity in the book: (1) self-contained sense-units which abut other units without any apparent flow of thought among them, (2) stylistic variety, (3) proverbial sayings apparently used to link two sense-units, (4) link-words used to join units without any other clear thought connection, and (5) differing vocabulary when discussing the same topic (although the perspective of the author remains the same).

This data means, then, that one can describe James in two ways. First, one may examine the work form critically; this is the basic approach of Dibelius in his analysis of the epistle section by section. The important feature to note in his analysis is that two types of material appear: (1) oral discourses, which he labels diatribes, and (2) sayings, including proverbs, which may be joined into series of sayings.[78] This analysis is basically correct; this commentary takes issue with Dibelius on only two points (although in the commentary individual issues may be challenged): (1) "diatribe" is probably not the correct term for the longer discourses. Even if Prof. Jocelyn is not correct in rejecting the term "diatribe" as a literary category,[79] one must still face the data marshalled by W. W. Wessel, who argues that the features of the diatribe are in fact the features of the Jewish synagogue homily, as best it can be determined from the available sources: dialogue (including such features as rhetorical questions, questions and answers, and an imaginary opponent); the direct address of the auditor (e.g. "my brethren"); variety in subject matter; and harsh speech.[80] Thus it is as logical to speak of a series of homilies in James as to speak of diatribes. James contains oral discourse, and only the context imagined for such discourse will reveal whether the Greek or the Jewish term is more applicable. Reinforcing this conclusion are data which are beginning to emerge and which point to possible parallelism underlying the rhetorical structure of some of these discourses (e.g. 2:14–26);[81] such parallelism would make the Jewish origin even more likely.

(2) The sayings and proverbs are not as unrelated or jumbled together as Dibelius, 6, believes. The analysis below and in the commentary will show that many sayings follow a common theme or join units together (e.g. 2:13) and so, while originally separate, now form part of a greater whole. It is also important to note that the style of James differs markedly from the wisdom style of Sirach, Wisdom, or Proverbs.

Second, having done the form-critical study, one may examine the work as a whole. It is at this level that several hypotheses have been

78. Dibelius, 1; Ropes, 10–18.
79. See above, n. 40.
80. Wessel, 71–112. Much of the evidence for the form of the synagogue homily is later than AD 70, but comparison with traditions in the Dead Sea Scrolls, Josephus, the gospels, and other early material make it likely that the basic features remained constant. Cf. Marmorstein, 183–204.
81. Burge; Mussner, 30–31.

advanced. Older works viewed James as wisdom literature,[82] but the pattern of wisdom literature hardly fits the type of exhortations, the connected oral discourse, and the radical tone of the epistle. Later works have tended to see the work as parenesis, i.e. as part of the genre of moral exhortation common in the ancient world, beginning with Isocrates' *Ad Nicoclem*.[83] As such it is viewed as a series of isolated units, not simply as moral exhortation. That this is a total picture of the work is important, for no one denies that James is basically a moral exhortation, nor could one deny that James *contains* parenetic catalogues,[84] but that is not to admit that the basic literary character is parenesis. If, as Dibelius argues, the basic characteristics of parenesis are: (1) "a pervasive *eclecticism*," (2) a "*lack of continuity*," (3) "*the repetition of identical motifs in different places*," and (4) "the inability *to construct a single frame* [i.e. audience and set of circumstances] *into which they* [all the moral exhortations] *will all fit*,"[85] James only partially fulfils the requirements. There is a repetition of themes, but in a definite pattern which fits a clear enough *Sitz im Leben*. The eclecticism is only apparent when one fails to move beyond form criticism to redaction criticism.

At this point it would be instructive to compare the progress of outlines used in the study of James. Dibelius and Cantinat naturally see simply a series of unrelated sections. Their outlines reveal no subordination. Mussner shows a step forward in discovering subordination and larger units in several sections. Logically, he follows this up with a series of essays on theological themes in the epistle *as a whole*. Adamson, 44–45, comes up with the fullest outline of the book, seeing a consistent rondo pattern throughout.

The analysis of the epistle in this work has been arrived at in three ways. First, there is my independent analysis. Second, this analysis was confirmed and widened when I discovered the work of F. O. Francis, which added the needed historical dimension. Finally, this analysis has been reconfirmed in many of its particulars by an independent discourse analysis of the epistle from a linguistic point of view.[86]

At face value James claims to be an epistle. But it is clear that it is a literary epistle, i.e. a tract intended for publication, not an actual letter, e.g. the epistles of Paul to specific churches. This means: (1) the epistle will reflect the *Sitz im Leben* of its place of publication, not that of its "recipients" (i.e. those for whom it is published), and (2) the form of the

---

82. E.g. Carpenter.

83. Dibelius, 3–11; Cantinat, 14–16.

84. Cf. commentary on 3:13–18.

85. Dibelius, 4–11 (emphasis his). He cites Tobit, the Two Ways sections of the Didache and Barnabas, Ps.-Isocrates, Ps.-Phocylides, Ps.-Menander, and Test. XII.

86. Cf. Hill and Torakawa, both of whom worked at the International Linguistics Center in Dallas, Texas. This commentary differs from them only in places in which it perceives theological connections among the larger units. Cf. Ekstrom and Rountree.

epistle will differ from that of the actual letter, especially in its lack of personal detail, but also in other ways.

What Francis has demonstrated is the following: (1) the opening formulae of both literary and actual letters are often doubled (Jos. *Ant.* 8:50–54; Euseb. *Praep. Ev.* 9.33–34; 1 Macc. 10:25–45; Phm. 4–7; 1–2 Thessalonians); (2) the opening formulae often contain blessing/thanksgiving formulae; (3) the opening often uses the device of cognate words to link it to the greeting; and (4) themes in the opening are often repeated in the rest of the letter or may indeed structure it. As for the closing paragraphs, the following become clear: (1) in both James and 1 John the closing paragraphs begin with an eschatological injunction; (2) the closing paragraphs of letters often have a thematic reprise, (3) πρὸ πάντων plus a health wish or an oath formula is frequent in the closing of Hellenistic letters, and (4) Christian letters (e.g. Paul) often end with something about prayer.[87]

If Francis is correct, James is far from a random collection of thoughts and sayings, but is a carefully constructed work. When the work is studied in detail, this proves to be the case. In other words, scholarship must move beyond Dibelius's form-critical view of James, valuable as that is, and discover the redactional level.

As a unit, then, James begins with an epistolary introduction (1:1) and moves via a catchword into the double opening statement (1:2–27). The first segment introduces the themes of testing, wisdom, and wealth (1:2–11). The second segment recapitulates these themes in terms of testing, speech, and generosity/doing (1:12–25), with a summary and transition segment (1:26–27). It is important to note that the second segment is not mere recapitulation, but that as the themes are taken up again they are developed and merged. Thus the testing theme discusses the problem of failure in the test (i.e. testing God), the wisdom theme is developed in terms of pure speech (as will also happen in 3:1–18), and the wealth theme is developed in terms of obedience and sharing. The inner unity among the themes begins to appear, with the result that the borders between the themes merge, as will also happen in chap. 4.

The major blocks of material in the book take up the themes in reverse order, giving a chiastic effect. As the introduction ended with the command to obedience (at least in part with respect to wealth), the first block of the body is a two-part specification of what this means in terms of partiality and charity. As the end of the introduction virtually merged obedience in terms of wealth with that in terms of speech, so the second topic to be taken up is speech and wisdom (3:1–4:12, divided into four sections). As part of this topic the evil impulse (testing theme) is again

---

87. Francis. Only the more accessible examples have been cited; for papyrus evidence one must refer to his study.

discussed, this time with a special focus on greed. Thus the final block must deal with the outworking of greed in terms of how Christians succumb to the spirit of the age in their own use of their wealth (4:13–17) and of how non-Christians put pressure on the church through their use of wealth (5:1–6; cf. 2:5–6).[88]

The closing statement consists, then, of an eschatological exhortation coupled with a thematic reprise (5:7–11), which could have ended the letter. But the author continues with topics normally in epistolary closings: πρὸ πάντων plus an oath formula (or in this case a rejection of all oaths, 5:12) and a health wish (in this case directions as to how to obtain health through prayer, 5:13–18). The topic of prayer is included because it not only fits the topic of health, but also is a frequent final topic in Christian letters. The final verses (5:19–20) also show how closely prayer is related to the purpose of the author, to turn others from sin. It is these verses which contain his goal in writing the epistle.

In this work we cannot discuss but only mention briefly the striking parallels between James and 1 John in both form and content. Both have the doubled opening, the thematic chiasmus in the body, and the discussion of prayer and health in the conclusion (with a short appendix, which may give the purpose). Both are ethically dualistic, utterly rejecting the world; both are based on communal concern; and both deal with the topic of generosity. The differences would seem to point to 1 John as a later use of this form and thematic materials, for alongside the ethical concern there is now a doctrinal concern (absent in James) associated with protognostic teachers.[89] There is also more caution in 1 John than in James about the efficacy of prayer (cf. Jas. 5:15 and 1 Jn. 5:14–15 and possibly 16–17). Thus while the literary style and some of the interests of the two works are totally divergent, there is a close enough similarity on some points to argue that 1 John knows the same stream of tradition in both form and content that James knows.

A similar formal relationship exists between James and 1 Peter.[90] That is, 1 Pet. 1:6–7 uses a chain-saying very similar to that in Jas. 1:2–4. Likewise there is close contact in several other passages (e.g. Jas. 4:6–10 and 1 Pet. 5:5–9; Jas. 5:20 and 1 Pet. 4:8; Jas. 1:18 and 1 Pet. 1:23; Jas.

88. There are two major places where this analysis disagrees with that of Hill and Torakawa. First, not knowing the Hellenistic letter form, they join 1:19ff. to 2:1–3:18, sensing the thematic unity, but missing the summary and transition structure in 1:26–27. Second, they separate 1:19–3:18 from 4:1–5:20 as the former is termed individual and the latter communal. There is more of a communal focus in 4:1ff. in comparison to 3:1–18, but as Ward has shown, the whole of the epistle exudes a concern for communal interests, not an individualistic ethic.

89. Schammberger disagrees, for he believes that James is a strong antignostic polemic. Yet there is little evidence for any gnosticism in James not read into the work by him.

90. On the relationship of the two works cf. Spitta, 183–202; Mayor, cii–cvii; Ropes, 22–23; Dibelius, 30–31; and Wifstrand.

4:1 and 1 Pet. 2:11; Jas. 1:10 and 1 Pet. 1:24–25). Yet as the works cited show, while there is enough overlap in thought to assert that James and 1 Peter know many of the same traditions (e.g. Jas. 5:20, which for this reason is thought by some to be a dominical saying), use the same citations from the OT (Jas. 4:6–10; Jas. 1:10–11), and know some of the same favorite forms (Jas. 1:2–4), there is neither real macrostructural similarity between the works nor enough contact to assert borrowing. In macrostructure 1 John is far closer to James. But James does share many of the traditions known to 1 Peter, which is to be expected given James's *Sitz im Leben*.

The Epistle of James — Analysis

I. Epistolary Introduction—1:1

II. Opening Statement 1:2–27
    1. First segment: testing, wisdom, wealth 1:2–11
      a. Testing produces joy 1:2–4
      b. Wisdom comes through prayer 1:5–8
      c. Poverty excels wealth 1:9–11
    2. Second segment: testing, speech, generosity 1:12–27
      a. Testing produces blessedness 1:12–18
      b. Pure speech contains no anger 1:19–21
      c. Obedience requires generosity 1:22–25
      d. Summary and transition 1:26–27

III. The Excellence of Poverty and Generosity 2:1–26
    1. No partiality is allowable 2:1–13
      a. Illustration: judicial assembly 2:1–4
      b. Rational argument 2:5–7
      c. Biblical argument 2:8–12
      d. Call to obedience (transition) 2:13
    2. Generosity is necessary 2:14–26
      a. Illustration: poor Christian 2:14–17
      b. Rational argument 2:18–20
      c. Biblical argument (two-part): Abraham; Rahab 2:21–26

IV. The Demand for Pure Speech 3:1–4:12
    1. Pure speech has no anger 3:1–12
      a. Warning against self-exaltation 3:1–2a
      b. Warning about the power of the tongue 3:2b–5a
      c. Warning about the doubleness in the tongue 3:5b–12
    2. Pure speech comes from wisdom 3:13–18
    3. Pure prayer is without anger/in trust 4:1–10(12)
      a. Prayer with anger and desire 4:1–3

  b. Condemnation of compromise 4:4–6
  c. Call to repentance 4:7–10
 4. Pure speech is uncondemning 4:11–12

V. *Testing through wealth 4:13–5:6*
 1. The test of wealth 4:13–17
 2. The test by the wealthy 5:1–6

VI. *Closing Statement 5:7–20*
 1. Endurance in the test 5:7–11
 2. Rejection of oaths 5:12
 3. Helping one another through prayer/forgiveness 5:13–18 (health)
 4. Closing encouragement 5:19–20

See further Boismard; Bultmann; Burge; Ekstrom; Exler; Forbes; Francis; Gertner; Gertner, "Midrashim"; Hill; Souček; Thyen; Wessel.

III. A POSSIBLE *SITZ IM LEBEN*

It is obvious that this work cannot offer the final answer to the *Sitz im Leben* of James. It is also clear that everyone proceeds with some setting in mind, although a few, like Dibelius, 47, almost totally abandon the attempt to find such a setting or to discuss the local conditions, believing the material to be so traditional as to rule out any more specific setting than the Diaspora Jewish Christian church and thus not Palestinian.[91] Moffatt, on the other hand, definitely locates the work in Egypt because of alleged wisdom affinities. Reicke and Laws are so impressed by similarities to Hermas and alleged Roman coloring that they confidently set the work in Rome, although at different dates.[92] Many others would place James somewhere within Palestine-Syria, e.g. Caesarea.[93] Although each setting is different, it is this setting which colors exegesis.

In the present examination of James we cannot find a clear and specific historical situation. We observe neither a definite crisis in the epistle such as those which called forth 1 Thessalonians or 1 Corinthians nor a specific persecution such as those which called forth 1 Pet. 4:12 and (probably) the book of Revelation; Jas. 1:2 covers any persecution which the church may happen to undergo. Again, the situation described in Jas. 2:2–4 is simply a parabolic narrative used to introduce a teaching, not an actual report of historical occurrences such as Cloe made to Paul. Nor

91. Cf. Bultmann, *Theology*, II, 143, who discovers a Jewish document from the Hellenistic synagogue reworked by a Christian. Such theories of dual composition are not uncommon.
92. Laws, 22–26, also Marshall, 227–247; Reicke, 6 (cf. Reicke, *Diakonie*, which develops his thesis): Laws dates James prior to Hermas, while Reicke dates it with 1 Clement.
93. Ropes, 49. Since Origen first cites James explicitly in his Palestinian period, Ropes believes that these data fit a local circulation theory.

STRUCTURAL DIAGRAM OF THE EPISTLE OF JAMES

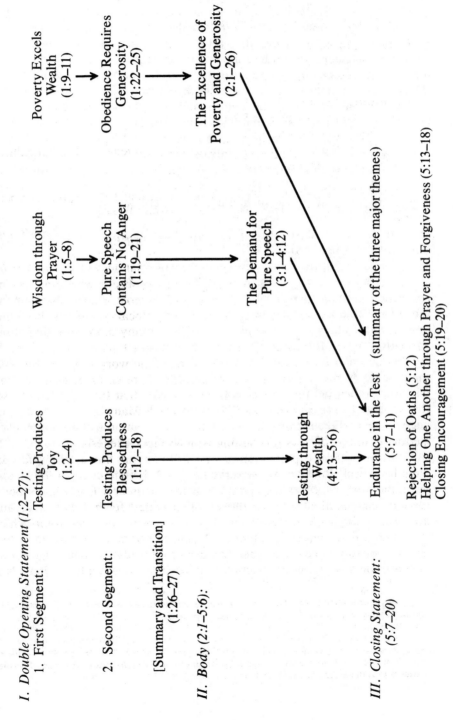

I. *Double Opening Statement (1:2–27):*
  1. First Segment:

  2. Second Segment:

  [Summary and Transition]
    (1:26–27)

II. *Body (2:1–5:6):*

III. *Closing Statement:*
    (5:7–20)

Testing Produces
Joy
(1:2–4)

Wisdom through
Prayer
(1:5–8)

Poverty Excels
Wealth
(1:9–11)

Testing Produces
Blessedness
(1:12–18)

Pure Speech
Contains No Anger
(1:19–21)

Obedience Requires
Generosity
(1:22–25)

The Excellence of
Poverty and Generosity
(2:1–26)

The Demand for
Pure Speech
(3:1–4:12)

Testing through
Wealth
(4:13–5:6)

Endurance in the Test   (summary of the three major themes)
(5:7–11)

Rejection of Oaths (5:12)
Helping One Another through Prayer and Forgiveness (5:13–18)
Closing Encouragement (5:19–20)

do we suppose that Jas. 5:1–6 is limited to one group of wealthy men. The author is largely dependent upon the traditional portrayal of the wealthy in OT prophecy.[94] But at the same time it is hard to understand how the choice of this material could not reflect the *Sitz im Leben* of the author, his readers, or both. An author would not use a theme of rich men as persecutors if he perceived the church situation as one in which the rich were members of or tolerant of the church. Nor would he portray the wealthy as farmers if he understood that the really wealthy were merchants. It is true that if an author is passing on preformed units (written or oral) from a stream of tradition his material may tell more about the situation when the units were formed than about the present situation, but if he is trying to speak to a contemporary audience (rather than serve as a literary archivist), his selection of the units will be limited to those which are relevant to his own time. Therefore one has every right to believe that the cultural descriptions in James's material describe something of the general situation in which the author of the epistle finds himself (or his readers).[95]

The basic cultural data appear in the "woe" sections in Jas. 4:13–5:6. These sections describe two groups of people: a mercantile group (4:13–17), and an agricultural group (5:1–6). James stigmatizes the latter group with the title οἱ πλούσιοι. Jas. 2:6–7 adds to the description of οἱ πλούσιοι, indicating that they have enough authority in the community and enough antipathy toward the Christians to persecute them.

While Palestine is not the only land which this cultural data may fit, the data do fit the situation in Palestine exceedingly well, especially that which prevailed before AD 70. Although Josephus (*Ap*. 1:60) claims that the ancient Israelites were simply farmers, not traders, the economic necessities of life and the needs of their land turned many Jews into traders and merchants. A limited area with a growing population simply cannot retain its total population in agriculture. Thus many younger sons were forced off the land to allow their older brothers to earn a living. At the same time the influx of Hellenistic goods attracted many to gain their fortune in trade.[96] In urban situations, especially in Jerusalem, a Jewish mercantile group arose, and trade came to be seen as the quickest means

94. Feuillet, "sens," 277.

95. Cf. Mussner, 80–83. Adamson, "Inductive," 7–52, 60, gives a fuller exposition of James's economic situation. This commentary differs with Adamson in arguing (1) that Adamson narrows the time span too closely and (2) that he overestimates the Hellenistic influence upon James. The same general picture appears in Martin, 97–103, although he appears to take Hegesippus's narrative too seriously and thus suggests a priestly setting in the 60s, which unnecessarily narrows the time span as well.

96. Schürer, II, 52–80, presents the fact of the influx of Hellenistic goods. Not only are coins and governmental terms Greek, as one would expect in an occupied land, but commercial terms and even names for common domestic items appear in Aramaic as Greek loanwords. These data suggest an influx of trade from surrounding countries, especially during the pre-70 period of prosperity. Jesus also witnesses to such trading activity (e.g. Mt. 13:45–46). Cf. Jeremias, *Jerusalem*, 30–57, 195, and G. Smith, I, 367–373.

of becoming wealthy.[97] Outside the urban centers agriculture remained the main activity of the people. In the coastal towns the physical location led to commercial activity; in Jerusalem it was simply the religious importance of the city as the center of Jewish life that made it an important trading city. Thus its commercial importance and with it much of the internal commerce of the land ceased with the destruction of the temple.[98]

James has strong words for the materialism of the merchants in the church. He accuses the merchants in essence of ignoring God and boasting in their seeming self-sufficiency.[99] But in reality this is a boast in a situation of weakness and instability. These men have failed to follow the Christian tradition enshrined in the synoptics; they have failed to place the whole of their future in the hands of God.[100]

The rich agricultural group is not a new occurrence in Palestine.[101] Palestine has been an agricultural land since primitive times, but the concentration of land in the hands of a wealthy minority stems from the setting up of the monarchy. The ancient tradition was that God alone was the owner of the land and had given it to tribal groups for division into inalienable family plots.[102] The economic changes brought about through king and conquest produced men who, with power derived from the centralized authority of the king, were able to amass large estates.[103]

97. The evidence for this situation is collected in Grant, 72–76; Heichelheim, 150 (although one must be cautious over the degree to which this work reads rabbinic descriptions back into the period before AD 70); G. Smith, I, 310–336; and Klausner, 184–192.

98. Schürer, I, 514–528, describes the postwar impoverishment. On the natural disasters which compounded the economic problems and caused something of a decline in the prewar period, cf. Jeremias, *Jerusalem*, 140–144. On the postwar depression see also Heichelheim, 182; Baron, II, 102–108. A certain amount of normalcy speedily returned to the land, despite the talmudic sayings about famine. Since most of the farms were not expropriated, agricultural life was probably back to normal c. AD 75, although population reduction due to the war probably meant the easing of some food shortages and led to other permanent changes. Trade recovered more slowly, and in Judea much of the trade never recovered, for it had depended upon the temple and the political and religious activity it attracted to Jerusalem. In places in which the rabbis had effective control, the trade restrictions they imposed for religious reasons, e.g. m. A. Zar. 1, must have limited commercial activity.

99. The term ἀλαζονεία, used to characterize these people in 4:16, means a proud or empty boast, arrogance, or pretension. Cf. commentary and BAG, 34.

100. Cf. the parable of the rich fool (Lk. 12:16–21). Paul has a similar teaching, e.g. 1 Cor. 4:19; 16:7. Cf. Mussner, 191. Two other factors are worthy of note: (1) James does not call these men οἱ πλούσιοι, and (2) he does not accuse them of exploiting others. It is true, as Adamson, "Inductive," 15–17, points out, that merchants often gained a reputation for exploitation, including profiteering in hard times (Jeremias, *Jerusalem*, 122). But James attacks only their materialism; he does not produce an attack against large-scale economic ventures as such or a proletarian protest against the wealthier classes. For him the merchants are as honest—and as sinful—as Jesus' rich fool.

101. As argued above, pp. 13–14, and shown in the commentary, the Palestinian background of either the author or the readers or both is seen in the references to the autumn and spring rains in Jas. 5:7, a weather phenomenon limited to the eastern Mediterranean coastal plain and lowlands. Cf. Krauss, II, 149–153.

102. Dalman, II, 41–46.

103. Mi. 2:2; Is. 5:8; cf. Mussner, 77; Davids, 111–112.

While the exile broke up the large estates and impoverished or destroyed their owners, it did not change the character of the people. Thus the process of the concentration of wealth repeated itself through the various circumstances of the Persian, Greek, and Roman periods; only the source of the political power, which often enough made or broke fortunes, changed. Thus despite the fact that Herod, for example, had the distressing habit of executing men and confiscating their wealth, fortunes continued to be gained (and lost), and land, because of its ancient and important place in Jewish religion and culture, continued to be the most prestigious investment.[104]

In pre-70 Palestine, then, and to a large extent in post-70 as well, one finds a cultural situation in which the majority of the population consists of peasants subsisting on a small plot of land. The size of their plots and conditions favoring a growing population forced all males but the eldest son into trade (if they were lucky) or unskilled labor. Even the resources of the eldest son were so small that given the occurrence of drought or similar calamity he was often forced to mortgage his fields to survive. (Religious regulations compounded the economic pressure upon him.) Continued poor harvests and the economic power of the wealthy landowner (who had loaned him seed or money at rates favorable to the landowner) would frequently force him off his land. Many of these landless peasants became hired laborers or tenant farmers—often on the land they had once owned—who were open to continued economic exploitation by the wealthy. The rapaciousness of the leading political figures, including the family of the high priest, was notorious during this time. The weight of heavy taxation and misgovernment added to the other economic burdens.[105]

This situation of oppressed but "free" labor prevailed because, as Heichelheim shows, unlike Italy, in Palestine landlords used hired laborers rather than slaves to work their large estates. This practice was partly due to the religious requirements connected with slaveholding. The preference for hired labor may explain the lack of references to slavery by James, who is otherwise concerned about oppressed classes, despite the fact that such prophets as Jeremiah addressed themselves to this situation and that slaves were members of the gentile church (as the *Haustafeln*

104. Jeremias, *Jerusalem,* 91, and Krauss, II, 161, point out the high value placed upon agricultural work. Cf. Test. Iss. 3:1; 6:2. Adamson, "Inductive," 7–9, 17, asserts that it was the spread of the culture of the Hellenistic bourgeoisie (called the πλούσιοι in fourth-century BC Greece) into Palestine that caused this cultural pattern. No doubt this group did spread in the Greek world and the influence of Hellenism led by the Greek language was felt in Palestine, but that the cultural phenomenon of Hellenism did anything more than influence the pattern of luxury and display among the wealthy absentee farmers of Palestine is questionable. The actual existence of these farmers and their oppressive labor policies was much older than the Hellenistic influence.

105. For the details of the taxation cf. Klausner, 179–184; Grant, 64–68; and Heichelheim, 146–150, 164–165.

show): even in the Jewish Christian church there would have been no problem with their membership, for all slaves bought by Jews were to be circumcised.[106]

After AD 135 there was a rise in industry within Palestine and an exodus of Jews from agriculture. This meant a lessening of the import trade plus a further sharp decrease in population. During both of the Jewish wars the large landholders remained more or less undisturbed, although they all suffered from heavy taxation and a few suffered confiscation. The extent of total economic recovery between the wars may perhaps be judged by the reputations of some of the rabbis from this period for wealth (although some of these reports are certainly exaggerated).[107]

This information means that one can easily picture a setting for James during the last three decades before the first Jewish War. It was after the death of Herod Agrippa I that there was a severe deterioration in the internal stability of Palestine as well as a series of famines. Also, as the Pauline collection shows, the church itself was impoverished in this period. During the last decade of this period even the temple clergy were at odds, the wealthy high-priestly families siding with the Romans and depriving the lower clergy of their tithes, while the lower clergy were impoverished and sided with the Zealots.[108]

One can picture what this situation did to the church in Palestine. On the one hand, the church naturally felt resentment against the rich. They had "robbed" many of the members of their lands; they probably showed discrimination against Christians in hiring their labor; and they (at least the high-priestly clans) were the instigators of attempts to suppress the church (which was probably viewed as a revolutionary movement). On the other hand, if a wealthy person entered the church or was a member, there would be every reason to court him. His money was seen as a means of survival. Certainly one should not offend *him*.[109]

Given the external situation, one would also expect internal effects. The generosity of the 30s and 40s had worn off. The church is now routine. Under financial pressure people tend to hold orthodox belief, but also to grasp tightly to whatever money they have. Naturally this orientation would mean a proliferation of schemes to gain more financial security, i.e. a love for the world in James's view. The class warfare outside the church led to the struggles between the Zealots and the pro-Roman parties. Within the church it would lead to complaining, bitterness, and

---

106. That slavery did exist (although the evidence is from nonagricultural urban settings) Jeremias, *Jerusalem*, 110–111, shows.

107. Cf. Baron, II, 104–105, 123, and Büchler, 33–40.

108. Jos. *Ant.* 20:180–181; Martin, 99.

109. Cf. Burchard, "Jakobus," 29–35.

party struggles, along with the temptation to join the Zealots. After all, Zealots were for the poor, as their incineration of the debt records shows.

James fits such a setting. In Acts James the Just is portrayed as a mediator, a moderator (15:13–21; 21:18–26). The book fits this picture. Against the rich, James levels stinging eschatological denunciation in line with the strongest words of Jesus (Lk. 6:24–26). His church is the church of the poor. The Jewish *ᵃnāwîm* piety shines through, but it is coupled with fervent eschatological expectation. Yet for all his sympathy for the poor, James refuses to join the Zealots. He demands that Christians give up the world. The desire to find financial security is in fact demonic, a test. Furthermore, he calls for the rejection of hatred and strife (4:1–3), abusive words (3:5b–12), and anger (1:19–20). No oaths are to be taken (5:12), including those to the Zealot cause.

The focus of these demands is, of course, on the community. James is most concerned about the breakdown of unity, love, and charity within the church. The tests of faith were breaking the church apart as people yielded to pressure. The call is for internal unity and charity with an attitude of prophetic denunciation toward the rich yet a refusal to engage in hatred and violence. The Lord's intervention, not man's, is sought. The outward collapse raises eschatological expectation.[110]

Although one can never be sure of the setting of James, this appears to be the most likely one. This commentary assumes, then, that the original traditions appeared during the early part of this period, i.e. late 40s and early 50s. They were gathered together during the latter part to solidify the church's position. Thus the work is perhaps the last picture one has of the Palestinian church before the storms of war closed over it.[111]

See further von Campenhausen, "Nachfolge"; Carroll; Polhill; Prentice; Reicke, *Diakonie*; Stauffer.

IV. THEOLOGY

As soon as one admits that there is a unity to the Epistle of James, one must also begin to look for a theology, for no matter how fragmentary and disunified the sources may have been, the end product is a redacted whole.[112] This conclusion, of course, does not mean that one can extract

---

110. If the tradition of the flight of the church to the Transjordan area is to be accepted, it clearly fits with this picture. Eventually the warring between the factions grew too intense for the church to survive. It withdrew to await divine intervention.

111. A prewar setting for the book is chosen because on the redactional level the book does not appear to be just the collected teachings of a revered leader, but a tract against the problems described above.

112. This is also true for Mussner, who sees no overall plan to the epistle, and for Hoppe, who sees the epistle as a series of large units joined together, for there is a theology within these units.

a complete picture of the author's theology or that it is systematic. It does mean that one can explore seven areas on which the author does speak and try to extract a systematic account of what he thinks.

See further Bieder; Brooks; Cranfield; Eichholz, *Jakobus*; Henderlite; Kromrei; MacGorman; Maston; Noack; Obermüller, "Themen"; Reicke, *Diakonie*; Rendtorff; Schammberger. Except where supplemental bibliography appears useful, this discussion will simply summarize and leave the detailed argument and documentation to the commentary proper.

1. Suffering/Testing

The first major theme encountered in the Epistle of James is that of suffering or testing, πειρασμός. One cannot miss it in the opening verses or in 1:12ff., but it is quite possible to forget its presence from then on. Yet the theme does not disappear, but in fact underlies much of the rest of the epistle. It is connected to the eschatological waiting of 5:7 (and likewise the need to return the erring one in 5:19–20); it is taken up in the transition verse of 4:17; it underlies the defection of 4:1–10; and it is behind the two parts of chap. 2. Thus the problem of testing forms the thread which ties the epistle together, although like the thread in any necklace, the pattern of the specific ornaments is more often seen than the thread itself.

The background of the idea of testing/suffering in Judaism cannot be more than summarized at this point. The literature is far too vast to attempt any in-depth development, but several strands can be observed. First, the earliest material in Judaism normally connects suffering to sin, individual or corporate. God has been offended, so the person suffers until the offense is removed. On the other hand, the righteous person is marked by good fortune in life. Thus Joseph, for example, always ends up on top, despite the machinations of others. Although true in many situations, this explanation did not form a universally valid description of suffering.

Second, out of the experience of the divided monarchy (especially the experiences of the prophets) and the exile, Judaism became aware that suffering is often the lot of the righteous and thus rooted not in personal sinfulness, but in spiritual realities larger than the individual. It is in this context that the testing tradition belongs, a tradition itself older than the context—the testing of Abraham (Genesis 22) and the testing of Israel in the wilderness are eloquent here. But as the tradition developed (e.g. in the prose narrative of Job), God is seen as allowing his choicest servants to endure suffering at the hands of a Satan figure. As part of this development the older traditions were rewritten to remove God as the direct cause of suffering and to introduce Satan (Belial, Mastema; e.g. 1QM 16–17; Jub. 17–19). Thus suffering became the field of conflict: if the person who suffers gives in and blames God, God (and he) loses, but if the person remains firm, God wins and the person is rewarded. Furthermore, even in works like Sirach and Wisdom in which the dualism of Jubilees never appears, suffering has a positive value, for it refines and tests the pious so that they come out of it with more virtue and worthy of greater rewards. In all of these accounts two individuals stand out: Abraham (who has 10 tests in many accounts) and Job. In fact, these saints are used to show that suffering is the *normal* experience of the pious rather than a foreign experience.

See further Batley; Carmignac; Carmignac, "théologie"; Crenshaw; Davids, 1–184; W. Eichrodt, "Vorsehungsglaube"; Flusser; Gerhardsson; Leaney; Peake; J. A. Sanders; Scharbert; Stamm; Sutcliffe; Wichmann.

Third, closely related to the problem of suffering is that of the origin of sin. Here there are two developments which are important for this epistle. On the one hand, sin was increasingly seen as a force within the human being, an evil impulse of *yēṣer*. This impulse is simply pure, undirected desire and thus part of the created nature. But desire alone is a dangerous force, for it grasps all it can by whatever means are available. Thus the evil impulse leads into sin in that it breaks the bounds of the legitimate. What is needed, however, is not the total removal of all desire, but a counterforce (variously described as the law, the good impulse, or the Holy Spirit) which channels and limits the evil impulse into doing good. The struggle within is won when the person gives the upper hand to the good impulse.

On the other hand, the problem of sin was also increasingly externalized. Satan (by whatever name he was designated) was viewed as being in a contest with God for people. This dualistic picture was not absolute, of course, for within Judaism the outcome was certain (e.g. 1QM). The strategy of the evil force was to use whatever spirits or other means were available to lead people astray and to make to suffer those who remained faithful to God. The seriousness of such a challenge to faith by Satan is clearly reflected in the final pair of petitions in the Lord's Prayer.

Given these two directions, one must not think of them as mutually exclusive. Paul, for example, was clearly aware of both the evil *yēṣer* (Romans 7) with its counteragent of the Spirit (Romans 8) and of the role of Satan in temptation and apostasy (e.g. 2 Cor. 2:11). The link between the internal and external testing and the coexistence of the ideas that one belongs to the elect group and yet is sinful are both found in the DSS. Thus the NT has no exclusive claim on the conjunction.

See further Davids, 1–93; Davies, *Paul*, 17–35; Edlund; Hadot; Malina; Murphy; Porter; Seitz, "Spirits"; C. Smith; Stacey; Tennant; N. Williams; Wolverton.

James uses this theology in his own creative way. He is well aware of the connection between sin and suffering, especially illness. This he addresses in 5:14–16, which allows that confession of sin may in fact be part of the healing process. Yet the conditional sentences he uses point to his deeper concern: there is a danger that suffering may lead one into sin or that one may sin to avoid suffering.

The real burden of the epistle, then, appears in 1:2–4, 12–15. The community he addresses is facing the problem of suffering. The suffering is not acute persecution, but circumstances which the author sees as a test, πειρασμός. The test ought to create eschatological anticipated joy, for God's purpose is not in any way malevolent but purificatory. They will show the virtue of patient endurance and thus come through with a greater perfection than before: they will be the tried and true (i.e. δόκιμος, 1:12).

On the other hand, there are evidently some in the community who find the situation hard. They are tempted to blame God in the testing situation as Israel did in the wilderness. This act signals failure, a giving in to the evil impulse. Such people are sternly warned that God is not to be put to the test (1:13). Their failure is due to their own internal impulse (ἐπιθυμία), not God. He is not the one leading them to evil.

Three other factors also appear in the testing context. First, one of the pressures upon the group is economic. It is no accident that Abraham and Job, heavily tested individuals known in popular tradition for their approved character and great charity,[113] are both cited. Desire will lead some to compromise and seek financial security in the world. True faith will remain charitable whatever the pressure. Second, it is the evil impulse (ἡδονή) which is also the source of internal community strife (4:1ff.), for the internal strife is the product of the desire to have. Here the compromise with the world is far clearer, and it is denounced in absolutely explosive terms. Third, the external tempter is not forgotten by James. In chap. 1 the tempter does not appear, but in 3:15 he is first seen as the source of the "wisdom" which is dividing the community. Then in 4:7 those led astray by the evil impulse are told to resist the devil. Clearly James does not stress this dualism for pastoral purposes, but just as clearly he recognizes the power of spiritual-demonic evil behind the internal evil in the person. James shares the ambiguity of Qumran and Paul in recognizing the propensity to evil within the person while acknowledging the suprapersonal forces of evil in the world. He shares with late Judaism the desire not to attribute the testing situation to God, while at the same time he refrains from directly involving Satan because of his interest in calling people to repentance and responsibility. Yet the presence of the devil is not entirely masked.

---

113. Cf. Davids, "Tradition," for a fuller discussion of these examples.

The proper reaction to suffering, then, is not to give in to the evil impulse and accuse God, but to endure patiently. The ὑπομονή of chap. 1 is the μακροθυμῶ of chap. 5. Patient endurance is repeated three times in two verses and then is taken up again two verses later with a repetition of ὑπομονή. This is the call of the book both in its introduction and its thematic reprise. The what and how appears between the two sections.

Thus James falls squarely into the testing/suffering tradition. The tests can lead to maturity if endured, yet they do not come from God, but from the evil one. The tests involve suffering, but the suffering will lead to glory, as in the case of Job.

See further Nauck; Thomas.

2. Eschatology

In discussing the suffering/testing theme which underlies the whole book, one could not help but notice the eschatology. It was argued above that the suffering theme fits into a dualistic context similar to the one found in Qumran. A similar type of dualism underlies the gospels with their clear battles between Jesus and Satan, light and darkness, and it may also be discovered in Paul. It is not surprising then to find that the eschatology behind these works is also reflected in James.

The strongest eschatological passage in James is the thematic reprise of 5:7–11. Here the Christian is called to suffering and enduring with a patient attitude in the face of the παρουσία τοῦ κυρίου. This παρουσία is said to be ἤγγικεν (5:8). Thus the author sees the church standing at the end of history. The tension between this age and the age to come is high. The inbreaking of the new age is imminent. The need of the moment is not resistance to evil, but perseverance in the good. The church needs to hold together in the face of the intense pressures upon it while it, like Job, awaits the resolution of the eschatological battle.

Having described the attitude of the church, we must quickly move on to point out that the coming day is a call to faithfulness in the face of judgment. To those who would break the unity of the church by grumbling about their brothers, the message is, "the judge stands before the door." For the persecutors of the poor (i.e. the Christians) the message is a reflection of the OT prophets: the eschatological judgment is so near that their wealth is already moth-eaten and rusted; they have treasured up indeed, but in the last days (there is no distant future); the cries of those they have defrauded have already entered the ears of the Lord; and they have feasted "in the day of slaughter" indeed, but now it is in fact the day of eschatological slaughter. In this context the call to be patient until the parousia of the Lord is ominous. The comfort that coming will bring the poor Christians can be no comfort at all for the rich. The tones are the somber ones of the OT judgment oracles as reflected through NT apocalyptic tradition.

Literarily, then, James's eschatology lives in the world of Mark 13, Matthew 24–25, 2 Thessalonians 2, and the book of Revelation. This is a world of intense apocalyptic expectancy; the return of Christ is awaited without any thought of parousia delay.[114] The call is for faithfulness to the end; the coming of Christ will bring the desired judgment and justice. There is hardly a breath of realized eschatology.

Yet eschatology is not the burden of the book; it is the context of the book. James shares a thought-world with his readers, so there is no need to give detailed instruction. This community, like Paul's (cf. 2 Thessalonians 2), has seen to it that the apocalyptic teaching is among the basics of the faith. Without an appreciation of the foundational role this teaching played in the Christian world view of James's church, one could hardly understand the joy referred to in 1:2, 12. This is, as J. Thomas has aptly put it, *"eschatologische Vorfreude,"* anticipated joy in the face of trials because of the reward which one knows is fast approaching. It is no wonder that the reward in 1:12 is expressed in the same terms used in Rev. 2:10. Whatever the date of the final form of James, the work is solidly within the tradition which Schweitzer saw in Jesus and which later flowed into the book of Revelation.[115]

See further Aland; A. Moore, 149–151; Obermüller, "Themen."

3. Christology

If the Lord is coming, there is some use in asking who this Lord is. That is, what is the nature of the Christology of the letter? Here utmost caution must be exercised, for the Christology of James is an assumed Christology. The author refers to ideas as needed; he feels no compulsion to explain Christology. Thus one cannot be sure the picture which emerges fully represents his thought.

Two explicit christological passages exist in James. In 1:1 he refers to himself as a κυρίου Ἰησοῦ Χριστοῦ δοῦλος and in 2:1 he refers to a faith "of our glorious Lord, Jesus Christ" (τοῦ κυρίου ἡμῶν Ἰησοῦ Χριστοῦ τῆς δόξης). While the grammar of these passages is difficult and their authenticity has been disputed, they reveal the clearest christological affirmation of the letter.[116] The passages show that like Paul (Rom. 1:1;

---

114. The role played by parousia delay anywhere in the early church outside of 2 Peter is debatable; cf. Smalley. But even if Smalley were wrong, there is no hint of a problem with delay in James.

115. His eschatology may have been one reason James was poorly accepted at first, for a similar resistance met the book of Revelation.

116. Only scholars like Spitta and Meyer, who wish to deny the Christian character of the work, deny the authenticity of these verses. Cf. Introduction, 2–22, and the commentary.

Phil. 1:1) the author considers himself not only a servant of God but also
of Jesus Christ. There is also a faith which concerns this person, apparently meaning a body of doctrine and practice, if the same meaning for
faith is intended in 2:14ff. as well.

The key statement the author makes occurs in the term κύριος, for
this is obviously his favorite term for Christ (11 times in the epistle). This
fact means that he thinks of Christ primarily as the resurrected Lord, the
one to whom all people should submit. Obviously this view of Christ fits
well with Pauline thought, although it was in existence long before Paul
flourished,[117] as the *Maran*-type formulae indicate (e.g. 1 Cor. 16:22; cf.
Acts 2:26).

Given the author's view of Jesus as the ascended Lord, one notes
the absence of a *theologia crucis,* a son-of-God Christology, or a savior
Christology (which absence eventually put his work on Luther's black-
list). The reason for this absence is clear enough. First, the *theologia
crucis* appears to be Paul's special contribution *in his epistles.* If Acts
represents anything of the early Christian preaching, it represents it as
based upon a proclamation of Jesus as Lord and Christ, not upon the
detailed arguments about the cross found in Paul. The latter became necessary because of Paul's conversion experience on the one hand and his
need to deal with the law-grace issue on the other. Thus it was properly
the concern of his controversial epistles and played a much smaller role
if any within Jewish Christian communities.[118] Second, it is clear that the
author is interested in showing Christians their proper role at the end of
the age under the threat of the return of the exalted Lord. The other
christological formulations simply do not fit into this picture. The parallel
in 1:1 between God and Christ makes one suspect that a son-of-God
concept would not have been foreign to the author, but it obviously did
not serve the purposes of the epistle.

What, then, is said about the Lord? (1) The Lord is the source of
spiritual gifts of wisdom, etc. (1:7); (2) the Lord is the one before whom
one should be humbled (4:10); (3) the Lord is the one who controls history
and personal destiny (4:15; 5:4, 10, 11); (4) the Lord will come and end
history (5:7, 8); and (5) the Lord is the one in whose name the sick are
anointed and who will heal them (5:13–16). It is apparent from these
references that they do not all refer to Christ. As the commentary will
show, probably those grouped under (1), (2), and (3) refer to God, while
the others are more probably christological.[119] To these one should add
the reference to the "royal law" of 2:8 as another possible reference to

---

117. Bultmann, *Theology,* I, 124–126, ranked this title among the pre-Pauline ideas
taken over by Paul.

118. Longenecker, *Paul*; Stendahl; and E. Sanders add clarification on this point.

119. The variant in 1:12 refers to Christ as the giver of the "crown of life" in harmony
with "judge" in 5:9, if the parallel in Rev. 2:10 is any guide.

Christ, noting, however, that although it would then refer to a word of the earthly Jesus, the adjective βασιλικός says no more than Χριστός and κύριος do. A final addition is the title κριτής (5:9).

The conclusions one may draw from this list are relatively limited. The picture of God which one obtains (θεός appears 17 times in chaps. 1–4) is fairly standard in Jewish and Christian thought. God is one (2:19), the creator (1:17; 3:9) of unchanging character who revealed himself to Abraham (2:23) and through the prophets (5:10). God has elected the Christian, i.e. the poor (1:18; 2:5), and grants him the heavenly wisdom and other good things (1:5, 17). God is the proper object of worship (3:9), who never leads people astray (1:13). His sovereign will is not to be challenged (1:13). God has a righteous purpose which is not served by human anger, but by human charity (1:20, 27). This purpose means he is diametrically opposed to the world and all human pride (4:4, 6) and is the righteous leader of the hosts of heaven in judgment (5:4), but is also ready to receive all those who submit to him, all those who humble themselves and repent (4:7, 8).

The picture of Christ is that of (1) the leader of the church whose sayings still provide guidance for it,[120] (2) the exalted Lord in heaven in whose name the community is baptized (2:7) and through whom healing is available, and (3) the coming Lord and judge, who will execute the justice of God within the church and upon the earth, presumably setting up God's righteous kingdom as his anointed one.

This picture is hardly a developed Christology, but it is a Christology. It has all the usual ambivalence of the early church in that lines are not clearly defined; what is attributed to God in one case may be a function of his Christ in another. Yet it is a consistent picture. If one other phrase might describe it that would be "primitive and un-Pauline," for it is certainly among the simplest Christologies in the NT, showing no trace of Pauline developments. This fact can hardly be used as a firm dating tool, however, for we do not know if James believes more than he expresses, and we suspect Paul's influence was much less pervasive in large areas of the early church than has often been thought true.[121]

See further Mussner, "Christologie."

4. Poverty-Piety

The christological affirmations in James as well as the problem of suffering with which he deals are all related to the piety-poverty equation. It is obvious that this is one of the key themes in the book.

120. This conclusion stems from the extensive contact between James and the sayings tradition, not only in 2:8 and 5:12, but throughout the epistle. See below, pp. 47–48.

121. A further fruitful study could compare James and the Johannine tradition. There are many similarities between James and 1 John in doctrine and between James and the Fourth Gospel in Christology (e.g. John 5, judge and lawgiver).

The background of the concepts in James is deeply rooted in Jewish thought. Naturally there are parts of the OT which glorify wealth as a reward from God (e.g. the Abraham cycle), and these point to the fact that neither OT nor NT is ascetic. Yet it was clear to the biblical writers by the period of the prophets that piety often led to poverty as ruthless people took advantage of the honest and upright person. It was also clear that the same people took advantage of the weaker classes in society in general, forcing them first from their land and then into slavery. It is this process, one which was perfectly legal according to the civil law of that period but morally abhorrent according to religious law, that drove the prophets to cry out against the wealthy oppressors of the poor:

> For crime after crime of Israel
> I will grant them no reprieve,
> because they sell the innocent for silver
> and the destitute for a pair of shoes.
> They grind the heads of the poor into the earth
> and thrust the humble out of their way.
> (Am. 2:6–7 *NEB*; cf. 5:10–13; 8:4–6)

This was the iniquity of your sister Sodom: she and her daughters had pride of wealth and food in plenty, comfort and ease, and yet she never helped the poor and wretched.

(Ezk. 16:49 *NEB*)

Three factors should be noted in these passages, which are selected from a host of possible examples. First, the action of the wealthy in taking advantage of the poor or *simply in failing to help* them is a crime, a sin. The wealthy are not condemned for their wealth *per se* but for how they use it. Second, the word pair *'ānî we'ebyôn* ("poor and wretched") had come into use as a technical designation of the poor by the exilic period. Third, the concept of poor was readily paired with that of innocent (or righteous, *ṣaddîq*).

The basis of the prophetic denunciation of the wealthy who failed to help the poor is embodied in Israelite law: God loves and cares for the poor. First, "the Book of the Covenant declares it to be Yahweh's will as Ruler that there should be no permanent or hopeless poverty in the community."[122] Second, because of this fact God declares himself to be the protector of the poor, often naming their typical classes: widow, orphan, foreigner, and Levite.[123] Third, a demand to act like God in this respect was built into the covenant and tied in with the fundamental act of redemption, the exodus, so to ignore the demand (i.e. to fail to help the poor or to take advantage of them through interest on loans, etc.) was a

122. E. Bammel, *TDNT* VI, 889–890; Ex. 21:2; 23:10.
123. Cf. Eichrodt, II, 357; von Rad, I, 400–401.

fundamental breach of the covenant with God. Thus in Dt. 10:16–19 one reads:

> So now you must circumcise the foreskin of your hearts and not be stubborn any more, for the Lord your God is God of gods and Lord of lords, the great, mighty, and terrible God. He is no respecter of persons and is not to be bribed; he secures justice for widows and orphans, and loves the alien who lives among you, giving him food and clothing. You too must love the alien, for you once lived as aliens in Egypt.[124]

It is obvious that the conviction that God cares for the poor and defends them against their oppressors, fundamental as it is in Hebrew covenantal formulae, would form a fine basis for the prophetic denunciation of those who ignored it. But even if less obvious, it was equally true that the same fundamental principle formed the basis for the response of the oppressed to God in the Psalms. Thus there was not only a theology about the poor, but also a theologically informed piety of the poor.

Two images emerge in the Psalms with respect to the poor. The first is that the ideal king will act like God and defend the rights of the poor (e.g. Ps. 72:1–2). The second is that the poor (often using the compound title 'ānî wᵉ'ebyôn) call boldly upon God and assume his help because they are poor. They know "the Lord listens to the poor" (Ps. 69:32–33) and thus on this basis the pious call upon him:

> Turn to me, LORD, and answer;
>   I am downtrodden and poor.
> Guard me, for I am constant and true;
>   save thy servant who puts his trust in thee.
>
>   (Ps. 86:1–2 NEB)

This latter fact means that downtrodden pious individuals and groups found the term "the poor" an acceptable self-designation, which formed a basis for its future development.

Within the intertestamental period three basic developments took place. First, the traditional piety of the need to care for the poor remained strong and became a fundamental religious duty (Sir. 4:1–10; Tob. 1:8; Wis. 19:14–15). Second, the wealthy were increasingly viewed as unlikely to be pious and in at least one work were roundly cursed (Sir. 31:5; 13:2–8; Test. Jud. 19; Eth. Enoch 94–105; 108:7–15). Third, the poor were increasingly viewed as being pious (Sir. 10:22–24; 13:15–20), and this close association of piety with poverty made "the poor" either a name or a popular self-designation of pious groups who felt oppressed (Pss. Sol. 5, 10, 15, 18; Test. Jud. 25:4; 1QpHab 12:3, 6, 10; 4QpPs37; 1QM 11:9; cf. Gn. Rab. 71:1). Even when the term was used as a self-

---

124. NEB; cf. Dt. 16:3; 26:7, which follow from Ex. 3:7; 4:31.

designation, however, it did not lose its original sense: a pious group
would use this term only when they perceived themselves in some sense
as oppressed or impoverished.

It was this admittedly rich and multiform background upon which
Jesus and the early church called. Whether one thinks of Jesus and his
band (e.g. Mt. 8:20), the Jerusalem community (Gal. 2:10; Rom. 15:26),
or the Pauline churches (1 Cor. 1:26ff.; 2 Cor. 8:1ff.), the early Christian
groups found themselves generally in the category of "the poor." They
also were frequently oppressed for one reason or another, and their oppressors had the requisite power and wealth to be effective.[125] Thus the
traditional material on the piety of the poor fitted their sociological situation well, even though they never used the term "the poor" as a formal
community name.

Jesus himself gave a fresh impetus to the piety-poverty tradition in
the early church, particularly in the version of his teaching in Luke, but
also in the other gospels. That he valued charity and set an example which
led to the Spirit-inspired economic sharing mentioned in Acts is not in
the least surprising (e.g. Mk. 12:4–44; 14:3–9). On the other hand, it is
equally clear that he was known as a person who moved with some ease
among wealthy and disreputable people. It thus comes as a natural development that he would bless the poor (Lk. 6:20–21),[126] particularly in
the light of his demand that his disciples give up all to follow him (Mk.
10:28–30 par.). The piety of the Psalms that views God as caring for the
poor is characteristic of Jesus, yet it does surprise us when he curses the
rich (Lk. 6:24–25). There are in fact a number of sayings which support
this passage, so we are not dealing with an isolated text.

Three aspects of Jesus' thought lie behind the curse on the rich.
First, in a whole set of sayings Jesus commanded his listeners not to
worry about wealth (Mt. 6:19–34 par.). Not to worry about wealth means
not to store up wealth, but to seek righteousness and to put treasure in
heaven. The rich almost by definition have their wealth stored on earth
and thus are not rich toward God. The parable of the rich fool flows out
of this line of thought (Lk. 12:13–21). Second, we have the whole reversal-
of-fortunes theme: "the first shall be last and the last first." When this
is applied to the economic circumstances of the disciples, we discover
that the poor have eschatological blessedness and the wealthy conversely
have received their reward already. The beatitudes obviously are based

125. The accounts in the gospels list the chief priests and other powerful groups as
opposing Jesus, while in Acts Paul's oppressors are often the leading men and women of
a given city. In 2 Corinthians 11 Paul lists sufferings including several punishments which
would arise only if powerful officials were involved.

126. The parallel in Mt. 5:3 has the other side of this theme. The basic characteristic
of the pious poor is their total dependence upon God. Matthew exegetes the saying in terms
of this inner quality in parallel with the expression in 1QM 14:5–8. Cf. Yadin, 327; Davids,
253–259.

on this concept, particularly in their Lucan form, as is the parable of the
rich man and Lazarus (Lk. 16:19-31), for the poor man is blessed because
he suffered and the rich man suffers because he enjoyed his goods (Lk.
16:25), the implication being that he should have shared them with the
poor and thus received his reward in heaven (possibly the meaning of Lk.
16:9; so Hiers). Third, there is the warning against wealth and the world,
or the divided heart. Thus the rich can hardly enter the kingdom because
they are tied to wealth (Mk. 10:24–25). The disciple is called to forsake
all for Christ even to the point of taking up his cross. The world is such
an uncompromising foe that one cannot serve God and mammon. It is
either one or the other, never both.[127] The important thing is that one's
"eye" be "single," i.e. that one be generous because one is totally fixed
on God.[128]

Obviously much more could be said about the teaching of Jesus, but
this is not the context for a full development of the material.[129] Yet enough
has been said to indicate that although "the poor" was hardly a name for
the church, it was a description of the community, and thus a theology
of the poor fits well in the teaching of Jesus.[130] It was natural for the
leaders of the early church to pick up the major themes of poverty theology and apply them in their own situations.

James applies the teaching of Jesus within the context of the themes
of testing and suffering already developed. In doing so it becomes clear
that the major pressure upon the community is economic pressure, and
the major test has to do with the world.

It is clear first of all that James has great sympathy for the poor and
that the term is virtually identical in his mind with "Christian," probably
due to the community's circumstances and the traditional piety-poverty
link. In 1:9 it is the humble or poor brother (ταπεινός = 'ānî) who in the
reversal of fortunes receives eschatological exaltation. This is a cause for
anticipated joy, the *eschatologische Vorfreude* found also in 1:2, 12.[131]
Similarly, in 2:5 God has chosen the poor "rich in faith and heirs of the
kingdom which he has promised to those who love him" (the last clause
also appears in 1:12 with respect to those enduring the test). The elect
are the poor. The same point is also made in 5:7 where the "brothers"
exhorted to patience are surely those suffering at the hands of the rich
denounced in the previous paragraph. Thus each place identifies the community with the poor and oppressed group. Also, each of these passages
sets the promise within an eschatological or even an apocalyptic context.
In the first passage the poor are already exalted, in the second a coming

127. Mt. 6:24 par. Lk. 16:13. Cf. Schnackenburg, 125.
128. Mt. 6:22–23. Cf. Cadbury.
129. Cf. Davids, "Poor."
130. Keck, 111; Dibelius, "Motiv," 190; Bornkamm, 76.
131. So Thomas.

reward is promised, and in the third they are waiting for the coming of the judge who will set things right.

Second, James also has the reverse side of the theme: οἱ πλούσιοι are the wealthy persecutors of the church. It is not that the church does not contain some wealthy individuals: the sections 4:13ff. and 2:1ff. refer to them. But in each of these cases the author referred to them by circumlocutions which avoid the use of the offensive term πλούσιος (in 2:1–4 the description is hyperbolic as well). Those named "the rich" are mentioned three times. In 1:10–11 they are described by the reversal-of-fortunes motif: they are "humiliated" while the poor are exalted. This is complemented by the addition of the Is. 40:6–7 saying about their fading as grass. They will "perish."[132] Surely that is no description of the community member to whom the next verse holds out the promise of a crown of life. In 2:6–7 they appear again. Here there is an ironic accusation, for the Christians, i.e. οἱ πτωχοί, have become the persecutors of the poor through their favoritism and thus taken the role of the rich. It is the rich who are accused of (1) oppression, (2) legal persecution, and (3) blasphemy of Christ. These rich are not Christians, but rather the enemies of the church.[133] In 5:1–6, using highly traditional language, the author roundly cursed the rich and threatened them with hell. The very fact that the language is so full of the OT makes the term οἱ πλούσιοι more outstanding, for in the OT this is never a name for the persecutor; only Eth. Enoch and Jesus specifically curse the rich. Here again the rich are on their way to perdition and stand in contrast to the Christian community (ἀδελφοί).

The reason for the sharp dichotomy and stress on economic distinctions appears in three places. First, 1:22–27 makes it clear that one concern of the author is that belief lead to action, to a doing which includes charity. The problem is then explicitly dealt with in 2:14–26, where the author rules that those who fail to practice charity, i.e. who do not show actions in accord with what they profess, have a totally worthless (i.e. nonsalvific) faith. In this context Abraham as the great example of charity appears. Finally, 4:1–8 attacks the root theology. These people are unwilling to share because they really are motivated by desire and love the world. They are thus making themselves enemies of God. Over them is written the charge: "to the one knowing to do good and not doing it, it is sin" (4:17).

The test, then, is especially the test of charity. Will the Christian really stand the test and share with the rest of the community? Or will the person show himself to be of a divided heart and really a lover of the

132. = damnation. Cf. Laws, "Scripture," 214.
133. The three charges may not be separate; the rich may have hauled the Christians into court and spoken disrespectfully of their belief to gain the sympathy of the court. That may have been their only oppressive action.

world, an adulterer (apostate) from God? The issue is set in the sharpest terms by the use of the piety-poverty theology.

See further E. Bammel, *TDNT* VI, 885–915; Betz; Birkeland; Bolkestein; Causse; Cronbach; P. Davids, 184–305, 448–509; Degenhardt; de Vaux, 68–74; Gelin; E. Gerstenberger, *THAT* I, 19–25; Hengel; Humbert; Jocz; Koch; Kuschke; Laws, "Ethics"; Legasse; Martin-Achard; Navone, 170ff.; Noack, "Jakobus"; Osborn; Percy, 45–108; Rahlfs; van der Ploeg; von Waldow.

5. Law, Grace, and Faith

The issue of law and grace not only colored the previous discussion, but also has made James most famous. This issue is problematic for several reasons: (1) the terms are critical catchwords in the theologies of most biblical interpreters; (2) the terms have been underlined by discussion from Luther on; and (3) the terms are multivalent in that they have a wide field of semantic possibilities. Thus, although this essay is summarizing the discoveries of the commentary, it must proceed carefully.

First, it is clear that the law is not an issue for James's community. The law is mentioned in three passages: 1:25; 2:8–12; and 4:11–12. In each of these passages the validity of the law is not argued, but simply assumed. In 1:25 it is quite simply νόμος τέλειος, the law as a perfect guide for life. In 2:8 it is νόμος βασιλικός, the sovereign law or the law as interpreted by Jesus. Here is an attitude toward the law similar to Matthew's (Mt. 5:17–20), but in no way as defensive. James has no need to argue about the law, but simply works from it.

The contact between James and the law is similar to Matthew in another way as well. Like the Sermon on the Mount, James has no interest in the ceremonial aspects of the OT, but simply in moral imperatives, as the following chart illustrates:

JAMES AND THE SYNOPTIC TRADITION[134]

James	Matthew	Luke	Source
1:2	5:11–12	6:23	Q
1:4	5:48		
1:5	7:7	11:9	Q
1:6	21:21		Mk. 11:23–24
1:12	10:22		
1:17	7:11	11:13	Q
1:20	5:22		
1:21		8:8	
1:22	7:24	6:46–47	Q
1:23	7:26	6:49	Q
2:5	5:3, 5; 11:5	6:20; 7:22	Q
2:6		18:3	
2:8	22:39–40		

134. Sources for this chart include Davies, *Setting*, 402–403; Mayor, lxxxv–lxxxviii; and Mussner, 48–50.

JAMES AND THE SYNOPTIC TRADITION

James	Matthew	Luke	Source
2:10	5:19		
2:11	5:21–22		
2:13	5:7		
2:15	6:25		
3:12	7:16	6:44, 45	Q
3:18	5:9		
4:2	7:7		
4:3	7:7–8; 12:39		
4:4	6:24	16:13	Q
4:8	6:22		
4:9	5:4 ?	6:25	
4:10	23:12	14:11; 18:14	Q
4:11–12	7:1	6:37	Q
4:13–14	6:34		
4:17		12:47	
5:1		6:24–25	
5:2	6:19–20	6:37; 12:33	Q
5:6		6:37	
5:8	24:3, 27, 39		
5:9	5:22; 7:1; 24:33		5:9b = Mk. 13:29
5:10	5:11–12	6:23	Q
5:12	5:34–37		
5:17		4:25	

MORE GENERAL PARALLELS IN THOUGHT

1:9–10; 4:10	18:4; 23:12	9:40; 14:11; 22:26	
1:26–27; 2:14–26	7:21–23		
2:14–16	25:31–46		
3:1–12	12:36–37		
3:13–18	11:19		
4:17	12:47		
5:5		16:19	
5:7			Mk. 4:26–29
5:19	18:15	17:3	Q

Of the 36 parallels listed, 25 are with the Sermon on the Mount and 3 others with the Sermon on the Plain. Only 8 are parallels to other teachings of Jesus. Furthermore, there is only slight contact with Mark or Q (other than in the Sermon). Thus Davies may well be right in stating, "The Epistle of James reveals that outside the Matthean, there were other communities where the words of Jesus not merely constituted a reservoir of moral cultivation in a generalized way, but also a new law."[135]

The law for James, then, is primarily ethical commandment. This

---

135. Davies, *Setting*, 404–405. This topic is the subject of future research by the author.

fact naturally says nothing about the ceremonial practice of his community: it may or may not have practiced circumcision or taken part in other aspects of the Jewish cultus as far as the data available are concerned.[136] It did accept the law as a normative guide for ethics, a position that Paul would not have found unacceptable in the proper context.[137]

The comparison with Matthew, however, should not be pushed too far. The two are alike insofar as they are interested in moral norms and argue the continuing value of a properly interpreted law. But there is no evidence of any literary dependence between the two, and in three ways James is closer to Luke's sermon.[138]

First, his vocabulary is similar. Of the words found only in James and the synoptic gospels in the NT, 22 are in common with Luke-Acts versus a total of 9 for the others. Thus about 70% of such words are in common with Luke-Acts, while only about 15% are in common with Matthew and about 15% with Mark.[139] In itself this datum means only that James has a grasp of Greek similar to Luke's—only a few of the terms are theological ones (ἀκαταστασία, δέησις, ζῆλος, ἡδονή, θρησκεία, μοιχαλίδος, ποιητής, προσωπολημψία, ταπείνωσις, ὑπομονή)—but it is suggestive of a further relationship between the two traditions.

Second, there is a close similarity in their eschatology. Both see this age as one of conflict with Satan. Both see the real hope for the age in the future consummation of the kingdom. Both demand perseverance in the face of trial.[140] The list could be continued, but the similarities are obvious.

Third, James's social outlook is close to Luke's. Only James and Luke in the whole NT contain curses on the rich. The material on wealth and its dangers and the call to give up all for the sake of the kingdom fill chapters in Luke (6, 12, 14, 16, 19). In James a similar view of wealth and poverty and a similar demand for charity appear in virtually every chapter. Both works are also concerned for communal solidarity rather than an individualistic piety (here Acts and James are similar). Again the list could be extended.

The result of this examination is not to say that James knew Luke or came from his community, but simply to argue for similarity. The lack of verbal parallels and the combined similarity to both Matthew and Luke point to James's having used the unwritten Jesus tradition freely. Insofar

136. If the assumption is correct that the community was Judean, then Jewish cultic practice is virtually assured, but that is data extraneous to the book and its interests. Laws, 14–15, disputes any notion that James's community accepted the whole law, including the cultic sections.

137. Cf. the extensive discussion in Drane.

138. Knox, 14–16, argued for this on a structural level, noting the opening beatitude and final exhortation.

139. Adamson, "Inductive," 293–295.

140. Cf. Brown, Lk. 22:28–46, and the πειρασμός theme in James.

as Matthew has preserved and enhanced its interest in the reinterpreted law, James is closer to Matthew. Yet for James it is not the gospels, but the words of Jesus himself that form the new law; indeed, Jesus' pervasive influence underlies the whole of James's teaching.[141]

Even if James assumed the value and validity of the law, he is not a legalist. He never argues that the essence of Christianity is anything other than a commitment to God in Christ or a reception of grace from God. The regeneration of the Christian comes through God's action in his word (1:18). Salvation comes through the "implanted word" which must be "received in meekness" (1:21). God gives grace to the repentant (4:6). None of these sentiments is at all at variance with Paul.

The problem with James arises because he stresses the results of commitment to Christ and uses much of the critical theological terminology in a way different from Paul. James has observed much verbal commitment to Christian affirmations without endurance and with a lack of practical follow-through.[142] The answer James gives is that "the proof of the pudding is in the tasting": the resulting obedience of the Christian is the proof of the sincerity of his or her repentance and commitment. Or, put another way, the verbal profession of "religion" is meaningless without the life to back it up (so 1:26–27); one remains simply a "hearer" until the word takes root in one's heart and produces a "doer." Grace which has no outward result is not grace at all.[143]

The critical passage in 2:14–26 bears this out. The argument is that verbal, intellectual assent to doctrine is meaningless unless an altered life-style reveals a truly salvific commitment. In arguing thus James appears verbally opposed to Paul, yet uses every critical term differently. Πίστις in James has previously indicated a trust in God (1:3, 6; 2:5; 5:15) or the content of such trust (2:1), both meanings similar to Paul's. Now the same term is used 12 times in 13 verses and the verb twice to indicate intellectual assent to doctrines such as "God is one." Even the demons are more personally involved—at least they tremble (2:19)! This is far different from Paul's use of πίστις.

A second term is ἔργα. For Paul the ἔργα he is against are always ἔργα νόμου, either explicitly stated or clearly intended in the context. These are never moral prescriptions, but rather ceremonial rites added to the work of Christ. In James ἔργα are always moral deeds, especially acts

141. Many scholars have argued that some or all of the following may be agrapha: Jas. 1:12, 17; 4:5–6, 17; 5:20. If this is the case, the teaching of Jesus is pervasive indeed in this work. Cf. Adamson, "Inductive," 301–303.

142. There is some similarity between this idea and the Johannine concern of remaining in Christ and his words (although in that corpus a doctrinal as well as an ethical sense is intended), as well as Hebrews' worry about apostasy under pressure.

143. Paul shows a similar attitude, e.g. 1 Corinthians 5, 10, where he argues that certain actions are incompatible with Christian profession and should result in excommunication.

of charity, the type of things Paul would command people to do (e.g. Gal. 6:6, 10), for they flow naturally from true faith. Thus there is no essential conflict between Paul and James at this level.

The final term is δικαιόω (2:21). Here again there is no real contact. Paul uses this term in his own special way as a forensic term, "declare to be just" or "declare not guilty." James's usage, as the commentary will show, is like its normal use in the LXX, "show to be righteous." The person who is righteous shows the fact by his works of righteousness. Because of this great difference in meaning the two writers focus on different incidents in Abraham's life, Paul on Gn. 15:6, an initial experience where Abraham believes and is justified, and James on the final event of the testing of Abraham, where the salvation of Isaac showed for Jewish tradition that Abraham had been righteous. That both use Abraham is hardly unusual—various parts of the Abraham tradition were frequently cited in Christian literature.

It is possible that James is reacting to Paul, but if so it is a Paulinism so garbled and misunderstood that every term is redefined and no trace of a conflict over Jewish cultic rites remains. James exists blithely unaware that the issue was circumcision. Such a misunderstanding of Paul could as easily be early (during Paul's period in Antioch and Tarsus) as late. But the differences between the two in terminology do not require such a hypothesis of misunderstanding. At the least the two agree in substance if not in terminology.

In summary, then, James believes that through a gracious act of God one becomes a Christian. One's response to this act is repentance and faith from one's entire being. This commitment ought to be expressed through appropriate moral action, the fruit of the renewed life. The authoritative guide to the character of this action is the law, particularly as interpreted by and in accordance with the sayings of Jesus. An intellectual faith which lacks such fruit is not salvific; it is an abomination showing a lack of endurance and a double mind.

On James and the law see further Bieder; Eckart; Eichholz; Hamann; G. Kittel, "Jakobusbrief"; Lindemann, 240–252; Lohse; Luck, "Weisheit"; Moulton; Powell; Robinson, 126; Schmithals; Seitz, "James"; Trocmé.

On James and other works see further Eleder; Gnilka; Knox; Pearson, 13–14; Schwarz; Seitz, "Relationship"; Selwyn; Shepherd; Young.

6. Wisdom

One of the aspects of grace in James not yet discussed is wisdom. It is relatively obvious that this is an important concept for the author, but often it is not related to other concepts in the book. For this reason the function of wisdom in James is often poorly understood, and James is passed off simply as Christian wisdom.[144]

144. Cf. Halston.

"Wisdom" appears in three passages in James. In 1:5–8 it is the gift requested from God in the context of πειρασμός. In 3:13–18 it is something which descends from above and produces certain virtues. In 1:16–18 there is reference to a good gift and a perfect giving from above. While the reference in this case is not explicitly to wisdom, in the context of the book the chief gift the reader should surely think of is wisdom.[145] The context is parallel to that of 1:5–8, namely πειρασμός.

To put these three passages into perspective, one must again turn to the background. Wisdom in the OT is very closely tied on the one hand to practical action and on the other to God. It is the "Spirit of God" which grants the wisdom to make the tabernacle (Ex. 31:3). Similarly, wisdom relates one to God, not by an increase of theoretical knowledge, but by producing obedience to his commands, i.e. the "fear" of God or deeds of righteousness (Jb. 28:28; Pr. 1:7; 9:10; Je. 4:22). Since God is all skillful and grants wisdom to humans, he is the supreme example of wisdom, which is particularly displayed in his creation of the world (Pr. 3:19; 8:22–31).

Already an interesting aspect of wisdom has appeared: it is closely related to God's Spirit. Whether one looks at Exodus, the Joseph cycle (Gn. 41:38–39), or the prophecy of Isaiah (Is. 11:2), Spirit and wisdom are linked. In some cases wisdom may actually replace the divine Spirit as the agent of activity, partly because wisdom comes to be highly personified (Pr. 8:22–31). Interestingly enough, in Proverbs wisdom is the good woman who delivers one from the foolish/strange woman, who appears to embody lawless pleasure (and possibly idolatry as well).[146]

In the intertestamental period wisdom developed in a variety of ways. First, building on Dt. 4:6 some texts identify wisdom with the Torah (e.g. Sir. 24:23; Bar. 3:29–4:1; 4 Macc. 1:16–17). The result is that in the rabbinic literature wisdom virtually disappears as an independent idea, for Torah has absorbed its functions. Second, wisdom, building on her role in creation (Wis. 7:22; 8:1, 6; Sir. 24:3–5), takes over more of the realm of God's Spirit (Wis. 1:5–7 = Holy Spirit). Thus Wis. 10 can reinterpret the whole of patriarchal and Mosaic history as wisdom's action. In other words, there are two possible mediators in these works between the increasingly remote God and man: spirit and wisdom. Where one is developed, the other tends to fade.

Because wisdom is primarily *God's*, it is a gift of his grace. Solomon in wisdom seeks for the grace, but it is only when his search becomes a humble petition that he attains. More importantly, in the apocalyptic literature wisdom is an eschatological gift to the righteous (Syr. Bar. 59:7; 44:14; 2 Esd. 8:52). As Eth. Enoch 5:8 says:

145. Hoppe, 50, 71. It is no accident that this passage is often seen as heavily colored by Hellenistic wisdom concepts.
146. Pr. 7:14; cf. Rankin, 259ff.

And then there shall be bestowed upon the elect wisdom,
And they shall all live and never again sin,
Either through ungodliness or through pride;
But they who are wise shall be humble.

But the elect do not really have to wait, for Eth. Enoch 91–105 makes it clear that it is already their possession. This means that the present age has two groups: the wicked or the rich, who live in luxury and persecute the other group, and the righteous or wise, who suffer now but will receive blessings in the age to come.

A similar pattern exists in Qumran's literature. On the one hand, wisdom is the hidden knowledge of God's eschatological plan, which means that it is more than simply the Torah, but includes both the Torah and its proper interpretation. Together these yield not a gnostic salvation, but proper action in the light of the real significance of the times.[147]

On the other hand, wisdom is clearly a gift given now to the covenanters by a spirit from God (i.e. since wisdom is not personified, it is mediated through God's Spirit). This is particularly true of the Teacher of Righteousness (1QH 12:11–13; 14:25), yet because this wisdom is mediated by him to the whole community, they are collectively "the wise" (1QH 1:35; CD 6:3) just as they are collectively "the poor." This doctrine does not mean that they are perfect and thus need no more wisdom—they look forward to its purification in the eschaton (1QS 4:22)—but the sons of light do have the spirit of wisdom now and so discern the wiles of the enemy, the proper action needed, and the signs of the times (1QS 4:2–6).[148]

Naturally, such a background colors the NT as well. In a variety of "Q" and "L" passages, for example, Jesus is portrayed as the one who possesses wisdom or who is the mouth of wisdom itself (Lk. 7:35 par. Mt. 11:19; Lk. 11:31 par. Mt. 12:42; Lk. 11:49 par. Mt. 23:34; Lk. 10:21, 22 par. Mt. 11:25–30). Here he functions in a way not dissimilar to that of the Teacher of Righteousness. In Paul Jesus is wisdom, for the wisdom found in him contrasts radically with that of this world (1 Corinthians 1–3). The latter the rulers of this age possess and it also determines the behavior of the ψυχικοί. The former only the τέλειοι or πνευματικοί (i.e. the church) receive. The spiritual, then, are also the truly wise.[149]

A similar picture is also true of Ephesians and Colossians. In the former, wisdom is the revelation of God's eschatological-salvific plan, a

147. Nötscher, *Terminologie*, 39–41, 43–44; Reicke, "Gnosticism," 138–141; and Davies, 129–136.

148. There is one exception to this picture: 11QPsᵃ154, otherwise known as Syriac Psalm II, does personify wisdom and locates the dwelling of wisdom in the gatherings of a group called the perfect (*tmymym*) or poor (*'ny*). While this psalm is obviously a wisdom psalm, it must have been congruent with the covenanters' theology.

149. Barrett, 17–18; Conzelmann, 231–244; Baird, 430. Pearson, 13–14, believes James depends on this Pauline passage in 3:15.

revelation which strengthens the commitment of the believers, being mediated to them by the Spirit (Eph. 1:17–19; 3:10). In the latter the believers' wisdom is the new, eschatological life-style of the Christian rather than God's past deeds: wisdom is the way the believer must live to please God and to accord with his knowledge of God's future consummation. One could almost call it skill in living in the light of the eschaton[150] (Col. 1:9; 3:16; 4:5).

With this background, one can begin to see the function of wisdom in James. First, wisdom is a gift of God to the Christian. It descends from above (3:15; cf. 1:17) and thus the person cannot obtain it apart from grace. Unlike OT wisdom, this cannot be searched out, but must be prayed for.

Second, wisdom results in a series of virtues. Here we are not talking about gnostic enlightenment, but about the ability to live a life-style which pleases God. Wisdom, then, results in a list of community-preserving virtues (3:17), producing a virtue catalogue which may be compared with others:

James 3	1QS 4	Matthew 5	Galatians 5
πραΰτητι σοφίας	humility	πραεῖς	πραΰτης
ἁγνή	admirable purity	καθαροὶ τῇ καρδίᾳ	
εἰρηνική	patience	εἰρηνοποιοί	εἰρήνη
ἐπιεικής			μακροθυμία
εὐπειθής	discernment		χρηστότης
μεστὴ ἐλέους	abundant charity	ἐλεήμονες	
καὶ καρπῶν	unending goodness		ἀγαθωσύνη
ἀγαθῶν			
ἀδιάκριτος	steadfastness	πεινῶντες . . .	
	of heart		
ἀνυπόκριτος		δικαιοσύνην	
			ἀγάπη
			χαρά
			ἐγκράτεια

It is clear that this comparison chart gives no evidence of direct dependence, but it does show an interesting parallel among the lists indicative of their common background in Judaism.[151] Significantly, three of the four lists connect the virtues with a gift from God (especially with the Spirit) and contrast the virtues with vices they attribute to ἐπιθυμία or its equivalent and link to the demonic order (the flesh for Paul).

150. Thus it is very similar to the wisdom of the covenanter at Qumran, who also learns how to live in the light of the coming consummation (although the presence of Christ considerably changes the character of the Christian's wisdom).
151. For further data see the commentary and Wibbing, Kamlah, and Easton.

If wisdom is expressed in such concrete virtues, one suspects that it has the ability to meet the concrete situations faced by the readers. It is here that the passage in 1:5–8 is significant, for 1:2–4 ends by describing the person who endures as τέλειος, "lacking nothing," and the next phrase suggests that if one has a lack of wisdom one should pray for it. The question arises, then, whether the lack of wisdom is to be connected with enduring in the test. Although Dibelius rejects such an idea and Mussner suggests a loose relationship,[152] two other authors have suggested a closer tie. U. Luck states, in line with much wisdom thought, that suffering (i.e. πειρασμός) *produces* wisdom. The problem with this position is not background is lacking, but that James does not appear to be stating this truth. J. A. Kirk, however, comes to a more fruitful conclusion when he argues that wisdom is the "something" the lack of which could cause one to fail in the test.[153] That this fits James is clear, but it is not clear in Kirk's article whether there is any precedent which would make the implicit connection explicit to the readers. Yet there are passages in which the wisdom tradition does point to such a link between wisdom and endurance: Wis. 10:5, perhaps Test. Jos. 2:7, and 4 Maccabees. The latter is virtually a treatise on the subject, although it differs from James in the meaning it assigns to wisdom. Both believe wisdom controls the passions, but 4 Maccabees interprets this in a Stoic/Platonic way, while James does it in a less dualistic Hebraic way; James comes closer to Qumran, where the "perfect" have wisdom (i.e. a correct interpretation of the OT) which enables them to live properly in the face of the testings of the age.

Thus wisdom has a variety of functions: (1) it produces the virtues of the Christian life; (2) it is related to standing in the test and being perfect; and (3) it is contrasted to ἐπιθυμία as the good gift of God which leads to life (1:17). This latter reference does not speak explicitly of wisdom, but if the observations on structure made above are correct, 1:17ff. resumes 1:5–8. What good gifts could come down in James, if not wisdom (3:15)? There is a fascinating parallel observed in the commentary between desire's actions leading to death and God's actions leading to life. Thus similar to Romans 7–8 wisdom appears to function as the counterforce to the evil *yēṣer* and to produce life where death once reigned.

From this conclusion it is rather simple to understand what one might request that would produce these results. As Lk. 11:13 states,[154] God gives the Holy Spirit to those who ask. The identification of wisdom and Spirit in earlier literature makes this identification here expected, even if the parallels in function had not given it away. If some works have a

152. Dibelius, 106. Mussner, 68, cites Wis. 1:4; 3:6–11; 7:15; 8:21; 9:4–6; 11:9–10; and Sir. 4:17 as parallels.
153. The author is indebted not only to Kirk, but also to Gowan for some of the following wisdom references.
154. Cf. Hoppe, 148; Davids, 428–429.

wisdom Christology, James has a wisdom pneumatology, for wisdom in James functions as the Spirit does in Paul: wisdom helps one stand, delivers one from "the flesh" (i.e. ἐπιθυμία in James), and produces the fruit of the Christian life.

See further Bieder, 111; Davids, 397–447; Feuillet; Halston; Hoppe; Kirk; Luck, "Weisheit"; F. Nötscher, *Terminologie*, 39–44; Obermüller, "Themen"; Rankin; Rylaarsdam; Ziener, 99–104.

7. Prayer

The way to gain wisdom is prayer. There are in fact two and possibly three functions of prayer in James: (1) to request wisdom (1:5); (2) to obtain healing (5:13–15); and possibly (3) to seek material goods (4:2–3). The third must remain only possible, since the parallel between 1:5–8 and 4:1–3 suggests that while they are requesting material benefits, their materialism is worldly and they might better be asking for the wisdom to resist the world than for the goods to join it. Still, in the light of the words of Jesus on prayer (e.g. Mt. 6:5–15, 25–34; 7:7–12 par.) and the thought of other NT writers, it is not unlikely that James believed prayer for material needs was appropriate if the person was sincerely devoted to God and not motivated by the world and desire.

It is not possible to produce a complete theology of prayer from James, but several points should be mentioned. First, James is very likely interacting with the gospel promises on prayer (e.g. Mt. 18:19–20; 21:22 par. Mk. 11:24; Jn. 14:13–14; 15:7; 16:23). The significant factor here is that these are apparently unlimited promises. James's action appears not to be a limiting of the promises (i.e. what is possible) but an "exegesis" of their implied conditions (i.e. to whom they apply). Thus he points out that it is the person of wholehearted commitment to God, not the compromiser with the world, to whom the promise applies. This is not the result of disillusionment with the results of prayer, but an attempt to prevent those who would turn prayer into a magical ritual divorced from the moral qualities of their life from continuing their practice or from abandoning prayer altogether. For the author prayer "works," but *he* knows what it presupposes.

Second, two of the foci of prayer are on the relationship with God, rather than on the material world. On the one hand, James is like Luke in his redaction of the "Q" tradition, where Luke applies the encouragement to ask-seek-knock to the request for the Spirit (Lk. 11:9–13; cf. 10:21–24; one should also remember that Acts repeatedly connects the coming of the Spirit or his infilling with prayer). For James the primary focus of prayer is the request for wisdom/Spirit. On the other hand, James is like 1 John, who applies the blanket promises of Jesus (e.g. 1 Jn. 3:22) to the forgiveness of sin (1 Jn. 5:14–17). Illness is connected to sin in James, and his primary interest appears to be the root cause, the sin, rather than the surface symptom, the illness. This emphasis needs to be maintained in any use of the Jacobean material that is true to the book.

Third, it is clear that in the context of prayer James has institutionalized what for Paul was a charismatic activity.[155] In 1 Cor. 12:9 Paul indicates that gifts of healing are charismata in no way associated with office. Even the later Pauline literature does not connect healing with an office (teaching, perhaps prophecy, but not healing). In James one does not call healers, but elders. They have *ex officio* the right to pray for the healing of disease and the forgiveness of sin. The reason for this may be that the community is the true possessor of the Spirit (wisdom) and thus the elders (who may be the truly wise teachers of chap. 3) are those who possess the divine power in the full. Interestingly enough, it is the same type of prayer (prayer of faith, i.e. trust) which raises the sick as that which calls down wisdom. Perhaps, then, one is correct in supposing that for James divine wisdom (Spirit) is a possession of the community as much as of the individual.

See further Cooper; Hamman.

With prayer we finish the theology of James, not as an exhaustive study, but as a survey. James is concerned about the testing of faith in situations of economic deprivation. He sees the test made critical by the presence of the evil impulse, the tempter within, who answers to the devil without. The setting is the dualistic conflict of Christ and the world/devil. The apocalyptic consummation is imminent. In order to stand, the community must remember they are the community of the poor and thus be charitable and impartial. They must remember true faith yields works of charity and peace. They must seek wisdom (the Spirit) who enables them to produce the necessary virtues and to stand in the test. And above all, they must patiently wait and pray with single-minded devotion to God.

V. LANGUAGE AND TEXT

1. Language and Style

Given the composite nature of this work (as has been argued), we must say something about its language, style, and text. It would be quite possible to produce a long and detailed discussion, but this would only repeat

---

155. To say that prayer and healing are institutionalized is to say nothing about the date of James, but only that James was not functioning in the Pauline churches when Paul was. It shows the diversity of early Christianity more than its development.

the work of others;[156] a brief summary of the results of the commentary should suffice.

It is clear that the writer of the epistle is an able master of literary Koine. This can be concluded from a host of observations: the use of subordination (with conjunctions) and participial constructions rather than coordination, the careful control of word order (e.g. the placing of the stressed object before the verb, the separation of correlated sentence elements for emphasis as in 1:2; 3:3, 8; 5:10), the relative lack of barbarisms and anacolutha, the use of the gnomic aorist (1:11, 24), and choice of vocabulary (e.g. ἔοικεν in 1:6, 23; χρή in 3:10; κάμνω in 5:15; the accusative with ὀμνύμαι in 5:12; the careful use of ὅστις in 2:10; 4:14; the use of τινα in ἀπαρχήν τινα in 1:18). All of these point to a developed literary ability.

Furthermore, a variety of elements belong to good rhetorical style and show that the author was a master not just of literary grammar, but of oral composition as well: paronomasia (χαίρειν-χαράν, 1:1–2), parechesis (ἀπελήλυθεν-ἐπελάθετο, 1:24), alliteration (πειρασμοῖς περιπέσητε ποικίλοις, 1:2), rhyme (ἀνεμιζομένῳ-ῥιπιζομένῳ, 1:6), and similarity in word sounds (note the grouping in 3:17). To this one can add rhythm; in many cases the shift of sentence elements (e.g. placing of the genitive in 1:13 and 4:4) and the choice of vocabulary appear to serve the flow and euphony of the sentence rather than its meaning.

In addition to the above there are a number of further indications of oral style: relatively short sentence structure, frequent use of the imperative (49 in 108 verses) and the forms of direct address (17 occurrences of the vocative, mostly ἀδελφοί), vivid examples, personification (1:15; 2:13), simile (1:6, 10–11; 5:7), rhetorical questions (2:6–7, 14, 17; 4:1, 5), and negative terms (2:20; 4:4, 8). All of these examples together show that despite its careful literary crafting, the letter partakes of the characteristics of oral rather than written discourse.[157]

A further characteristic of James is his unusual vocabulary. Dibelius, 35, is certainly correct to say that much of this data is circumstantial—other NT writers simply do not pick the same figures of speech, but the words themselves must have been common in the language—yet the data are striking in both quantity and source. There are, according to Mayor, ccxlvi–ccxlviii, 63 NT *hapax legomena* in James. Of these 13 appear in James for the first time in Greek: ἀνέλεος (2:13), ἀνεμιζόμενος (1:6), ἀπείραστος (1:13), ἀποσκίασμα (1:17), δαιμονιώδης (3:15), δίψυχος (1:8;

156. Mayor, ccvi–cclix, produces a detailed description of James's grammar and vocabulary. A technical linguistic description appears in Amphoux, "description." Shorter studies are found in Wifstrand; Dibelius, 34–38; Cantinat, 12–14; and Mussner, 28–33.

157. Both Dibelius and Mussner speak of this feature in terms of the diatribe style, although Dibelius carefully points out that such an analysis must be qualified. This work prefers to speak of oral discourse, for there seems no way to separate a "diatribe" from a synagogue homily or other forms of oral exhortation.

4:8), θρησκός (1:26), πολύσπλαγχνος (5:11), προσωπολημπτέω (2:9), προσωπολημψία (2:1), ῥυπαρία (1:21), χαλιναγωγέω (1:26; 3:2), χρυσοδακτύλιος (2:2). Some of these may have been in the language previously, while one or two James may have coined himself (e.g. χρυσοδακτύλιος). Of the remaining terms 45 are found in the LXX; thus another characteristic of his language is the use of biblicisms and Semitisms.

The problem of Semitisms in James is complicated by the data above. Terms like ποιεῖν ἔλεος (2:13), ποιητὴς νόμου (4:11), and ἐν ταῖς πορείαις αὐτοῦ (1:11) are Semitic, but are probably derived from the language of the LXX.[158] Other phenomena are harder to explain on this basis: parallelism (1:9, 11, 13; 4:8–9; 5:4), the frequent placement of the possessive pronoun immediately after the noun, repetition of pronouns (2:6), frequency of the imperative participle (e.g. 1:1, 6, 21), frequent use of ἰδού, the pleonastic use of ἄνθρωπος and ἀνήρ (1:7, 12, 19), the frequency of the use of the genitive of an abstract noun instead of an adjective (e.g. 1:25; 2:1; 3:13; 5:15), subordination without use of conjunctions or the use of paratactic constructions where the logic is hypotactic (2:18; 4:7–10; 1:25; 2:2–3; 3:5; 4:17), the use of periphrastic conjugations with εἶναι (1:17; 3:15), the use of the dative similar to the Hebrew infinitive absolute (5:17), and individual terms and expressions (γέεννα, 3:6; σῴζειν ψυχήν, 1:21; 5:20; passive used to avoid God's name, 1:5; 5:15). All of these are not of equal worth. Many are not un-Greek, for it is only their frequency which makes their use important. Others could come from Jewish culture or church terminology. Yet the impression remains that behind the fine Greek of the epistle lies a Semitic mind and thought pattern. Dibelius naturally explains this as due to the traditional character of Christian parenesis. Mussner suggests a Greek scribe. The position taken above is that speeches and sayings of James (either in Greek or Aramaic, quite possibly the former) were edited into a finished document. The polishing and editing have been sensitive to the rhetorical quality, but have not fully covered the Semitic origin of much of the thought.[159]

See further Amphoux; Beyer; Kennedy; Meecham; Thyen; Wifstrand.

2. Text

Because of its obscurity during the first few centuries, there is no Western text of James. The important texts which exist are the following:[160]

---

158. Mussner, 31, lists 20 such expressions.

159. This discussion has not cited several misused Greek phrases (i.e. not used in their original sense): e.g. τροχὸς τῆς γενέσεως (3:6), ψυχικός (3:15), ἔμφυτος λόγος (1:21). This phenomenon may indicate misunderstanding or the use of such phrases in popular or Christian culture as opposed to philosophical schools.

160. The symbols used here follow those used in Nestle[26]; publication information on the manuscripts appears in the footnotes in Dibelius, 57–61.

p[20]	2:19–3:2; 3:4–9	3rd cent.	Egyptian text[161]
p[23]	1:10–12, 15–18	3rd cent.	Egyptian text
p[54]	2:16–18, 21–26; 3:2–4	5th–6th cent.	Egyptian text
p[74]	virtually total epistle[162]	6th–7th cent.	similar to A
א	complete epistle	4th cent.	Egyptian text
A	complete epistle	5th cent.	Egyptian text
B	complete epistle	4th cent.	Egyptian text
C	1:1–4:2	5th cent.	Egyptian text
K	complete epistle	9th cent.	Koine text
L	complete epistle	9th cent.	Koine text
P	complete epistle	9th cent.	Koine text
Ψ	complete epistle	8th–9th cent.	Koine text
0166	1:11	5th cent.	
0173	1:25–27	5th cent.	
33	complete epistle	9th cent.	similar to P
326	complete epistle		related to 33
81	complete epistle	AD 1044	
1175	complete epistle	11th cent.	
1739	complete epistle	10th cent.	

Other minuscules: 6, 42, 69, 104.
Old Latin: ff (Corbeiensis, similar to B with 21 differences)
         s (Bobbiensis, 1:1–2, 10, 16–3:5; 3:13–5:11, 19)
         m (Pseudo-Augustine, 1:19–20, 26–27; 2:13–17, 26; 3:1–8, 13; 14:1, 7, 10–13; 5:1–3, 5)
         p (Perpinianus)

Other translations: Coptic (Sahidic and Bohairic), Armenian, Ethiopic, Syriac (Peshitta, Philoxenian, Heraclean, Palestinian [1:1–12 only], Vulgate.[163]

The textual history of James is hard to reconstruct. It was obviously far better known in the East than in the West. The best existing witness today appears to be B, but this uncial has at least one emendation (4:14) and several peculiar readings in common with ff. א is also valuable, but has more mistakes than B and some Koine text influence, as well as one slip into Hellenistic Greek (5:10). A is a valuable support to א and B and suggestive where it agrees against them with other Egyptian texts. C is basically Egyptian with Koine traces. Of the other witnesses **p**[74] and 33 are the most valuable along with ff (the peculiar readings of which were so impressive in the late 19th century—as well as the basis of a thesis that

161. "Egyptian text" means basically א B C.
162. Cf. Mussner, 54–55, for a detailed comparison of **p**[74] with the Nestle[25] text (28 different readings).
163. Cf. Belser, "Vulgata."

James was originally an Aramaic work—that Mayor prints it in full).[164]

The conclusion to be drawn, then, is that James has a relatively unified text, which can be reconstructed with fair accuracy from ℵ A B C. However, it is unclear where some of the other pieces of the textual pieces fit in, and it is even more problematic as to what happened to the text of James during the "dark period" when it was not widely cited. As a result there is more room for conjectural emendations in James than in most other NT works; yet such conjectures should be made only in cases where the text as it stands makes no sense at all.

See further Belser, "Vulgata"; Klostermann; O'Callaghan; Sanday; Wordsworth.

164. Wordsworth; Sanday.

EPISTOLARY INTRODUCTION 1:1

THE greeting formula presents James the Just, the brother of the Lord, writing to Jewish Christian congregations scattered outside of his "home" district of Palestine. The author (whether James or an editor of material stemming from him; cf. Introduction, 12–13) uses a typical Greek greeting style, a form which appears in both literary (e.g. 1 Macc. 10:25; Euseb. *Praep. Ev.* 9.33–34) and actual (e.g. 1 Thes. 1:1) letters of the period.

(1) The author names himself James or Jacob (Hebrew *y'qb*). As has been argued above (Introduction, 5–6), such a title could refer to only one person in the early church—James the Just (*contra* Meyer and Kürzdorfer). This title itself is very interesting. The term δοῦλος is by no means unusual on the lips of an apostle (e.g. Rom. 1:1; Gal. 1:10; Phil. 1:1), coming as it does from Jewish literature (e.g. Gn. 32:10; Jdg. 2:8; Ps. 89:3 [88:4]; Is. 41:8; Je. 26:7; Am. 3:7). It is both an indication of humility, for the servant does not come in his own name, and of office, for the bearer of the title is in the service of a great king (cf. Mussner, 60–61). But the reference to Ἰησοῦ Χριστοῦ is unusual, for "Christ" is now not a title, but a name. That use of the word would be surprising for a Jew who spent most of his time in Jerusalem where the titular use would have been meaningful, but it is very similar to the normal Pauline (i.e. Hellenistic) usage. Thus it is an indication that this verse stems from a Hellenistic Christian, that the editor has at least heavily shaped it. There is no reason to suppose (*contra* Spitta) that Ἰησοῦ Χριστοῦ is an interpolation, for the form and order of words is also found elsewhere (e.g. Rom. 1:7; 5:1, 11; 1 Cor. 1:3; 2 Cor. 1:2; Gal. 1:3).

In using the phrase αἱ δώδεκα φυλαί, the author looks on the recipients of the epistle as the true Israel. The church has quite naturally appropriated the title, for it was the work of the Messiah to reestablish the twelve tribes (Je. 3:18; Ezk. 37:19–24; Pss. Sol. 17:28), and Christians recognized themselves as the true heirs of the Jewish faith (Romans 4; 1 Cor. 10:18; Gal. 4:21–31; Phil. 3:3). While such a term for the church would fall quite naturally from the lips of a Jewish Christian, Paul also uses it in his letters to gentile churches.

The second part of the title, however, produces some controversy; the term διασπορά was used by Jews to indicate that part of Judaism living outside of Palestine (cf. K. L. Schmidt, *TDNT* II, 99–101), but what would such a term mean to Christians? On the one hand, it is possible that they adopted the term and used it metaphorically to indicate their state as "strangers and pilgrims" upon the earth (cf. Heb. 11:13; 13:14; and 1 Pet. 1:1, 17; 2:11). Thus Dibelius sees the book addressed to "the true Israel, whose home is in heaven, but for whom the earth is only a foreign land." This would be the most likely meaning of the term if the work were written outside of Palestine (and a possible meaning if it were written within that land). On the other hand, if one assumes not only a Palestinian, but a *Jewish* Christian provenance for the work, it would be unnatural to leap over the literal meaning. What other term would such a group have used to refer to Christians outside of Palestine, i.e. to Christians living "in the Diaspora"? This was the logical and natural way to do so. As a result, we conclude with Mussner that although the metaphorical sense is attractive, accepting as we do the Jewish Christian origin of this epistle, the most natural way of reading this phrase is as an address to the true Israel (i.e. Jewish Christians) outside of Palestine (i.e. probably in Syria and Asia Minor).

The greeting itself is at first glance not very significant, for it is the standard Greek epistolary greeting. But when compared with the Pauline greetings it is surprising. Paul uses the double formula χάρις ὑμῖν καὶ εἰρήνη, which shows both Jewish-oriental (*šālôm*; cf. Dan. 4:1 Theod.) and Christian liturgical practice (in the style and use of χάρις; cf. H. Conzelmann, *TDNT* IX, 393–394). Why are these influences absent from a Jewish Christian letter? The author has simply used the conventional Greek term, either because he lacked Paul's creativity and mastery of Greek or because the Hellenistic redactor/scribe had principal responsibility for v 1 and did not think in Paul's more Aramaic terms.

OPENING STATEMENT 1:2–27

1. FIRST SEGMENT: TESTING, WISDOM, WEALTH 1:2–11

JAMES presents the first statement of his main themes in 1:2–11. The first of the three major concepts which he brings together is that the genuineness of faith will be tested. James argues that this testing is for the benefit of the individual, for it produces the approved character. The second concept is that the "wisdom" needed to discern the test and stand fast under pressure is the gift of God to the person who seeks him with a single heart, i.e. with his total being. "Wisdom" functions for James in an analogous position to that which "Holy Spirit" occupies for Paul (cf. Introduction, 51–56). The third concept is that one major situation in which belief is tested is the use of wealth. Faith is the great equalizer, but can the wealthy Christian stand the test? Will he share with his poorer brother? Will he try to compromise when his radical adherence to the faith threatens his economic circumstances? These issues begin to emerge in this opening paragraph.

a. Testing Produces Joy 1:2–4

Verses 2–4 cover the first theme of this section, using a chain-saying form which carries the thought on from step to step. Similar statements in both form and content occur in Rom. 5:2b–5 and 1 Pet. 6–7:

Rom. 5:2b–5	*Jas. 1:2–4*	*1 Pet. 1:6–7*
καυχώμεθα ἐπ' ἐλπίδι		(3 ἐλπίδα ζῶσαν)
τῆς δόξης τοῦ θεοῦ.		
3 οὐ μόνον δέ		
ἀλλὰ καὶ	2 **πᾶσαν χαρὰν**	6 ἐν ᾧ [σωτήρ?]
καυχώμεθα	**ἡγήσασθε**	**ἀγαλλιᾶσθε**
	ἀδελφοί μου	
		ὀλίγον ἄρτι εἰ δέον
		ἐστὶν λυπηθέντες
ἐν ταῖς **θλίψεσιν**	ὅταν **πειρασμοῖς**	ἐν **ποικίλοις**
	περιπέσητε ποικίλοις	**πειρασμοῖς**

Rom. 5:2b–5	*Jas. 1:2–4*	*1 Pet. 1:6–7*
εἰδότες ὅτι ἡ θλῖψις ὑπομονὴν κατεργάζεται	3 γινώσκοντες ὅτι τὸ δοκίμιον ὑμῶν τῆς πίστεως κατεργάζεται ὑπομονήν·	7 ἵνα τὸ δοκίμιον ὑμῶν τῆς πίστεως πολυτιμότερον χρυσίου τοῦ ἀπολλυμένου, διὰ πυρὸς δὲ δοκιμαζομένου
4 **ἡ δὲ ὑπομονὴ** δοκιμήν ἡ δὲ δοκιμὴ ἐλπίδα· 5 ἡ δὲ ἐλπὶς οὐ καταισχύνει	4 **ἡ δὲ ὑπομονὴ** ἔργον τέλειον ἐχέτω	
ὅτι ἡ ἀγάπη τοῦ θεοῦ ἐκκέχυται ἐν ταῖς καρδίαις ἡμῶν διὰ πνεύματος ἁγίου τοῦ δοθέντος ἡμῖν	ἵνα ἦτε τέλειοι καὶ ὁλόκληροι ἐν μηδενὶ λειπόμενοι	[ἵνα] εὑρεθῇ εἰς ἔπαινον καὶ δόξαν καὶ τιμὴν ἐν ἀποκαλύψει Ἰησοῦ Χριστοῦ

All of these passages, as J. Thomas points out, contain part of a common tradition of "eschatological anticipated joy," a theme which James brings out even more clearly in 1:12 and 5:7–8 (Thomas, 183–185). All three also see a test of the genuineness of faith taking place. But there the similarities end. James is verbally closer to 1 Peter, but his thought is closer to Paul's in that both he and Paul value the virtues produced by the trying circumstances rather than the test itself, which Peter values (perhaps because it produces a heavenly reward). (Peter comes a little closer to James in thought in 1 Pet. 4:12–13, but here Peter is christocentric and ends in hope, while James is theocentric and ends in a virtuous character.) The best explanation of both the similarities and the differences among these passages is that all three employ a common traditional form circulating in the early church. Each has modified the form to bring out his own emphases. This form, which probably stems originally from some saying of Jesus (e.g. Mt. 5:11–12; cf. below on 1:2), may have circulated as part of Christian baptismal instruction, having been taken over from Judaism (so Daube, 113, 117–119). At any rate, James pieces this form into his epistle via the catchword device apparent in vv 2 and 4.

(2) The author couples his opening paragraph to the greeting by the play on words χαίρειν-χαράν. This allows him to jump from a formal greeting into his subject of concern, which has no obvious connection to it. That wordplay is a favorite literary device of the author becomes ap-

parent in vv 4 and 5 where the author again makes a transition using the same device.

The readers are addressed as "brothers." This is another character-istic of James's style, one which he shares with Paul. In a Christian context the term means that he addresses those within the church: this is not an epistle addressed to the world at large. The brothers are to rejoice or "count themselves supremely happy" (NEB) whenever they face πειρασμός. The author assumes that this is a context for the Christian life, and that testing comes in a variety of forms (ποικίλοις).

Jews, of course, have a long tradition about testing, reaching back to Abraham (Genesis 22), the prime example of one who passed the test, and to the Israelites in the wilderness (e.g. Nu. 14:20–24), the prime example of failure. This tradition was amplified under the experience of exile and persecution. Sir. 2:1–6 advises:

My son, when thou comest to serve the Lord, prepare thy soul for temptation. Set thy heart aright and endure firmly, and be not fearful in time of calamity. . . . Accept whatsoever is brought upon thee, and be patient in disease and poverty. For gold is proved in the fire, and men acceptable to God in the furnace of affliction. . . .
(Cf. Jud. 8:25; 1QS 10, 17; 1QH 5:15–17; 1QM 16:15–17:3.)

Jesus anticipates a similar test of faith in the "Q" saying:

Blessed are you when men revile you and persecute you and utter all kinds of evil against you falsely on my account. Rejoice and be glad, for your reward is great in heaven, for so men persecuted the prophets who were before you. (Mt. 5:11–12 par. Lk. 6:22–23)

Jesus' words also show similarities to James: both look on sufferings as an external trial, neither sees suffering as something to be sought, and both see an eschatological benefit in the suffering (cf. Jeremias, *Theologie*, 229–233). James is here, like Jesus in Matthew, instructing his readers to get the proper perspective, i.e. an eschatological perspective, on the sit-uation in which they find themselves. One can easily picture a *Sitz im Leben* for both sayings in the early church as soon as the church began to face social, economic, or physical persecution (which for practical purposes one may date from the stoning of Stephen; cf. also the situation reflected in Jn. 9:22, 34–35; we must reject Laws, 3, who connects the trials to daily life rather than persecution).

Joy is the proper perspective for the test of faith: "consider it sheer joy." (On this use of πᾶς cf. BDF, § 275[3].) This joy, however, is not the detachment of the Greek philosopher (4 Macc. 9–11), but the eschatolog-ical joy of those expecting the intervention of God in the end of the age

(Jud. 8:25). Suffering is really experienced as such, but it is viewed from the perspective of *Heilsgeschichte*. It is this perspective that Jesus gave the church in the Sermon on the Mount (cf. also 2 Cor. 8:2; 12:9).

(3) James immediately turns to give the reason why an eschatological perspective produces joy: the catechetical teaching of the church (the probable referent of the circumstantial participle γινώσκοντες) has instructed them that the test produces the virtue of ὑπομονή. The term for the test, however, has shifted from πειρασμός to δοκίμιον, resulting in a shift in tone. This shift is necessary because now the "means of testing" are in view, and the likely background is the refiner's fire (Pr. 27:21 LXX, the same root in Sir. 2:5; cf. b. Pes. 118a). But this implies that there is something genuine that will survive the refining process, an idea which 1 Pet. 1:7 also shows to be latent in the terminology: James already assumes that the Christian will pass the test.

Although some manuscripts read δόκιμον one should accept the reading δοκίμιον because: (1) the manuscript evidence strongly favors δοκίμιον (despite the fact that p⁷⁴ has been thought at various times to favor both readings); (2) the reading δόκιμον shows a tendency to regularize the unusual δοκίμιον, which occurs only here and in 1 Pet. 1:7; and (3) δοκίμιον, the means of testing, fits better in this context.
We agree with Dibelius that δοκίμιον has two meanings: in 1 Peter it means "genuineness" and here "means of testing." These meanings fit with the general characteristic of this type of neuter noun, which indicates the result, object, or instrument of the verbal root (MHT II, 341). In the LXX there are two possible places where δοκίμιον indicates result, i.e. "genuine" or "refined," 1 Ch. 29:4 and Zc. 11:13; but the two certain occurrences of the word both indicate instrument, i.e. "furnace" or "crucible," Ps. 12:6 (11:7) and Pr. 27:21. Peter apparently has chosen the former meaning and James the latter. Ropes's hypothesis of "act of testing" appears impossible; but cf. Laws, 52, and also Hort, 5. Cantinat and Marty observe that one has in this term a definition of πειρασμός in the direction of purification as Paul in Rom. 5:3 defines it in the direction of affliction using θλῖψις.

Like gold from a refiner's fire, then, ὑπομονή "fortitude," *NEB*; "patient endurance," *RSV*) comes out of the testing situation. It is a new facet of the believer's character that could not exist without testing. In classical Greek it "means above all perseverance in the face of hostile forces" and in the LXX "nerving oneself . . . to hold fast to God and not to mistake his power and faithfulness" (F. Hauck, *TDNT* IV, 583–584). Thus Dibelius is correct when he points out that it is active, a "heroic endurance." This is the virtue of the much-tested Abraham (Jub. 17:18; 19:8), of Joseph (Test. Jos. 2:7; 10:1; in reality the whole Test. Jos. is a midrash upon this theme), and above all of Job, whom James will later cite, probably referring to traditions now recorded in the Test. Job (cf. comment on 5:11). The Christian church valued this virtue, for only those with such a tested character knew that they would stand to the end. That Paul values it is evident from the 16 times that he uses the term (e.g. 2 Cor. 6:4; 12:12; 1 Thes. 1:3) and naturally it occurs frequently in Revelation (e.g. 1:9; 2:2; 13:10; 14:12). The battle-tested soldier, the heroic warrior for the faith, is highly valued. Or, to change to a more accurate metaphor, the tempered metal is more precious than the raw material. So, says James, testing does a service for the Christian, for the virtue of fortitude comes out of the process, however slow and painful it may be. (Both the multiplicity of tests implied in v 2 and κατεργάζομαι in v 3 indicate that process, not instant perfection, is in view.)

(4) Fortitude is not the end for James. It is indeed an important virtue, but it leads to something even more important. James joins it to the concluding member of his chain with an imperative preceded by δέ, which has here a more conjunctive than adversative force, ending the concatenation with exhortation rather than the more usual declarative climax (cf. Rom. 5:5 and the examples Wibbing cites, 104ff.). One must not short-circuit fortitude, James exhorts, perhaps now meaning the virtue-forming process as a whole, but rather let it come to its culmination, its "perfect work." This statement raises the expectancy that James will name some particular virtue as the "perfect work," and thus many suggestions have been given about its nature. For Ropes it is the fruit of the Christian life (citing Gal. 5:6 and Rom. 6:22), but for Marty this suggestion is too passive—he prefers "deeds of moral integrity" (a theme which one must agree lies close to James's heart). Now it is clear that James almost tempts one to name a superlative virtue, and one is drawn to Cantinat's suggestion that love would fit very well (cf. Rom. 13:8; 2 Pet. 1:6)—James surely includes the idea in the epistle—but the fact remains that no single virtue is actually named. The perfect work, as Mayor, Mitton, Laws, and Dibelius all agree, is not a single virtue, but the perfect character, which James describes in the following clause: ἵνα ἦτε τέλειοι καὶ ὁλόκληροι, ἐν μηδενὶ λειπόμενοι.

As the schema of concatenation has led one to expect and as James underlines by the catchword pair τέλειον-τέλειοι, the Christian himself is the perfect work: "*You* are that perfect work" (Dibelius). Fortitude leads to perfection. But what does James mean by perfection? It is obvious that James likes the adjective, for no NT book uses it as much as this epistle. While it is also a favorite term for Philo (e.g. *Spec. Leg.*4.140 and *Flacc.* 15), in both use and content James is dependent upon the Jewish apocalyptic tradition rather than the Hellenistic philosophical tradition. Noah is *the* perfect man of Jewish tradition: "Noah was a righteous man, blameless [Heb. *tāmîm*] in his generation; Noah walked with God" (Gn. 6:9; cf. Sir. 44:17; Jub. 23:10). He was a man who kept God's law or, in other words, was "of a stable integrity not contaminated by divergent motives or conflicts between thoughts and deeds" (Du Plessis, 94–99). "Perfection," meaning a full-blown character of stable righteousness, is the virtue of the righteous man.

This term was also beloved by one Jewish circle contemporary with James, the Qumran community. One scroll alone (1QS) uses *tāmîm* some 18 times. The group saw themselves as the "perfect of way" (1QS 4:22; 1QM 14:7; 1QH 1:36), those who were walking in the *imitatio Dei* (1QS 2:1–2; cf. Davies, 115), yet those who longed for a still fuller perfection (1QS 4:20–22; one sees here, then, a present-future ambivalence). Deasley, 330–334, sums up the nature of this perfection: "This consisted of a fusion of the ritual and the moral, the legal and the spiritual, the outward and the inward, so intimate that neither was complete without the other." The NT use of the term has some of these same characteristics. Paul, for example, maintains the present-future tension in that he can look on Christians as "the perfect" but also see the "perfect man" as the end of the process of Christian maturing, which is certainly not complete until the eschaton (1 Cor. 2:6; Eph. 4:13; Col. 4:12; Phil. 3:15). The Matthean redaction of the gospel puts Christian perfection in terms of *imitatio Dei* (Mt. 5:48; cf. Davies, *Setting*, 212–213; Yoder, 119–120), which it later reinterprets in terms of *imitatio Christi* (Mt. 19:21). Since it has already been argued that James is influenced by a primitive form of the sayings tradition (cf. Introduction, 47–50), it is not hard to see the relationship between the ideas in this tradition and the point James is making. James sees the culmination of Christian life not simply in the secure holding of the faith, but in a fully rounded uprightness, an approach toward the character of God or an imitation of Christ. In expanding this goal of maturity James adds ὁλόκληρος, a synonym for τέλειος that stresses the incremental character of the process. That is, perfection is not just a maturing of character, but a rounding out as more and more "parts" of the righteous character are added (Ezk. 15:5; Wis. 15:3; Philo *Abr.* 34 and 47; cf. Trench, 74). In this vein James adds the final phrase, "lacking nothing," which is virtually an expansion of ὁλόκληρος.

One sees, then, a pattern of eschatological perfection in James. The Christian partakes in the testings which are part of the struggle between the ages. But rather than mourning, he rejoices in that he knows that this testing will produce the virtues prized in Jewish and Christian circles. From the terms he uses one sees that "the 'perfectionism' of James is eschatological!" (Mussner). The reader is called to encourage the process to reach its conclusion (ἐχέτω), for its goal is none other than eschatological perfection (notice the goal-directedness of ἵνα ἦτε), which Paul would describe as "Christ being formed in you" (Gal. 4:19).

See further Rigaux, 237–249.

b. Wisdom Comes Through Prayer 1:5–8

Verses 5–8 form the second subsection of the opening. They revolve around two concepts which will appear again later in the text, wisdom (cf. 3:13–18) and double-mindedness (cf. 4:8). Neither idea is unimportant for James. James argues that the gift of wisdom is granted to those who trust God, who are not double-minded. In asserting this, he is arguing that those who compromise their faith, who look to *both* God and the world for their norms and security, are in reality lacking the essence of any faith at all. If they had faith they could have wisdom, which, the context implies, would make them perfect (probably by helping them to discern the situation of testing and react to it properly).

(5) Structurally this phrase links the passage to the preceding one by the catchword device λειπόμενοι-λείπεται. We agree with Dibelius that this is an editorial technique to join originally separate units, in this case a traditional chain-saying and a short piece of instruction. Mussner is also probably right in his suggestion that ἐν μηδενὶ λειπόμενοι in 1:4 may be an editorial addition to supply the first catchword. But despite the original independence of the two units it does not necessarily follow that it is "futile" to try to "establish some internal connection in thought" in this redacted form (Dibelius). If, as has been argued above (Introduction, 22–28), James does have a definite structure of three related themes, then it would not be surprising to see the themes joined here in the opening as well as later in the body of the work. The key to applying such an understanding to this passage rests in one's view of its main theme: for Dibelius it is the theme of prayer, and wisdom is only an excuse to introduce the subject; for Mitton wisdom is the subject, but this leads him to connect James with the literary genre of Proverbs, a disconnected collection of sayings; this commentary, however, agrees with Mussner and Kirk not only that wisdom is the subject, but also that the passage is closely related to the preceding section in thought, i.e. the author is forging a unity among the ideas with which he is working.

The author views the real possibility that his readers lack wisdom. But what is this wisdom which they lack? It is the gift of God which enables one to be perfect or, in James's conception, to stand the test. To a certain extent this idea is found in such passages as Sir. 4:17 and Wis. 7:15; 8:21; and 9:4, 6, but Dibelius is correct in not finding these parallels fully satisfactory. Rather, one discovers that in line with the eschatological ring of 1:2–4 such parallels as 2 Bar. 44:14; 59:7; 2 Esd. 8:52; Eth. Enoch 5:8; 98:1–9; and 100:6 (which probably in turn depend upon the *maśkîlîm* in Daniel 11–12) are more pertinent. Here there is a tension between wisdom as the gift of the age to come and wisdom as the present possession of the righteous remnant, as that which enables them to resist and endure the tests of this age. These same ideas appear in the DSS in 1QS 11; CD 2 and 6:3; 1QH 12:11–13 and 14:25; and 11QPs[a]154 (Syriac Psalm 2). Thus someone with a Jewish background would have every reason to pray for wisdom in the testing situation. Wisdom would make or keep him perfect or enable him to stand. Similarly, in the NT wisdom is closely associated with understanding the divine plan and responding to it. In 1 Corinthians, for instance, Christ is the manifestation of wisdom, especially in his sufferings (e.g. 1 Cor. 1:24). There is also a contrast between human wisdom (κατὰ σάρκα) and the divine perspective (κατὰ πνεύματα). The Corinthians are the "perfect" because they recognized the divine wisdom in Paul's preaching (1 Cor. 2:4–6). Wisdom, then, is the possession of the believer given by the Spirit that enables him to see history from the divine perspective. One notices that James never mentions the Spirit, but frequently mentions wisdom, which such passages as Proverbs 8, Wisdom, Eth. Enoch, and CD 2 show can be a fluid equivalent for the Spirit as his gift. This relationship to the Spirit illuminates the significance of wisdom for James, who believes that failure in the test may be related to a need for this gift of eschatological power, the lack of which can keep one from being perfect (cf. Introduction, 51–56; Kirk).

The description of wisdom as a gift of God logically leads to the command to ask for it. The focus, however, is on the character of God as a basis for assurance that the request will be fulfilled. God, the author is saying, is the most gracious and perfect of givers; he is not a "fool," whose "gift will profit you nothing, for he has many eyes instead of one. He gives little and upbraids much, he opens his mouth like a herald; today he lends and tomorrow he asks back; such a one is a hateful man" (Sir. 20:14–15; cf. Sir. 18:15–18; 41:22c–25; like James, all these passages use ὀνειδίζω). Rather, God fits the Jewish picture of the good giver (Pr. 3:28; *Abot R. Nat.* 13; Did. 4:7; Hermas *Man.* 9). Yet, if the meaning of ὀνειδίζω is clear, what is the meaning of the *hapax legomenon* ἁπλῶς? Two meanings have been suggested: (1) "generously" (Hort, Mitton, Cantinat) or (2) "without mental reservation," "simply," "without hesitation" (Mayor, Dibelius, Mussner). The root certainly can mean "generosity," as Test. Iss. 3:8; Jos. *Ant.* 7:332; and 2 Cor. 8:2 and 9:11 show, but on the other side one can marshal excellent evidence for "simply," "with an undivided mind," or "sincerely." Epictetus states, ". . . stop letting yourself be drawn this way and that, at one moment wishing to be a slave, at another not, but be either this or that *simply* and with all your mind. . ." (Epict. 2.2.13). To this we may add the evidence of Rom. 12:8 and the long discussion in Hermas *Man.* 2 (which Laws, 55, believes is dependent on James; cf. Mayor's citation of Philo and many Greek authors; Did. 4:7; Barn. 19:11; and also Spicq, 217–219; and Edlund, 100–101). This evidence when added to the parallel term μὴ ὀνειδίζοντος makes one lean toward the second meaning of ἁπλῶς, namely "without mental reservation." (Furthermore, as shall appear in vv 6–8 below, it prepares one for the description of the vacillating petitioner, whose divided loyalty prevents his prayer from being heard.)

God is, then, one who gives sincerely, without hesitation or mental reservation. He does not grumble or criticize. His commitment to this people is total and unreserved: they can expect to receive. In so arguing James is surely dependent upon sayings of Jesus such as the "Q" saying in Lk. 11:13: "If you then, who are evil, know how to give good gifts to your children, how much more will the heavenly Father give the Holy Spirit to those who ask him" (par. Mt. 7:7–8). God gives sincerely to his children who ask. In fact, he will even give the Holy Spirit or divine wisdom. Here is the picture of the truly good father.

See further Brandt, 189–201; Daniélou, 362–365.

(6) Having described the willing father, James turns to the other side of the transaction, the waiting child. The mild adversative δέ lets the reader know that another part of the picture is in view. James has already informed him that the reason why the request is not fulfilled does not lie with the father; now he discovers that it does lie in the child, who is undergoing a crisis in faith. But what type of faith is in question? Dibelius, believing that Hermas *Man.* 9 is a decisive parallel, argues that the faith in question is that of trust in God's willingness to give. The petitioner must not doubt that he will receive from God. In so arguing Dibelius rejects any comparison of the faith here with the faith in 2:14–26 and views the expectation expressed in 1:7 as purely rhetorical. But this argument overlooks the redactional level in James and thus the entire context. (Since it is very possible that Hermas may depend upon James, the parallels with *Man.* 9 are less impressive than Dibelius believes, especially since Hermas in 9.6 and 9.9 indicates that earlier in the tradition the double-mindedness he speaks about was more serious than simply doubt when praying, but had to do with salvation itself.) Surely James is reworking a concept found in Mt. 21:21 (par. Mk. 11:23), and in doing so he appears to be carrying the tendency of the Matthean redaction (where the faith-doubt contrast is sharpened from Mark) a little further to the point where he sees behind the doubt the root distrust of God: the petitioner really has no faith in God, for his whole attitude toward God is divided (cf. 1:8) and he thus lacks fortitude. He is "ὁ διακρινόμενος . . . a man whose allegiance wavers" (Ropes) or "one who lives in an inner conflict between trust and distrust of God" (Mussner). This person is in no way ἁπλῶς toward God (cf. Paul in Rom. 4:20).

The instability of the doubter is reinforced by the use of a vivid metaphor of "the restless swaying to and fro of the surface of the water" in the sea (Hort). The imagery of a billowing sea, wind driven and blown about, is so popular in Greek literature that it would be rash to suggest a source for this metaphor, but a similar idea does appear in Sir. 33:1–3: "No evil befalls the man who fears the Lord, but in trial he will deliver him again and again. A wise man will not hate the law, but he who is hypocritical about it is like a boat in a storm. A man of understanding will trust in the law. . . ." (Cf. Eph. 4:14; Philo *Gig.* 51; Is. 57:20; Dibelius and Mayor also provide long lists of classical Greek parallels.)

(7) The petitioner is to ask out of trust in God because (γάϱ) the one who does not trust God (the Semitism ὁ ἄνθϱωπος ἐκεῖνος, the tone of which suggests the author's disapproval, clearly refers back to the doubter of 1:6) will receive nothing, however much he may expect to receive something. The man who expects (οἶμαι, used only 3 times in the NT, is equivalent to δοκέω) to get something from God despite his lack of commitment is simply deluded. (Note that at this point in James κύϱιος means God rather than Christ, in contrast to Paul's normal usage.)

(8) James adds to the statement above two descriptions of "that person." (With the majority of commentators we read ἀνήϱ and ἀκατάστατος as appositives.) First, "that person" is ἀνὴϱ δίψυχος, a two-souled man. The pleonastic ἀνήϱ is, like ἄνθϱωπος in the preceding verse, a Semitism; the use of ἀνήϱ where the generic ἄνθϱωπος would be more appropriate is known from the LXX, particularly in Psalms and Proverbs (cf. Ps. 32[31]:2 = ʼāḏām). This usage is so characteristic of James that Windisch remarks that this literary style is "developed by men and in the first place shaped for men" (cf. 1:12, 23; 2:2; 3:2; Ps. 1:1).

The term δίψυχος, which does not appear in Greek literature earlier than James, has its background in Jewish theology. In the OT one finds that a person is to love God with an undivided heart, a perfect or whole heart (Dt. 6:5; 18:3). Over against this is set the hypocritical or double heart (lēḇ wᵉlēḇ—Ps. 12:1, 2; 1 Ch. 12:33; cf. Ho. 10:2). Sir. 1:28–29 also speaks against the faithless man who is not wholly devoted to the fear of God, and in 2:12–14 he describes the double-hearted man as one who loses his ὑπομονή. This theme of "either-or" single-hearted devotion, which is closely associated with two-ways teaching (cf. Sir. 33:7–15), is also found in both its positive and negative forms in the DSS (e.g. 1QS 2:11–18; 5:4–5; 1QH 4:13–14) and the Test. XII (Test. Lev. 13:1; Test. Ben. 6:5–7b). In rabbinic materials the teaching on the single heart means the total rejection of the evil yēṣer in favor of the good (cf. Introduction, 35–38; Schechter, 257). With this in view, we reject the need to read back the meaning of this term from the Didache or Hermas (Did. 4:4; Barn. 19:5; 1 Clem. 9:2; 23:2; 2 Clem. 11:3; 40 times in Hermas), for both have developed this theology beyond James (and away from Judaism); rather we look to the Jewish material for background (*contra* Seitz, "Spirits,"

82–95, and Laws, 60–61 = Marshall, "Δίψυχος," who sees it as a local Roman idiom).

The δίψυχος-type of person, then, is one whose allegiance to God is less than total, whose devotion is not characterized by ἁπλότης. Such a one, claims James, is "unstable in all his ways." Here is another Semitism, ἐν πάσαις ταῖς ὁδοῖς αὐτοῦ (cf. Ps. 91[90]:11; 145[144]:17; 1QS 1:8; 3:9–10; 9:9), which is related to the two-ways type of literature; it means that the total conduct or way of life of the person in question is unstable or vacillating. The double-minded person is "vacillating in all his activity and conduct" (Dibelius). (The root of ἀκατάστατος was later used of demonic activity in Hermas *Man.* 2.3; 5.2.7; cf. how Paul uses the noun in 1 Cor. 14:33; 2 Cor. 12:20. James uses this root again in 3:8, 16.)

The author, then, concludes his description of this doubter with a strong condemnation: his divided mind, when it comes to trusting God, indicates a basic disloyalty toward God. Rather than being a single-minded lover of God, he is one whose character and conduct is unstable, even hypocritical. No wonder he should expect nothing from God! He is not in the posture of the trusting child at all. For James there is no middle ground between faith and no faith; such a one, he will later argue (4:8), needs to repent.

See further Edlund; Marshall, "Δίψυχος"; Seitz; Seitz, "Antecedents"; Seitz, "Relationship"; Wolverton.

c. Poverty Excels Wealth 1:9–11

Verses 9–11 form the third subsection of the opening. Now the author introduces the topic of the rich and the poor, to which he will devote more than an entire chapter later in his epistle. The poor, he argues, are highly honored when they are Christians, for God has given them a high position despite their low state in the world. The wealthy, however, may seem powerful now, but God will bring them low in the end unless they humble themselves now. Here is a reversal of status indeed; such a reversal finds its Christian parallel in the Lucan beatitudes and the Magnificat.

This subsection is again introduced by δέ. Despite Dibelius's argument, 84, that "one must avoid pushing for some sort of logical significance of the introductory δέ," its use is a quite interesting editorial device. An apparently "free-floating" δέ appears in 1:5, 9, 19, 22, but on closer examination one discovers that each of these points marks a transition between subsections within the two parts of chap. 1. In other words, the mild adversative has just the proper force to make the transition between sections while at the same time signaling that they must be held apart (cf. BAG, 170, s.v. δέ, 2—transitional use).

(9) James turns first to ὁ ἀδελφὸς ὁ ταπεινός. Two facts stand out. First, this person is a Christian, for the title "brother" is used. He is a member of the community. Second, this person is poor. The term ταπεινός by itself does not necessarily mean "poor," for it usually means "low," "humble," "unimportant" (in the social sense), as in 2 Cor. 7:6 and 10:1, but in this context its meaning "poor" is clear, for it stands in parallel to πλούσιος. Both these meanings are well attested in the LXX; the meaning "low" is found repeatedly in Leviticus 13 as well as elsewhere (e.g. Jdg. 1:15; Ezk. 17:24), but the word also translates six Hebrew terms meaning "poor," "crushed," or "oppressed" (e.g. Jdg. 6:15; Pss. 10:18 [9:39]; 18:27 [17:28]; 34:18 [33:19]; 82[81]:3; Pr. 3:34; Am 8:6; Is. 11:4; 49:13). That Pr. 3:34 occurs in this list is especially significant, for James quotes this verse in 4:6, indicating that it is precisely such folk whom God receives.

James exhorts these poor Christians to boast or glory (καυχάσθω) in their exaltation. The use of this term here and in 4:16 is surprising, for all its other uses in the NT are in Paul (35 times), where it often means pride or boasting in the negative sense, as also in 4:16 (e.g. Gal. 6:13; Eph. 2:9; Rom. 2:23; 1 Cor. 1:29; 2 Cor. 5:12). But it also has the positive meaning of rejoicing or glorying in God, which comes from the OT (Pss. 32[31]:11; 149:5). Paul thus speaks of boasting in God (Rom. 5:11), in the Lord (1 Cor. 1:31, dependent on Je. 9:23), or in Christ Jesus (Phil. 3:3). It is significant that he uses καυχώμεθα in Rom. 5:3 (having just used it in 5:2) parallel to James's Πᾶσαν χαρὰν ἡγήσασθε and Peter's ἀγαλλιᾶσθε (1 Pet. 1:6; a similar parallel use appears in Ps. 32[31]:11, for there it indicates an eschatological joy that transcends the present suffering, which is viewed as an indication of coming blessedness. Here in James the poor person is called upon to exult because God has chosen him for an exalted position (cf. 2:5; Mt. 5:3, 5). This Christian must overlook the present circumstances in which it is the rich who boast (as in 4:16 and Ps. 49[48]:7) and see life from an eschatological perspective in which the one who really has the exalted position and who is really rich is the Christian, the poor person.

(10) The irony of this situation is underlined in the next clause, which contrasts the rich man's situation to that of the poor Christian: the rich person must boast in humiliation or abasement! The concept of reversal of fortunes is clearly present (as in 1 Sa. 2:7, the Magnificat, or Luke's Beatitudes) rather than the milder warning of 1 Tim. 6:17–18 (cf. Schrage, 17). So far the passage appears clear.

Yet this clarity is deceptive. First, who is this wealthy person? Is ὁ πλούσιος a modifier of an understood ὁ ἀδελφός in parallel with v 9, or does one encounter a poor/humble brother and a rich non-Christian? Structurally the former alternative appears most likely, for the sentence demands that καυχάσθω be understood as the verb of v 10. In this case the wealthy Christian is instructed to take no pride in possessions or position, but rather to think on his self-abasement in identifying with Christ (i.e. repenting) and Christ's poor people. This is how most scholars have interpreted the phrase (e.g. Adamson, Cantinat, Mayor, Mussner, Ropes).

On the other hand, some scholars looking at the form of James's thought believe the passage speaks of non-Christians. In this case ὁ ταπεινός is virtually a synonym for ὁ ἀδελφός, and together these words stand in contrast to ὁ πλούσιος. Dibelius, 87, points out the similarities to Jewish thought, where the rich are often contrasted with the poor remnant of Israel. Michl, 29, reminds us that the one indisputable use of πλούσιος in James (i.e. 2:7) presents the rich as non-Christian (cf. Laws, 63–64; Windisch, 7; Spitta, 26). Perhaps, then, this may be an originally Jewish saying (similar to Sir. 10:21–11:1) which James has modified by placing it in the context of his work. In the original version both are members of the same community, but in the setting of the polemic use of πλούσιος in the epistle (cf. Introduction, 45–47) we doubt that the πλούσιος was considered by the writer truly Christian, for he is given no future hope. This rich person is called with a sharp ironic twist to understand the humiliation in which he lives, existing like the rich fool (Lk. 12:13–21) in luxury in this age only to discover the true system of values in the coming age, which will be unexpectedly thrust upon him. There may also be the suggestion that if the rich would really embrace humiliation (i.e. the outward situation of the followers of Jesus), he would *really* have something to boast about.

Whether the rich person is a brother or not, the following proverbial statement invites us to consider the meaninglessness of wealth in the face of death (cf. Jb. 15:30; Pr. 2:8; Sir. 14:11–19; Syr. Bar. 82:3–9; Mt. 6:19–21; 19:21). The saying is very similar to Is. 40:6–7 (cf. 1 Pet. 1:24), but it is also close to Ps. 103(102):15, 16. Perhaps some rough allusion to these two passages is intended—both the Psalm and Isaiah contrast the mortality of humanity with the permanence of God—but one cannot press this, for the verbal parallels are equally close to both passages and the saying had certainly been or become a common proverb. (Test. Job 33 and Pliny *Nat. Hist.* 21.1 illustrate how widespread such imagery was; 1 Pet. 1:24 is a direct citation of Isaiah.) James quite naturally more or less conforms his citation of the proverb to the biblical style.

(11) The proverb itself refers to phenomena observed most dramatically in Palestine: the sun rises and the anemone and cyclamen droop and wither, becoming fit only for fuel (cf. Bishop, 184, and Baly, 67–70). The one problem in the picture is the meaning of καύσωνι. One can translate this quite easily "with its burning heat," the definite article substituting for the possessive pronoun (cf. BDF, § 221; MHT III, 172–174; cf. 179), but

it is also possible to translate this rare word (only 2 times in the NT and 10 times in the LXX) "with the burning (wind)" (or sirocco). First, it certainly has this latter meaning at least 7 times in the LXX (e.g. Jb. 27:21; Ho. 12:1; Je. 18:17); second, in Is. 49:10 it is paired with ἥλιος (translating the Hebrew šārāb, "mirage" or "burning heat") and could well be intended to complement it (i.e. they will be smitten with sirocco and sun); and third, Ps. 103(102):16 refers to πνεῦμα, which could therefore have been in the back of James's mind. The real question, though, is the grammar of the passage. The sirocco has nothing to do with the rising of the sun, but blows constantly day and night, usually for a three- or four-day period, during the spring and fall transitional periods in Palestine. Thus while it is tempting to see this as a specifically Palestinian touch in James (so Hadidian) and one cannot rule that out absolutely, it is more likely a proverbial reference to the obvious effects of the sun's heat.

The proverb, couched in the typical proverbial style of the gnomic aorist, contains two Semitisms in ἡ εὐπρέπεια τοῦ προσώπου and ἐν ταῖς πορείαις αὐτοῦ (cf. 1 Clem. 48:4; Hermas Sim. 5.6.6). The latter is a common expression for "way of life"; it would be stretching it too far to refer it to the travelling merchants of 4:13ff. as Mussner, Mayor, and Hort do.

But what is it that happens to the rich person? Μαραίνω is particularly fitting in this context, for it refers to both the withering of plants (Jb. 15:30; Wis. 2:8) and the death of persons (Jos. War 6:274; see further BAG, 492). Originally, then, the proverb meant that the rich person would die and all his deeds would crumble, leaving no trace of his former exaltation. Yet James implies something more, although he will not make it explicit until 5:1–6, where he describes the torments awaiting the rich at the last judgment. The rich will be scorched in the sun's heat, a scorching indicative of God's judgment which will follow and turn the "fading away" into an eternal fact.

2. SECOND SEGMENT: TESTING, SPEECH, GENEROSITY 1:12–25

With v 12 one begins the second section of the opening with each theme being repeated in order. Naturally, the author does not simply repeat, but indicates enough overlapping ideas to remind the reader of the previous section and then moves on to develop each concept further. In many cases one will discover that this second statement of a theme couples directly into the following development in the main body of the epistle. The problem with this division is determining where the first and second subsections divide. As seen below, the exposition runs smoothly until v 18, and then there follows an apparently disjointed section, vv 19–21. But the development in chaps. 3 and 4 will show that vv 19–21 deal with a theme closely related to that of vv 16–18, so the commentary will deal with them keeping this link in mind without ignoring the fact that 1:12–15 and 1:16–18 are a double paragraph unit giving two sides of a single issue.

a. Testing Produces Blessedness 1:12– 18

i. The Results of the Evil Impulse 1:12–15

James now returns to the theme of πειρασμός that was first discussed in 1:2–4. After a brief recapitulation in traditional terms, he goes on to argue that one dare not blame God for failing the test. One fails because of giving heed to the evil impulse (yēṣer) within. In saying this James disassociates God from the test, as many Jewish writers had already done, but instead of appealing to the devil as the source (which is the normal Jewish solution and one which he will later indicate he believes), he calls to his aid the Jewish teaching on the evil impulse in man which allows him to keep the responsibility squarely on the individual.

(12) It is certainly true that James begins this section with a verse that is "almost a mosaic of stock language" (Marshall, 181), although this may be true because it is one of the more apocalyptic sections of the book. Μακάριος ἀνὴρ ὅς is a literal translation of (and the most frequent way of rendering) the Hebrew 'ašrê hā'îš (or 'āḏām) 'ªšer in the LXX (it occurs 6 times in Psalms, beginning with 1:1, and twice in Proverbs). James has taken over this "biblical" language, ignoring the pleonastic ἀνήρ (which the LXX often uses where ἄνθρωπος would be more appropriate; it would be even better Greek to simply write μακάριος ὅς, as the LXX occasionally does). The phrase pronounces a blessing (certainly eschatological, for the situation precludes the thought of material blessing in this world) upon the person who endures a test of faith.

While the form is similar to the Psalms (and a host of other literature), Schrage correctly sees the background of this blessing in apocalyptic Judaism (thus it is most frequent in Revelation). Cantinat cannot have taken the context into account when he calls this sapiential. The ὑπομονή of 1:2–4 is present in verbal form, and the same comments which were made there are pertinent. The Christian is enduring an external test, which in Jewish tradition could be caused by God (as in the canonical Gn. 22:1) but is usually charged to the demonic figure (Mastema in Jubilees and Beliar in Test. Ben. 3:3). The goal is to pass the test (i.e. keep genuine faith) and become approved, δόκιμος, which is a favorite term of Paul's for human or divine approval (5 times in Romans and Corinthians; cf. 2 Tim. 2:15 for an interesting parallel). Dibelius misses the point when he states that endurance is not a condition for receiving the blessing, but is simply assumed for the pious, for in the parallels cited only those who endure are counted pious. Similarly Dan. 12:12 Theod. (μακάριος ὁ ὑπομένων . . .) has the idea of enduring until the end (of the Seleucid persecution) as being the sign of the pious character which will receive the reward. It is possible that James is thinking of this passage (so Windisch), but the idea may have been widespread. (Cf. *Ex. Rab.* 31:3: "Happy is the man who can withstand the test, for there is none whom God does not prove." This passage describes testing through wealth and poverty in terms similar to Ec. 5:13 and Pss. Sol. 16:13–15; cf. also Korn, 72.)

Such a tested person will receive a crown of life as his reward. The future tense in λήμψεται reminds one that the author has his focus on the consummation of the age (as does the author in 1 Pet. 5:4, who promises τὸν ἀμαράντινον τῆς δόξης στέφανον when "the chief shepherd appears"). The actual reward is salvation itself, for (eternal) life is certainly the content of the crown (so Laws, Mussner, Mitton, Schrage). It is useless to speculate whether this is a victor's crown (in battle or athletic competition, the normal use of στέφανος) or a royal crown (a use of στέφανος found in Revelation, e.g. 4:4; 6:2; 12:1), although the former would fit best in this context if 2 Tim. 4:8 is any parallel, for the image is a stock one in apocalyptic writings for the eternal reward (Rev. 2:10; the imagery of m. Ab. 6:7; Wis. 5:15; and elsewhere illustrates that "crown" could also be used of any generalized reward).

Ὅν ἐπηγγείλατο τοῖς ἀγαπῶσιν αὐτόν has engendered some speculation. Mayor, Adamson, and Resch have suggested that this could refer to an unwritten word of Jesus (seen also as the background of Jas. 2:5 and Rev. 2:10), but we doubt that this is the case. The suppression of the subject of the clause shows a typical Jewish reluctance to name God: one does not encounter this reluctance about Jesus. What is more, the background appears to be the generalized OT promises (cf. Ex. 20:5–6; Dt. 7:9; Pss. Sol. 4:25; Eth. Enoch 108:8; 1 Cor. 2:9; Eph. 6:24), for "those that love him" frequently stands for the pious, being at times an exegesis of Dt. 6:5 in rabbinic literature (Gerhardsson, "Parable," 169). The pious are those that stand the test, for real love of God naturally comes out in action in James's view.

(13) Turning from those who pass the test, the author addresses a stern warning to those who are about to abandon their resistance. For the first time in the work he drops into a so-called diatribe style with imaginative dialogue and closing exhortation. Yet the relationship of this verse to the preceding one is vigorously disputed: is it not true that here πειραζόμενος has a completely different meaning from πειρασμόν in 1:12 ("being tempted" versus "test") so that at best one is encountering a radical contrast in meanings (Adamson, 70; Marty, 30)? Spitta, 31, and Dibelius, 90, argue that what has happened is that a new section begins with this verse, the two words from the same root being used simply as link-words to join unrelated material.

We must, however, dissent from this analysis. First, the use of link-words does not necessarily mean a break in continuity, as has already been argued for 1:2–8. Second, the formal analysis of the epistle into a doubled opening statement plus body would militate against the insertion of unrelated material (for the epistle is too carefully written) or the beginning of a new paragraph here. Third, the sharp contrast between v 12 and v 15 suggests that they begin and end a section, and the contrast between 1:12–15 as a whole and 1:17–18 suggests that these two sections are bound together in the same structure. These considerations mean that one cannot speak of an interpolation at this point.

But that does not solve the problem of the meaning of the words. Most commentators agree that there is a change in meaning, although Laws, 69, states James is playing on the ambiguity of the root and Schrage, 18, argues that v 12 is speaking of temptation, not testing, and so solves the problem while leaving 1:13 speaking of temptation. But if v 13 is speaking of God's tempting persons, then James is simply repeating a common maxim of Jewish lore (Sir. 15:11–20; Philo *Fug.* 79; *Leg. All.* 2.78; b. Men. 99b; b. Sanh. 59b). One wonders why he would add it here. If, however, both verses refer to testing, there is every reason for this section. In the OT God is responsible for testing (Gn. 22:1; Dt. 8:2; Ps. 26:2), but in later Judaism there is a tendency to refer this to another source, especially the devil. (Gn. 22:1 is restated in terms similar to Job in Jub. 17–19; a similar reinterpretation went on in 2 Sa. 24:1 and 1 Ch. 21:1. 1QM 16–17 presents Satan as the active agent in the test.) The Christian tradition also pictures God as the tester in the Greek form of the Lord's Prayer, μὴ εἰσενέγκῃς ἡμᾶς εἰς πειρασμόν (this refers to the eschatological test rather than daily temptations; cf. Jeremias, *Prayers*; Lohmeyer; Schürmann; Manson). Either this petition or the Jewish tradition would give ample ground for one to blame God for his failure in the test. It is not necessary to posit a nascent gnosticism with its evil creator-god (*contra* Adamson, 69). Jeremias, *Prayers,* 104, argues that James is making a direct reference to the Lord's Prayer. But it is not necessary to posit this either. If he is, it would be to the *Greek* form, for the Aramaic form could be understood to say "cause that we do not enter into the test''; cf. Carmignac, 289.

James is naturally interested in blocking this charge (cf. Eth. Enoch 98:4; 1 Cor. 10:13, each of which blocks this in a different way), and he does so by denying that God actively tests anyone. (It would be wrong to consider this a theodicy: James is not explaining how a good God can permit evil, but whether God is the efficient cause of the impulse to abandon the faith. His focus is practical rather than theoretical; cf. Schrage, 18.) What makes a given situation a test is not that God has put one there—James will later argue that God gives good gifts (1:17), so presumably he wills good in any given situation—but that the person is willing to disobey him (cf. Schlatter, 126). Thus no one who finds himself being enticed to abandon God (πειραζόμενος) is to claim that this enticement is from God (ἀπὸ θεοῦ; Mayor, 40; Ropes, 155; and Schlatter, 126, are not correct in distinguishing ἀπό from ὑπό as remote versus proximate cause; rather, as Dibelius, 90; MHT I, 102; Robertson, 634, argue, this is simply a case of ἀπό beginning to take over functions of ὑπό. (The slight textual uncertainty probably reflects orthographic similarity rather than differentiation in use.)

The reason why one must not make this charge is twofold: God is ἀπείραστός . . . κακῶν, and πειράζει . . . αὐτὸς οὐδένα. The introductory γάρ lets the reader know that these are indeed reasons, while the δέ joining the two indicates that they are different reasons, not tautological. Yet the translation of the first phrase is as various as the commentators. Ruling out the tautological possibility, which accepts an active sense for ἀπείραστος and appears in the Vg and some older commentators ("God does not tempt to evil"—Deus enim intentator malorum est), one is left with three types of possibilities: (1) "God cannot be solicited to evil" (e.g. Laws, 71; Mussner, 87; Dibelius, 121–122), (2) "God is inexperienced in evil" (Hort, 23), or (3) "God ought not to be tested by evil persons" (Spitta, 33–34). All of these are grammatically permissible, for they accept a not unusual passive sense for a -τος verbal adjective (cf. MHT I, 221–222).

The first possibility certainly provides the antithesis between the two reasons that δέ expects and fits well with Philonic statements about God (cf. Dibelius), but it does not fit smoothly in the logical sequence nor does it fit with OT statements that some people did test God. Furthermore, this meaning for ἀπείραστος never appears in later literature (the word is a *hapax legomenon* in the NT, appearing elsewhere only in Greek literature later than James), where the passive meaning "untested" or "untried" appears (e.g. John Dam. 3).

The second possibility has the advantage of (1) showing an analogy to the familiar ἀπείρατος κακῶν, and (2) appearing in later literature (e.g. Maximus 256 A), but it also has its problems. To be a cogent argument it assumes the syllogism: God is inexperienced in (doing) evil; testing is evil; therefore God does not test. Would a person who knew how often God is the subject of πειράζειν in the LXX really be prepared to call this action evil? One would expect some qualification or definition of πειράζειν. Also this meaning would make one expect ἄρα, ἄρα γε, or οὖν rather than δέ, for even if δέ is seen as providing no disjunctive force, it makes a weak transition in this type of argument.

One comes, then, to the third possibility: "God ought not to be tested by evil persons." This meaning fits some later uses of the term (e.g. Act. Jn. 57) and it also fits the grammar of the passage: γάρ introduces a cogent reason (God ought not to be tested; ipso facto you should cease from doing it) and δέ introduces a somewhat different reason (*he* does not test anyone anyway, so you are also wrong in accusing him). Furthermore, this translation shows that James is drawing upon an important theme in Jewish theology: people in tight places tend to turn and challenge God, and they ought never to do so (for it is unfaith). This theme is summed up in the deuteronomic command, "You shall not put the Lord your God to the test, as you tested him at Massah" (Dt. 6:16), which concept appears repeatedly in Jewish literature from that time on, including the NT. When James hears the person start to accuse God, his mind flashes back to Israel in the wilderness and out comes the indignant rebuke, "God ought not to be tested by evil people."

See further Davids, "Meaning"; Gerhardsson, 28–31; H. Seesemann, *TDNT* VI, 23–36.

The last phrase in the verse, πειράζει δὲ αὐτὸς οὐδένα, carries us forward to a different place in Jewish tradition. While he does not say that testing is evil or that God is not involved somewhere in the testing process, James does assert that God is not directly responsible. The reader expects the reason to be that God allows Satan to test people, which would be in line with how 1 Chronicles reinterprets 2 Samuel and how Jub. 17–19 reinterprets Genesis 22. But while James believes in some demonic involvement (as will appear in 3:15 and 4:7), he does not want to introduce it here. God does not test you, he argues; rather, you test yourself!

(**14**) James introduces this contrasting statement with δέ, which here has its disjunctive sense. Each person is put to the test ὑπὸ τῆς ἰδίας ἐπιθυμίας. Note that desire (ἐπιθυμία) is singular. This fact, as well as the whole flow of thought, indicates the meaning which the phrase has for James. What puts a person to the test is the evil impulse (*yēṣer hārā'*) within. James has excluded, or at least strategically ignored, the tempter without (cf. Cadoux, 87), but only to point to the traitor within underlined by the emphatic ἰδίας.

As many commentators have noted, this is one of the clearest instances in the NT of the appearance of *yēṣer* theology (e.g. Windisch, 8; Cantinat, 86–87). In Jewish theology the evil impulse is not per se evil, but is simply undifferentiated desire. Desire by nature will transgress the limits of the law; thus the uncurbed *yēṣer* will certainly lead to sin. A Jew could easily have written what James says about desire. Furthermore, it is clear that desire could lead to blaming God, for in some streams of Jewish theology God created the evil impulse (*Gn. Rab.* 9:7; b. Yom. 69b). Desire is necessary for human life. To prevent it from becoming destructive God gave the Torah (*Abot R. Nat.* 20) and the good impulse (b. Ber. 5a).

See further Introduction, 35–38; Porter.

This impulse, which is differentiated from the human ego (Schlatter, 126), is characterized by ἐξελκόμενος καὶ δελεαζόμενος. Both words come from the realm of hunting and fishing. Some commentators have felt difficulty with these terms, for while δελεάζω means to entice by bait, ἐξέλκω suggests a fish being drawn out of the water by a line (Hort, 25; Hdt. 2.70). Adamson, 72, rebels at the drawing out preceding the enticing and, rejecting Hort's suggestion of a metaphorical meaning for ἐξέλκω parallel to that demonstrable for ἕλκω (e.g. Xen. Mem. 3.11.18), suggests emending the text to read ἐφελκόμενος, "attracted," as in the proverb in Homer Od. 16.294 and Thuc. History 1.42. This seems an extreme solution, being totally without textual support. In 1QH 3:26 and 5:8 the author merrily mixes metaphors of nets and snares (this multiplying of types of traps is also done in the OT, e.g. Ec. 7:26; 9:12; Ezk. 12:13; 17:20), and there is no reason to believe James would not do the same: in the first word he pictures the person enticed to a hook and drawn out (here Hort's suggestion that only the enticing is in James's mind may well be true) and in the second the person attracted to a trap by delicious bait.

Grammatically ὑπὸ τῆς ἰδίας ἐπιθυμίας can fit with either the verb or the participles. Spitta, 34–35, demands that it be joined only to the verb, for, he argues, the evil impulse outside the person, i.e. ἁμαρτία (cf. Gn. 4:7), is the subject of the participles. But this fails to see that ἐπιθυμία is the evil impulse, external to the ego but not to the person. There is no need to impart a second agent. The grammar is deliberately vague, for ὑπὸ . . . ἐπιθυμίας fits well with either the verb or the participles.

(15) The metaphorical character of the bait or enticement is quite apparent in this first phrase. Ἐπιθυμία, which was very active in enticing the person in v 14, now turns out to be a seductress who, having enticed the person to her bed, conceives a bastard child by him. The personification may draw on Proverbs as its background, although the description of desire as seductive is a rather common image which, given the feminine gender of ἐπιθυμία, could suggest itself without precedent, as would the sexual nature of the evil yēṣer, which was consistently associated with adultery (Schechter, 250; Porter, 111). The figure of wisdom in chaps. 1–9 and particularly the contrast with the loose woman in chaps. 5 and 7 may lie behind the imagery here: note that Pr. 7:22, 23 uses the picture of a snare and an arrow, most appropriate in terms of the words used in Jas. 1:14; cf. Marty, 33; b. Yeb. 1036 and b. Shab. 146a picture yēṣer hārā' as stemming from adultery between Eve and the serpent, which could be another association; there was also a strong tendency in Jewish tradition to personify the evil impulse and make it interchangeable with Satan; cf. b. Sukk. 52b; b. B. B. 16a).

Spitta, 35–39, and others would like to make this verse an explicit reference to Eve as interpreted through Jewish literature, i.e. to the attack of Satan (Beliar) upon the soul (ἡ διανοία in the Test. XII: Test. Ben. 7; Test. Reub. 2; 4 Macc. 18:7f.; Apoc. Mos. 19:3; Edsman argues that the reference is to a gnostic creation myth, an interpretation very similar to Spitta's). But in such mythological genealogies the paternal element is normally very clear (cf. Od. Sol. 38:9; Dibelius, 93), while in this case it is entirely absent. Furthermore, the stress in this verse is on the result of desire, not on its origin. Finally, there is a role reversal here. The female desire is the perpetrator of the crime: the "male" person is the acquiescent second party. There is no room for an external Satan except to the extent he is already wrapped up in desire. Spitta does show the popularity of seduction-conception motifs to describe the origin of sin, but here only the form remains as part of an original chain-saying.

The word pair συλλαβοῦσα/τίκτει may be a Semitism, *wattahar wattēled* appearing 24 times in the OT for conception and birth; they are also used figuratively, e.g. Ps. 7:14; cf. Schlatter, 126–127; Marty, 34.

'Η . . . ἁμαρτία ἀποτελεσθεῖσα . . . completes the chain, bringing it to an emphatic conclusion. The δέ makes the transition by underlining the fact that sin is not the end. The child grows up (ἀποτελέω, used in the NT only here and Lk. 13:32, is quite appropriate, for it fits not simply the maturing of an individual, which the metaphor demands, but especially the complete development or fulfilment of a hope, plan, or desire, which fits the nature of sin) and produces offspring (ἀποκύω, only here and 1:18 in the NT, is often a synonym for τίκτω, but can also be used for single-parent or monstrous births, as Hort, 27, shows: one must not stress the latter aspect, but it may have some relevance in the context since no father is named). The offspring of sin is death. This result is well known in the NT, for Paul has a similar progression in Rom. 7:7–12 (cf. Rom. 5:12; 6:21; Gn. 2:17; Ezk. 18:4). James differs from Paul only in that he enshrines this in a metaphorical (or mythical, if one sees James as *creating* the myth) form in a chain-saying. (On the chain-saying form, cf. Dibelius, 94–99; Marty, 35.)

James has thus completed the first stage of this argument. The chain ἐπιθυμία-ἁμαρτία-θάνατος forms a stark contrast to πειρασμός-δόκιμος (or ὑπομονή)-ζωή in 1:12. Two ways appear to the individual: endure and live or curse God and die. The contrast ties the passage together and prepares for the further development below.

ii. The Results of God's Grace 1:16–18

Since God does not send the test, the way is open to discuss what he does send: he gives good gifts, which is probably a reference to his gift of wisdom or the spirit which will help one in the test, for that is his unchanging nature. In fact, this truth has already been demonstrated by the new birth through the gospel by which the Christian is the firstfruit of the redemption of God's creation.

(16) The problem appears when one tries to locate 1:16 in relation to the argument. Calvin, Schlatter, Dibelius, Laws, Adamson, and Mitton take it as introducing the new paragraph (as does the UBS[3] text), while Cantinat (citing 1 Cor. 15:33) and Windisch take it as concluding the preceding one. The reason for this uncertainty is clearly that it is a hinge verse: the admonition not to err picks up the problem of 1:13 and carries it forward to its contrast in 1:17, tying the two paragraphs together.

The admonition μὴ πλανᾶσθε refers neither to some simple intellectual non sequitur nor to a moral failure, but to a serious error which strikes at the heart of faith itself (1 Cor. 6:9; Gal. 6:7; 1 Jn. 1:8; Epict. 4.6.23; cf. Windisch, 9; H. Braun, *TDNT* VI, 242–251 [although Braun accepts the form μὴ πλανᾶσθε as a borrowing from the Stoic diatribe, he still holds that it refers to serious moral error]; Brown, 27, and Wibbing). James may not feel that the person is about to fall from faith (yet cf. 5:20), but at the least a serious failure is in view with a background in Jewish apocalyptic warnings (cf. the use of πλανάω in Revelation or πλάνη in 2 Pet. 2:18; 3:17; 1 Jn. 4:6; Rom. 1:27; etc.). The address is an amplification of the form in 1:2, a characteristic of the homiletic style of the work. It shows that the author still considers himself addressing Christians; they have not yet left the faith.

(17) The formula in 1:16 is used by Paul in 1 Cor. 15:33 to introduce a quotation, and it probably does the same here: πᾶσα δόσις ἀγαθὴ καὶ πᾶν δώρημα τέλειον form a hexameter quotation, which was probably originally a pagan proverb (H. Greeven; Amphoux, 127–136, claims the quotation runs until φώτων [τοῦ οὐρανοῦ], but he has to alter the text so much that he fails to convince; Ropes, 159, gives a good demonstration of the poetic form). In that case the saying originally meant "every gift is good and every present perfect" (roughly equivalent to "don't look a gift horse in the mouth"), but James has altered it by adding the awkward ἄνωθέν ἐστιν, making it "every good gift and every perfect present is from above" and bringing it in line with much Jewish and Hellenistic thought (cf. Philo *Sacr.* 63; *Migr. Abr.* 73; *Post. C.* 80; Plato *Rep.* 2.379). The construction is admittedly difficult, but Hort's suggestion, 27–28, that ἄνωθεν modifies τέλειον and ἀγαθή appears more difficult because (1) it would not fit the hexameter pattern and so could not be part of the original saying; (2) it would be grammatically unusual, especially since ἔστιν would then have to fit with καταβαῖνον, forming a periphrasis for καταβαίνει; and (3) ἄνωθέν ἐστιν may have been a common expression. If James is modifying a quotation, that would explain the awkward style; Schlatter, 132, views the verse as a Palestinian formula (cf. Hermas *Man.* 9.11; 11.5; Dibelius, 100). Because of the poetic and proverbial nature of the text, no distinction ought to be drawn between δόσις and δώρημα, for they simply make for proper style (*contra* Mayor, 58).

The author uses a participial phrase to explain ἄνωθεν: καταβαῖνον ἀπὸ τοῦ πατρὸς τῶν φώτων: "from above" means that good things come down from God. The circumlocution "father of lights" refers to God as the creator of the stars (Gn. 1:14–18; Ps. 136:7; Je. 4:23; 31:35; Sir. 43:1–12; the sun and moon were probably considered the greatest of the stars); whether or not James thought of the stars as animate beings is not clear, but may be supposed from the general Jewish belief (Jb. 38:7; 1QS 3:20; Eth. Enoch 18:12–16; cf. G. Moore I, 403; Schlatter, 133). In any Jewish mind the imagery of light and stars would associate with God and the good (H. Conzelmann, *TDNT* IX, 319–327; Amphoux, 131–132, suggests the classical poetic φῶς = ἀνήρ and thus "father of men" as a possibility, but the astronomical terms following would rule this interpretation out). The phrase "father of lights," found elsewhere only in some versions of the Ass. Mos. 36, 38, is probably built from the creation narrative and the fact that God was thought of as light (1 Jn. 1:5; Philo *Som.* 1.75) by analogy to many similar statements about God (Jb. 38:18; Test. Abr. 7:6; Philo *Spec. Leg.* 1.96; *Ebr.* 81; CD 5:17–18). The idea is certainly Jewish both because of the creation reference and because Hellenistic thought apparently did not use φῶς to designate heavenly bodies.

The final phrase of the verse both fits the metaphor developed in "father of lights" and makes the argument coherent: if God gives good and does not change, he cannot be trying to trap people into evil (not all Jews would have agreed: some believed God gave evil gifts as well; *Gn. Rab.* 51:3). While this sense is clear enough, the exact meaning of the words has caused endless difficulty. The use of παρά to express an attribute is not common, but is known (Rom. 2:11; 9:14; Eph. 6:9); ἔνι is not problematic (= ἔνεστιν; cf. 1 Cor. 6:5; Gal. 3:28; Col. 3:11; BDF, § 98); παραλλαγή, τροπή, and ἀποσκίασμα form the real problems. All of these words could be used to refer to astronomical phenomena, but none of them (with the exception of τροπή in certain limited contexts) is a technical term. Thus confusion results when one tries to determine to which astral phenomena James refers. This confusion is reflected in a textual uncertainty: whether to read τροπῆς (most manuscripts) or τροπή (614 and a few other minuscules) or ῥοπή (some versions) or ἀποσκίασμα (אᶜ A C K and most witnesses) or ἀποσκιάσματος (א* B p²³). Of these readings, only ἢ τροπῆς ἀποσκίασμα makes any sense unless one is prepared to emend the text (Metzger, 679–680; Dibelius, 102; Ropes, 162–164; cf. Schlatter, 133–134, who emends the text to read ἢ τροπῆς ἀποσκιάσματος, which still makes little sense; Dibelius suggests [ἢ] τροπῆς ἢ ἀποσκιάσματος as a counsel of despair; and Adamson, 96–97, tries τροπῆς ἢ ἀποσκίασμα· αὐτὸς . . .), but commentators have searched in vain to find to what phenomena it refers: (a) shadow of the changing constellations (G. Fitzer, *TDNT* VII, 399); (b) shadow of an eclipse (Cantinat, 94), or (c) shadow of night (Mussner, 92; Spitta, 43–45). Perhaps all of these are looking for too specific a referent. The father of lights is God. God neither changes (παραλλαγή) nor is changed (darkened by a shadow from change). The terms suggest a general reference to astronomical phenomena, particularly to the sun and moon (for Mussner, 91, is surely right in noticing the creation reference, and the sun and moon alone are called lights in Gn. 1:18), which were well known for changing (Sir. 17:31; 27:11; Epict. 1.14.4, 10; Wis. 7:29; Eth. Enoch 41, 72; Test. Job 33), while God was unchanging (Philo *Deus Imm.* 22; *Leg. All.* 2.33; Jb. 25:5). They thus serve as a general illustration in accord with the imagery, while the only specific referent is God.

This verse, then, serves to give a positive counterbalance to the negative statements of 1:13–15: does God send tests? No, he actually sends all good things and, since he is unchanging, could never send evil. But one notices that the argument could be more direct and clear. The reason for this form of counterbalance may be that the author is also thinking of 1:5–8. What is the best gift from above (ἄνωθεν, 3:17) if not wisdom, which God gives to enable people to stand in the test? God does not change, but people fail to receive wisdom because they waver (1:6–8) and even accuse God for their own failings (1:13–15). This verse ties together several lines of thought. But its creation reference points forward to the next step in the argument.

See further Amphoux; Greeven; Hatch; Metzger.

(18) God gives good things and has an unchanging character; an example of his goodness is in order. The author leads off by pointing out that God wanted to do something for people: "in accordance with his will" (Dibelius, 103) or "wanting us " (Reicke, 64, implies this possibility, but carries it one step further to "with good will"; *contra* Reicke, the idea that God willed is not at all out of keeping with the context; Adamson's conjecture, 75–76, is also improbable). In the light of the general overlap in use between θέλω and βούλομαι, one must not stress the choice of vocabulary (James uses βούλομαι 3 times and θέλω twice, using θέλω for God's choice in 4:15 and both words for human volition, 4:4; 2:20; cf. G. Schrenk, *TDNT* I, 632–633, and Elliott-Binns, "James I. 18"). Nor should the emphatic position of the participle be stressed, except to note that this is the normal position for the participle in Philo when referring to the creative decree of God (*Op. Mund.* 16.44.77; *Plant.* 14; cf. Mussner, 93). James's point is not simply that God chose, but what he chose to do.

That God chose "to bring us forth" is the center of endless debate. Ἀπεκύησεν is properly applied only to a female (as *yālaḏ* in the *qal* in Hebrew), but this does not warrant the conclusion of Edsman or Schammberger, 59, that the passage must therefore refer to the gnostic idea of a male-female primordial God. First, as Dibelius, 104, shows,

Edsman's patristic citations fail to show that ἀποκυεῖν cannot be used metaphorically (see especially Iren. *Haer.* 1.15.1). Second, multiple streams of Jewish tradition refer to God bearing his people or the world (Dt. 32:18a LXX—θεὸν τὸν γεννήσαντά σε; Pss. 22:9; 90:2; Nu. 11:12; 1QH 9:35–36; Philo *Ebr.* 30; Tanhuma on Ex. 4:12; cf. also the female imagery applied to God in Is. 66:13; Od. Sol. 8:16; 19:3), so this imagery is far from unparalleled. Third, birth or new birth theology is attested in all forms of Christian tradition, whether in Paul (Eph. 1:5; Rom 12:2; 1 Cor. 4:15; Tit. 3:5), Peter (1 Pet. 1:3, 23), or John (Jn. 1:13; 3:3–8; 1 Jn. 3:9; 4:10). Fourth, the choice of ἀποκυέω rather than γεννάω (which would have been the more usual term) was dictated by a need to parallel 1:15. Sin produces death, but God produces life, the quality of this life being specified by the context (cf. G. Bauer, *DNTT* I, 187, who shows even τίκτω can be used metaphorically, though it is less suitable than ἀποκυέω; cf. also A. Ringwald, *DNTT* I, 176–180).

Having established that God can properly be said to bear or bring forth, we still have the question of what he does bring forth: (1) humanity as the peak of creation (Elliott-Binns, "James I. 18"; Windisch, 9–10; Hort, 32; Spitta, 45–47; Cadoux, 21–23), (2) Jews as chosen out of creation (Mayor, 155–159), or (3) Christians as the first in God's process of redeeming creation (Dibelius, 104–105; Mussner, 94–95; Adamson, 76–77). We agree with Elliott-Binns that the author intended some reference to creation: Philo (*Ebr.* 8; *Leg. All.* 3.31, 51) does speak of God's begetting the world (the reference to the "Father of lights" in 1:17 is certainly an allusion to Gn. 1:3; Ps. 33:6; Is. 55:11; Wis. 18:15; Sir. 43:26), creation in Genesis was "by the word" of God, and κτίσμα does refer to the whole creation, not just humanity (Elliott-Binns, "James I. 18," 154–155, believes this last point is "the nearest approach to anything decisive"). Yet is it not the case that redemption in the NT is often seen as a new creation, the creation terminology being used for effect? It is this fact that has persuaded most recent commentators that the regeneration reference is intended, although Laws, 78, entertains the possibility that both creation and redemption are in view.

The word of truth, then, could be a reference to God's word in the OT, which is frequently called true (Ps. 119:43; but also Je. 23:28; Dt. 22:20; Pr. 22:21); in the NT, however, while never becoming a univocally technical term, the word of truth does frequently mean the gospel (2 Cor. 6:7; Eph. 1:18; Col. 1:5; 2 Tim. 2:15; 1 Pet. 1:25; this use may have come from previous Jewish use in Test. Gad 3:1; Pss. Sol. 16:10), and in 2 Cor. 6:7 it appears with this meaning without the article. Thus while one has precedent for creation by the word of God or for calling God's word (i.e. the law) a word of truth, only Christian and post-Christian sources provide real parallels to James's "bringing forth by the word of truth." This fact secures the reference to the gospel and regeneration.

God naturally brings forth for a purpose: εἰς τὸ following βουληθεὶς underlines this good purpose clearly (BDF, § 402 [2]). The Christian is to be "a type of firstfruit" (for the use of τίς to soften a metaphorical expression see BDF, § 301 [1]). The OT background is that of the firstfruit of people, animals, and plants, which belonged to God and were either redeemed or offered to him (Ex. 22:29–30; Nu. 18:8–12; Dt. 18:3; 26:2, 10; Lv. 27:26; Ezk. 20:40; cf. Greek parallels: Homer *Od.* 14.446; Hdt. 1.92; Thuc. *Hist.* 3.58). Israel was pictured as God's firstborn (Ex. 4:22; Je. 2:3; Philo *Spec. Leg.* 4.180; *Ex. Rab.* 15:6) and thus specially belonging to him (G. Delling, *TDNT* I, 484–486). This picture, both as the first ripe fruit which promises the coming full harvest and as the special possession of God (often also thought of as the best of the harvest as well), was frequently used in the NT both temporally (Rom. 16:5; 1 Cor. 15:20; 16:15) and theologically (Rev. 14:4; 2 Thes. 2:13) with a soteriological sense (cf. Dibelius, 106).

"We" are a "firstfruit of his creation." Κτίσμα originally referred to the foundation of a city (cf. LSJ), but in the LXX it is frequently used of God's creation or the creatures in it (Wis. 9:2; 13:5; 14:11; Sir. 36:20; 38:34). In this sense it also appears in the NT (1 Tim. 4:4; Rev. 5:13; 8:9) and thus in James. Elliott-Binns, "James I. 18," 154–155, is correct in noticing that it always has a wider scope than simply humanity, but he fails to notice that humanity can be joined to creation in redemption contexts. James, like Paul (Rom. 8:18–25), sees Christians (Mussner's suggestion, 96, that it is especially the Jewish Christians does not flow from the text) as that part of creation first harvested by God as part of his new creation. They have been reborn by the word of truth, the gospel. It may well be that James also sees them as the special possession of God. But redemption does not stop here, for the full harvest will follow the firstfruits and the consummation will include the whole creation.

The God who is redeeming creation is a gracious God. Such a gracious God is not one who is trying to lead people to fall, but one who would use his giving to preserve them in the test.

Mussner, 95–96, sees this text rooted in such NT baptismal texts as 1 Pet. 1:23; Col. 1:10; Eph. 2:15; 4:21–24; 5:26. The "word of truth" refers the believer to the gospel heard in the catechetical training. This interpretation is certainly possible—the eschatological context is present in James—but Dibelius's caution, 105, seems warranted, when he points to the lack of a "mystical" understanding of rebirth in James and of an explicit reference to baptism. Mussner's suggestion remains interesting in that it is possible such language appears in baptismal contexts elsewhere and, if one accepts these as baptismal texts, James may be counted as a possible baptismal allusion as well.

See further Elliott-Binns, "James I. 18."

b. Pure Speech Contains No Anger 1:19– 21

The shift from God's word to human words is easy, especially since chap. 3 shows how closely God's gift of wisdom is tied to how people speak. Rather than arguing and debating, Christians should be listeners, for their "righteous indignation" will never bring about God's justice. They should reject such evil and instead meekly submit to God and his instruction in the gospel.

(19) Immediately the text presents a problem: אᶜ A B C it. Vg read ἴστε, while K P Ψ syr. Byz. all read ὥστε. Although Adamson, 78, accepts the latter reading because it would join vv 18 and 19, we, along with most other commentators, accept the former: (1) while James's use of imperatives to begin paragraphs is frequent, he never so uses ὥστε; (2) v 19 does not appear to follow v 18; (3) it is easier to explain the shift from ἴστε to ὥστε as an attempt to get a smoother style than vice versa; (4) there is a formal parallel between vv 16–18 and 19–21, both beginning with imperative and vocative and both ending with a reference to the word in the context of redemption (cf. Cantinat, 99; this tells against Dibelius's analysis which groups v 21 with vv 22–25); and (5) the vocative (ἀδελφοί μου ἀγαπητοί) in James is generally associated with an imperative (ἀδελφοί appears 15 times: 9 times it follows an imperative; twice it precedes one; once it introduces a clause leading to an imperative; twice it is in a question; and only once, in 3:10, does it come in a declarative sentence). For the last two reasons named above one must also read ἴστε as an imperative, not an indicative. "Know (this), my beloved brothers," calls James, and then turns to his three-part saying.

Reicke, 19–20, who translates "Although you have knowledge . . ." and refers it to Christian "gnosis," fails to convince both because of his absolute use of οἶδα and because he walks roughshod over James's style.

In the next clause one must accept the more difficult reading, ἔστω δέ, with p⁷⁴ א B C against K P Ψ etc., which drop the δέ. This δέ and the tripartite proverbial style of the rest of the verse are the key to its form: the introductory address has led to the citation of a proverb, a quotation of a familiar thought from Jewish oral or written parenetic tradition. The difficult δέ probably fitted in easily enough in the context from which the saying came, but now appears awkward in its new setting.

On the proverbial form cf. Dibelius, 111–112, who points to it in *Pirqe Aboth*, and Cantinat, 100–101, who points to examples in Egyptian wisdom.

The content of the proverb is simply that one ought to listen carefully and neither speak rashly nor get angry, advice as wise now as then. While the saying is probably from a Palestinian Jewish context, for the Semitism πᾶς ἄνθρωπος (kol 'āḏām) appears instead of the more Greek πάντες, the concept appears in both Hellenistic and Jewish contexts: Pr. 13:3; 15:1; 29:20 ("Do you see a man who is hasty in his words? There is more hope for a fool than for him"); Ec. 7:9 ("Be not quick to anger, for anger lies in the bosom of fools"); Sir. 1:22; 4:29 ("Do not be reckless in your speech . . ."); 5:11 ("Be quick to hear, and be deliberate in answering"); 6:33 ("If you love to listen you will gain knowledge, and if you incline your ear you will become wise"); 6:35; 21:5; Pss. Sol. 16:10; 1QS 4:10; 5:25; m. Ab. 2:10; 5:12; Test. Lev. 6; b. B. B. 16a; Dio Chrys. 32 ("Don't be quick to anger but slow"); Lucian Dem. 51; Diog. Laert. 8.23; Ovid 1.2.121; Seneca Ira (cf. Mussner, 100).

To point to this ample background, however, is not to give the meaning of this text. How can one evaluate Adamson's assertion, 78, that the text means to listen to the teachers who preached the word of 1:18 and that the speaking and wrath refer forward to the slander of chap. 3, or Reicke's claim, 21, that the anger refers to political agitation (i.e. Zealotism)? Doubtless one must interpret this verse first within a wisdom context which valued listening and careful speech in all areas of life, as a perusal of the references already cited or even a casual reading of Proverbs or Sirach would prove. On the other hand, in the light of 3:1 and the known problem with channeling charismatic (or self-willed) ministries in the church (1 Corinthians 14; 1 Thes. 5:19-22; 1 Tim. 1:3ff.; cf. Cantinat, 100), one cannot resist the feeling that James is letting his concern with communal harmony surface (cf. Ward, 183-189). To push for such a specific reference as political agitation appears to go beyond the thought-world of James and to set it in a foreign context (Introduction, 28-34); to see a reference to 1:18 would appear to violate the structure and the break between 1:18 and 1:19; but to see this passage as introducing the theme to be dealt with in chap. 3 (not simply slander, but also the urge to set oneself up as a teacher, to speak in the church) appears justified by the structure of the book (Introduction, 22-28). This also obviates Dibelius's problem, 111, as to why James should quote such a saying in this context; contra Dibelius, rather than calling the last two sections of this quotation an unwanted part, one should consider them to be his point and remember that the hearing-doing theme first appears in 1:22.

(20) James elaborates on the proverb with a comment which shows where his interest lies: one should be slow to get angry, for human anger does not produce God's righteousness. The use of ἀνήρ for generic humanity is typical in James; cf. 1:8, 12; as in v 8 here it comes quickly after ἄνθρωπος, giving variety to the style; still, Hort, 36, Adamson, 93, and Cantinat, 101, may be right that James is thinking of the anger of an individual person, "petty passion" rather than human anger in general as

opposed to divine anger. That human anger is in fact undesirable and destructive is clearly an ancient Jewish or Hellenistic idea (cf. 1:19; note b. Pes. 66b; m. Ab. 5:11; Test. Dan 4:3; and H. Keinknecht, *TDNT* V, 384–385, who points to the particular rejection of anger by the Stoics). James may have received it from that background, but it was certainly underlined for him by the teaching of Jesus (e.g. Mt. 5:6, 20; 6:33). But what does James mean by "the righteousness of God"? Several possibilities suggest themselves: (a) God's righteous standard, (b) the righteousness God gives, (c) righteousness before God, or (d) God's eschatological righteousness. It is obvious on this point that one cannot interpret James by Paul (cf. Dibelius, 111; Ziesler, 9–14), but even internally in James one could have two possibilities. Jas. 5:7 refers to the eschatological justice of God for which one is to wait patiently; precisely in the light of this event Paul denies retribution to Christians (Rom. 12:19). In view of his strong eschatology James may have this in mind. But there is also Jas. 3:8–12, where the author condemns cursing one's brother (a theme of conflict carried on into chap. 4). Since 1:19 has been dealing with speech and since the structure of the work points toward chap. 3 (Introduction, 22–28; cf. Adamson, 79–80), it is probably the latter he has in mind, the angry outburst against another Christian. This sense is close to the first meaning above: the human outburst of anger does not produce the type of righteousness which reflects God's standard. It does not meet his demand (cf. G. Schrenk, *TDNT* II, 200 and 195–196, where he points to this concept in ancient Israel).

(21) "Therefore," says James, and draws his conclusion to this subsection together. Up to this point he has been using common proverbial material: he concludes with material from Christian parenesis. Dibelius, 122, takes this verse with what follows, but that is to ignore διό and the parallel in structure between 1:16–18 and 1:19–21; it also means that he must force a hearing-doing theme back into this verse. Cantinat, 102, and Mussner, 101, are surely correct in pointing out the parallels in other parenetic literature, particularly the virtue and vice catalogues studied by E. Kamlah such as 1 Pet. 1:22–2:2; Rom. 13:12–14; Col. 3:8; Eph. 4:22–23. James has picked up the stock terminology of Christian exhortation to apply in this situation. This fact probably explains some of the awkwardness when the terminology falls together (cf. Dibelius, 113–114; Mussner, 101, argues for a baptismal context, but appears to exceed the evidence: 1 Peter may imply a baptismal setting, though there is no agreement on this point, but that certainly need not imply that every appearance of the stock terminology implies such a *Sitz im Leben*).

The first section of the verse is the vice catalogue listing what the Christian is not to do, although it may have characterized his former way of life. Ἀποτίθημι, whose original meaning was to take off clothing, introduces several examples of the rejection of vices (1 Pet. 2:1; Eph. 4:22; 1 Clem. 13:1; Philo *Post. C.* 48); in the Christian examples it refers to the familiar idea of total conversion, the complete change of life-style. What one removes is ῥυπαρία, dirt, filth, moral uncleanness, especially greediness (cf. BAG, 745; its cognates are used in a variety of contexts for moral evil, e.g. 1 Pet. 3:21; Epict. 2.16.25; Philo *Deus Imm.* 7; *Mut. Nom.* 49 and 124) and abundant malice or vice. From the parallel in 1 Pet. 2:1 one suspects that malice rather than simply wickedness or vice is the correct meaning of κακία. This meaning also fits with the previously mentioned anger and the theme of chap. 3, to which this section runs parallel (Mayor, 67; Hort, 36; Cantinat, 104). The noun περισσείαν is more difficult, for "abundant," "excess of wickedness," or "advantage of wickedness" from the usage in the LXX (all in Ecclesiastes) does not seem to make good sense. This led some earlier commentators to posit hendiadys, e.g. "the whole dirty mass of wickedness" (Windisch, 10–11; cf. Mayor). Either some meaning like Mayor's "overflowing of malice" (citing Lk. 6:45 for the picture and interpreting Rom. 5:17; 2 Cor. 8:2; 5:17 accordingly), Dibelius's "profuse wickedness," 113, or Laws's "great mass of malice," 81, must be intended, or else James has used another common meaning of the περισσευ-stem, "remainder," and therefore means "every trace of malice" (Cantinat, 104). This latter meaning must remain speculative, for it cannot be definitely established for περισσεία, though it would fit admirably in the context. The general meaning is clear: Christians must turn once for all (an imperatival use of the aorist participle) from evil and malice, i.e. they must repent; the expression includes the anger just mentioned, but is certainly not limited to it; the whole pre-Christian life is in view.

On the meaning "remainder" cf. Ex. 10:5 LXX and many other places in the LXX where this root translates the Hebrew root *ytr,* which means either "abundance" or "remainder"; περισσεία translates this root in Ecclesiastes 12 times and may have taken on for James the dual meanings of that root.

Instead of the pre-Christian life of evil (including, as chaps. 3 and 4 will show, cursing, anger, self-aggrandizement, and attacking others) the Christian must "receive in meekness." The idea of receiving has already been implied in vv 5 and 17, where gifts from God appear. This attitude shows that faith is indeed involved and that virtue, although it must lead to action, is primarily a gift from above. That it is necessary to receive in meekness is almost redundant. Dibelius, 112, sees in this phrase the main point of the passage, for meekness contrasts so strongly with anger (structurally this phrase is similar to Jas. 2:1 and Sir. 3:17, ἐν πραΰτητι τὰ ἔργα σου διέξαγε). Meekness is indeed important in the passage, not so much because of its contrast to anger but because it is the attitude of those who

are God's poor, the '*ānāw* or "*nāwîm* of the OT and the Pss. Sol. and
the DSS, who have come to the end of their resources and wait humbly,
trustingly upon God (cf. Causse; Dupont; Hauck; and S. Schulz, *TDNT*
VI, 645–651). It is such people who will receive the kingdom (Mt. 5:5),
and these people demonstrate the Spirit in them (Gal. 5:23; cf. Jas. 3:13).
While James may not have had the full depth of this theology in mind, he
certainly recognized this virtue of trusting receptivity as incompatible
with anger and of cardinal importance in the Christian parenesis ("meekness" appears 11 times in the NT, mostly in parenetic contexts).

    What one is to receive is the implanted word. Here there has been
a lively discussion over whether ἔμφυτον means "engrafted" (so the AV
and some older commentators but now abandoned for lack of evidence)
or "implanted" (Adamson, 98–100; Mussner, 101; Dibelius, 113; Schrage,
21). Certainly the word can mean "innate," "inborn," as in Wis. 12:10
(the only other biblical use) and much Hellenistic literature (Jos. *War*
1:88; *Ant.* 16:232; Philo *Deus Imm.* 22; Ps.-Phocyl. 128; cf. Dibelius, 113).
This would involve reading the passage as a Stoic expression of inborn
reason (Knox, 14–15) or an inborn capacity to receive revelation (Hort).
The problem is, however, that something inborn could have nothing to do
with receiving nor does it fit well with the context of hearing before and
after this verse. The λόγος here can be obeyed or not, done or not done,
which is not what one would expect of Stoic reason (cf. Bonhöffer, 97).
But if one thinks of this word as implanted (with Hdt. 9.94; Barn. 1:2;
9:9; Ps.-Ign. 17:2), it immediately fits, for that which is implanted is the
preaching of the gospel. (For the imagery see Dt. 30:1; 1 Thes. 1:6; 2:13;
1 Cor. 3:6; Mt. 13:4–15, 18–23; 1QH 4:10). The call to receive the word
of the gospel which they have already implanted in them sounds contra-
dictory. But the stock characteristic of the language of receiving the word
(meaning accepting and acting on it, as in the examples above) and the
fact that the gospel consists of both a word about Jesus and ethical content
(which is James's main concern; cf. Mussner, 102) point to the sense "act
upon the word you accepted at conversion" (or baptism, if one accepts
Mussner's baptismal context).

    That the gospel, if obeyed, is able to save a person's self (ψυχή here
does not contrast with the body, but means the whole of the person as in
Dt. 6:5; Jb. 33:28; Is. 42:2; Mk. 8:35; Jn. 10:11; Acts 2:41) is certainly a
truism of the NT. The salvation is future, therefore salvation from the
apocalyptic hour of the judgment of God, fitting with the general tone of
James. Thus the God who regenerates (begets) the Christian by the word
of truth, will save him by the same word implanted in him if he receives
it.

    See further Elliott-Binns, "James i. 21."

c. Obedience Requires Generosity 1:22–25

The author turns to his theme of works, particularly charitable works, pointing out by argument and illustration that the only faith which will save (make a person blessed) is that which results in obedience to Christ's directives. This argument positions him to address the issues which concern him in chap. 2.

See further Sisti.

(22) The temptation in 1:22 is to assume that James is explicating the previous section: "When I say receive the word, I mean do the word, not just listen to it." This may in fact be the case (Mussner, 104; Reicke, 21–22), but one should not put too much stress on the use of δέ. James uses it six times to introduce imperatives (1:6, 9, 19, 22; 4:7; 5:12) and frequently to make transitions between thoughts; it is hard to guess how closely they are joined.

"Be doers of the word," says James. The imperative γίνεσθε regularly substitutes for ἔστε (which does not appear in the NT; cf. Jas. 3:1; Mt. 10:16; Rom. 12:16; 1 Cor. 7:23; 2 Cor. 6:14; Eph. 5:1) and so the verse has a continuous force with a charitable assumption ("continue being") rather than the ingressive "become" which γίνεσθε might be thought to imply. A doer, ποιητής, is a Semitic use of the Greek, for ποιητής properly means a maker or composer (Plato *Rep.* 597; *Phdr.* 234; Heracl. 2.53; LSJ; Windisch, 11) and ποιητής λόγου a writer, poet, or orator (e.g. 2 Macc. 2:30). The Jews, however, often spoke of doing the law ('*āśâ hattôrâ*: Dt. 28:58; 29:28; etc.), which the LXX translated literally ποιητής νόμου (1 Macc. 2:16; Sir. 19:20; Rom. 2:13). The transition from law to word was easy for one who felt Christ's teaching was a new law (1:25; 2:8; cf. Rom. 8:2; 1 Cor. 9:21; Gal. 6:2). James calls the Christian to obey the gospel, which in this case means primarily the ethical teaching of Jesus. James has a particular liking for ποιητής (4 of 6 times in the NT) and ἀκροατής (3 of 4 times in the NT; cf. Rom. 2:13), a classical term for an auditor or pupil (Thuc. *Hist.* 3.38; Plato *Rep.* 536c; Plut. *Thes.* 1; *Lyc.* 12; Dem. *De Cor.* 18.7; Aristotle *Pol.* 1274; although Marty, 54, claims it was not used elsewhere in Hellenistic literature until the fourth century).

The concept, of course, is very much at home in the Jewish world in more than a linguistic sense. Besides the OT citations commanding one to do the law, there are Josephus (*Ant.* 20:44: "for you ought not only to read [the laws of Moses], but rather to practice what they command you"); b. Shab. 88a; m. Ab. 1:17 ("not the expounding [of the law] is the chief thing but the doing [of it]"); 2:7; 5:14; 1QS 2:25–3:12; 1QpHab 7:11; 8:1; 12:4; 4QpPs37 2:14, 22 (all referring to "the doers of the law"); and

Philo *Praem*. 79. Thus all strands of Jewish teaching witness to the idea that one must do the law, not just hear it. James, however, despite his knowledge of Jewish tradition, probably refers in the first place to the teaching of Jesus (Mt. 7:21–27; Lk. 6:46–49; Origen *Hom*. Gn. 2:16 even believed this verse was an agraphon of Jesus; while not impossible when one considers Jas. 5:12, this theory is not provable), for it is the word, the gospel message, one is to do, not the law. The hearing would parallel the listening to the law in the synagogue reading, but would in fact mean the learning of the traditions of Christ, both as they were recited and explained in the church and as one had opportunity to learn privately (cf. Cantinat, 108, who refers only to the liturgical use of the tradition, and Laws, 85, who denies contact with the Jesus tradition).

To hear and not to practice is to deceive oneself. Παραλογίζομαι occurs elsewhere in the NT only in Col. 2:4, where it means to lead one astray from the faith. Here it must mean to deceive oneself as to one's salvation (so Dibelius, 114, though he wrongly assumes παραλογιζόμενοι goes with γίνεσθε rather than μόνον ἀκροαταί, and *contra* Mussner, 105, who limits it to knowledge about true piety), for that fits best with James's total view (cf. 2:19, which assigns orthodoxy to demons!) and also with the possibility that James is explicating what 1:21 means by receiving the word: it means not simply to hear but to do, and anyone thinking it to be less than that deceives himself that he has received the word.

(23) James began v 22 with the positive command both to stress it and to put μόνον ἀκροαταί at the end of the sentence, for now in v 23 he will pick up on the negative example before returning to the positive example in chiastic fashion in v 25.

James begins by stating the situation (loosely linking the whole illustration to the preceding by ὅτι, a weak "for"—BDF, § 456): "if someone is a hearer of the word and not a doer." This statement recapitulates the situation of v 22 (the οὐ with ποιητής after εἰ is not unusual; οὐ is the normal negative for individual words and phrases, cf. BAG, 594, BDF, § 426; Mayor's long explanation, 70, is unnecessary). Given this assumption of hearing without doing, the author propounds a proverb: οὗτος ἔοικεν (while it is true that ἔοικω appears with this meaning only here and in Jas. 1:6 in biblical literature [in Jb. 6:3, 25; Jos. *Ap*. 2:175, it means "seem"], the structure, i.e. the subject of the comparison plus verb of comparing plus dative, is like those in Matthew 13 or Mark 4). Since this is the case, one expects a point to be illustrated, rather than allegory, although allegorization is a tendency to a greater or lesser degree in many commentators (e.g. Mussner, 106–107; Adamson, 82–83).

The proverb is simple. Such a person is like one who looks at his face in a mirror (there is no thought of "glance at" as opposed to "look carefully at" as Mussner, 106, and Adamson, 82, seem to feel, for κατανοέω commonly means "contemplate" or "observe carefully," as in Mt. 7:23; Lk. 12:27; 20:3; cf. BAG, 416; Ropes, 175; Cantinat, 109; Laws, 86, points out that linguistically the "glance" is at the *law*, the "careful look" at the mirror). While the use of mirrors as illustration is common in religious and philosophical literature (e.g. 1 Cor. 13:12; Sir. 12:11; Wis. 7:26; cf. Mayor, 71–71), James is not relying on any fixed tradition or previous literature. Rather, as mirrors of polished copper or bronze (less often silver) were typical toilet articles, they formed useful items for illustrations for all teachers. James's illustration, in fact, is quite unlike Paul's (1 Cor. 13:12), for the clarity of the mirror or lack thereof is of no consequence to him nor is what is seen of consequence. The point will come in the next verse. Here James simply paints the picture: a man (again the use of ἀνήρ for generic "person"; cf. 1:8) looks at his natural face in a mirror.

With Dibelius, 116, we take πρόσωπον τῆς γενέσεως as "natural appearance"; 2:9; Wis. 7:5; Jud. 12:18; Philo *Post. C.* 29; any attempt to refer this specifically to birth or physical as opposed to spiritual appearance, as Adamson, 83, and Laws, 86, do, would overinterpret the Semitic noun plus genitive construction which is common in James; e.g. 1:25; 2:1; 3:13; cf. Cantinat, 109.

(24) James explains his point of comparison, using gnomic aorists (κατενόησεν, ἐπελάθετο) and the perfect (ἀπελήλυθεν) over against the two momentary states of "seeing" and "forgetting." The latter may be used to stress the continuing state of "departedness" (Ropes, 177; MHT I, 144); or it may be used simply to mix forms for stylistic variety (BDF, § 344). The person sees himself, departs, and forgets what sort of a person (ὁποῖος; cf. BAG, 579) he was. The point is that the impression is only momentary: the look in the mirror while combing one's hair may be temporarily absorbing, but it normally bears no practical results when one engages in the business of the day. It is useless. The momentariness and lack of real effect is the point of the parable, not a comparison with a different type of mirror or a different way of seeing. The next verse will carry on the metaphor in the first verb (παρακύψας), but only as this picture is later qualified by a term far from the metaphor (παραμείνας) does the point of contrast appear.

(25) The contrast implied in δέ at the beginning of v 25 carries one back, not to v 24, but to the beginning of v 23. This person, as the author will explain in the next phrase, is the one who hears and *does*. He looks at the law and continues. It is on this enduring occupation, i.e. the doing, that James's emphasis lies, as enduring in many senses is important to James (notice his use of ὑπομένω and μακροθυμέω), for it is this aspect which contrasts with hearing and forgetting.

Παρακύψας is a simple carrying-on of the simile, a link-word between parable and further discussions; Dibelius, 116; Mussner, 106; and Cantinat, 110, point to Pr. 7:6; Sir. 14:23; 1 Pet. 1:12; Lk. 24:12 and argue that this term suggests a more attentive looking than κατανοέω; but even if these examples did demand special attentiveness, Gn. 6:8; Sir. 21:23; and others do not; more importantly κατανοέω can equally well indicate careful attention, e.g. Gn. 3:6; Sir. 23:19; Heb. 3:1.

The blessed person looks into "the perfect law of liberty"; this expression is a major interpretive problem for James. On the one hand, it is well known that the Stoics saw life according to the rule of reason, i.e. the law of nature, as a life of freedom (so Epict. 4.1.158; Seneca *Vit.* 15.7; Cicero *Parad.* 34; cf. H. Schlier, *TDNT* II, 493–496; J. Blunck, *DNTT* I, 715–716). Thus it is quite reasonable to see James's phrase as linguistically possible in the Stoic world, although this expression has not yet been found (cf. Dibelius, 116–117). It is also true that Philo took the Stoic concept and identified it more or less with the law of Moses (*Op. Mund.* 3; *Vit. Mos.* 2.48) and correlated the keeping of that law with freedom (*Omn. Prob. Lib.* 45; cf. 4 Macc. 14:2), so that even within some Jewish circles such Stoic influence was possible. On the other hand, there is absolutely no question that Jews saw their law as perfect (Pss. 19:7; 119; Aristeas 31; Rom. 7:12), that they found joy in its observance (Pss. 1:2; 19:7–11; 40:6–8; 119; Sir. 6:23–31; 51:13–22), and even that they saw the law giving freedom (m. Ab. 3:5; 6:2; B. K. 8:6; b. B. M. 85b). E. Stauffer, "Gesetz," claims to find the very expression "law of freedom" in 1QS 10:6, 8, 11, and this has been supported by S. Légasse, 338–339. But while Légasse's general point of the freedom which the sectaries found in their law is true enough, Nauck, "Lex," and Nötscher have convincingly proved that this exact citation must be translated "inscribed law" as in Ex. 32:16 *before* rabbinic exegesis, which Nötscher believes to be a reaction to Christian claims. Still, even without the exact phrase, these Jewish parallels mean that although the author freely uses words and phrases from the general Hellenistic pool to which the Stoics added their share, unless one finds specific Stoic concepts (such as natural law or passionless life) it is more likely that he is still within a Jewish Christian world (cf. Bonhöffer, 193: "With the exception of individual expressions and the relatively good Greek in which it is written, one will hardly discover a trace of Hellenistic influence in James").

It is within this Jewish world that one can understand the phrase. For the Jewish Christian the law is still the will of God, but Messiah has come and perfected it and given his new law (cf. Davies, *Torah*). Thus one finds the Sermon on the Mount (especially Mt. 5:17) and other similar passages in the early Christian tradition that present Christ as the giver of a new or renewed law. James's contact with the tradition behind the

Sermon on the Mount is certain (see Introduction, 47–48), and one must agree with Davies that James sees Jesus' reinterpretation of the law as a new law (cf. 2:8, royal law; Davies, *Setting*, 402–405; Schnackenburg, 349–352). Similar conceptions of Jesus' teaching appear in Barn. 2:6; Hermas *Vis.* 1.3; Iren. *Haer.* 4.34.4; but they also are not lacking in Paul. Certainly Paul was against legalism, the use of the law as a way of salvation—that could only lead to death—but when it came to the ethical life of the Christian, it was another matter. On that topic Paul draws on the earlier Christian tradition in terms similar to James (Gal. 5:13, which combines freedom and law; Gal. 6:2; 1 Cor. 9:21; and 1 Cor. 7:10, 25, where a dominical saying ends the discussion; cf. Dibelius, 119). Although in James one is in a different area of Christianity than in Paul, he nonetheless finds similar ideas, especially when looking at what Paul says about James's sphere of concern (cf. Eckart, 521–526).

The one who looks and remains in the law of freedom, i.e. the OT ethic as explained and altered by Jesus, is clearly defined: he is one who does not simply hear and forget, but practices what he hears. Both expressions are unusual Greek: ἀκροατὴς ἐπιλησμονῆς (the latter word found in biblical literature only in Sir. 11:27) is a Semitism, "hearer of forgetfulness," and ποιητὴς ἔργου is apparently built so as to make an obvious parallel (the problem is that there is a change from a genitive of quality to an objective genitive; cf. Mayor, 74; but while the Greek is unusual the meaning is clear enough; cf. m. Ab. 3:8 and the citations in Str-B III, 754).

Such an obedient Christian is pronounced μακάριος (another term with a Semitic background as in 1:12; Matthew 5; Psalm 1; Is. 56:2, etc.) in his deeds (οὗτος is for emphasis: *this* person, the doer, in contrast to the hearer only). Does this eschatological type of pronouncement refer to blessing as one acts or a future joy at the parousia (Schrage, 23)? The future ἔσται, the use of μακάριος in 1:12, and the normal eschatology of James make one agree with Mussner, 110, that this saying is future-oriented: there is an eschatological blessing in store for the one whose deeds (ποιήσις, *hapax legomenon* in the NT) are the doing of the law of freedom, the teaching of Jesus.

See further Eckart; Nauck, "Lex"; Nötscher; Stauffer, "Gesetz."

d. Summary and Transition 1:26–27

The final section of this introductory chapter sums up what has preceded and bridges between it and chap. 2. The subject has been true Christianity, and three marks stand out: (a) a true Christian must control his tongue (1:19–21, but also chap. 3 and with it the wisdom sayings, 1:5–8), (b) he must engage in charity, which was certainly the teaching of Jesus (1:22–25, 9–11; chap. 2), and (c) such a one must resist temptation, i.e. the world (1:2–4, 12–15; chap. 4). The summary first states (a) negatively, then (b) and (c) positively. Because of their summary character and the use of unusual vocabulary not appearing elsewhere in the work, these verses are probably part of the final redaction of James.

See further Johanson; Obermüller, "Themen"; Roberts; Taylor.

(26) The summary begins with a common introductory hypothesis, a structure appearing in this section of James in 1:5, 23, 26 (a similar construction appears in 5:19): "if someone thinks he is pious" (δοκεῖ could mean "seems [to others] to be pious" or "thinks himself"; in the light of ἀπατῶν καρδίαν αὐτοῦ, it appears that the person himself, not others, is deceived and thus considers himself pious; cf. Mitton, 74–75). Θρησκός (hapax legomenon in biblical literature) as θρησκεία later (Wis. 14:18, 27; Sir. 22:5; 4 Macc. 5:6; Acts 26:5; Col. 2:18; Jos. Ant. 4:74; 5:339; 9:273–274) focuses on religious performance, in either a negative or a positive sense (1 Clem. 45:7 is positive, as is the Gallio inscription and many cases in Josephus, but Col. 2:18, the occurrences in Wisdom, and Philo Spec. Leg. 1.315 are negative; cf. K. L. Schmidt, TDNT III, 155–159). The specific practices James has in mind are unclear, but would include the religious activities of prayer, fasting, and worship of his community (and perhaps the keeping of the ritual law as well, assuming it was a Jewish Christian community). Whatever they are, the person has the outward practice of religious activity and so considers himself pious.

The problem, however, is that the person does not control his tongue (that χαλιναγωγέω appears here [for the first time in Greek] and then again in 3:2 indicates the relationship between the two sections; cf. also Hermas Man. 12.1; Polycarp 5:3 and χαλινόω in earlier literature; Mayor, 76). That this failure is evil appears repeatedly in Jewish literature (Pss. 34:13; 39:1; cf. the comment on 1:19), but James has more than a general concern with virtue. Some group, posing as teachers (3:1, 13), appears to be causing dissension and factions in the community (chaps. 3 and 4). Here, as in 1:19–21, the author rebukes these people sharply (that these were Jewish Christians opposing the Pauline gentile community as Mussner, 112, believes, is doubtful, for that would place James at an untenable date and in a wrong relationship to Pauline doctrine; cf. Introduction, 19–21).

The phrase ἀλλὰ ἀπατῶν καρδίαν αὐτοῦ is grammatically difficult for, first, καὶ instead of ἀλλά would seem more appropriate, and second, the phrase would appear better grammatically if it were joined to the apodosis. Mussner, 111, however, is probably correct in suggesting that (1) the reason for this construction is rhythm or euphony, and (2) ἀλλά coming after the negative statement means "but only" (German *sondern nur*). The fact, states James, is that such religion without works (i.e. a controlled tongue in this example) is self-deception (καρδία here stands for the person, particularly his thoughts; cf. J. Behm, *TDNT* III, 612, who notes that here and in 5:5 it stands for the reflexive pronoun as in Mk. 2:6=2:8).

Therefore, concludes James, this person's religious practice is empty (μάταιος, Je. 2:5; 8:9; 10:3; Acts 14:15; 1 Cor. 3:20; 1 Pet. 1:18; most of these examples refer to idolatry). Religion which does not have ethical results, particularly in this case control of the tongue, is totally useless before God: such faith is dead, not salvific, as James will say later (2:20, 26). Here is a critique of religion similar to that of the prophets (Ho. 6:6; Is. 1:10–17; Je. 7:21–28) and of Jesus (cf. his sabbath controversies or the command of love [Mk. 12:28–34; Jn. 13:34], which James will take up in 2:8).

(27) In contrast to this empty religious practice (v 26), which indeed has the proper ritual and doctrine but fails in ethical results, the author places a correct religious practice, which also assumes ritual and doctrine (these are neither questioned nor discussed but rather assumed in the whole of the epistle) yet leads to the proper ethical action as well.

Dibelius, 121–122, points out that this verse can be understood in many ways: as a Jewish call for proper legal observance and ethic, as a protest against Pharisaic ritualism (Windisch, 13), or as a denunciation of Zealotic Christians who fail to practice the law of love (Reicke, 25). Here as much as anywhere in James the total context of the book must determine the interpretation.

Dibelius sees the lack of cultic and ritual interest here as a decisive blow to Jewish Christian authorship, but that means that he must understand 2:14ff. as depending on Pauline formulations and interpret Gal. 2:12 as presenting James the Just as a strong ritualist, both of which assumptions are questionable; cf. Introduction, 2–22 and below at 2:14.

True religion is described as "pure and unblemished before God." The description καθαρὰ καὶ ἀμίαντος is also found elsewhere (Plut. *Per.* 39.2; Philo *Leg. All.* 1.50; Hermas *Man.* 2.7 [where the context is an ethical one similar to James and Did. 1:5]; *Sim.* 5.7.1; cf. Marty, 64, and Mayor, 76) and may be an idiom for absolute purity as Cantinat, 116, claims; since both words have a long established ethical usage and fit together as positive and negative statements of the same thing, they form a natural hendiadys (F. Hauck, *TDNT* IV, 644–647; cf. Heb. 7:27; 1 Pet. 1:4; and F. Hauck, *TDNT* III, 425–426). It is certainly the ethical and not the cultic sense which is intended here, particularly when one considers the call for cleansing in 4:1–10. It is pure παρὰ τῷ θεῷ καὶ πατρί; the formula translates the Hebrew *lipnê* and thus is probably a septuagintalism (1 Ch. 29:10; Wis. 2:16) meaning "in God's eyes" (Adamson's "to win account with God," 86, apparently misses this fact). That God is designated father (the single article joining the two terms to designate one thing) is not unusual either in James (1:17; 3:9) or in Judaism (Is. 63:16; 1 Ch. 29:10; Sir. 23:4; Wis. 2:16; Ps. 68:5; 3 Macc. 5:7; Philo *Leg. All.* 2.67; cf. the covenant formula in 1 Sa. 7:14 and the many places God speaks of Israel as his son) or in early Christianity (e.g. Jesus' use of *'abbā'* and the Lord's Prayer). But here as in the other places in James this designation may indicate the universal creatorship of God, that he is just as much father of the one who is slandered or insulted or of the widow who is not helped as of the Christian who professes "true religion."

James focuses on two elements of true piety that illustrate the doing of the word of 1:22–25 and lead into chaps. 2 and 4 respectively. The first is "to visit orphans and widows in their distress." That this act of helping orphans and widows was commanded in the OT and early church is clear (Is. 1:10–17; Dt. 14:29; 24:17–22; Je. 5:28; Ezk. 22:7; Zc. 7:10; Sir. 4:10; Jb. 29:16; Acts 6:1–6; 1 Tim. 5:3–16); it is also clear that these were typical examples (along with the foreigner and levite, who were perhaps overlooked in a Diaspora situation; cf. Rahlfs, 74) for all who suffer distress and oppression. True piety helps the helpless, for God is the God who secures the rights of those who have no hope (Dt. 10:16–19; 16:3; 26:7; cf. Kuschke, 33–36, and especially the mass of evidence gathered and partially digested in Miranda, chaps. 2–4). This will be the theme of the next chapter.

But the second element of true piety is "to keep oneself unstained by the world." (We reject the suggestion of Roberts that we should read ὑπερασπίζειν αὐτοὺς ἀπὸ τοῦ κόσμου with p⁷⁴ because it agrees better with James and the NT as a whole; cf. Johanson, 118–119.) The concept of keeping oneself unspotted has a cultic ring, clearly seen in its association with ἄμωμος in 1 Pet. 1:19 (ἄμωμος is very frequent in the LXX, ἄσπιλος only in Symmachus of Jb. 15:15), but as with many cultic concepts this became moral in the NT usage (2 Pet. 3:14; 1 Tim. 6:14; Hermas *Vis.* 5.3.5; even 1 Pet. 1:19 probably refers to Christ's sinlessness; cf. A. Oepke, *TDNT* I, 502). Likewise the world (κόσμος) in James is moral: "a widespread disposition and power in mankind for evil in opposition to God" (Johanson, 118–119). This is a dualistic (but not in a creation-rejecting gnostic sense) use of the term characteristic of Paul and John (1 Cor. 1–3; 5:19; 11:32; Eph. 2:2; Jn. 12:31; 15:18ff.; 16:8ff.; 17:14–16; 1 Jn. 2:15–17); these ideas are found in Jewish literature, but only rarely and often in passages which may have Christian influence (e.g. Eth. Enoch 48:7; 108:8; Apoc. Abr. 29:8; Test. Iss. 4:6; cf. H. Sasse, *TDNT* III, 889–895). In agreement with Paul (e.g. Rom. 12:2) James states that true piety keeps free from the evil influences in the surrounding culture; what may be in his mind is the desire to possess and gather, the service of Mammon, for that is his reference in 4:4. Keeping free from this will lessen community strife (1:26) and pave the way for charity (as in the preceding clause): it will also remove the underlying motivation for the abuses discussed in the next chapter.

THE EXCELLENCE OF POVERTY AND GENEROSITY 2:1–26

HAVING set the stage in his introduction, James now turns to discuss one of the major themes he has introduced, that of wealth and charity. This discussion expands the previous statements in 1:9–11 and 1:22–27 and forms the basis for the strong denunciations of chaps. 4 and 5. Chap. 2 itself breaks into two parts, 2:1–13, which begins with an illustration (2:1–4) and leads into a discussion based on OT precedent, and 2:14–26, which likewise begins with theme sentence and and illustration (2:14–17) and ends with a discussion based on the precedent of Abraham and Rahab. The first part argues that one must honor the poor and the second that one ought to share with them.

1. NO PARTIALITY IS ALLOWABLE 2:1–13

a. Illustration: Judicial Assembly 2:1–4

James clearly believes that the poor have a very important place in the church because of the leveling effect of the Christian gospel. True faith has no place for the social distinctions of the world. In fact, if a Christian church-court should so much as consider these distinctions, it becomes by that act evil and sides with the wealthy who persecute Christians.

See further Burchard, "Jakobus"; Rost; Ward, "Partiality."

(1) The author begins this new section with his common homiletic introduction "my brethren" (cf. 1:2) as used in the early church and in Judaism in general (Wessel, 82–85). As is normal in James, the address comes with an imperative, μὴ . . . ἔχετε. . . . The proscribed behavior is focused in the phrase ἐν προσωπολημψίαις. This term is not found in either secular Greek or the LXX. It is apparently a creation of the early Christian parenetic tradition to translate the common Hebrew term for favor/favoritism, nāśā' pānîm (LXX πρόσωπον λαμβάνειν or θαυμάζειν πρόσωπον) used in the OT in both a positive (1 Sa. 25:35; Mal. 1:8) and a negative sense, particularly in judicial contexts (Dt. 1:17; Lv. 19:15; Ps.

82:2; Pr. 6:35; 18:5). God shows no partiality (Dt. 10:17), so neither should human judges. This theme is repeated in the NT (Gal. 2:6), and the coined expression for favoritism, προσωπολημψία, entered the NT tradition first as a characteristic of God's judgment (Col. 3:25; Eph. 6:9; Rom. 2:11; Acts 10:34; cf. 1 Pet. 1:17) and then (as in the OT) as a mandate for human justice. This meaning naturally continues in church tradition (cf. E. Lohse, *TDNT* VI, 779–780; Mayor, 78–79).

The phrase τὴν πίστιν τοῦ κυρίου ἡμῶν Ἰησοῦ Χριστοῦ τῆς δόξης is the center of one of the turmoils over James. The expression ἔχειν . . . πίστιν is not surprising; in fact, it will appear again at 2:18. Nor is the concept of "the faith" unusual (cf. R. Bultmann, *TDNT* VI, 213). But the genitive qualifier of πίστιν is quite unusual, which leads Spitta, 4–5, and Windisch, 13–14, among others to consider ἡμῶν Ἰησοῦ Χριστοῦ to be a later interpolation. Certainly the phrase reads awkwardly, but this solution appears extreme for the following reasons: (1) the phrase is difficult enough that one would have to posit an interpolator with an unusual lack of ability, (2) the expression κύριος τῆς δόξης does indeed have its parallels (see Spitta), but τὴν πίστιν τοῦ κυρίου is a Christian, not a Jewish, expression, (3) this interpolation theory is normally used to support Jewish origin for the work, which is too much weight for such a tentative hypothesis to bear, and (4) the piling up of titles and descriptions is well known in liturgical and homiletic usage.

But that still leaves the problem of τῆς δόξης and what it modifies (if one does not excise it with 33 429 sa). The following options are possible: (1) τῆς δόξης modifies τὴν πίστιν, yielding either "the glorious faith" or "faith in the glory of. . . ." This option is taken by 614 and the Peshitta and gains support from other examples of such word order (Acts 4:33) and the connection of the preached gospel with glory in 2 Cor. 4:4. But the reading is unnatural and the emphasis on glory in this context seems to make no sense; the stress in the following verses will be on Christ. (2) Τῆς δόξης modifies κυρίου, meaning "faith in our Lord of glory Jesus Christ." But despite the parallel to "Lord of glory" in 1 Cor. 2:8, where it is applied to Jesus, having been transferred from God (cf. Eth. Enoch 22:14 and Spitta, 4), it is unlikely that James would have expressed himself so awkwardly (but cf. the *RSV* and perhaps the *NEB*). (3) Τῆς δόξης is an appositive to Jesus Christ, i.e. "our Lord Jesus Christ, the Glory" (Hort, 47–48; Laws, 95–97; Mayor, 80–82). Despite the parallel form in Jn. 14:6 ("the Truth") and its later use by Justin (*Dial.* 128.2), there is no instance of such a title being applied to Jesus at this period of history. (4) Τῆς δόξης is a genitive of quality modifying "our Lord Jesus Christ" and yielding "our glorious Lord Jesus Christ" (Dibelius, 128; Cantinat, 121; Ropes, 187; Mussner, 116; *NIV*). While awkward, this genitive function has a precedent in 1:25, and it allows one to explain the word order as a qualifying (and amplifying) addition to a standard title, as in Eph. 6:24.

Adamson's emendation, 103–104, to read "the Lord Jesus Christ our glory" (cf. 1 Tim. 1:1), appears without basis either in the manuscript evidence or in the given word order. It simply conveniently rearranges the text.

To speak of Christ as glorious is to speak of his reputation, fame, or honor. But this is not simply to say that "our Lord" is most honorable or exalted, for to one who knew the LXX the term would immediately recall the OT use of δόξα to translate the Hebrew kābôḏ, characteristically meaning "the luminous manifestation of God's person" particularly in his bringing salvation to Israel (Ex. 14:17–18; Ps. 96:3; Is. 60:1–2; Ezk. 39:21–22; Zc. 2:5–11; quotation from S. Aalen). Thus it is a term of exaltation, revelation, and eschatological salvation. These meanings are also common in the NT usage of the term, especially the eschatological sense (Mt. 16:27 par.; Mt. 24:30 par.; Tit. 2:13; 1 Pet. 4:13; cf. Lk. 9:32; 24:26; Jn. 1:14; 17:5; Rom. 8:17; 1 Cor. 2:8; Phil. 3:21). The idea in James, then, is probably related to this area of the term's meaning, for James clearly thinks about the exalted Christ and his return to judge (e.g. 5:7ff.). Thus those who hold "the faith of our glorious Lord" with partiality are not debasing just any belief, but rather a faith-commitment in the one exalted Lord Jesus whose glory will be fully revealed in eschatological judgment. As the tone implies, this is no matter for casualness or trifling; final judgment is at stake.

See further S. Aalen, *DNTT* II, 44–48; Brockington; G. Kittel, *TDNT* II, 247–251; Lührmann.

(2) The preceding verse has pointed out that faith in Christ cannot be combined with partiality. The author now provides an example of just how the church can slide into partiality. One must remember that this is an example, not an actual instance known to the author; the descriptions of the two individuals are stylized, and a certain degree of hyperbole is involved. Because of this fact one must reject Reicke's argument (27, and in expanded form in *Diakonie*, 342–343) that this is a descriptive example of a Roman politician being favored as he tries to influence the church. It would also be wrong, however, to conclude with Dibelius, 129, that no historical information can be gathered from the text. The ἐὰν γάρ may point to a hypothetical situation, but it does introduce an example of something. The very examples one uses and how one expresses them may indicate one's cultural context better than any other feature of one's speech.

The example, structured as the protasis of a conditional sentence with v 4 as the apodosis, presents two persons entering "your synagogue." The use of συναγωγή raises the questions of why ἐκκλησία was not used (cf. 5:14), and what the meaning of the term actually is. Ἐκκλησία is by far the more common term in the NT, for this is the only use of συναγωγή for a Christian meeting. From this fact plus the frequent occurrence of συναγωγή for Jewish congregations or places of worship some scholars have concluded that James belongs to a stage of Christianity before its clear separation from Judaism (Adamson, 105). But while this usage would not be inconsistent with such a hypothesis, it does not demand it. First, several Christian writers of the first two centuries referred to a Christian gathering as a συναγωγή (Ign. *Pol.* 4.2; *Trall.* 3; Hermas *Man.* 11.9, 13, 14; W. Schrage, *TDNT* VII, 840–841), which shows this term was so used at a much later date than anyone would place James. Second, as will be argued below, a special type of gathering, noncultic in character, is intended by James, which indicates the reason why the less specific term was used. As to the second question, it is clearly possible for συναγωγή to designate either a place of worship or the congregation. Either meaning is possible in this context, but the meaning "gathering" or "assembly" is more likely on the basis that the context refers to an act of the group but not to any special feature of the place (Mussner, 117).

The two persons who enter this assembly are described as first, "a man wearing gold rings and shining clothing," and second, "a poor person in filthy clothing." It is quite possible if one accepts a Roman *Sitz im Leben* and a nonhyperbolic description to see the first person as a Roman of equestrian rank wearing the *toga candida* (e.g. Polyb. 10.5.1) and seeking adherents (Reicke, 27; cf. Judge, 53). But this interpretation is hardly necessary. The *hapax legomenon* χρυσοδακτύλιος is a strikingly descriptive term (perhaps a neologism, for although a similar description occurs in Epict. 1.22.18, χρυσοῦς δακτυλίος ἔχων πολλούς, this form is not found elsewhere) and can just as easily be understood in terms of the custom of wealthy Eastern Jews and others (cf. G. Humbert, *DAGR* I, 296–299; E. Saglio, *DAGR* I, 293–296; and Betz, 197–198). The ἐν ἐσθῆτι λαμπρᾷ may well have been a conventional expression for expensive clothing; certainly no one suspects angels of wearing the *toga candida* (Lk. 23:11; Acts 10:30; cf. Lk. 24:4; Acts 10:21; which together with James account for all occurrences of ἐσθής in the NT; the expression does not occur in the LXX, but Betz, 197–198, argues that this term plus the ring form a composite stylized description of a wealthy person). What is significant, however, is that while the term πτωχός is used for the poor person (and the following description of the person is both conventional and realistic), the term πλούσιος is not used for the wealthy one. Rather, a circumlocution is used both here and in 4:13, the only two places where wealthy *Christians* are mentioned.

(3) When the two people enter, one is seated well (κάθου ὧδε καλῶς) and the other relegated to standing or sitting on the floor (or perhaps at a lower level in the building if a synagogue structure such as that at Capernaum is envisioned; cf. Dibelius, 132). That much is clear (the textual problem appears to be an attempt to balance ἐκεῖ either with another ἐκεῖ or with a contrasting ὧδε; the given text takes the rougher, more difficult reading; cf. Metzger, 680–681). But even if these are conventional descriptions of places of rank and disgrace (ὑπὸ τὸ ὑποπόδιόν; cf. Pss. 99:5; 110:1; 132:7; Is. 66:1; La. 2:1; Mt. 5:35; that the people speak [plural, εἴπητε] of "my [μου] footstool" is probably a deliberate allusion to the OT text where enemies are placed in a similar position), showing attitudes rather than actual statements (Dibelius, 132; Adamson, 106–107), a question remains. If this is an assembly for worship, would some stand and others sit? And if these are Christians entering a service of worship, would they need to be told where to go? And is there any realism in describing a wealthy non-Christian visiting a church? Would that situation not be unusual enough to make this a poor example?

Clearly the two people are strangers, at least to this type of meeting, for otherwise they would not need to be directed to their places. To this extent Laws, 99–100, is correct to call them visitors, although Burchard, "Jakobus," 28–30, is probably more accurate in terming them new converts (or perhaps catechumens), since it is unlikely that people were admitted to Christian congregations even as observers until they had made some initial profession of faith. But this explanation is insufficient, for it still does not answer the question of whether differential postures were allowable in early Christian worship. Nor does it resolve the question as to why clothing and postures in particular were selected for this example: why did James not simply write, "a poor man came in and was insulted; a rich man came in and was honored"?

The probable solution to these questions is that of W. B. Ward (78–107, or "Partiality"). The problems remain only so long as one looks on this as a worshiping congregation. If instead one remembers that partiality in biblical literature almost exclusively concerns judicial settings (cf. the citations for 2:1) and posits a *Sitz im Leben* of a church-court (1 Cor. 6:1–11) built upon and finding its legal basis in the Jewish synagogue's *beth-din*, the example clarifies itself. The assembly is a judicial assembly of the church and both litigants are strangers to the process. The conventional nature of the descriptions and the exaggeration involved in the ἐν ἐσθῆτι λαμπρᾷ are paralleled in Jewish descriptions of judicial partiality (differences in clothing, *Dt. Rab. Shofetim* 5:6 on Dt. 16:19; b. Shebu. 31a; differences in standing versus sitting, *Sipra Kedoshim Perek* 4:4 on Lv. 19:15; b. Shebu. 30a; t. Sanh. 6:2; *Abot R. Nat.* 1:10). Thus the details of the example are explained, and one is prepared for the apodosis.

(4) The author phrases his apodosis in the form of a two-part question, but the interrogative οὐ with which he begins leaves no doubt that the question is rhetorical and the charges true. The parts of the accusation are linked by the wordplay διεκρίθητε-κριταί, but the exact meaning of the two words is debated. First, it is obvious from 1:6 that διακρίνω can mean "doubt," and some would translate this "don't you doubt in your own mind?" (BAG, 184; Chaine, 44; Ropes, 192). But this fits poorly with the second clause, as does the second translation, "are you not divided in yourselves?" (i.e. in your heart, Mayor, 85). Becoming judges requires some activity, and thus the sense "discriminate" or "make a distinction" is intended. The ἐν ἑαυτοῖς is most naturally taken as equivalent to ἐν ἀλλήλοις, "among yourselves" (Dibelius, 136; contra Mussner, 119, "inside yourselves," or Laws, 102; cf. Cantinat, 125; Schrage, 26; Mitton, 84, suggests not unreasonably that since both wavering and discrimination were common ideas in James, both may have been intended here). James, then, accuses them of "discriminating among yourselves" (which would mean that both parties were Christian) and thereby becoming "judges of evil thoughts." The phrase is awkward, but the sense is clear in the parallel phrase and the context of Jewish thought about judges. They are "evilly motivated" or "evil-thinking judges" (cf. κριτὴς τῆς ἀδικίας of Lk. 18:6; Dibelius, 137, suggests that this construction like the genitive in 1:25 may be a Semitism; cf. Moule, 175). Clearly their wickedness is that they are distinguished from the God who judges righteously and is not prejudiced (Pss. Sol. 2:18; cf. b. Ber. 6a; Ex. Rab. 30:24; Pr. 18:5; and the many passages cited at 2:1 and in Ward, 41). This description ties the paragraph together, for as προσωπολημψία in 2:1 suggested judicial partiality, so the example works that idea out and 2:4 concludes the theme with a near synonym (διακρίνω ἐν ἑαυτοῖς) and the accusation of being wicked judges. The application of this passage is certainly not limited to judicial partiality, but this situation appears to be James's main concern.

James may have had a specific scripture in mind in terming them "evil-minded judges," i.e. Lv. 19:15: "You shall do no injustice in judgment; you shall not be partial to the poor or defer to the great, but in righteousness you shall judge your neighbor." Laws, 102, believes this verse is the reason James uses the term "judges," having been suggested to James by its proximity to Lv. 19:18 which he was planning to cite in 2:8. But that seems to assume a tortuous train of thought to produce a simple word; it is more logical to conclude that having thought first in terms of this verse as a basis for his attack on their judicial procedure, he then selected another verse from the same passage to move his argument ahead to the next step.

b.-d. Rational and Biblical Arguments, Call to Obedience 2:5-13

If these Christians discriminate against the poor in such a fashion, they show themselves not on the side of the God who chose the poor, but on the side of the rich who persecute the church. Far from being judges, they are found to be lawbreakers and thus in danger of judgment for their unmerciful actions.

This segment breaks into three parts: vv 5–7, a rational argument concerning the rich and poor; vv 8–12, a biblical argument concerning the royal law; and v 13, a concluding summary proverb which drives the point home.

b. Rational Argument 2:5–7

(5) As in 1:16, 19 and eight other places in James the imperative precedes the vocative address. But, as in the two verses cited, the imperative serves simply to underline what follows so that the readers will pay careful attention (cf. the longer ὁ ἔχων οὖς ἀκουσάτω of the gospels and Revelation). Yet in all three cases the stark, severe address is softened by ἀγαπητοί. The rebuke may be stern, but the author is a preacher and pastor who is personally concerned about the lives of his congregation.

Again James begins a discussion with a rhetorical question, "Has God not chosen the poor. . . ?", using the interrogative οὐ as in 2:4. This question about the poor parallels two about the rich that are dialectically posed against it to drive the point home (2:6–7). In each case the particle indicates the expectation of an affirmative answer. The church knew well that *God* had chosen the poor. The concept of election was deeply rooted in both Jewish and Christian thought. God chose Israel (Dt. 4:37; 7:7; 14:2) and thus the Jews thought of themselves as God's elect (at times to their own detriment; cf. L. Coenen, *DNTT* I, 539). Likewise God has chosen groups for his new people (Acts 13:17; 15:7; 1 Pet. 2:9; Eph. 1:4), and one of the favored groups is "the poor." This election is based on the OT passages in which God is said to care for the poor (e.g. Dt. 16:3; 26:7; cf. Kuschke, 31–57) and the resulting fact that "poor" became a term for the pious (cf. van der Ploeg, 263–270), not only in the OT, but also in the intertestamental and rabbinic literature (Sir. 10:22–24; Pss. Sol. 5; Eth. Enoch 108:7–15; 1QpHab 12:3, 6, 10; 1QH 3:25; *Gn. Rab.* 71:1 on 29:31; *Ex. Rab.* 31:13 on 22:24; *Lv. Rab.* 13:4 on 35:6; cf. E. Bammel, *TDNT* VI, 895–898; Percy, 45–70, 73–81). This background naturally stands behind Jesus' declaration of the election of the poor (Lk. 6:20), and Jesus' declaration is certainly behind James's statement.

That the aorist ἐξελέξατο is used might refer to some eternal election of God (Eph. 1:4) but probably refers to the declarations of Jesus and reflects the constituency of the church. These Christians were largely the πτωχοὺς τῷ κόσμῳ, a situation which was true everywhere (e.g. 1 Cor. 1:26), but particularly in Palestine (Gal. 2:10; 2 Cor. 8:9; Acts 11:29). God has chosen these poor "rich in the sphere of faith" (cf. Dibelius, 136, thus rejecting Cantinat's "rich in faith," 126, for one does not know that they had much faith, and the contrast is explained by the next accusative as that of a real eschatological wealth), which means (using a type of hendiadys) "heirs of the kingdom" (i.e. the kingdom of God promised to the poor in Lk. 6:20; Mt. 5:3; cf. Mt. 25:34; 1 Cor. 6:9, 10; Gal. 5:21). The world sees only their poverty; God sees their exalted state because of his election of them to eschatological exaltation, for they are those who love him and thus receive his promise (cf. the comment on 1:12). The term "the poor," then, has as Bammel observes (*TDNT* VI, 911) picked up a religious quality, for it is virtually a name for the true believers (the Matthean version of the beatitude in Mt. 5:3 is an accurate interpretation in part). But it does so without losing the quality of material poverty, for it is a materially poor person who has been discriminated against.

Πτωχοὺς τῷ κόσμῳ is a *dativus commodi*, "poor in the view of the world," not "poor with respect to worldly belongings" as Schoeps, 350, believes; Moule at first takes Schoeps's option and then on 204 backs away; note that the readings τοῦ κόσμου A² C² K L P and ἐν τῷ κόσμῳ in some minuscules appear to be attempts to smooth out this grammar.
See further G. Schwarz.

(6) God has chosen the poor, but these Christians (the ὑμεῖς δέ underlines the contrast) have dishonored him. The aorist plus articular τὸν πτωχόν refers back to 2:2–3, but certainly the application is now wider, for discrimination is not limited to a judicial situation (cf. 1 Cor. 11:22), even if that is the primary one in view. The term ἀτιμάω is also used in the OT for the oppression of the poor, which action is roundly condemned (e.g. Pr. 14:21; Sir. 10:22). The heinousness of this action is now further underlined by the following contrast.

The Christians do not simply discriminate against the poor, but they do so in favor of the rich. This means that they are siding with the very class which both historically and at present persecutes the impoverished believer. They have made the church into a tool of persecution; they have, in effect, sided with the devil against God.

Again the οὐχ indicates that James expects agreement as he details three charges against the wealthy: oppression, legal persecution, and blasphemy. The rich as a class are seen as outside the church (they oppress ὑμῶν . . . ὑμᾶς, who are the elect πτωχούς; in contrast to this *class* distinction the church has only oppressed τὸν πτωχόν, an individual, for he is of their "group"), so now the term πλούσιοι is used instead of the circumlocution previously used to indicate a wealthy Christian (cf. Ward, "Partiality," 95–97). The rich oppress the church; no distinction is made between oppression because they are poor and oppression because they are Christian. Nor should there be, for the charge stems from the OT tradition of the oppression of the poor by the wealthy. This is precisely the context in which the verb καταδυναστεύω frequently appears in the LXX (Je. 7:6; 22:3; Ezk. 18:7, 12, 16; 22:7, 29; Am. 4:1; 8:4; Hab. 1:4; Zc. 7:10; Mal. 3:5; Wis. 2:10; 17:2). The verb, meaning "exploit" or "oppress," appears only twice in the NT (here and Acts 10:38). The old charge against the rich is still true (and it will be made more specific in 5:4).

The OT rarely calls the oppressor "the rich" but rather "the violent." The OT does describe the oppressor as wealthy and powerful, however, and so it is not surprising to find the title "rich" used in the intertestamental period; cf. E. Bammel, *TDNT* VI, 888.

The second charge is virtually a variety of the first, and again one cannot determine whether the Christians are exploited as poor or as Christians, but certainly the disfavor people earned as Christians would do nothing to hinder their being hauled into court on trumped-up charges, either civil or criminal (although in that age they probably would not have made that distinction in types of charges). The persecutors are emphatically the same (καὶ αὐτοί), and the injustice of their cause is indicated by the strong ἕλκω (cf. Acts 21:20; 16:19; this verb is not used similarly in the LXX but cf. Ps. 10:9; Jb. 20:28; Je. 14:6; normally ἄγω would mean to arrest or haul into court). While Acts records instances of persecution by the rich (e.g. the Sadducees of Acts 4:1; 13:50; the owners in Acts 16:19), the probable reference is to being hauled before synagogue-courts (the legal basis for 1 Cor. 6:2, 4, the other NT use of κριτήριον; the classical term is δικαστήριον) or other local jurisdictions for civil actions to rob the Christians "legally" of what was rightfully theirs.

(7) The author brings up the third charge with the same emphatic αὐτοί: *these* people blaspheme. That is, they insult "the good name," which certainly shows a religious motivation and for which a wide variety of causes could be supposed, from fear of losing control of a synagogue (if Jewish), to dislike of Jews (if gentile), to dislike of Christian morality, to dislike of the "superstitions" of one's slaves or tenants (cf. Dibelius, 139–141). "The good name called upon you" is certainly the name of Jesus (not necessarily the name Christ or Christian, *contra* Adamson, 112–113). The phrase "to call a name upon one" is a septuagintalism, indicating possession or relationship, particularly relationship to God (Am. 9:12; Dt. 28:10; 2 Ch. 7:14; Is. 43:7; Je. 14:9; Pss. Sol. 19:18; of a wife, Is. 4:1; of children, Gn. 48:16). For Christians the name of Jesus was substituted for that of Yahweh, or Yahweh translated as κύριος was simply transferred to Jesus (Hermas *Sim.* 8.1.1; 8.6.4; 9.12.4; etc.). And the "calling upon" became a fixed point; namely it was called over the believer in baptism (Acts 2:38; 8:16; 10:48; Hermas *Sim.* 9.16.3). This may be the reason for James's use of the aorist. Thus the blasphemy referred to indicates the reviling of the name of Jesus (whether explicitly or by implication, e.g. "those followers of a cursed criminal"), which was the

baptismal "seal" of the Christian. By siding with the rich the church was siding with blasphemers! James has held the worst charge until last.

c. Biblical Argument 2:8–12

The person who favors the wealthy has failed to love his neighbor, the poor, and therefore is a lawbreaker (for to break a part of the law is to break the whole), who should know that he will be judged by that very law which was broken.

(8) The particle μέντοι (the most common -τοι compound in the NT, used 8 times) points out that James does not begin a new topic when he uses the argument from the royal law: he continues the discussion of discrimination against the poor by showing that it violates the law of love. The particle appears to bear the force of the English concessive "however" (German *aber*; Mussner, 123) in a semi-ironic contrast of their actual behavior with that presupposed in this clause, underlining the standard of judgment.

On the translation "however" cf. Mayor, 89; Schrage, 24; and Mussner with BDF, § 450 (1) and Robertson, 1188; *contra* Adamson, 113–114; Dibelius, 142; Cantinat, 131; Laws, 107; and Hort, 53, who read "indeed" or "really," German *freilich*. Only "however" will fit in the other 7 NT uses, e.g. Jn. 4:27; 7:13; 2 Tim. 2:19; Jude 8. It seems unnecessary to posit a different, more original meaning here, for one can preserve the contrast with the following δέ of v 9 without reducing μέντοι to μεν and losing the connection to vv 2–7.

If they fulfil the νόμον βασιλικόν they do well, James states flatly. But what is that law? It is a "sovereign law," i.e. it has royal authority (Dibelius, 143), but more than that the anarthrous νόμον indicates a particular law with, as Mayor, 90, argues, a stress on its character. Would it be possible to read this in a Jewish Christian context without thinking of the kingdom of God (2:5) and the kingship of Yahweh that was in Christian thought invested in Jesus? Is it not most natural to see a reference to the whole law as interpreted and handed over to the church in the teaching of Jesus, i.e. the sovereign rule of God's kingdom (cf. Matthew 5)? That would seem more likely than both the parallel Dibelius cites in 4 Macc. 14:2 and Mussner's tempting suggestion, 124, that this refers to the royal rank of this command among the others in the law, although not in the sense of main command as in Mt. 12:31. The use of νόμος instead of ἐντολή makes it appear decisive that the whole law rather than a single command is intended (Furnish, 179–180).

This kingdom law, then, is κατὰ τὴν γραφήν, which indicates that Lv. 19:18 is being cited, although Jesus' endorsement of the law and of this law in particular was certainly in mind: "You shall love your neighbor as yourself" (cited 6 times in the synoptics and also in Rom. 13:9 and

Gal. 5:14). In other words, this command is no whim and not just simply a law, but part of *the* law, carrying the king's authority. This point is made here in the way the command is introduced; later it will be made by showing that to break one command (i.e. this one) is to destroy the whole law. The choice of the commandment is first because it fits the case and second because for James the poor person *is* the neighbor (cf. Pr. 14:21; Mussner, 123), for the context makes this point abundantly clear: the poor is elect, a neighbor, in a way the rich is not.

Spitta, 67, argues that this particular law is not the point. Rather, "you do well if you keep this law, but [2:9] its neighbor passage in Lv. 19:15, You shall not be partial to the poor, nor show favoritism to the mighty, condemns partiality and one cannot obey one without the other." This explanation seems oversubtle, for while v 9 refers to favoritism, it does not appear to cite or even use the exact terminology of Lv. 19:15. It is possible, as Dibelius, 142, suggests, that the presence of 19:15 was in the back of James's mind because it may have been connected to 19:18 in Jewish parenetic tradition. But since there are no examples of this connection, although the poem of Ps.-Phocyl. comes close in drawing upon Leviticus 19, such reasoning must remain no more than an attractive hypothesis. See further M. Smith; Furnish, 175–182.

(9) One does well if he fulfils the law, i.e. loves his neighbor as himself, *but* (and here the δέ plus the parallel structure underlines the contrast) if instead of loving the neighbor (i.e. the poor Christian) the person shows favoritism, the royal law is broken. The author expresses the favoritism concisely, using προσωπολημπτεῖτε, the verbal form of the προσωπολημψία of 2:1, a *hapax legomenon* in biblical Greek (also not found in pre-Christian secular Greek). By this choice of wording he ties 2:9 to 2:1 and thus further unifies the passage; he also underlines the point that favoritism (particularly in a court situation) is the negation of the command to love.

This connection between love and caring for the poor was also made in Jewish literature: Test. Iss. 5:2, "Love the Lord and your neighbor and have compassion on the poor and feeble"; cf. G. Moore, II, 84–88.

Such a person commits sin (cf. 4:17; 5:16, 17, 20). The expression is stark and crystal clear in its accusative force (cf. Mt. 7:23, οἱ ἐργαζόμενοι τὴν ἀνομίαν; also Acts 10:35; Rom. 2:10; 13:10; Gal. 6:10; Jas. 1:20, and κατεργάζεται in Jas. 1:3). But as if it were not clear, James explains it as "being convicted by the law as a transgressor," using a type of appositional phrase. The passive expression personifies the law in a mild way (unlike Paul in Rom. 2:25, 27, but with a similar effect), but in so doing παραβάται stands out in bold relief at the end of the sentence. The term is not found in the LXX (although Symmachus uses it for *sôrᵉrîm*, "rebellious," in Je. 6:28 and for *rāšā'*, "wicked," in Ps. 139[138]:19), and it is rare in the NT (twice in Romans, Gal. 2:8, and twice in this section of James), but the meaning is clear (Mayor, 91, shows that this is good classical idiom; however, the use in Paul would indicate that Christians used the expression at least occasionally). To transgress the law was a serious rebellion for the Jew and Jewish Christian. It was to throw off the yoke of heaven and to stand under the judgment of God (b. Shab. 11a; b. Yom. 36b; *Sipre* on Dt. 32:29; Schechter, 219–241, especially 229–230, which identifies unjust judgment and other mistreatment of the poor as murder, one of the three cardinal sins).

(10) James amplifies his flat statement of 2:9 with an explanation (therefore using γάρ) which shows just how seriously he takes the idea of παραβάται. This explanation moves the argument to a deeper level of seriousness and introduces one of the most Jewish sets of ideas into the letter.

The form of this clause is a little strange, for the indefinite relative pronoun ὅστις is normally followed by ἄν and the subjunctive. James uses the aorist subjunctive, a type of gnomic aorist, but he leaves out ἄν, which never occurs in James, although ἐάν does 7 times (cf. 4:4; 5:19); this mixed grammatical structure may come from the merging of the indefinite and simple relative forms: Moule, 123–124; MHT III, 106–108, citing Mt. 10:33 as a similar case. The unusual grammar has led to the attempt to change the subjunctive to future indicative in the Byzantine text and in A, πληρώσει, and Ψ, τελέσει.

The statement itself is more or less a truism, even if the form is Jewish. Although penalties may vary, one is counted a criminal no matter which particular section of the code one may have broken. Thus James notes that even if one keeps the whole law (τηρέω is the normal expression for this; cf. Mt. 19:17; Acts 15:5), but transgresses with respect to a single commandment (πταίω is usually used absolutely in this moral sense; cf. 3:2; 1 Pet. 1:10), he is guilty (ἔνοχος, used either with respect to the penalty attached to the transgression, Mt. 26:66; Mk. 3:29; 14:64; or the commandment transgressed, 1 Cor. 11:27) of it all. That this unitary conception of the law was held by Jews is clear, for it first occurs in the LXX of Dt. 27:26 and then in a variety of later Jewish writings (Philo *Leg. All.* 3.241; 4 Macc. 5:20; Test. Ash. 2:5; b. Shab. 70b; *Sipre* on Dt. 187; *Pesiq. R.* 50:1; *Nu. Rab.* 9:12 on Nu. 5:14; cf. Str-B III, 755). More important is the fact that the Jesus tradition contains the same idea (Mt. 5:18–19; 23:23) and so does Paul (Gal. 5:3), which means this unitary concept of the law was current in Christian circles as well. (Dibelius, 145, cites a similar Stoic concept, but the examples he gives are not at all parallel to James; besides, the concept is too Jewish to need to look elsewhere.)
It is obvious that such an idea bothers modern commentators (es-

pecially Adamson, but also Dibelius and Mitton), but one must remember two factors. First, as pointed out above, the statement is in part a truism (i.e. one speaks of breaking *the* law, not a law); an attitude toward the law and the authority behind it is revealed in any transgression. Second, the unitary concept is found in arguments, not in treatises on morality. It is a forceful way of stating that every command is important, even if in unskillful (i.e. casuistic) hands it can lead to an overemphasis of minutiae (which the rabbis avoided through their use of the opposing concept of heavier and lighter commands). James uses the idea skillfully to point to the underlying attitude and cut away any grounds the person may have for a flippant disposition toward the commands against partiality ("After all, I'm keeping the decalogue very well").

(11) James now points to two facts in support of the unity of the law. One is the *ad hominem* argument that people recognize all crime under the one heading of lawbreaking (παραβάτης; cf. the comment on 2:9). The second is that the one lawgiver expresses his will in each command (notice the use of εἰπών . . . εἶπεν καί, a circumlocution in Jewish style to avoid naming God, the choice of verb pointing to the law as the orally pronounced personal command of God). The commands only have force insofar as they express his will. And his will is violated no matter which command is broken. The law is a unity because the lawgiver is one.

The examples James selects show he is not at all concerned with ritual commands or minutiae. Rather, he selects the central ethical commands of the decalogue as examples. The order in which he cites them may be significant in that these two commands come in this order in some manuscripts of both the LXX and Hebrew text (B of Dt. 5:17, 18; a Hebrew papyrus in Burkitt, "Papyrus") and may lie behind other citations of the commandments (Philo *Decal.* 51, 121, 168, 170; cf. Dibelius, 147). Yet the order appears in some Christian literature (Lk. 18:20 against Mt. 19:18; Mk. 10:19 has the reversed order only in D and Irenaeus; Rom. 13:9) and it might be a case of either loose citation or a common Christian parenetic tradition, if a minority one. At the least, the selection of the commands is far from accidental. "You shall not commit adultery" *may* have been chosen because of their adultery with wealth (cf. 4:4), but probably only its proximity to murder is the reason. Murder, however, is frequently associated with discrimination against the poor and failure to love the neighbor (Je. 7:6; 22:3; Sir. 34:26; Test. Gad 4:6–7; 1 Jn. 3:15; Am. 8:4; cf. the literature cited on 2:9). Thus, while the commandments serve as an example, the "if" in the context of the accusation James is making is a very real possibility (cf. 4:2; 5:4–6).

See further Kilpatrick.

(12) The considerations mentioned above lead logically to James's conclusion: take into account the final judgment in all of your actions. The speaking-doing pair of terms covers all the actions of a person (Acts 1:1; 7:22; 1 Jn. 3:18; Test. Gad 6:1), in this case being particularly focused on the discrimination against the poor (Cantinat, 136; *contra* Mussner, 126, who understands "speak" as "exhort one another"). The οὕτως ("in such a way," "with this in mind," "so"; οὕτως occurs with a following ὡς also in 1 Cor. 3:15; 9:26) is repeated to stress the solemnity of the statement (cf. βραδύς in 1:19). The whole verse sounds very like a solemn catechetical pronouncement (Dibelius, 147) and may reflect such language. Certainly the concept that one's words and deeds would be judged is deeply rooted, not only in James (words: 1:19, 26; 3:1–12; 4:11–16; 5:12; deeds: 1:27; 2:1–26; 4:1–10; 5:1–6), but also in the gospel tradition (Mt. 12:36; 25:31–45).

The standard for action is set in the knowledge of a sure judgment. In this case the μέλλω does not so much indicate the nearness of judgment (as the Vg *incipientes judicari* would indicate, although 5:7–8 show that James did believe the parousia was near at hand) as its certainty (cf. Robertson, 870). This certain judgment will be according to (διά, as in Rom. 2:12) "the law of liberty," which, as has already been observed (cf. 1:25), is nothing less than the law of Moses as interpreted (and to some extent altered) by Jesus and the early church, which took its cues from Jesus. This standard, which focuses on the example of Jesus and thus the command of love, should cause all to examine their lives and channel them into obedience to Jesus' commands (cf. Mt. 7:15–23; Lk. 6:43–45).

Adamson, 118–119, strangely contrasts the "law of liberty" in 2:12, which is chosen by showing pity, with the "law of ordinances" of 2:10, 11, apparently believing that James is discussing a law-grace contrast. For this there is no support in the text.

d. Call to Obedience (Transition) 2:13

(13) Despite the γάρ, one rightly concludes from the shift from imperative second person to gnomic third person, from the pithy form of this verse, and from the sudden appearance of ἔλεος that 2:13 originally existed as a free-floating proverb (Dibelius, 147–148; Mussner, 126). But one must not conclude with Dibelius that it therefore has no connection to its context. The γάρ indicates that the author did see a relationship; it makes an excellent bridge in that it captures and summarizes aspects of what precedes and yet throws thought forward into the topic of charity, which the following verses will take up.

God, according to this saying, will judge the unmerciful without mercy (ἀνέλεος, occurring also in Test. Abr. 16, is a biblical *hapax legomenon* but is a regular formation from the classical ὁ ἔλεος). Judgment without mercy would be strict justice, every sin getting its full punishment, a prospect which the Jews feared (cf. Urbach, 448–461, on the rabbinic development of the relationship of God's attributes of justice and mercy; it would be unwise to hazard a guess at the relationship of these attributes in the period of James as Adamson, 119, does, yet certainly both concepts were present). The one who does not show mercy would be the person failing to care for any creature or other person (a duty derived from the requirement of copying God's attribute), especially the failure to help the poor. That God was merciful is frequently repeated in the OT (Ex. 34:5–6; Dt. 4:31; Ps. 103:8ff.). That people must also show mercy is also common in the OT (Je. 9:26; Ho. 6:6; Mi. 6:8) and in the teaching of Jesus (Mt. 5:7; 12:7; 18:29, 34; 25:45–46).

Moreover, the connection between forgiveness at the last judgment and one's having shown mercy was clearly stated long before James (Sir. 27:30–28:7; Tob. 4:9–11; cf. Test. Zeb. 8:3 and b. Shab. 151b: "Rabbi Barabbi said, 'To him who is merciful to the created, Heaven is merciful, but to him who is unmerciful to the created, Heaven is also unmerciful'''; cf. Adamson; Windisch, 16–17; Str-B I, 203ff.), although for him the statement of Jesus in Mt. 5:7, "Blessed are the merciful, for they shall obtain mercy," was surely of first importance. Here, then, is the negative statement of that saying phrased in good Jewish form, juxtaposed (thus the lack of any connective particle) with a positive proverb flowing from it: "mercy triumphs over judgment" (Sir. 3:20; cf. Mayor, 95; Mussner, 127; Cantinat, 138; for "triumph" as a meaning of κατακαυχάομαι, see BAG, 412; R. Bultmann, *TDNT* III, 653–654, "boast in triumphant comparison with others"). Certainly the connection must be that in humiliating the poor (whom God honors) and in transgressing the law of love (thus breaking the law) they are also failing to show mercy. As such they could expect no mercy in the final judgment. Yet showing mercy reminds one primarily of helping the poor materially. This pulls the argument on to the next section.

2. GENEROSITY IS NECESSARY 2:14–26

A "faith" which is purely doctrinal and does not result in pious action (i.e. charity) is a dead sham, totally useless for salvation. True faith reveals itself in pious deeds of love, as the examples of Abraham and Rahab show. The form of the argument is that of an opening statement plus a supporting dialogue like the Stoic diatribe or the synagogue homily (Introduction, 12; the work of G. M. Burge suggests the latter, for he finds a careful parallelism in two parts, each of two stanzas: Part 1 = vv 14–17, 18–20; Part 2 = vv 21–24, 25–26). This may indicate that this section was separately composed as a self-contained unit, but such a hypothesis should not lead one to conclude with Dibelius, 149, that it has no connection to its context. Rather, the author has placed it here because he saw such a connection, as the exegesis will make clear.

See further Burge; Ward, "Works."

a. Illustration: Poor Christian 2:14–17

(14) The opening sentence introduces the theme of this section and presents the partners in the imaginary dialogue: (1) the author, (2) the Christian readership (ἀδελφοί μου being a now familiar mode of address at the beginning of a new section of argument), and (3) τις, an imaginary member of the community who embodies the attitude James wishes to combat (this "straw man" stylistic device is widely found in Greek literature; cf. Mussner, 130). The theme under discussion is that of a faith which does not produce works. The examples in 2:15–16 and 2:21ff. will show that the works being considered are not those of the ritual law, which were the works Paul opposed, but the merciful deeds of charity that 2:13 has already suggested (cf. van Unnik, 984ff.).

Τί τὸ ὄφελος is a regularly occurring phrase in such a dialogical style (1 Cor. 15:32; Sir. 20:30; 41:14; Philo Post. C. 86: τί γὰρ ὄφελος λέγειν μὲν τὰ βέλτιστα, διανοεῖσθαι δὲ καὶ πράττειν τὰ αἴσχιστα; Epict. 1.4.16; 1.6.33; 3.7.30; 3.24.51; cf. Marty, 91, who notes that all the citations except 1 Cor. 15:32 lack the article, as does the text in B C 99, and suggests the text here is an assimilation to 1 Corinthians; yet haplography plus assimilation to the common idiom better explains the article's absence in the minority manuscripts), always expecting a negative answer: it is no use at all. In a Christian context such as this, however, the "use" takes on serious consequences, for it is salvation which is at stake. What James is asking is whether a certain faith will help one in the final judgment (the κρίσις of 2:13). The implied "no" fits with the "no" expected in the final clause of this passage: "can such a faith [i.e. a faith lacking works] save him?" The eschatological ring of such a question is unmistakable (cf. 4:12; 1:21; 5:20 and W. Foerster, TDNT VII, 990–998, especially 996).

That which will be useless in the final judgment is a faith lacking works. The hypothetical situation introduced by ἐάν is described as a person "claiming to have faith." And a claim it is, for whatever the content of the faith in terms of orthodox belief, pious expressions, prayers, etc., it appears only in the person's verbalizations (and ritual actions) but not in such deeds as would prove the reality of an eschatological hope. The emptiness of such profession is not new in the NT. One has only to scan the prophets to discover a condemnation of ritual piety without practical justice for the poor (cf. Miranda, 111–160). John the Baptist is also reported as demanding deeds be added to faith (Lk. 3:7–14), and Jesus warned that it would not do to enter the last judgment merely verbalizing his lordship (Mt. 7:15–27; cf. 5:16). Paul also reiterates this theme (Rom.

1:5; 2:6–8; 6:17–18; 1 Cor. 13:2; 15:58; 2 Cor. 10:5–6; Gal. 6:4–6). James has already mentioned this theme in 1:22–27; here he underlines it. Works are not an "added extra" to faith, but are an essential expression of it; cf. the importance of deeds of love alongside proper faith in late Judaism (m. Ab. 1:2; b. B. B. 9a; 10a; *Lv. Rab.* 31:3 on 22:24; Schechter, 214; Str-B IV, 559ff.; G. Moore, II, 168–169). Some of this emphasis in Judaism, however, first appeared in the post-70 period when charity became a means of atonement.

(15) At this point the author introduces an example of what faith without works is, an example so self-evident that it is virtually a parable (Ropes, 206; Mussner, 131; Dibelius, 152–153). But it would be wrong to follow the latter two scholars in supposing that because it is a comparison (the οὕτως καί of v 17 makes this point clear) the comparison is entirely to the spoken words of charity of v 16 which lack works. Rather, the parabolic nature is evident in the fact that this is such a crass example of faith without works that the nature of any such situation becomes clear to all.

The ἐάν makes it clear that the situation is hypothetical, so as to allow the reader to hear the example without becoming defensive. The example considers, however, a situation of faith: it is a brother or sister who comes, one of the poor mentioned in 2:5 who belongs to the community, and it is "one of you" (τις . . . ἐξ ὑμῶν) who responds, also a member of the community (cf. Mt. 12:50; Rom. 16:1; 1 Cor. 7:15). James is dealing with those who hold the faith and with an intracommunity situation (cf. Cantinat, 141–142). The person is in a typical situation of need, as portrayed in numerous OT passages: γυμνοὶ ὑπάρχωσιν (having insufficient clothing; in rags or without the outer garment which kept one warm at night; Jb. 22:6; 24:7; 31:9; Is. 20:5; 58:7; Mt. 25:36; 2 Cor. 11:27; Jn. 21:7) and λειπόμενοι τῆς ἐφημέρου τροφῆς (lacking daily bread; the adjective, which is a biblical *hapax legomenon,* is common enough in classical Greek: Diod. Sic. 3.32; Dion. Hal. 8.41.5; cf. Mayor; Dibelius, 21; and Adamson, 122, although other terms are more common in the NT; cf. Mt. 6:11, etc.). The description, then, is stylized, although one should not doubt that such examples of lack existed in the early church as in most marginal societies.

(16) The response to this need is also hypothetical (εἴπῃ), yet it is calculated to shock the reader. The suppliants (there is already in v 15 a shift from the singular brother or sister to the plural) are dismissed with friendly words (ὑπάγετε ἐν εἰρήνῃ =lᵉkû lᵉšālôm, the common Hebrew farewell found in Jdg. 18:6; 1 Sa. 1:17; 20:42; 29:7; cf. Jud. 8:35; Jub. 18:16; Mk. 5:34; Lk. 7:50; Acts 16:36) and a wish that the persons should be clothed warmly (θερμαίνομαι refers to warmth from clothing in 1 Ki.

1:1; Hg. 1:6; and Jb. 31:20 LXX) and well filled with food (χορτάζω means "to satisfy hunger" in Koine Greek as opposed to its use for animals or animallike men alone in classical Greek). While the form could be either middle or passive (Mayor, 97–98, and Adamson, 123, argue for the latter, yet a middle sense appears to be the normal case in both verbs in biblical Greek), Dibelius, 153, is correct that such a question makes little difference, for the point is that the Christians fail to give the needy ones what they lack (the reference broadens still farther in δῶτε to include the whole community which James addresses). Again James uses an NT *hapax legomenon*, ἐπιτήδεια, which is broad enough to include both food and other bodily needs (cf. 1 Macc. 14:34; 2 Macc. 2:29; Thuc. *Hist.* 8.74; Dibelius, 153). He concludes with the same expression found in 2:14, τί τὸ ὄφελος ("what's the use?"). In doing this he produces a type of *inclusio*: catch-phrase statement, statement repeated as an example, catch-phrase.

(17) The example was crass and would have shocked many pagans, let alone people accustomed to the OT prophets and the application of the laws of charity in late Judaism. It was clear that such a person could not have heard the teaching of the community; his faith was empty. James now expresses this conclusion.

Οὕτως καί is James's regular way of applying a metaphor or example (1:11; 2:26; 3:5), and the application is direct: faith which has no works is "dead," i.e. it is useless (ἀργή, 2:20; μάταιος, 1:26; unable to save him, 2:14; a similar use of νεκρός appears in Epict. 3.16.7 and 3.23.28, but Dibelius's interpretation, 153, of it as "barren, unfruitful" is too weak, for James sees it as totally useless, as Epictetus views useless philosophical speech). It is dead καθ' ἑαυτήν, which probably means "by itself" (i.e. per se, without works; cf. Gn. 30:40; 43:32; 2 Macc. 13:13; Acts 28:16; Rom 14:22; *contra* Ropes, 208, "in itself," "inwardly").

For James, then, there is no such thing as a true and living faith which does not produce works, for the only true faith is a "faith working through love" (Gal. 5:6; cf. Mussner, 132). Works are not an "added extra" any more than breath is an "added extra" to a living body. The so-called faith which fails to produce works (the works to be produced are charity, not the "works of the law" such as circumcision against which Paul inveighs) is simply not "saving faith."

Both Laws, 120–121, and Burchard, "Jakobus," see a correspondence between this illustration and the reality in the community and thus place this situation within a corporate (plural you) setting, although not as specific a setting as Reicke, 32, and Trocmé, 663, who see in the expression "Go in peace" the blessing by a deacon at the end of the Holy Communion. For Burchard in particular the situation must be read in the light of 2:1–4: the church has received a rich person as a new convert, and, rather than demanding from him the normal "fruit of repentance," they soft-pedal the demand of full righteousness or works "in this special case" and simply accept the person as he is. Although it is debatable that the link between the two passages is that specific, Burchard is surely correct in understanding the unity of the whole passage 2:1–26, as the structural and thematic analysis in this commentary shows, and in seeing that the demand of charity is involved in both halves of this chapter. He is further correct in pointing out that James does not argue for faith instead of works or works instead of faith or even works above faith, but for faith and works. Both are important and must equally be present or else the other alone is "worthless," just as body and spirit are each "worthless" when separated from one another.

b. Rational Argument 2:18–20

(18) At this point James begins the argument which develops the theme begun in 2:14–17, yet it is this verse which Dibelius, 154, claims to be "one of the most difficult New Testament passages in general." This is not a *crux interpretum*, for, as Mitton, 108, has observed, the general sense of the verse is clear enough in its context, but the exact nuance of the words is indeed difficult, especially in the first part.

The initial clause, "But someone will say," obviously introduces some type of imaginary interlocutor into the situation, a typical device of a homiletic style. The style predisposes the reader to view this person as a hostile or erring voice, for it is in this way that Paul uses the clause (1 Cor. 15:35 and similarly Rom. 9:19; 11:19; Lk. 4:23) and also other Greek writers (Jos. *War* 8:363; 4 Macc. 2:24; Barn. 9:6; Xen. *Cyr.* 4.3.10), and of course the Stoics (cf. Ropes, 12; Bultmann). Yet the following clauses do not seem to oppose James's concepts. How are these data to be reconciled? Spitta, 77–79, and Windisch, 16–17, claim that the objection has disappeared from the text; only James's reply remains. Because of the difficulty of the other position, this solution is not to be rejected out of hand. Yet since it lacks manuscript evidence, it must remain a counsel of desperation for those who can accept no other solution.

Dibelius, 155–156, Marty, 96, Ropes, 208–214, Mitton, 108–109, Michl, 154, Schrage, 31, Laws, 123–124, and others argue that the problem is the proper interpretation of the σὺ . . . κἀγώ pair. As in the case of Teles, 5–6 (quoted fully in Dibelius, 156), the reference of σύ and κἀγώ is neither clear nor important. The point is that the interlocutor is claiming that faith and works may exist separately, as the many gifts of 1 Cor. 12:4–10. It is this separation which James then attacks. The strength of this interpretation is that it takes the introductory clause as referring to an opponent, as is the case everywhere else it has been observed. It also fits with the response in v 18b. Yet if this is what James means, he has expressed it very awkwardly, for ἄλλος . . . ἄλλος (or ἕτερος) would have done much better (cf. the quotation of C. F. D. Moule in Adamson,

137: "To tell the truth, I cannot think of a less likely way to express what J. H. Ropes wants the James passage to mean than what there stands written").

Mayor, 99–100, Mussner, 136–138, Adamson, 124–125, 135–137, and perhaps Cantinat, 146, argue that to take the *content* seriously the interlocutor must be favorable to James and expand upon his position in v 17 in another voice in 18a: "You (claim to) have faith, and I (you admit) have works. Show me your 'faith' apart from your works (you can not, naturally), and I. . . ." If this is what the verse intends, then the ἀλλ' which introduces the verse cannot be adversative, but rather must be an emphatic particle following the negatives implied in 2:14–17. This use of ἀλλά has been argued by many grammarians and commentators: Chaine, 61; BAG, 37–38; MHT III, 330 ("yes, indeed," giving as examples Jn. 16:2; 1 Cor. 3:2; 2 Cor. 7:11; 11:1; Phil. 1:18); Thrall, 78–82. It is obvious that on the basis of this evidence one could see no adversative relationship, but rather emphasis: "Indeed, someone will say. . . ."

Yet this reading, attractive as it is, also has its problems. First, why introduce a third person here? Can it be simply for rhetorical effect? Does James use such a device out of modesty? But in this case the "quotation" would have to extend at least to the end of 2:19. Second, while such a reading is grammatically possible, it appears linguistically improbable, for no one has yet been able to find a case where this common stylistic introduction did not introduce an opposing or disagreeing voice. The evidence just is not strong enough to make this the one exception.

It is obvious, then, that none of the solutions to this passage is without its problems. On the whole it appears that the second solution, that of Dibelius, is the most likely, for it is grammatically possible and yet explains the problems in interpretation. If that should not be persuasive, some version of the first solution should be the second choice, for it is posssible that something was lost through an early haplography or, assuming that the Greek is an edited version of an Aramaic synagogue homily, that the translator/redactor left out a clause. But because such a solution is hypothetical it must remain a second choice.

The passage, then, introduces an objection. The gist of the objection is that faith and works need not be connected, that charity and faith are separate spiritual gifts (the works here are the same as those in 2:14–17— not the Pauline works of the ceremonial law, but the works of charity assumed in the teaching of Jesus and the early church). James responds to this objection with a challenge familiar in the diatribe style: δεῖξόν μοι (e.g. Epict. 1.4.10, 13; Ps.-Cal. 3.22.10; 1 Clem. 26:1; BAG, 171), meaning "prove to me." "Prove to me this (so-called) faith of yours apart from deeds." It is obviously impossible, for the reality of faith can only be seen in life-style. So Paul in 1 Corinthians 13 claimed that faith needs love. "*I*," continues James, using the emphatic κἀγώ, "will demonstrate my faith by my works." The contrast is clear: no works, no faith. But James wants to close even more avenues of escape, so he continues in the next verse with the *reductio ad absurdum* of the interlocutor's implied position.

(19) Again the author uses the conversational device of addressing an imaginary opponent. Significantly he indicates an intellectual commitment on his interlocutor's part to a creed (πιστεύεις ὅτι) rather than the distinctively Christian personal trust and commitment which would include obedience (πιστεύεις plus dative, ἐν, or εἰς; cf. R. Bultmann, *TDNT* VI, 210–212). In this he is indicating something far different from the Pauline concept of faith and thus not addressing the Pauline doctrine at all. The content of this faith is also significant, for it is not a clearly Christian confession, but the *Shema*ʿ of Judaism, recited twice daily (Dt. 6:4; cf. m. Ber. 1; Aristeas 132; Jos. *Ant.* 3:91; Philo *Op. Mund.* 171; *Decal.* 65), which was also basic to Christian belief and formed a great distinction between Christians (whether Jewish or not) and pagans (Rom. 3:30; 1 Thes. 1:9; Hermas *Man.* 1), although some pagan philosophers had also reached this conclusion (cf. Dibelius, 159; Windisch, 18). The assumption of this orthodox creed does not mean that James's readers believed nothing more; rather, he picks the most basic formula of Jewish belief, for he knows that he can compare the following statement about demons to this and receive assent.

There is a difficult textual issue here: did the original text read εἷς ἐστιν ὁ θεός p⁷⁴ ℵ A etc.; εἷς θεός ἐστιν B etc.; εἷς ὁ θεός ἐστιν C etc., or ὁ θεός εἷς ἐστιν K Byz. Lect. and many minuscules? While there is not much difference in meaning among these readings, the first is probably original, for the last is weakly supported, the middle two, which are really versions of the same reading, appear to be more "philosophical" versions of the first, moving closer to gentile Christian faith, and the first is the most primitive, as well as best supported, being a version of the *Shema*ʿ but not a citation of the LXX; cf. Metzger, 681.

The confession is in accordance with true belief, so James adds a semi-ironic καλῶς ποιεῖς (the author certainly believed this truth with all his heart, following the tradition of Jesus, Mk. 12:29). Such belief is indeed necessary, but not enough for salvation. The demons themselves are quite orthodox, but they tremble in fear of judgment. That all things, including demons, shudder (φρίσσω) before God is clear in Jewish literature (Test. Abr. recension A, 9; Jos. *War* 5:378; Hermas *Man.* 4), but the special fear of demons before God is attested at least soon after the NT period and probably existed within it, as magical papyri, which use God's name against demons, and Christian literature show (Leiden Magical Papyrus J 384, 239–240; Justin *Dial.* 49.8; Eth. Enoch 13:3; 69:1, 14; Heb. Enoch 14:2; Clem. Alex. *Strom.* 5.5; cf. Dibelius, 160; BAG, 873–874;

Windisch, 18; Peterson, 295–299; Deissmann, 260). More importantly, the NT knows of the monotheism of demons (Mk. 1:24; 5:7; Acts 16:17; 19:15) and their fear before Christ, whom they recognize (Mk. 1:23, 24; 5:7). The point is that the knowledge of who God is does not save them; in fact, it is this very knowledge which makes them shudder (and that very name which was used by exorcists to drive them out)! A faith which cannot go beyond this level is worse than useless.

See further Deissmann, 256; Jeremias, "Paul," 370; Peterson, 295.

(20) On first glance one might think that this question in 2:20 underlines the point just made in v 19 about workless "faith" being demonic, but that would demand οὖν or a similar particle. The δέ pictures the still-furrowed brows of the imaginary interlocutor who needs more evidence. James introduces the clinching evidence from the history of Israel. The θέλεις . . . γνῶναι, then, is more "Will you recognize?" or "Do you want to be shown?" (Mussner, 139; Dibelius, 149; cf. Cantinat, 148) than "Do you realize?" (Adamson, 127).

The address "O foolish person" is part of the strong, direct style of both the diatribe (Bultmann, 60–61; cf. Hermas *Vis.* 3.8.9; Epict. 2.16.31–32) and the discourse of Jewish teachers (1 Cor. 15:36; Mt. 23:17; Lk. 24:25; Gal. 3:1; cf. Wessel, 80–82) and James (4:4, μοιχαλίδες). The term κενός itself (used in a different sense in 4:5) is the linguistic equivalent of ῥακά (Mt. 5:22) and has overtones not only of intellectual error (Mussner, 140; Cantinat, 148), but also of moral error (Jdg. 9:4; 11:3 LXX), thus coming close to μῶρος (one must beware of taking the root meaning of κενός, "empty," "useless," out of context, to produce the implication "lacking works," as Adamson does, 127; cf. A. Oepke, *TDNT* III, 659).

The error involved (which is moral as well as intellectual in that it puts the person on the side of demons with a useless faith) is not to see "that faith without works is sterile." The reading ἀργή (B C it.) is superior to νεκρά (א A K etc.), for (1) the latter reading is a harmonization with 2:17 and 2:26 and (2) the former is a wordplay (ἀργή-ἔργων) of which James is certainly fond. The idea, then, is that work-less faith is sterile or useless (cf. BAG, 104); it will not produce the hoped-for salvation, but is totally without result.

c. Biblical Argument (Two-Part): Abraham; Rahab 2:21–26

(21) The example of Abraham serves to prove the above. The author refers to him as "our father," which would be most natural in a Jew's mouth (Is. 51:2; 4 Macc. 16:20; Mt. 3:9; Jn. 8:39; m. Ab. 5:2) and may thus add to other evidence that a Jewish Christian wrote this letter. Yet such an expression was not impossible for a gentile (e.g. 1 Clem. 31:2), since Christians considered themselves the true Israel, descendants of Abraham by adoption (Romans 4; Gal. 3:7, 29).

The crucial concept in the verse is οὐχ ἐξ ἔργων ἐδικαιώθη. The οὐχ obviously expects a positive answer to the question, so one should read it as a statement. But what does ἐξ ἔργων ἐδικαιώθη mean? Here it is certainly correct to bracket Paul's definitions and first of all search for answers in the Abraham tradition. The works are plural, which could indicate simply the class of actions leading to being declared δίκαιος, but which in the case of Abraham may well refer to his 10 testings, especially since testing (πειρασμός) is of such interest to James. In fact, the incident of the binding of Isaac ('Aqedah) which James cites forms in Jewish tradition the capstone of a series of tests (Pirqe R. El. 26–31; Abot R. Nat. 32; m. Ab. 5:3; 1 Macc. 2:52; Jub. 17:17; 19:8), and the fact that Isaac is bound and then released is seen as evidence not only of Abraham's obedience to God, but also of the value of his previous acts of mercy, of charity:

> The angels then broke into loud weeping, and they exclaimed: "The highways lie waste, the wayfaring man ceaseth, he hath broken the covenant. Where is the reward of Abraham, he who took the wayfarers into his house, gave them food and drink, and went with them to bring them on their way? . . . for the slaughtering knife is set upon his throat."

(see Ginzberg, I, 281; Ward, "Works," 286–290; and Davids, "Tradition," 113–116). That is, the release of Isaac is itself a declaration of righteousness. The Jewish reader considering Abraham and God's final declaration of his righteousness in Gn. 22:12 would think not on the declaration of Gn. 15:6 (which was considered an anticipatory statement and thus a result of merit), but on the hospitality of Abraham in Genesis 18 as vastly amplified in the course of tradition (Test. Abr. recension A, 1.17; Tg. Ps.-J. on Gn. 21:33; Abot R. Nat. 7).

These data mean that neither the works which James cites nor the justification which results are related to Paul. Rather, the works are deeds of mercy (which therefore fit with the opening verses of this section) and the ἐδικαιώθη refers not to a forensic act in which a sinner is declared acquitted (as in Paul), but to a declaration by God that a person is righteous, ṣaddîq (which is the implication of the "Now I know" formula of Gn. 22:12; cf. Is. 5:23; Gerhardsson, 27; Dibelius, 162). Adamson is correct in seeing that a moral rather than a primarily judicial emphasis is intended (although of course there is some judicial tone in any declaration of standing by "the judge of all the earth"; cf. Marshall, 148). The point of James's argument, then, has nothing to do with a forensic declaration of justification; the argument is simply that Abraham did have faith, which here unlike other places in James means monotheistic belief—for this Abraham was famous in Jewish tradition—but he also had deeds flowing from that faith. His faith was not just "saying," but "saying and doing."

He had responded to the "implanted word" (1:21; cf. Burchard, "Jako-bus," 41, and *contra* D. Via, who tries to set the message of 1:18–24 in contradistinction to that in 2:14–26). Abraham did acts of mercy because of faith that God is one, and thus God put his approval on Abraham's life and declared him righteous.

The interpretation above gives a new focus to the final phrase of the verse, "offering his son Isaac upon the altar." This test of the reality of the faith forms the point at which God's verdict becomes clear, for while Abraham starts to offer Isaac, God ratifies the covenant by sparing the boy's life. The "offering" ends with the "binding," for Abraham was in fact righteous and obedient in all of his relationship with God. This con-cept is a long way from Paul and Hebrews (where a proleptic, typological resurrection is in view, Heb. 11:17–19), but just such a difference must be taken into account if one is to explain James's unique point of view.

(22) In 2:22 James quickly makes his point. Βλέπεις shows that he is still in the homiletic style of 2:20 (θέλεις δὲ γνῶναι) and 2:19 (σὺ πιστεύεις . . .); the same imaginary person is being addressed. "You see" draws the conclusion from the example much as οὖν might in less dra-matic prose.

The point is that faith assisted (συνήργει, not the συνέργει of ℵ A etc.) his works (as the Spirit of love assists the law in Test. Gad 4:7 and the Logos assists deeds in Musonius 21–22: συνεργεῖ μὲν γὰρ καὶ τῇ πράξει ὁ λόγος). One might conclude from this that the main factor in reaching the goal was works. Their necessity may be the stress, but James turns right around and states that Abraham's faith is perfected (ἐτελειώθη, doubtless meaning "is brought to maturity" and thus indicating the un-finished state of faith without works) through his works (ἐκ τῶν ἔργων). Here, then, is a balanced statement. James wishes to reject *neither* faith *nor* works. Both are individually important. Yet for the person to receive God's declaration that he is righteous (2:21 presents the goal in ἐδικαιώθη) they must mix together. Faith assists works, works perfect faith (notice that perfecting, as in 1:4, 15, not completing, is in view).

But, one may ask, from where does Abraham's faith suddenly ap-pear? Two answers must be given. First, it is clear that the author knows of Gn. 15:6 and its place in the Abraham tradition, which 2:23 will explain. For Dibelius, 163, this alone answers the question: the Jewish haggadic tradition used this verse, so James also uses it. No dependence upon Paul is implied. Yet, second, one can inquire more deeply into this tradition and ask if James might not have *already* given hints of Abraham's faith. The answer is not hard to find if one remembers the stories about Abra-ham in *Gn. Rab.* 38; Jub. 11–12; Philo *Leg. All.* 3.228; *Virt.* 216; and Jos. *Ant.* 1:154–157: Abraham was known as a man who had turned from idols to serve the one God (for Josephus he is the discoverer that God is one).

This accords exactly with James's definition of faith in 2:19 (εἷς ἐστιν ὁ θεός). So the mention of Abraham's faith would have received ready assent from the readers: every Jew knew how Abraham had committed himself to the one God (and how he had tried to convert others as well). Thus this verse not only leads the discussion forward, but also unifies the two themes of the Abraham tradition: Abraham's faith and his works are complementary.

(23) Because of the above James can draw a further conclusion, that Gn. 15:6 is "fulfilled" in the event mentioned. This is typical of the midrashic method: a primary event or text is cited, the text is discussed, and then a secondary text is added to the discussion (cf. Adamson, 131, citing Guillaume, 394, and Longenecker, *Exegesis,* 32–38). Thus it would be incorrect to see ἐπληρώθη simply functioning in the form of prophecy-fulfilment (*contra* Mayor, 104; Ropes, 221), but rather in the sense that the scripture in Gn. 15:6 says the same thing that James has been arguing.

The form of the citation in James conforms to the LXX with the addition of δέ as also in Rom. 4:3; Philo *Mut. Nom.* 33.1; 1 Clem. 10:6; Justin *Dial.* 92; the LXX in this case has transformed the active *wayyaḥše̊ḇehā* into a passive, perhaps as an antianthropomorphism or because it knows the tradition of angels writing such decisions, and has translated the tetragrammaton by θεῷ.

The use of this particular scripture is not surprising quite apart from Paul, for Jewish exegesis frequently joined Gn. 15:6 to the Abraham tradition (including the '*Aqedah*) as a type of timeless sentence written over the life of Abraham (*Mek. Beshallah* 4[35b] on Ex. 14:15 and 7[406] on Ex. 14:31; Philo *Abr.* 262; *Deus Imm.* 4; Jub. 18:6; and 1 Macc. 2:52: Ἀβραὰμ οὐχὶ ἐν πειρασμῷ εὑρέθη πιστός, καὶ ἐλογίσθη αὐτῷ εἰς δικαιοσύνην; cf. Dibelius, 168–174). The problem is not *that* James uses the passage, but *how* he uses it.

First, there is no evidence that James uses the passage precisely as rabbinic exegesis did, for they considered the faith of Abraham itself a work (cf. *Tg. Ps.-J.* on Gn. 15:6). Certainly in this passage in James faith and works are separate, however closely they may be related.

Second, James does not use the passage the way Paul does. Two possibilities commend themselves: (a) since 2:22 has already joined faith to works, showing that Abraham had a faith which included works, his type of faith in God could therefore be considered righteousness (Mussner, 144), or (b) since the two parts of the sentence had already been separated in midrashic fashion in Jewish exegesis (1 Macc. 2:52), James does the same, with the first clause referring to the faith of Abraham (perhaps even his conversion from idolatry) and the second clause to the fact that his deeds were accounted righteous in heaven (Dibelius, 164–165).

He is certainly right that λογίζω means "to enter in the heavenly books" (cf. H. W. Heidland, *TDNT* IV, 284–292), but whereas Dibelius refers the sentence to the binding of Isaac, it is more likely that Ward, "Works," correctly argues that the successful outcome of this event was seen as a reward for his *previous* righteous deeds of charity, as in the citations mentioned on 2:21. To James scripture witnesses to the faith-works combination in Abraham's life.

Third, while καὶ φίλος θεοῦ ἐκλήθη is not a direct biblical citation, James apparently uses it as a paraphrase of the biblical sense (in such passages as Is. 41:8 and 2 Ch. 20:7), a paraphrase that had already become the common title in Judaism for Abraham as a result of his faithful deeds (Jub. 19:9; 30:20; 2 Esd. 3:14; Philo *Abr.* 273; cf. 1 Clem. 10:1; Cantinat, 154; Bowker, 209, 212; J. Jeremias, *TDNT* I, 8). Thus it rounds off his biblical citation with a summary which is itself biblical in a loose (midrashic) sense.

See further Berger, 181–182; K. Berger, *TRE* I, 373–374.

(24) James immediately moves to a concluding statement in his argument that sums up the results of the two scriptures previously considered. In so doing he comes closer than anywhere else in the epistles to directly contradicting Paul. Because of this possible conflict, 2:24 must be viewed as a *crux interpretum,* not only for James, but for NT theology in general.

The nature of the statement is apparent in its form. Ὁρᾶτε is on the one hand simply a variant of the βλέπεις of 2:22 (also found in Test. Jos. 10:14; cf. Epict. 1.4.16; 1.16.3; 1.28.20; 3 Macc. 12:4), but the shift to the second person plural shows that the argument with the imaginary opponent has been dropped, and the author has returned to directly addressing his readers (always thought of as plural, ἀδελφοί). This impression is confirmed in that he now speaks in general terms (ἄνθρωπος) rather than specifically mentioning Abraham. The example, then, ended with the preceding verse: this present verse is a general conclusion, the point of the whole argument.

Before looking in detail at the critical assertion, however, one must ask if it is really dependent upon Paul. J. T. Sanders, 115–128, for example, points to this verse as an example of a canonical writer's contradicting another on the basis of human feeling. Specifically, he argues that the language in James must reflect a knowledge of Rom. 3:20, 28 and 4:16. The critical portions are reproduced below.

It is evident that if James knows these verses in Paul he must intend to contradict them. On the other hand, it is unlikely that James had read these verses for the following reasons: (1) the vocabulary in James is not

Rom. 3:20	διότι ἐξ **ἔργων** νόμου
	οὐ **δικαιωθήσεται**
	πᾶσα σὰρξ ἐνώπιον αὐτοῦ

Ps. 143(142):2	ὅτι οὐ **δικαιωθήσεται**	*Jas. 2:24* ἐξ **ἔργων**
	ἐνώπιόν σου πᾶς ζῶν	**δικαιοῦται**
		ἄνθρωπος καὶ
		οὐκ ἐκ **πίστεως μόνον**

Rom. 3:28	λογιζόμεθα γὰρ
	δικαιοῦσθαι πίστει **ἄνθρωπον**
	χωρὶς **ἔργων** νόμου

Rom. 4:16	διὰ τοῦτο ἐκ **πίστεως**
	ἵνα κατὰ χάριν
	εἰς τὸ εἶναι βεβαίαν τὴν ἐπαγγελίαν παντὶ τῷ σπέρματι
	οὐ τῷ ἐκ τοῦ νόμου **μόνον**
	ἀλλὰ καὶ τῷ ἐκ πίστεως ᾿Αβραάμ

found in any single citation, but in a variety of verses in a variety of contexts spread over some 25 verses of text; (2) the vocabulary differs from Paul at critical places (e.g. νόμου does not appear in James, but while Paul can say ἐκ τοῦ νόμου instead of ἐξ ἔργων νόμου, he never says simply ἐξ ἔργων without indicating the law in the context, unless he means to use works in a quite different and positive sense, as in Gal. 5:19 and 6:4; likewise James's limiting expression μόνον is in a context quite different from Paul's); and (3) the two writers are discussing totally different subjects. Paul is justifying the reception of gentiles into the church without circumcision (cf. Stendahl) whereas James is discussing the problem of the failure of works of charity within the church (which may be totally Jewish). If James intends to contradict Paul, he has so misunderstood him that his use of biblical citations and the meanings of the similar expressions are totally different. This would hardly indicate that he had read Romans.

Cantinat, 155–157, makes a similar point, as does Mussner, 146–150, in his excursus on justification; cf. Laws, 131–133.

One is left, then, with two possibilities: either James writes in the period before the faith-works controversy existed in Pauline terms, or he operates in a part of the church where the issues were very poorly understood. In this latter case he could hardly have contacted a Pauline community, at least not until Paul's teaching had been thoroughly distorted, but it is possible that he had heard of the teaching second- or thirdhand before Romans was widely enough known to form a corrective. This second option assumes that James knows of a group claiming "faith, not works" as a slogan (Dibelius, 166). This may have been the situation, but it need not have been the case at all. The formulation in this epistle could as easily be James's own independent ideas arising from common Jewish tradition, just as Paul's belonged to him. All one need posit is that some were saying, "We believe; don't bother us further, especially about charity," or that the church was trying to court the wealthy by excusing them from works. The following exegesis works out this point of view (cf. Burchard, "Jakobus").

The point James is making is that it is from one's works (ἐξ ἔργων) that God declares one righteous in the final judgment (the passive δικαι-οῦται has God as the implied active agent): no question of the forensic justification of *sinners* arises, but rather of what pleases God. This is a normal meaning of this verb in the LXX (some 44 times; cf. the comment on 2:21). God is pleased only when confessed faith leads to action. Here the function of μόνον is clear. The confession is necessary (and faith does not have the full Pauline sense but rather is *simply* confession, simply intellectual)—the fact that μόνον appears shows this emphatically—but such faith in and of itself will not do. Faith must produce deeds. This is no more than what the Jesus tradition had taught James (cf. Mt. 7:15-21), and it would certainly have earned Paul's approval as well (Gal. 5:6; 6:4; 1 Cor. 13:2; 2 Cor. 9:8; cf. the parenesis in Eph. 4:17ff. and Col. 3:5ff.). One need look no farther than the situations envisaged in the Matthew 7 passage to find a suitable *Sitz im Leben*. The important point is that one must not read this verse with Pauline definitions in mind, but rather must allow James to speak out of his own background.

See further Allen; Lindemann, 240-252; Trocmé; Via for the opposing position; Burchard; Ziesler, 9-14; Jeremias, "Paul"; Walker.

(25) The author moves quickly on to a further example of how faith had to be put into action to earn the approbation of God and his salvation; the ὁμοίως δὲ καί serves to show that this is a second example with the same meaning as the first (not just a similar sense; Radermacher, 290).

Rahab was a person who fascinated the Jews (cf. Str-B I, 22-23; b. Meg. 14b-15a; b. Taan. 56; *Ex. Rab.* 27:4; *Sipre* Dt. 22(69b); Jos. *Ant.* 5:5-30). James says little about her, but much of what he does not say is assumed. For example, James does not mention her faith directly (cf. comment on 2:26), but not only does one have her speech in Jos. 2:9, 10 combined with the evidence of Heb. 11:31 and 1 Clem. 12:1, 8 to show that Christian tradition valued her as an example of faith, but also one finds in Jewish tradition that she was lauded as the archetypical proselyte, one "brought near" (*Nu. Rab. Bemidbar* 3:2; *Midr. Ru.* 2[126a]). Yet James naturally chooses to dwell on her deed, using the rhetorical question οὐκ ἐξ ἔργων ἐδικαιώθη to elicit the positive response from the reader. All her intellectual conversion would not have saved her life had she not protected the spies and followed their directions. Her actions are those of receiving hospitably (ὑποδεξαμένη in its classical sense) the spies (ἀγγέλους, normally used of heavenly messengers in the NT; the LXX follows the MT, using νεανίσκοι or ἄνδρες, while Hebrews and 1 Clement use the clearer κατάσκοποι) and then saving their lives (ἑτέρᾳ ὁδῷ ἐκβαλοῦσα, which contains the complex idea of her refusal to betray them to the king, her sending them out of the city through her window—thus the appropriateness of ἐκβάλλω—and her directing them to avoid the pursuit). This was seen in later Jewish literature as part of Israel's treasury of merit (Marmorstein, *Doctrine,* 86).

Obviously James has an excellent example in Rahab, but his mentioning her right after Abraham may not be accidental. In 1 Clem. 10–12 both are cited as examples saved διὰ πίστιν καὶ φιλοξενίαν. Note that (1) the two works are probably not dependent upon one another, (2) the same deeds of both characters are recalled in 1 Clement as in James, and (3) faith and hospitality (a form of charity for which Clement is arguing) are stressed in Clement and are necessary for James's argument. Thus H. Chadwick is probably right in claiming that both these works draw on a common Jewish tradition which cited these heroes as examples of charity (namely, hospitality; cf. Chadwick, 281). This is another clue as to the unity of this section, its theme of charity, and its dependence on Jewish tradition.

See further Jacob; Young.

(26) At this point James turns to sum up his argument, using a final comparison (ὥσπερ . . . οὕτως καί) which includes in its final clause a phrase which forms an *inclusio* with 2:17, neatly tying his midrashic exegesis together as a support for the main argument of 2:14–17. While the comparison may seem unnecessary at this point, a form of rhetorical overkill, it does bring the issue to a head.

Two points stand out in this verse (the final clause, ἡ πίστις χωρὶς ἔργων νεκρά ἐστιν is dealt with in 2:17). First, the γάρ indicates that the author does view his point as flowing out of the Rahab example. Thus he is clearly thinking of Rahab's faith as well as her works. This clue fills in the assumed background of 2:25. Second, the σῶμα-πνεύματος example assumes a typical Jewish Christian anthropology. The author likely refers to the concept rooted in the creation narrative of Gn. 2:7—the person is composed of body and breath (which could equally well be termed soul or spirit). The separation of the two produces not the longed for release of the immortal soul from the prison of the body, but the simple consequence of death (Jn. 19:30; Lk. 23:46; Ec. 3:21; 8:8; 9:5; cf. 2 Cor. 5:1–10, where Paul longs for resurrection rather than a disembodied state). Neither soul nor body is desirable alone; a body without its life-force is simply a rotting corpse. Likewise, says James, faith is useful when joined to works, but alone it is just dead, totally useless. Dead orthodoxy has absolutely no power to save and may in fact even hinder the person from coming to living faith, a faith enlivened by works of charity (i.e. acts of love and goodness).

See further Burchard, "Jakobus."

THE DEMAND FOR PURE SPEECH
3:1– 4:12

1. PURE SPEECH HAS NO ANGER 3:1– 12

A T this point James, having concluded his present discussion of the relationship of rich and poor, including the need for charity to enliven true faith, turns to a second theme of the work previously mentioned in 1:19–21 (and also in 1:5–8, although this section is really taken up more in 3:13), pure speech. Nothing could be more distressing to a community or more divisive than bickering and mutual verbal abuse, especially if the teachers of the community are those doing the sniping. James points out how inconsistent and evil such behavior is and even suggests that it may be an indication that the people in question are not as inspired by God's Spirit as they may think.

The passage naturally breaks into three segments. First, 3:1–2a is an introductory saying formed of one admonition plus a common truism which had perhaps become a proverb. It is possible that this complex was not originally part of the treatise, for the transition to 3:2b is rough enough and the specific topic of teachers far enough away in the remaining sections that it may well be that an originally general exhortation has been here specifically applied to teachers. Second, 3:2b–5a forms a supporting paragraph on the difficulty of controlling the tongue. The εἴ τις in 3:2b begins this segment (note the πταίει functioning as a catchword and the topic of the perfect person) and the οὕτως καί clause of 3:5 forms a natural conclusion (cf. 2:17, 26 for a similar stylistic feature). Third, 3:5b–12 forms a second supporting paragraph on the evil power of the tongue and its impropriety. The initial ἰδού plus proverb shows a typical use of an imperative to begin a paragraph (cf. 2:5; 1:16, 19); the ἀδελφοί μου at the end is an indication of the conclusion.

We must agree with Dibelius, 182, that there is much traditional material (proverbs, stock phrases, typical illustrations) in this section of text, which fact accounts for both its appealing universality and its literary roughness. But we must not be fooled into forgetting that the redactor wishes this section to be read as a unity. Only then will the reader see its coherence and its place in the context of the letter and chap. 3 in particular.

a. Warning Against Self-Exaltation 3:1–2a

(1) The topic sentence shows the intended application of the section. While it is quite possible that 3:2b–12 was originally a more general treatise on the problems of speech (as 1:19; Dibelius, 182), in its present context the segment focuses on teachers; their sins form the topic.

Using the by-now typical address ἀδελφοί μου (a sign of a new departure) the author advises them not all to seek the teaching office (properly, not many to become teachers). In saying this, we reject Mussner's suggestion, 159, that πολλοί is to be understood adverbially (as πολύ; cf. 5:16 —here Mussner follows BDF, § 243 and § 115 (1), where πολυδιδάσκαλοι is a suggested reading, or Völter, 328, who conjectures ἐθελοδιδάσκαλοι as in Hermas Sim. 9.22.2; cf. Col. 2:23). While Mussner certainly gives an attractive idea, "do not teach much," the more usual translation also makes good sense, making his suggestion less likely.

In the early church the charismatic office of teacher was valued and thus high in status. This naturally built upon the role of the teacher in Judaism, as is reflected in the gospels. The title rabbi is known in the gospels (Jn. 1:38; 20:16; Mt. 8:19), as were other titles of similar import, e.g. γραμματεύς, Mt. 2:4; διδάσκαλος, Lk. 2:46; νομοδιδάσκαλος, Lk. 5:17; cf. Mt. 23:2; Jeremias, Jerusalem, 241–245. One does not need to posit the later system of rabbinic training and ordination to recognize that even pre-70 the scribe/teacher was highly esteemed (cf. m. Ab. 4:12; B. M. 2:11). The leading role in Christianity was probably thought of as rabbinic or scribal in some communities (e.g. Mt. 13:52), but of course it was charismatic as well (1 Cor. 12:28). Clearly it was an office of some social rank (mentioned with prophets in Acts 13:1; cf. Did. 13:2). Thus there was quite an impulse for those fit and unfit to press into this office. This situation posed a problem, for the church had to cull out the true teacher from the false. It is obvious that this task is going on in 1 John 3; 1 Pet. 2:1; 1 Tim. 6:3 (cf. 4:1ff.); 2 Tim. 4:3; and Jude, but one should also include Paul's struggles with the circumcision party in Galatians and elsewhere. While some of the false teachers were doctrinally subversive, many are cited as ethically subversive (see K. Wegenast, DNTT III, 766–768; Laws, 140–143).

In this passage, then, the author deals with people wishing to put themselves forward as teachers because of the status and other rewards of the position (cf. Hermas Sim. 9.22.2). This process could and did lead to rivalries and divisions as teachers tried to secure a following. Not so, says James, for not many should be teachers. Only a few are called. What is more, such a role means not simply honor and a following, but responsibility, for "to whom much is given from him much is required." If Jesus had said that every word would be judged (Mt. 12:36; cf. m. Ab. 1:11) and that the false teachers of the Jews would be most severely judged (Lk. 20:47; Mk. 12:40; cf. Mt. 23:1–33), it must have been a common teaching that teachers would be held to a stricter standard (εἰδότες refers to something already taught in the church, underlining its traditional character; cf. Rom. 5:3; 6:9; 1 Cor. 15:58; 2 Cor. 4:14; Eph. 6:8). And that is only right in that the teacher has the possibility of greater damage and claims to have a more perfect understanding of doctrine and ethics.

The author reveals his own position at this point in λημψόμεθα, for he includes himself among the teachers; whatever else one knows of the redactor of this work, he considered himself a teacher and had a proper humility about his position. He would also be judged for his teaching (a similar concept is expressed by Paul in 1 Cor. 9:27, where he refers to the possibility of teaching others, but then being declared ἀδόκιμος himself).

(2a) The judgment would necessarily find something to condemn, for the author (he is still using the first person plural to include himself) notes that "we all sin often" (ἅπαντες refers to all people, not just teachers; πταίω is used only here, 2:10; 2 Pet. 1:10; and Rom. 11:11 in the NT; Hermas *Sim.* 4.5, πολλὰ καὶ ἁμαρτάνουσι). Πόλλα probably refers to all types of times as well as sheer frequency (cf. Dibelius, 184; Mussner is not wrong in saying "in many respects," 160; cf. BAG, 695). The whole expression is not so much a humble confession as a proverbial observation which should warn the teacher to take care in the face of the coming judgment. This proverbial character is abundantly clear when one considers the wide variety of writers in which the idea is found, both Jewish and pagan (Soph. *Ant.* 1023; Thuc. *Hist.* 3.45.3; Epict. 1.11.7; 2.11.1; Seneca *Clem.* 1.6.3—*peccavimus omnes, alii gravia, alii leviora*; Philo *Deus Imm.* 75; Pr. 20:9; Jb. 4:17–19; Ps. 19:13; Ec. 7:20; Sir. 19:16; 1QH 1:20–21; 2 Esd. 8:35; Rom. 8:46; 1 Jn. 1:8). James will now join to this observation the specific sin against which he wishes to warn the teachers.

b. Warning about the Power of the Tongue 3:2b–5a

(2b) "If someone," begins James, using a formula for a hypothetical instance which he frequently used to begin paragraphs within a larger context (1:5; 2:26), "does not stumble with respect to speech, this person is perfect." The verb πταίω (see 3:2a) forms the catchword link between the topic statment of 3:1–2a and the first supporting paragraph. There is a slight transition in thought from 3:1, for while λόγος is surely chosen because of its apt application to teachers (Mussner, 160) it is not limited to error in teaching (Dibelius, 184) but includes all speech in general, a synonym for γλῶσσα of 3:5. Τέλειος occurs here as in 1:4 to designate completeness in virtue, not sinlessness; the ἀνήρ is pleonastic, a typical feature of James's style first observed in 1:12.

The high value placed on the control of the tongue here is not only quite appropriate to the problem James sees in multiple teachers, but also very common in Judaism (Sir. 19:16; 20:1–7; 25:8; Pr. 10:19; 21:23; Ec. 5:1; m. Ab. 1:17—see also Philonic and other Greek citations in Dibelius, 184). James uses the teaching to recapture the truth of 1:26 and to function as the topic sentence of the paragraph, for the following examples are to prove this point (they are admittedly traditional and quite probably frequently associated together, as Dibelius argues).

This concluding description of the perfect person confirms the previous assertion. Χαλιναγωγέω, used elsewhere in the NT only in 1:26, serves both to recall forcibly 1:26 and to provide the point to which the χαλινός of the illustration in the following verse can link. At the same time it teaches the well-known virtue of the control of the body and its passions (e.g. m. Ab. 4:1; cf. Jas. 1:13 and the whole *yēṣer* concept), of which James wished to make control of the tongue the chief aspect. Here one is solidly within the early Jewish Christian parenetic tradition, which is being applied to teachers with a special concern for community harmony.

See further Bauer.

(3) James immediately launches into an illustration, but it is difficult to decide how he structures it, for the textual problem is extremely unclear. C P and many versions read ἴδε; א* reads εἶδε γάρ (=ἴδε); and A B K L it. Vg, etc. read εἰδέ. The problem is that due to itacism (ει pronounced like ῑ, although in B it also serves for ῑ) one cannot be sure whether the ειδε spellings mean εἰ δέ or ἴδε. Hort, 68–69; Dibelius, 184–185; Schrage, 32; Mussner, 158; Marty, 119; and Cantinat, 167, opt along with UBS[3] (cf. Metzger, 681–682) and Nestle[25] for εἰ δέ and view the other reading as an attempt to assimilate to the ἰδού of 3:4, 5. Adamson, 141; W. F. Howard (MHT II, 76–77; cf. BDF, §§ 22–23); Laws, 146; Mayor, 108–110; and Ropes, 229, all argue that ἴδε is correct because it fits the style indicated by ἰδού and James's Semitic preferences and the εἰ δέ does not make good sense. In the stylistic data of James, εἰ δέ appears 5 more times (only chap. 5 lacks it) while ἴδε does not appear again (as opposed to 5 appearances of ἰδού). As a result one cannot claim *lectio difficilior* for either reading: εἰ δέ does not fit as well in the context while ἴδε does not fit well with James's style. The probabilities appear to be in favor of εἰ δέ for one reason: it was argued that εἴ τις in 3:2 is a paragraph introductory formula. The use of an imperative so soon thereafter (which could itself introduce a paragraph, but cf. 3:4) is less likely than the repetition of εἰ with δέ joining argument to statement.

The sense of the verse is clear, and the illustrations involved are common enough to have been the stock of writers (Plut. *Mor.* 33; Philo *Op. Mund.* 88) and wise men around the Mediterranean (or the Sea of Galilee; cf. Rendall, 38). The reference to the bridle (χαλινός) and horse comes first to give the link to χαλιναγωγῆσαι in the previous verse. The fact that by controlling the mouth the whole body is directed forms the rough analogy to the need to control the tongue and the positive results from doing so.

The analogy is rough, so Reicke, 37, proposes to make it clearer: human tongues do not control human bodies as bridles or tongue-shaped rudders do horses and boats. But since the boat is a favorite symbol for the church (1 Pet. 3:20; cf. the Apostolic Fathers) and since Paul frequently uses σῶμα for the church, James means that, if the church's "tongue," the teacher, is properly controlled, the whole church will be properly directed.

This suggestion is attractive, for the context of these verses does mention teachers, James does mention storms which may misdirect one (1:5–8), and the boat image does exist (Reicke does not mention the suggestion by H. J. Held in Bornkamm, *Tradition*, that the ship image is in Matthew 8 as well). Although one would expect that this saying in James would be often used in the church as Reicke suggests, the context does not allow this interpretation. There is nothing in James's use of σῶμα (3 times here plus 2:16, 26) to suggest Pauline usage, and the vices attacked later in this passage are not those of doctrinal error, but of personal rivalry. One may conclude that James did not feel a need for exactness in his analogy: everyone knows the bitter word precedes the schism. Everyone also knows that even if his actions are upright he has many words he wishes he could unsay.

(4) At this point one must consider Dibelius's hypothesis, 185–190, that these two verses plus perhaps 3:5 are derived from Hellenistic stock statements which have been shifted from their original meaning (thus explaining some of the roughness), but were probably originally connected as charioteer and helmsman. There is no doubt but that the vocabulary in this section is unusual; many of the words in this verse are *hapax legomena* in the NT or even in biblical Greek. It is likewise true that these verses find parallels in Hellenistic literature (4 Macc. 7:1–3; Philo *Op. Mund.* 88, 86; *Det. Pot. Ins.* 53; *Leg. All.* 2.104; 3.223; *Spec. Leg.* 1.14; 4.79; *Flacc.* 86; *Migr. Abr.* 67; *Cher.* 36; *Prov.* 1.75; *Decal.* 60; Soph. *Ant.* 477; Aristotle *Q. Mech.* 5; *Eth. Eud.* 8.2.6; Lucretius *De Rerum Natura* 4.898–904; Lucian *Jup. Trag.* 47; *Bis Accus.* 2; Cicero *Nat. D.* 2.34, 87; Stob. 3.17.17; Plut. *Q. Adol.* 33; *Gar.* 10, A; further examples in Mayor). The problem is evaluating these parallels. First, the parallels occur so widely that they must have been "in the air." It would require no great knowledge of Hellenistic literature to be aware of such proverbs wherever one lived. Second, since horses and boats were the sum total of what men steered in those days, the linkage of the two was so natural from common observation that there is no need for any given author to

depend upon a traditional usage (the horse metaphor shifts from horse alone to chariot-horse, further confirming this observation). One recognizes that the author of James knows his Greek well, so he undoubtedly had read some Greek literature. Also the use of traditional material is not unknown to him. But beyond this, one cannot determine whether he simply repeated the observation of others, used a common expression from his everyday speech, or actually referred to a literary tradition. One should suspect the latter only if contact with, say, Philo proved likely at several points.

The possibility that James might at least be referring to oral proverbs is strengthened by the fact that the proverbs do not fit exactly. "We control horses by controlling their mouths" and "we control a ship by controlling a small, tongue-shaped rudder" is not quite the same as "he who can control his tongue can control his whole body." On the other hand, the proverbs naturally lead into the following paragraph in which the tongue produces great evil, i.e. can misdirect the body and so *must* be controlled. The author's thoughts may be jumping somewhat ahead of himself. The evidence points toward the use of common proverbial sayings, for none of the *literary* parallels uses the imagery in exactly this way.

(5a) With his οὕτως καί James draws his point of comparison: even though the tongue is small, it is powerful. The initial conclusion is simply that James is amply justified in calling one who controls the tongue τέλιος ἀνήρ, for such a person controls the controlling member. On the other hand, a shift of thought already visible in the metaphors now makes itself clear: the tongue is indeed powerful, but it is not always used for good. With a nice alliteration (μικρόν-μέλος-μεγάλα) James moves toward the power of evil resident in the tongue. Whether one takes the probable reading μεγάλα (A B P etc.) or the somewhat less likely μεγαλαύχει (ℵ and the Koine tradition—probably a harmonization with Ps. 10:18 [9:39]; Ezk. 16:50; Sir. 48:18; Zp. 3:11; 2 Macc. 15:32) the meaning is the same: boasts greatly/great things (similar to the negative sense of καυχάομαι in Paul; cf. LSJ). The negative tone is evident. This is not so much a pessimistic change in usage (*contra* Dibelius, 190–191), but a slow shift in thought from the power of the tongue to the evil of the tongue to the need for proper control. It is not that the tongue steers the ship, but that the proper helmsman is often not in control.

c. Warning about the Doubleness in the Tongue 3:5b–12

(5b) After a transitional imperative James introduces his new paragraph with a proverb, much as 3:2 may also be proverbial. The structure ἡλίκον . . . ἡλίκην gives balance and symmetry to the expression (A C and the Koine tradition changed the first ἡλίκον to the easier ὀλίγον; the meaning would remain unchanged, for, as BAG, 346, points out, Antiph-

anes 166.1; Lucian *Herm.* 5; Epict. 1.12.26; and Philostr. *VA* 2.11.2 all
show the use of ἡλίκος for "how small" as well as "how large" in such
parallel constructions): how great a forest a little fire sets ablaze. One
observes, then, the contrast of spark and forest, of the unguarded fire
spreading into a roaring inferno. Elliott-Binns, "Meaning," 48–50, argues
that the picture is that of scrub or brushwood as found in Palestine, which
is accepted by Mussner, 162; Dibelius, 192; and Cantinat, 172; cf. Bishop,
186, who points to how quickly brushfires spread in the Palestinian dry
season.

Dibelius, 192–193, argues that originally this imagery was intended
to speak of the passions, producing the contrast of reason controlling
passion as a charioteer or helmsman, their vehicles of passion running
loose like a fire. The use of fire as an image for the passions is certainly
well attested (Plutarch *Co. Ir.* 4; *Gar.* 10; Lucian *Amores* 2; Diogenes of
Oinoanda 38.3; Philo *Spec. Leg.* 4.83; *Decal.* 32.173; *Vit. Mos.* 2.58; *Migr.
Abr.* 94.23; Phocyl. *Poema Admon.* 143–144; *Lv. Rab.* 16 on Lv. 14:4).
Something of that fire=passions imagery does seep into James's thought
(at least in terms of the evil *yēṣer*), as has been seen (1:13ff.) and will be
seen (see below 3:13–18; 4:1ff.). But all these passages compare the *passions* to the flame, while James will now point out that the tongue is the
flame, for which he has ample precedent in Pss. 10:7 (9:28); 39:1–3 (38:2–4);
83:14 (82:15); 120(119): 2–4; Pr. 16:27; 26:21; Sir. 28:13–26; Is. 30:27; Pss.
Sol. 12:2–3. It seems, then, much more likely that James is dependent
on the biblical tradition he knows (see especially Sir. 28:22). However,
his vocabulary is his own, not dependent on the LXX verses cited.
Ἀνάπτω appears elsewhere in the NT only in Lk. 12:49; ἡλίκος only in
Gal. 6:11; Col. 2:1; and ὕλη is an NT *hapax,* but appears frequently in
the LXX, e.g. Sir. 28:10. The proverb, then, is a common expression
which must certainly have been well used. Its application to the tongue
was natural for one steeped in the biblical literature.

(6) The proverb of 3:5b leads into one of the more perplexing structures of the epistle. It is true that the general sense of the passage is clear,
but scholars have not agreed on the detailed meaning or the structure of
the text. Three basic approaches to the text have appeared. First, Spitta,
96–98, Windisch, 23, Dibelius, 193–195, and Ropes, 233, all take the text
to be corrupt. Spitta suggests that καὶ ἡ γλῶσσα . . . ἀδικίας is in fact
the title of 3:6–12, while Dibelius concludes that ὁ κόσμος . . . ἡμῶν is
a gloss. Adamson, 158, follows a similar course in suggesting that the
Peshitta translation, "the tongue is fire, the sinful world, wood," is the
original form. Naturally, as the Peshitta suggests, both early versions and
scribes found the text difficult (thus the omission of the initial καί in א
and the addition of οὕτως or οὕτως καί before the second ἡ γλῶσσα in
some Koine manuscripts, all of which may be attempts to punctuate the

text). This difficulty could point to early corruption of the text, but before one resorts to the expedient of changing the text, he should be sure the given text does indeed make no sense.

Second, there have been attempts in some older commentators to take ὁ κόσμος in a sense other than the obvious one. Chaine, 81, suggests "an ornament of evil," i.e. the tongue makes evil attractive (cf. 1 Pet. 3:3; Isid. *Epis.* 4.10). The Vg along with Michl, 48, Bede, and many older commentators has *universitas iniquitatis,* "the universe" or "the totality of evil" (cf. Pr. 17:6). Such explanations are not linguistically impossible, but they are improbable, for James uses κόσμος 4 other times (1:27; 2:5; twice in 4:4) and in none of these places will such meanings fit. Instead, ὁ κόσμος τῆς ἀδικίας must be taken as a parallel construction to μαμωνᾶς τῆς ἀδικίας (Lk. 16:9, 11; cf. a similar form in Lk. 18:6) in which the genitive has substituted for the adjective ἄδικος (the frequency, but not the structure itself, is perhaps due to Semitic influence; it occurs at least 7 other times in James, all with feminine nouns). The evilness and anti-God character of "the world" is such a commonplace of early Christian thought that one could hardly see how an early reader could have taken this phrase otherwise (cf. J. Guhrt, *DNTT* I, 524–526; James's use of this term is one indication of his closeness to the parenetic tradition which also appears in 1 John).

Third, many commentators struggle with the traditional grammar and its obvious meanings. In this case one may either take ἡ γλῶσσα πῦρ as a nominal sentence, in which case ὁ κόσμος may either be an appositive (Alford, IV, 305) or the predicate complement of καθίσταται with ἡ γλῶσσα being the subject (Hort, 71, who suggests a parallel to 1:7, 8; Mayor, 113; Mitton, 125–126; Laws, 148–149, who points to the reflexive use of καθίστημι in 4:4); or, one may take καθίσταται as the implied verb with both uses of ἡ γλῶσσα (Mussner, 162–163; Schrage, 39). The former structure with the nominal sentence plus a clause with predicate-subject-verb order is more likely, for this would explain the article in ἡ σπιλοῦσα. The sense is the same in either case, however. The tongue is the danger-ous fire of the proverb in 3:5b. This sentiment was relatively commonplace in Jewish thought (Pr. 16:27; Sir. 28:22; Pss. Sol. 12:2–3; *Lv. Rab.* 16 on Lv. 14:2) and it naturally led to another comparison: the tongue represents the evil world itself among the parts of the body. In saying this the author may mean that it is the special seat of the evil *yēṣer,* for it is obvious that much of the book deals with community strife and that 3:8–12 points to doubleness (itself an attribute of the evil impulse) as a characteristic of the tongue (cf. b. Shab. 105b). Yet one must not press the statement into a formal declaration of his anthropology: the sense is simply that since speech is the hardest faculty to control it is there that one first observes "the world" in a person's heart. Jesus made a similar observation (Mk. 7:14–23 par.).

As in the teaching of Jesus, James states that the tongue stains the
whole body. This and the following participial phrase explain the exact
meaning of the main clause. The idea of staining the soul or body, i.e.
morally defiling it, was, as Dibelius puts it, "a very hackneyed expression" (195; cf. Test. Ash. 2:7; Wis. 15:4; Jude 23). What is stained is the
body in a typical Jewish sense, i.e. the whole person (cf. E. Schweizer,
TDNT VII, 1047–1048, 1058), for again it is clear that a person is morally
tarred with the brush of his tongue if not by the wider community. On
the other hand, the tongue does not stop there, for it sets fire to the whole
course of life, as anyone who has seen a plot develop into action or an
argument turn into a fight will testify; the origin of this fire is hell itself.

The problem of the expression τροχός τῆς γενέσεως has long been
discussed by commentators; one need only cite the excursuses in Dibelius, 196–198, Adamson, 160–164, and Ropes, 235–239. Their detail means
that we need merely to summarize the present state of the discussion. It
is clear, as Dibelius points out, that Orphic literature contains the idea of
a "circle of becoming" (κύκλος τῆς γενέσεως in Procl. *In Tim.* [5, 330 A]
3). The normal term, however, is simply κύκλος, although γενέσεως τρο-
χῷ does appear in one passage (Simplicius 2.168b; but here the term probably comes from the myth being interpreted). This literature is also very
early and thus the figurative expression had plenty of time to work into
later Greek and Jewish literature (Ps.-Phocyl. 27 = Sib. 2:87; *Ex. Rab.*
31:3 on Ex. 14:25; b. Shab. 151b; cf. Kittel, *Probleme,* 141ff.; Philo *Som.*
2.44). The conclusion thus must be that the phrase is a nontechnical term
which may be dependent upon an original Orphic formulation, but it is
now widely separated from its roots and inexactly used in discourse
around the Mediterranean. While the variety in usage among the literature
makes exact determinations of meaning impossible, most likely James
intended "the whole course of life" by the expression.

The concept of being set on fire by Gehenna is also a very interesting
one. Apoc. Abr. 14, 31 point to the existence of Azazel (Satan) in hell.
Thus by that date Satan had been identified as the present (as opposed to
future in Revelation) inhabitant of hell (cf. b. Arak. 15a; Laws, 152; but
also cf. W. Foerster, *TDNT* II, 80). James, then, could be an even earlier
reference to such a belief (especially if connected to 3:15 and 4:7), yet
the expression here goes even beyond that assertion. Gehenna (or Hades),
usually the place in which evil beings are tormented or imprisoned (cf. J.
Jeremias, *TDNT* I, 657–658), is now used as an expression for the source
of evil (cf. Rev. 9:1–11; 20:7–8). Two facts emerge: (1) this is a singular,
if clear and understandable, figure, for the prison now stands for the
imprisoned (perhaps as a warning to living people as well), and (2) the
evil in a person, already spoken of as the world or evil impulse, is now
traced for the first time to its ultimate source in Satan.

At this point the reason for the difficulty of this verse is apparent:

the author has piled up stock phrases and expressions which, if taken unidiomatically, are a mixture of metaphors and grammar but which would have impacted upon the original readers with rhetorical clarity. The same is often true of modern sermons.

See further Carr, "Meaning"; Kittel, τροχόν; Stiglmayr; van Eysinga.

(7) The picture of fire in the previous verse has suggested the wild, destructive nature of the tongue. Now James explains this image (the γαρ indicates as much) by use of another analogy from nature, which may indeed itself have been suggested by 3:3, 4. Dibelius's assertion, 200, that James shows his dependence "upon a diatribe which spoke of the mastery of human beings over their desires" has not been proved, for Dibelius shows only that the images were common, not that they were invariably linked.

James's first observation is that *every* (πᾶσα; cf. BDF, § 275 [3]) species of animal is domesticatable, as past (δεδάμασται) and present (δαμάζεται) experience shows. (The verb δαμάζω appears elsewhere in the NT only in Mk. 5:4, where the demon-driven man could not be subdued.) The meaning "species" for φύσις found in this verse is observable in Philo *Spec. Leg.* 4.116. Although ἐναλίων is a *hapax legomenon* in biblical Greek, the division of animals into four categories comes from scriptural tradition (Gn. 1:26; 9:2, which may be alluded to since they refer to the subject; Dt. 4:17–18; Acts 10:12; 11:6; Eth. Enoch 7:5; Philo *Spec. Leg.* 4.110–116). However, pride in the ability of humans to tame animals was quite common in the Greek-speaking world (Cicero *Nat. D.* 2.60.51–158; Seneca *Benef.* 2.29.4; Soph. *Ant.* 342; Epict. 4.1.21; Philo *Decal.* 113; *Leg. All.* 2.104; *Op. Mund.* 83–86, 148; Aelian 8.4). The ability proved to many ancients the superiority of human reason over strength or speed. James does not have to argue this point, but raises it to set up the following contrast.

(8) Using δέ for contrast and throwing τὴν γλῶσσαν into emphatic relief (that small member of man's own body in contrast to the great beasts and free birds of the previous verse), James pops the bubble of pride: no one is able to tame his own tongue (οὐδείς is separated from ἀνθρώπων to make it starker and more absolute, as Schlatter observes, 216). This problem was known to both Greek and Hebrew wisdom (cf. Plut. *Gar.* 14; *Lv. Rab.* 16 on Lv. 14:4; *Dt. Rab.* 5:10 on Dt. 17:4), and it is the source of common exhortation in Proverbs (Pr. 10:20; 13:3; 12:18; 15:2, 4; 21:3; 31:26; cf. Sir. 14:1; 19:6; 25:8). James now expands upon the problem with two nominative phrases which serve to explain the situation.

First the tongue is ἀκατάστατον κακόν, which compares with what

Hermas says about slander (ἀκατάστατον δαιμόνιον, *Man.* 2.3). The adjective has already appeared once in James (1:8 and nowhere else in the NT), where it refers to the instability of the double-minded. It is related to the noun ἀκαταστασία, which will appear in 3:16 as a characteristic vice of unspiritual men, but which is never a feature of God (1 Cor. 14:33; cf. Lk. 21:9; 2 Cor. 6:5; 12:20; in Pr. 26:28 LXX it is caused by the tongue), for heaven has perfect stability and peace (Test. Job 36 describes earth as unstable and heaven as stable; the normal antonym in the NT is εἰρήνη [cf. H. Beck and C. Brown, *DNTT* II, 780] or ἁπλότης as in Test. Iss. and Hermas *Man.* 2). Thus the tongue shows its demonic nature in its instability and lack of single-mindedness and peace. It is not, as James will explain in 3:9–10, that the tongue never speaks good, but that it speaks evil as well.

C 33 Syr. and the Koine witnesses all read ἀκατάσχετον, "unchecked." But not only does this reading fail to be supported by the Alexandrian text, but it also appears to be the substitution of a more understandable word, common in Greek, which ignores the deep rooting of ἀκατάστατον and δίψυχος in James and thus the wider context and style of the work.

Second, the tongue is full of death-dealing poison. Ps. 140:3 (139:4) contains a similar idea, and may be the origin of the metaphor (as in Rom. 3:13), although the idea was widespread in Jewish literature (1QH 5:26–27; Sir. 28:17–23; 10:11; Test. Gad 5:1; cf. Jb. 5:15; Ps. 58:4, 5; Sib. 3:32–33, the only place where θανατηφόρος ἰός appears). The metaphor is so appropriate for the dangers of the tongue (and naturally, as in the Act. Phil. [Mayor, 121], would suggest the serpent in Eden) that one can hardly speak of clear dependence at all (cf. Hermas *Sim.* 9.26.7 and O. Michel, *TDNT* III, 334–335).

(9) At this point James leaves the metaphors behind and clarifies his meaning of the tongue's instability. The issue is that the tongue is used for incompatible activities: on the one hand, it is very religious, but, on the other, it can be most profane in daily life. The need to avoid such duplicity in the tongue was a commonplace of Jewish and therefore early Christian ethics (Ps. 62:4 [61:5]; La. 3:38; Sir. 5:13; 28:12; Test. Ben. 6:5, which is similar to the δίγλωσσος of Did. 2:4; Philo *Decal.* 93; 1QH 1:27–31; 10:21–24; *Lv. Rab.* 33 on Lv. 25:1, which is similar to pagan narratives in Plut. *Gar.* 8; *Mor.* 506c; and Diog. Laert. 1.105).

The Jewish source of this thought is evident in the first part of the verse: men bless God with the tongue. Although the terminology τὸν κύριον καὶ πατέρα is not exactly duplicated in Jewish literature (1 Ch. 29:10; Is. 63:16 are close, but not exact; cf. Sir. 23:1, 4; Jos. *Ant.* 5:93; some Byzantine texts and the Vg have changed this to θεόν καὶ πατέρα, which does have exact parallels; cf. Laws, 155), the thought is certainly that of the OT (Bousset, 291–292), but copied by the church (e.g. Mt. 11:25). The blessing of God is another OT theme with εὐλογέω being used frequently in the LXX with God as object (Pss. 31:21 [30:22]; 103[102]:1, 2; etc.). In the NT God can be referred to simply as εὐλογητός (Mk. 14:61; Rom. 9:5), which certainly indicates common Jewish usage similar to the rabbinic "the Holy One, blessed be He" (cf. m. Ber. 7:3; Eth. Enoch 77:1; Dalman, Worte, 163–164). NT prayers often refer to God in this manner (Lk. 1:68; 2 Cor. 1:3; Eph. 1:3; 1 Pet. 1:3), reflecting a usage similar to that of the Jewish liturgy (cf. "Blessed art Thou" of the Eighteen Benedictions). In other words, this blessing is undoubtedly a liturgical blessing of God in the church services and private prayers rooted in the emergence of the church from the synagogue (which may not have been complete at the time James was written).

The second part of the verse likewise reflects Jewish and Christian usage. Cursing of people is common enough in the OT (Gn. 9:25; 49:7; Jdg. 5:23; 9:20; Pr. 11:26; 24:24; 26:2; Ec. 7:21; Sir. 4:5), although even there limits are placed on it and there is a certain uneasiness about it. In the NT one finds the words of Jesus forbidding cursing (Lk. 6:28), as well as those of Paul (Rom. 12:14), but apparently such prohibitions were not interpreted as absolute in all circumstances, for Paul certainly expressed at least curselike formulas (e.g. 1 Cor. 5; 15:22; Gal. 1:1) and Jude, to name another example, is virtually a long curse pronouncement on certain teachers. What James appears to be referring to is the use of a curse in anger, especially in inner-church party strife (contra Dibelius, 203, who supposes that this verse was taken as a whole from Jewish sources since the NT passages cited forbid curses: one suspects that never in the first centuries of the church's life were these strictures applied so as to forbid formal cursing of those excluded from the community and that the reason such teaching existed was that in practice early Christians resorted to curses in much less formal circumstances).

The idea that man was made in God's image refers to Gn. 1:26 LXX (καθ᾽ ὁμοίωσιν; cf. Gn. 9:6; Sir. 17:3; Wis. 2:23; 2 Esd. 8:44; Clem. Hom. 3:17, which have the same concept with different vocabulary). But it is important to realize that this fact was used in Jewish traditions to reject the cursing of men: Mek. on Ex. 20:26; Gn. Rab. 24:7–8 on Gn. 5:1; Sl. Enoch 44:1; 52:126; Sipra on Lv. 19:18. The connection is simply that one cannot pretend to bless the person (God) and logically curse the representation of that person (a human). Likewise the angry curse upon a person while liturgically blessing God makes moral and logical nonsense from James's theological standpoint. But humans are fallen and thus often do nonsense, and James feels close enough to such sin to identify with it in the editorial "we." We agree with Dibelius that this sin is not being limited to "we teachers" nor is this a personal confession of the author;

yet certainly in this redaction teachers are one specific group in mind and the author feels he shares the human weakness of the group enough to use the "we"; many early commentators could not accept weakness in such an author, and so attempted to weaken the force of the statement by making it a question.

(10) At this point the author draws his argument together into a compact statement. He has shown that the apparently differing objects of the blessing and cursing (now in nominal form) are actually irrelevant. The real issue is that they come ἐκ τοῦ αὐτοῦ στόματος, which proves his point that the tongue is ἀκατάστατος and falls under the rejection of διγλωσσία (Sir. 28:13; 5:9; 6:1; cf. the passages cited above in Test. Ben. and Hermas). Doubleness and instability are a sign of the evil yēṣer, of the demonic.

Mayor, 123, is correct that in essence this becomes an argument against all cursing (perhaps a form of καταλαλιά discussed in 4:11), building on the sentiments found in Jb. 31:29–30. When James states οὐ χρή, ἀδελφοί μου, ταῦτα οὕτως γίνεσθαι, he is not only using unusual language for the NT, but is also strongly rejecting those who curse, for he hardly intends to reject blessing. He probably thinks only about the angry or polemic curse, the uncontrolled tongue; he probably would have seen no connection to a solemn curse, although modern readers (if not in trying circumstances) may (cf. the woes on the rich in 5:1–6).

Χρή occurs only here in the NT, although it occurs in the LXX of Pr. 25:27; it is equivalent to ὀφείλομεν or δεῖ as in Mk. 13:14; 2 Tim. 2:24, and shows an educated use of classical terminology, fast becoming archaic; cf. Robertson, 124, 319.

(11) James illustrates his point with a series of three pictures from nature (or two if 3:12b is a condensation of 3:11) that not only clarify his meaning, but also show how monstrous a thing such instability of the tongue must be. Typically he uses the homiletic style of a rhetorical question introduced by the postclassical Koine μήτι (cf. μή in 2:14; 3:12; and μήτι in Mt. 7:16, a close parallel to 3:12; 26:22; Mk. 4:21; 14:19; etc.). It would be misleading to see a reference to the mixing of waters in the days of Messiah (Par. Jer. 9:16; 2 Esd. 5:9), the mixing of opposites (Test. Gad 5:1), Marah in the wilderness (Ex. 15:23–25), or other references which compare the mouth to a fountain (Philo Som. 2.281). Nor should one think of the tales in Pliny and Antigonus (Nat. Hist. 2.103 and Mirab. 148 respectively) in which they refer to fountains that do spew out fresh and brackish water. Rather, James is referring to a quite natural phenomenon commonly observed on the edges of the Jordan rift valley and similar geologically active locations around the Mediterranean that the same spring

does not put out two types of water, a sad fact of life in Palestine where water is in short supply (cf. Hort, 79; Hadidian, 228; Bishop, 187; although Palestine is not the only area in which this phenomenon is known).

The vocabulary is graphic: ὀπή is a reference to the split in the rock out of which the spring flows (also Heb. 11:38); βρύει, a biblical *hapax legomenon,* refers in classical Greek to the bursting forth in flower of a bud, but in the NT period was beginning to be used of springs bubbling forth as well (cf. Justin *Dial.* 114.4; Clem. Alex. *Paed.* 1.6.45; Clem. *Hom.* 2.45.2); and πικρόν substitutes for the more common ἁλυκόν or ἁλμυρόν (cf. 3:12, but also Rev. 8:11), probably because it also has a moral metaphorical meaning which James will use in 3:14. The picture condemns the evil speech while illustrating it, although one should not try to force an allegory into this passage, for it is more an apt picture than an allegory.

(12) It was quite fitting for James to follow the image above with one using plants, again driving the point home that a good nature or impulse cannot produce evil. The image of a plant producing according to its nature is widespread in Stoic literature (cf. Dibelius, 204–206, who cites M. Ant. 4.6.1; 8.15; 8.46; 10.8.6; Seneca *Ep.* 87.25; *Ira* 2.10.6; Plut. *Tranq.* 13; Epict. 2.10.18–19; only the last two are at all close parallels). One need not suppose, however, that there is any direct borrowing. First, the Stoic parallels are not close enough in content; second, the nature of the image is such that similar proverbial illustrations must have been common over the whole Mediterranean area; and third, the teaching of Jesus provides parallels which may have been in their oral form a basis for James's ideas (Mt. 7:16–20 par. Lk. 6:43–45; cf. Mt. 12:33–35 par. Lk. 6:45). While the teaching in James is not entirely parallel (the gospel sayings concern good and bad people and their respective works), a similar point occurs: a good nature or impulse will not produce evil, but only good, as a tree produces only according to its nature. The conclusions to be drawn from this fact have not yet been stated, but the illustration is already moving toward the two types of wisdom mentioned below.

Now the previous illustration of springs is brought into line with the agricultural illustration. The vocabulary has shifted back to the more usual ἁλυκόν from πικρόν. The choice of construction is admittedly difficult; the ἁλυκόν must stand for a brackish *spring* and the ποιῆσαι, at best unusual for what a spring does, must have been chosen to make the parallel with v 12a explicit. Nevertheless, the parallel does come across: springs like plants produce according to their natures (cf. Gn. 1:11).

The major problem with this phrase is what the text originally read. Several texts read οὕτως οὐδὲ ἁλυκόν (א C² it. Vg syr.) or οὕτως οὐδεμία πηγὴ ἁλυκὸν καί (K L P). The text interpreted above is supported by A B C. The Byzantine reading appears to be an attempt to smooth out difficulties by making v 12b repeat v 11. The text in ℵ is apparently an intermediate form. This commentary opts for the printed text because it is grammatically more difficult and yet fits the parallel in v 12a better and thus carries the thought on toward 3:13–18 (cf. Metzger, 682). James has moved from the impossibility of one nature producing two results to the observation that one's works reveal his true inspiration.

2. PURE SPEECH COMES FROM WISDOM 3:13–18

This concluding section of the chapter has been argued by Dibelius, 208–209, to be entirely independent of what precedes it. Structurally and grammatically this is quite possible, for in 5:13–14 a similar τις . . . ; plus imperative structure introduces a new unit. One must at least view this paragraph as a major subsection to the discussion of chaps. 3 and 4. In fact, since the vocabulary is not closely linked to that of 3:1–12 (except ἀκατάστατον in 3:8 and ἀκαταστασία in 3:16), it is likely that this segment was originally independent, an exhortation to peace circulating in the James tradition.

But, as Mussner, 168–169, points out, it would be quite a mistake to end the discussion on this level. The redactor has not erred by including the paragraph in this place. The σοφός and the διδάσκαλος (3:1) were in fact overlapping categories (cf. E. Lohse, *TDNT* VI, 963ff.; Schlatter, 321) and the "fire" of the disputes among teachers (3:5b–12) surely resulted in the bitter jealousy and party spirit which James now condemns (3:14). The passage is properly applied primarily to teachers and other leaders capable of dividing Christian communities (notice the σοφός terminology occurring in a different passage on community division—1 Corinthians 1), but naturally finds a wider application in the lives of all Christians.

Windisch, 25, has noticed that this unit also fits closely with 4:1–2 as "two sayings-segments against combativeness." This is also a correct observation, for the εἰρήνην at the end of 3:18 forms a contrast with the πόλεμοι of 4:1. The latter section makes the more general accusation of 3:13–18 pointed and specific. This means that while Dibelius is probably correct in arguing that 3:18 was originally an isolated proverb, in the context it is far from isolated, for, as Kamlah, 183–184, has argued, this verse now forms a summary of the preceding verses, which themselves are a virtue and vice catalogue, and thus an integral bridge to 4:1ff.

Teachers (and others), then, must not misuse the tongue. Specifically, they should be certain their speech and actions lead to community peace and solidarity; otherwise, the spirit inspiring them is clearly not God's Spirit. This in turn bridges into a discussion of what was actually happening in the community.

See further Burton, 205; Easton, "Lists"; Kamlah; Wibbing.

(13) As in Jdg. 7:3; Is. 50:10; Je. 9:11; Pss. 107(106):43; 106(105):2; and m. Ab. 4:1, the τις . . . ; (similarly the mî . . . construction in Hebrew) is essentially a vivid conditional relative clause (εἰ . . . would express the same idea in less vivid language). But this must not lead one to think that the section is purely an abstract warning. Surely the situation in Corinth and elsewhere in the early church, as well as among the Jews (1 Cor. 1:19; Rom. 1:14, 22; Mt. 11:25; 23:34), should lead one to conclude that the author knows of instances (and feels it is probably the case in the communities to which he writes) in which "spirit-inspired" men and women claimed godly wisdom and yet simply resulted in dividing the community, a problem as at home in newly formed churches full of the new wine of the Spirit as in more established churches.

The term ἐπιστήμων, a *hapax legomenon* in the NT, is likely a septuagintalism, for it appears in this combination with σοφός in the LXX of Dt. 1:13, 15; 4:6; Dan. 5:12, although since *ḥākām wᵉnābôn* is a frequent combination in the OT, this combination could as well be a Hebraism. Such people who claim to be spiritual leaders of the church (as was in fact the case in Deuteronomy) must have works to match their words. Two concepts are rather awkwardly combined here. First, true wisdom will show itself in the good deeds (i.e. works of charity) which flow from a proper (καλῆς) life-style (ἀναστροφῆς; cf. 1 Pet. 2:12; 3:2, 16; Gal. 1:13; so also Epict. 1.9.24; 1.22.13; 2 Macc. 6:23). Similar ideas were also well known in rabbinic Judaism (so Rabbi Eleazar ben Azariah in m. Ab. 3:18). This teaching is certainly neither new nor surprising in James, and, as the parallels in 1 Peter and Heb. 13:7 show, it is characteristic of early Christian parenesis. If the life-style does not match the profession, the latter is to be discounted.

Yet, second, the truly wise person will not only show works instead of just words, but will show them ἐν πραΰτητι σοφίας. This expression is somewhat awkward, probably showing, as Hort, 80, and Dibelius, 36–37, argued long ago, a preference for the Semitic-influenced genitive construction, but the meaning is clear: just as Moses (Nu. 12:3) and Jesus (Mt. 11:29; 21:5; 2 Cor. 10:1) neither displayed not defended themselves, so the Christian is exhorted to be characteristically meek, particularly in potential conflict situations (Gal. 6:1; Eph. 4:2; 2 Tim. 2:25; Tit. 3:2; 1 Pet. 3:15; cf. Jas. 1:21 and also Sir. 3:19; b. Sanh. 92a; Hellenistic writers saw meekness and humility as a vice; cf. Osborn, 32; Laws, 160–161). This cardinal virtue of NT vice and virtue lists (e.g. Gal. 5:23) is the sign of wisdom; therefore, this verse functions as a topic sentence to a paragraph which is itself a list of virtues and vices.

(14) James, unlike the authors of the catalogues in Did. 1 and 1QS 4, begins his catalogue with the vices, shifting as he does so to a rhetor-

ically powerful direct address ("if . . . *you* have") rather than the less direct form of 3:13 ("Who . . . among you? Let him . . ."). The εἰ δέ introduction (to which A P 33 etc. have added ἄρα to give even more emphasis) places a strong contrast between the reader addressed with his ζῆλον and the desirable πραΰτητι of the previous verse.

The vices being condemned are first of all "harsh zeal" (Ropes, 245) or "rivalry." Both of these translations are better than "jealousy," for ζῆλος, which often translates the Hebrew *qin'â* in the LXX, can have a positive sense in the OT (1 Ki. 19:10, 14; cf. also Sir. 48:2; 1 Macc. 2:54, 58; 4 Macc. 18:12; Jn. 2:17; Rom. 10:2; 2 Cor. 7:7; 11:2; Phil. 3:6). The problem is that zeal can easily become blind fanaticism, bitter strife, or a disguised form of rivalry and thus jealousy; the person sees himself as jealous for the truth, but God and others see the bitterness, rigidity, and personal pride which are far from the truth.

The second vice is ἐριθείαν, "the personal ambition of rival leaderships" (Hort, 82–83), or party spirit. The word ἐριθεία appears in Aristotle (*Pol.* 5.3, etc.), where it means "a self-seeking pursuit of political office by unfair means" (BAG, 309), but its meaning in the NT is not limited to the means of seeking political office, for the term appears in several NT vice lists after terms like ἔρις, ζῆλος, and θυμοί (Gal. 5:20; 2 Cor. 12:20) and apparently particularizes them in "party spirit" in which the jealous or angry leader forms a group which emotionally or physically withdraws from the rest of the church (cf. Phil. 1:17; 2:3; Ign. *Phil.* 8:2; F. Büchsel, *TDNT* II, 657ff.). Certainly the charge such a group would make is that the parent body has rejected wisdom and truth and thus those committed to the truth must withdraw. But the problem, says James, is not external, but "in your hearts," for the evil impulses within, not the Spirit, are the cause of all such sin (cf. 1:13ff.; Mk. 7:14–23 par.; Easton, "Lists," 11).

The person who claims wisdom but acts in this manner boasts and "lies against the truth." The expression is awkward, for it may mean "pride oneself" (in the negative sense of κατακαυχάομαι, Rom. 11:18), puffing oneself up over that which is really sinful, and thus lying against the truth (i.e. claiming to be wise when in truth one is foolish), as Ropes, 246; Mayor, 127–128; Mussner, 171; Laws, 160, all understand it, or as part of a hendiadys, "do not boast in defiance of the truth" (Dibelius, 210), or "do not boast, i.e. lie, against the truth" (Cantinat, 189). This problem has always bothered readers, for ℵ 33 syrᵖ all read κατακαυχᾶσθε (κατὰ) τῆς ἀληθείας καὶ ψεύδεσθε. Most likely the former group of commentators is correct (cf. Test. Gad 5:1 for lying against the truth), but the sense in any case is clear: those full of party spirit and bitter zeal ought at least to be honest and stop claiming to be inspired by God's heavenly wisdom.

(15) Making the above clear, James emphatically denies that the "wisdom" these sectaries (heretics would be the proper word, if it did not now have a purely doctrinal implication) claim is in any sense heavenly. *"This* wisdom is *not* that which descends from above." That divine wisdom comes from heaven, i.e. from God, was a commonplace of Jewish wisdom teaching (Pr. 2:6; 8:22–31; Sir. 1:1–4; 24:1–12; Wis. 7:24–27; 9:4, 6, 9–18), and James has already referred to the concept in 1:5, 17. It is also clear that because of the identification of wisdom with God's Spirit (Gn. 41:38–39; Ex. 31:3–4; Dt. 34:9; Is. 11:2; Jb. 32:7–10; cf. Rylaarsdam, 100; Wis. 7:7, 22–23; 1:5–7; Kirk, 32–54; 1QH 12:11–13; 1QS 4:2–6, 24; 11QPs 154) the claims to be wise, to have God's wisdom, and to be filled with the Spirit of God were virtually identical (Lk. 2:40; Acts 6:3, 10; 1 Cor. 1–3; 12:8; Eph. 1:17; Col. 1:9), at least as far as both the church and Qumran were concerned. Thus James is now making an emphatic denial that these critics are spiritual men, that they have God's wisdom. It is noteworthy that James never names what they do have: the term "wisdom" is reserved for God's gift, while the other so-called wisdom is only referred to obliquely, never with the noun (whereas Paul does speak of σοφία τοῦ κόσμου, 1 Cor. 1:20; 2:6; or σοφία σαρκική, 2 Cor. 1:12).

In contrast (ἀλλά) to the claim of a divine origin for their wisdom, James, using a type of antithetical parallelism reminiscent of the wisdom literature, declares through a series of three adjectives arranged in ascending order of strength that the sectarian "wisdom" is in fact demonic. First, he calls it earthly, ἐπίγειος. This word can be simply a neutral term (e.g. Philo *Leg. All.* 1.43, where earthly wisdom, τὴν ἐπίγειον σοφίαν, is a copy of the heavenly archetype), but in the NT the earthly is frequently the inferior (Jn. 3:12; Phil. 3:19; cf. 1 Cor. 15:40; 2 Cor. 5:1) and in this context the term is clearly a denial of heavenly inspiration (in Hermas *Man.* 9.11 ἐπίγειος is further defined as παρὰ τοῦ διαβόλου). Second, this wisdom is unspiritual or devoid of the Spirit, ψυχική. Dibelius, 211–212, in an excursus describes this word as a term with a gnostic background, but used by James in a nontechnical sense. One can certainly see that the dualism intended here, similar to the dualism of Qumran, is (as Schlatter, 234–236, and Mussner, 171, argue) more ethical than metaphysical in nature, and the meaning of the term in every other NT use is for that which stands in contrast to the spirit (1 Cor. 2:14—such people do not "receive" the "things" of God's Spirit: 1 Cor. 15:44, 46; Jude 19, ψυχικοί, πνεῦμα μὴ ἔχοντες; *contra* Pearson, 13–14, there is no literary dependence upon Paul by James). Thus James makes a clear denial that the Spirit has anything to do with such teaching, perhaps going so far as to suggest that these men do not even have the Holy Spirit (cf. Burton, 205). Third, this divisive teaching is "demonic," δαιμονιώδης. James has already alluded to this conclusion in 3:6 and he will be more explicit in 4:7. In claiming the people were lying against the truth (3:14) he had cited already another characteristic of demons (Jn. 8:46; Eth. Enoch 16:4). While it is possible that this biblical *hapax legomenon* means simply that such people do deeds similar to demons (so Laws, 161, 163; Cantinat, 190; Hort, 84), in the light of the closeness of this vice list to that in 1QS 4:1ff., the dualism observed elsewhere in James, and the use of the concept in the early church (cf. Hermas *Sim.* 9.22; 9.23.5; Mt. 6:13; cf. Davids, 39–79, who points to a long tradition connecting temptation to Satan) it would seem more reasonable to take James as intending that such deeds were inspired by demons. "You claim," says James, "to have the Holy Spirit. Impossible! You are inspired, all right—you are inspired by the devil!"

See further Davids, 397ff.; Ellis, 95; G. Fohrer, *TDNT* VII, 488; Lindblom, 193ff.

(16) As if to establish the previous point (although hardly as an aside to justify it, as Dibelius, 212, believes, for it is more a continuation with a somewhat less emphatic tone), James now adds a generalization: "for wherever jealousy and party spirit exist, there is also unrest and every sort of evil deed." The accusation is in itself self-evident, for how could party spirit do less than disturb the peace of the community? And who does not recognize the connection between jealousy and the justification of all types of evil deeds? (Φαῦλον here is used in the sense of κακόν as in Jn. 3:20; 5:29, and is opposed to ἀγαθόν; cf. Cantinat, 191.) But a deeper intention is surely present here as well. One knows from observation that James has a burden of communal unity (cf. Ward), so he would expect communal unrest to be a chief vice. This was true not only for James, but also for Paul (2 Cor. 12:20) and other groups (cf. 1QS 4:10). God, as Paul says, is a God of order and peace, not of unrest and disorder (1 Cor. 14:33). Furthermore, unrest is a characteristic of demons, and as such fits well with the accusation made in the previous verse (cf. the comments on 3:8 and 1:8 where the adjective ἀκατάστατος appears), and unrest is also paired with war (Lk. 21:9), which will appear in 4:1. Thus the term functions as a link-word which names another anti-Christian vice while bridging from the citation of the demonic to the coming citation of community disturbance.

One cannot be sure who the disturbers were. Obviously they were self-appointed teachers, although unlike those in Paul and Jude doctrinal error is not involved. Perhaps Mussner, 173, is correct in identifying them with the Judaizing type of disturbance, but in any case he is right in pointing out how well this verse agrees with the presentation of James the Just in Acts 15 and 21 as a mediator and peacemaker in church disputes.

See further F. Büchsel, *TDNT* II, 660–661.

(17) Having disposed of the so-called wisdom claimed by the disturbers of the churches, James now turns to characterize the true wisdom, which, as Windisch points out, 26, functions as πνεῦμα does in Gal. 5:22ff. It is also similar to ἀγάπη in 1 Corinthians 13 (cf. Furnish, 181). The enumeration structure is similar to Hermas *Man*. 9.8 (as is the emphasis on peace), which is another example of the similarity of early Christian virtue lists and the interchangeableness of σοφία and πνεῦμα, both of which come "from above" (Hermas *Man*. 11.5, 8, 9, 21).

The chief characteristic of true wisdom is purity. The meaning here is that of the OT in which God's words are pure (Ps. 12:6 [11:7]) or the ways of the righteous are pure as opposed to crooked (Pr. 21:8 LXX) or unjust (Pr. 15:26). This purity, then, means that the person partakes of a characteristic of God: he follows God's moral directives with unmixed motives. This person serves God alone, and so does not need the cleansing about which James will speak later (4:7–8; cf. 1:27; 3:6).

Moral purity is expanded by means of a list of adjectives arranged to take advantage of assonance (first initial ε, then initial α). Wisdom is εἰρηνική (elsewhere in the NT only in Heb. 12:11), "peaceable" (cf. Pr. 3:17). She is ἐπιεικής, "gentle," "noncombative" (Wis. 2:19; Epict. 3.20.11; Phil. 4:5; Tit. 3:2 and 1 Tim. 3:3 par. ἄμαχον; 2 Cor. 10:1 par. πραΰτητος), which means the wise person does not get angry, combative, or defensive even under provocation. She is εὐπειθής, a *hapax legomenon* meaning "tractable," "easily persuaded," "trusting" (Philo *Virt*. 5; Epict. 2.10.8; cf. the quotation of Musonius in Dibelius, 214; the opposite is ἀπειθής, Acts 26:19; Rom. 1:30, or δυσπειθής, Jos. *Ant*. 4:11), which does not indicate a person without convictions who agrees with everyone and sways with the wind (cf. 1:5–8), but the person who gladly submits to true teaching and listens carefully to the other instead of attacking him.

The next two virtues fit together in that ἐλέους is the practical mercy or concern for the suffering that manifests itself in alms (ἐλεημοσύνη), i.e. bears "good fruit" (cf. 1:26–27; 2:18–26). These certainly are virtues close to the author's heart. But he continues that wisdom is ἀδιάκριτος (a *hapax legomenon*), which may mean "impartial" (cf. 2:1ff.; Test. Zeb. 7:2; Mussner, 174; Michl, 50), "unwavering," "not doubting" (cf. 1:6; Ropes, 250; Schrage, 42), "not given to party spirit" (*unparteiisch*, cf. Spitta, 109; Windisch, 26), or "simple," "harmonious," "of a single outlook" (cf. δίψυχος; Ign. *Mag*. 15:1; *Trall*. 1:1; *Eph*. 3:2; Clem. Alex. *Strom*. 2.87.2; Dibelius, 214; Adamson, 156; Laws, 164). These meanings are relatively close to one another: the person with true wisdom is apparently nonpartisan: instead he is pure and absolutely sincere in his opinions and actions. This description fits with ἀνυπόκριτος, "without hypocrisy," "sincere" (1 Pet. 1:22; Rom. 12:9; 2 Cor. 6:6, where it is applied to love; 1 Tim. 1:5; 2 Tim. 1:5, where it is applied to faith), for such a person could not pretend or playact in order to influence people, but would act alike toward all. He would indeed be inspired by God and be a binding force in the Christian community.

(18) James now adds what may well have been a proverbial saying (and thus, as Dibelius, 214, argues, independent of the context) to sum up the virtues. Since the whole chapter has concerned those fighting, arguing, and disturbing the peace and unity of the community, this saying is hardly simply suggested by the catchword εἰρήνη-εἰρηνική, but rather forms a suitable conclusion underlining the main point and bridging forward to 4:1 and its wars and fighting.

"The fruit of justice/righteousness" is an expression common in biblical language (Is. 32:16–18; Am. 6:12; Pr. 11:30 LXX; 2 Cor. 9:10; Phil. 1:11; Heb. 12:11; cf. καρπὸς σοφίας, Sir. 1:16; καρπὸς πνεύματος, Gal. 5:22; etc.). The genitive is one of definition, i.e. the fruit which is righteousness, and thus allows the generic term in the genitive to be split into numerous fruit. For this reason it is useful and common in parenetic catalogues (Kamlah, 176–196; *contra* most commentators, who see the genitive as epexegetic; Laws, 165–166, follows Ropes in connecting Pr. 11:30 and 3:18 to argue that wisdom is the fruit of righteousness and that her presence is known by peace, for peacemakers possess her).

The sense here is to emphasize how such just and righteous deeds are to be done. It is "sown in peace by those who make peace." Certainly there is tautology here (cf. Cantinat, 194; Dibelius, 215; Laws, 165, who therefore prefer "*for* those who make peace"), but it is that type of emphatic tautology which is used for rhetorical effect. Who are those who in fact are doing justly? Those who make peace, who do their just acts in a peaceful way. The phrase aptly recalls Jesus' words in Mt. 5:9 to the reader: "Blessed are the peacemakers. . . ." Peace in the community, then, is the sum of the matter of doing justice.

F. Hauck, *TDNT* III, 615, follows Meyer, 263, in suggesting that God grants this fruit to those who seek wisdom. But neither the sowing-growing metaphor nor the connection to wisdom from above should be forced. The metaphor simply serves to describe those *really* doing justice; it does not form an allegory on the results of peacemaking.

3. PURE PRAYER IS WITHOUT ANGER/IN TRUST 4:1–10(12)

As a logical response to the section above James adds a section which will make the criticism he has already suggested more specific and pointed. Now he speaks of the community, not the tongue and teachers in general. The section breaks into four subsections, the last of which is semi-independent: vv 1–3, 4–6, 7–10, 11–12. The first and second diagnose the

causes of the infighting, the third calls to repentance, and the fourth gives
concrete practical advice.

The inner-community strife flows from the evil impulse, the lust
within, and thus blocks prayer. The Christians are adulterous, for they
have provoked God to jealousy. Therefore they must repent and turn from
the devil and his works. Concretely this will mean ceasing to criticize one
another, for in doing this they have assumed God's prerogative.

See further Townsend.

a. Prayer with Anger and Desire 4:1–3

(1) "From where do wars and conflicts among you stem?" begins
James with a pleonastic repetition of πόθεν (removed in the Byzantine
tradition for stylistic reasons) and a combination of ἐντεῦθεν with ἐκ for
rhetorical stress, revealing the original character of the work as impas-
sioned preaching. The wars and conflicts in question are not external to
the community (either within the Jewish community as Schlatter, 240–241,
believes, or as a Zealotic revolutionary force among Roman Jews, as
Reicke claims, *Diakonie,* 341–344); not only would such an interpretation
fail to fit the preceding and following contexts, but it would take ἐν ὑμῖν
in a most unnatural sense. The conflicts, then, are metaphorical and
within the Christian community. One cannot be sure to which conflict
this section originally referred; to this extent Dibelius, 216, is correct in
seeing it as contextless. However, in its present context it surely intends
to refer to the inner-community conflicts occasioned by the party spirit
of the teachers in the previous section (so Mussner, 176–177).

For the metaphorical use of "war" and "fighting" see πόλεμος in Philo *Gig.*
51; Pss. Sol. 12:3; Test. Sim. 4:8; Test. Gad 5:1; 1 Clem. 3:2; Epict. 3.20.18; and
μάχη in Test. Jud. 16:3; Test. Ben. 6:4; 2 Tim. 2:23; Tit. 3:9.

The community conflicts come not from a passion for truth or godly
wisdom, but from "your pleasures" or, better, "your desires." Here is a
shift in terminology from ἐπιθυμία of 1:14–15, but the meaning remains
the same. The term ἡδονή appears only 4 times in the NT (here; Lk.
8:14; Tit. 3:3; and 2 Pet. 2:13), but, as in Greek literature in general (cf.
G. Stählin, *TDNT* II, 909ff.), the term usually parallels ἐπιθυμία, as in
Tit. 3:3 where the former state of error is characterized as δουλεύοντες
ἐπιθυμίαις καὶ ἡδοναῖς ποικίλαις (in contrast to meekness, πραΰτητα),
and in Lk. 8:14 where in the interpretation of the parable of the sower
ἡδονῶν τοῦ βίου replaces the longer Marcan αἱ περὶ τὰ λοιπὰ ἐπιθυμίαι.
The reason for the use of the synonym here is harder to ascertain. On
the one hand, one is probably dealing with a source (or sermon; cf. Introduction, 12–13, 22–25) different from that in chap. 1, the ἡδονή indicating

one of the seams in the material; and on the other hand, the use of ἐπιθυμεῖτε in 4:2 may have kept the redactor from unifying his vocabulary. The source of conflict, however, is clearly the desire or *yēṣer* of the community members. No noble "fighting for the truth" this, but a disguised form of the evil inclination, the person's fallen nature.

The description of the desires is that they are "fighting in your members." Ropes, 253, takes this to mean the members of the church, a "war between pleasures which have their seat in the bodies of several persons." Yet this interpretation is unlikely, for (1) James has already used μέλος twice for a part of the human body; (2) the normal use of μέλος is for part of a human body (thus Paul must make the metaphorical sense of his argument clear in Romans 12 and 1 Corinthians 12); (3) the form of the argument is a movement from external conflict in the community to its internal basis (an interest of James; cf. 1:13ff.; 3:13ff.); and (4) Jewish *yēṣer* speculation forms a sufficient explanation for the military metaphor.

Later rabbinic tradition speaks of the *yᵉṣārîm* as having their seat in one or the other of the bodily organs, or warring against the body, or as controlling the 248 members of the body (b. Ned. 32b; *Ec. Rab.* 9:15 § 8; *Abot R. Nat.* 16). One would move cautiously on such late traditions if it were not that the Qumranic literature also speaks of a spirit of falsehood, etc., which must be driven out of the body (e.g. 1QS 4). The body is itself neutral, but it is often controlled by sin. This is precisely what Paul argues in Romans 6–8. Sin has to be conquered by Christ before a person can do what he wants with his body. Thus the fight is within the body of the individual Christian.

This struggle is not just against God and his Spirit (Spitta, 113, on the analogy of Test. Dan 5), or against the soul (1 Pet. 2:11, στρατεύονται κατὰ τῆς ψυχῆς, Hort, 88), for the self of these people appears to be being swayed by two forces. Rather, as Mussner, 177, argues, it is a war against "the better insight" or "the conscience" of the person, which in later Jewish terminology is the good *yēṣer*, in Paul's terminology the Spirit, and in James's terminology wisdom. The struggle, which will be set in a context of prayer as in 1:6–7, pictures the δίψυχος, the double-minded person, pushed this way by his conscience and that way by his evil impulse.

See further Davids, 366–376.

(2) This verse begins a substructure of the paragraph:

a   ἐπιθυμεῖτε
         καὶ οὐκ ἔχετε
b   φονεύετε καὶ ζηλοῦτε
         καὶ οὐ δύνασθε ἐπιτυχεῖν

b΄ μάχεσθε καὶ πολεμεῖτε

[καὶ] οὐκ ἔχετε διὰ τὸ μὴ αἰτεῖσθαι ὑμᾶς

a΄ αἰτεῖτε

καὶ οὐ λαμβάνετε διότι κακῶς αἰτεῖσθε ἵνα . . .

Naturally not all have recognized this structure: Hort, 89; Mayor, 136; Mitton, 147–148; Ropes, 254–255; Laws, 169; and Cantinat, 197–199, argue for the following structure on the basis of parallelism and the missing καί in 4:3 (bracketed above):

ἐπιθυμεῖτε, καὶ οὐκ ἔχετε· φονεύετε.

καὶ ζηλοῦτε, καὶ οὐ δύνασθε ἐπιτυχεῖν·

μάχεσθε καὶ πολεμεῖτε.

The pleonastic (on this reading) καί before ζηλοῦτε is explained as a Hebraism.

Two comments need to be made. First, as Mussner, 173; Dibelius, 218–219; and Adamson, 167–168, point out, the pleonastic καί on Hort's reading is at least as much of a problem as the lack of καί in the first reading. Furthermore, א P it. Vg syr and others do have the bracketed καί, thereby indicating the possibility that it was original or at least the way many ancient authorities read the text. Thus the more comprehensive structure appears to have the advantage.

Second, neither structure eliminates the problem of φονεύετε. How does murder fit into this series? Many would answer: "It does not fit!" Erasmus's conjecture that instead of φονεύετε an original φθονεῖτε stood in the text has found wide acceptance for three reasons: (1) no reason for a metaphorical "murder" has proved convincing, (2) the corruption is likely from the nearby references to wars and fightings and known occurrences of the same corruption (Test. Ben. 7:2 in *APOT* II, 357; 1 Pet. 2:1 in B and 1175; perhaps Gal. 5:21), and (3) the φθόνος-ζῆλος pair is frequent in biblical literature (1 Macc. 8:16; Test. Sim. 4:5; 2:7; cf. 4:7; Gal. 5:21; 1 Clem. 3:2; 4:7, 13; 5:2). Thus Dibelius, 217–218; Adamson, 167–168; Laws, 171; Windisch, 27; Spitta, 114; and Cantinat, 197–198, among others opt for the conjecture.

The conjectural reading is highly attractive, but Mussner's arguments, 178–179, must not be too lightly set aside. The conjecture has absolutely no textual evidence, so if another explanation makes sense of the text, it is preferable. One notes first that φονεύω is connected in a metaphorical sense to the sins of the tongue and to jealousy in many texts (e.g. Sir. 28:17, 21; Test. Gad 4:6; Did. 3:2; 1 Clem. 3:4–6:3). Second, one has the biblical tradition stemming from the Cain-Abel, Ahab-Naboth pairings to influence such a connection. Third, one has Christian warnings against murder (e.g. 1 Pet. 4:15 and many vice lists, which also include envy; in this light the Gal. 5:21 example could tell against Dibelius's argument). Fourth, one must take note of Jas. 2:11 (where the selection of commands is hardly arbitrary) and 5:6, at which places the commentary points out that the failure to care for the poor or the oppression of the poor was often called murder in Jewish tradition. This metaphorical sense of murder (cf. Did. 3:2) would fit well with the tone of the passage: they desire, yet never obtain. They oppress the poor (cf. 2:14ff.), either by legal oppression or by withholding needed aid, and envy those who are more successful, yet their desires slip between their fingers. All their struggles and intrigues among themselves (μάχεσθε καὶ πολεμεῖτε clearly reflecting the structure of 4:1) lead to nothing because they do not ask. The theme reminds one of Malachi: unjustly obtained wealth slips away as God withholds his blessing.

The asking is surely a reflection of such Jesus sayings as Matthew 7:7–9 (αἰτεῖτε καὶ δοθήσεται ὑμῖν . . .). Once again James brings the reader back to the topic of prayer and the promise of Jesus. The ἐπιθυμεῖτε has restated the ἡδονή (cf. 4:1) in the familiar terms of ἐπιθυμία of chap. 1. We will see below that this understanding will serve to explain the doubt-trust contrast of that chapter. Doubt is trusting in one's own machinations or worldly intrigues rather than in God. Rather than this useless fighting, arguing, competing, one ought simply to ask God for what one needs.

(3) "You ask and you do not receive," but these people *do* pray (there are not two classes of people here, one praying and the other fighting, as Spitta, 115, asserts), yet they seem simply to be "form prayers kissed to broken stone"—no blessing results. For James the reason is quite simple: evilly motivated prayers will receive no hearing by God. God is no magic charm which must help if the proper words are uttered.

For Dibelius, 219, this is evidence that the book is a reaction to dashed hopes aroused by the pneumatic consciousness and eschatological hopes stimulated by such passages as Mt. 7:7–11 (cf. Jn. 14:13; Mk. 11:23–24; Mt. 17:20). He notes the qualifications introduced in Lk. 18:7; 1 Jn. 5:14, 16; Hermas *Vis.* 3.10.6 and *Man.* 9.4 as being explanations of this failure.

Without arguing about the relative dates of the literature cited, there is evidence that such qualifications as those in James existed alongside the unqualified sayings from the beginning. First, the OT already gave specific promises of answered prayer to the just (e.g. Pss. 34:15–17; 145:18; Pr. 10:24). Second, the gospel tradition apparently had no trouble with juxtaposing the two types of saying (Mt. 7:7–11; the milieu that produced 1 John also produced John). Third, at least some parts of late Judaism also knew this problem (e.g. b. Sanh. 106b; b. R. Sh. 18a; b. Taan. 4a; m. Ber. 9:3—note that in b. R. Sh. especially it is prayer "with the whole heart" that is important). Thus the two types of sayings/teachings have

differing functions and would emerge together: the unqualified form simply encourages one to trust God and to depend upon him, while the
qualified form tells one *how* to pray and corrects abuses. The saying here
is parallel to the prophets' denunciations of Israel's cult: injustice makes
religious exercise meaningless. The unqualified form of promise will also
appear in Jas. 5:14–18.

In this context one might inquire why αἰτέω shifts from middle to
active and back to middle. Mayor, 138, sees the active as indicating words
without the spirit of prayer, while Hort, 90–91, argues the middle means
"ask for" and the active "ask a person." On the other hand, Dibelius
believes no difference exists, citing similar shifts (1 Jn. 5:15; Jn. 16:24, 26;
Hermas *Vis.* 3.10.7; cf. BDF, § 316 [2]; MHT I, 160–161). Yet Kittel,
89, may be right (as Mussner, 179, admits) in arguing that the active is
used instead of James's usual middle because of a conscious allusion to
the saying of Jesus (e.g. Mt. 7:7–11).

What makes the prayer evil is that it simply serves lust (ἡδονή here
makes a fine inclusion and thus neatly closes 4:1–3 as a unit). The use of
δαπανάω does not necessarily have a negative connotation, for it simply
means "to spend" or "consume" (cf. BAG, 169). The point is that the
good gift is not desired for sharing with others or godly ends, but simply
to gratify desire, the evil *yēṣer*. Thus the prayer will not be heard, for the
motives are totally selfish and worldly.

b. Condemnation of Compromise 4:4–6

(4) "Adulteresses!" the author cries, beginning his new unit. This
abrupt transition does not mean, as Cantinat, 201, supposes, that a new
tradition has been juxtaposed, but it does form a rhetorically emphatic
beginning to James's diagnosis of the true condition of such people: he
has broken off analysis and is now preaching repentance.

The term itself is not an indictment of the particular sin of the community, as ℵᶜ K P Ψ and others believed when they tried to include the
whole community with the inclusive terms μοιχοὶ καὶ μοιχαλίδες, nor is
it simply an illustration drawn from life with perhaps Mal. 3:5 as a background, as Hort, 92, believed, nor a turning from Zealots (4:1–3) to Jews
(4:4ff.) as Schlatter, 245, argues. Rather, the feminine vocative clearly
calls one back to the whole OT tradition of Israel as God's unfaithful wife
denounced in prophetic books and also—in an individualistic sense—in
late Judaism (Ho. 1–3; 9:1; Je. 3; 13:27; Is. 1:21; 50:1; 54:1–6; 57:3; Ezk.
16:38; 23:45—the Ezekiel and Jeremiah material, interestingly, combine
murder and adultery; cf. 4:2 above—*Mek. Baḥodesh* 8 on Exodus 20; cf.
Knowling, 98; Ziegler, 49–85; Eichrodt, I, 67–68, 250–258). This tradition
was picked up by Jesus, calling the Jews "an adulterous generation" (Mk.
8:38; Mt. 12:39; 16:4—γενεὰ πονηρὰ καὶ μοιχαλίς). In each case in both

Testaments the concept is applied only to Jews, never gentiles, for only those who have had or claim to have a covenant relationship with Yahweh can be included in such a condemnation. In the NT the basis for its application to the church comes in the bride-of-Christ imagery (2 Cor. 11:2; Eph. 5:22–24; Revelation 19, 21), as well as in the new-Israel imagery, but the plural here indicates an individual application which, although similar to Dibelius's claim of a Hellenistic individualization of piety (220, citing Philo *Cher.* 50; Clem. *Hom.* 3.27.3–28.1; and Rom. 7:1–3 as examples of the individualization of the OT ἱερὸς γάμος), points to a deeper level of reasoning. As at Qumran, the faithful remnant (here the church) remains by definition faithful. Individuals separate themselves from the church and from God by such apostate action. Thus the plural is far more appropriate than the singular.

That this self-seeking is tantamount to apostasy appears in the following parallel clauses, introduced by the typical reference to parenesis, οὐκ οἴδατε ὅτι (e.g. Rom. 6:16; 1 Cor. 3:16; 5:6; 6:2–19; 9:13–24; cf. 1 Thes. 3:3, 4; 4:2; 2 Thes. 2:6). Two diametrically opposed pairs are presented: friendship and enmity are used to underline the polar opposition between God and the world. Here is a radical ethical dualism of the type found in 1 Jn. 2:15–17 and elsewhere in the Johannine corpus. The world is not the created order or the earth, but the whole system of humanity (its institutions, structures, values, and mores) as organized without God. This concept is not unlike Paul's (1 Corinthians 1–3; Eph. 2:2; Col. 2:8, 20), but it has much more in common with the dualism of Qumran and other apocalyptic communities (Eth. Enoch 48:7; 108:8 describes hating the world; Jub. 30:19–22 talks of being a friend or adversary of God; cf. Spitta, 117). There is no middle point, no compromise. One is either God's friend or his enemy (Ropes's attempt, 260, to remove God's active opposition by calling these terms objective genitives is rightly rejected by Dibelius, 220; the friendship may be active or passive, but God's enmity is surely thought of as judgment). This is precisely the point Jesus made (Mt. 6:24; Lk. 16:13): one must be "100 percent." Even the attempt (βουληθῇ indicates that the world may not accept such a person either!) to cultivate the world is disastrous, for that inner disposition constitutes (καθίσταται) one not just a compromiser or a poor Christian, but an enemy of God! These people in the control of ἡδονή are in utmost danger.

Spitta, 116–117, argues that the first statement, ἡ φιλία . . . ἐστιν, is a quotation introduced by ὅτι, while ὅς . . . καθίσταται is the author's comment. The first statement is conceivable as either an allusion or a citation, in which case the most likely source would be a saying of Jesus, perhaps in a Johannine type of tradition. But although conceivable, Spitta's hypothesis can scarcely be proven, for a repetitious parallelism is not unlikely in an author such as James.
See further Davids, 380–393.

(5) In support of his bold assertion James, like most NT writers, cites scripture, connecting it to the foregoing by a parallel structure: οἴδατε (4:4) . . . δοκεῖτε (4:5). Scripture never speaks in vain, emptily (κενῶς, an NT *hapax legomenon*; cf. Mt. 5:17–19), so it should firmly establish the point the parenesis has taught. Yet precisely this citation forms one of the thorniest problems in the epistle, for if James cites scripture, which one does he cite? The citation of Pr. 3:34 LXX in 4:6 is obvious, but what is cited in 4:5?

One suggestion is that he does not cite scripture in 4:5, but instead is making some type of parenthetic remark or midrashic argument (so de Wette and others; cf. Dibelius, 221; Cantinat, 203). The latest form of this has been proposed by Laws, "Scripture," 214–215, who argues that the verse consists of two questions: "'Is scripture meaningless? (*v.* 5a). Is this envious longing (according to scripture) the proper manner of the soul's desire? (*v.* 5b)?' The answer implied, if the allusion to Ps 41:2 or Ps 83:3 LXX is taken, must be, surely not!" The thesis is fascinating and avoids some problems, but contains its own internal difficulties: (1) one would expect μή in such a negative rhetorical question (BDF, § 427), (2) such an interpretation brackets 4:4 and jumps back to 4:1–3, contrary to the epistle's structure, (3) the allusions are not close enough to be convincing, and (4) in every other case in the NT the γραφὴ λέγει formula introduces a direct quotation, not a sense quotation, allusion, or reference to scripture in general (which normally use a plural form of γραφή; Jn. 7:38 *may* be an exception to this rule). It is this last point which is fatal not only to Laws's thesis and the older works cited, but also to those who would see a loose sense quotation of scripture (e.g. Ex. 20:5; cf. Hort, 93; Mayor, 140; Coppieters, 40).

If the objections above are accepted, then two other options remain. First, James may quote some unknown version of the OT, although he usually quotes the LXX; Jeremias suggests Theodotion on Jb. 14:15b or *Frg. Tg.* on Gn. 2:2; Ropes, 262, suggests an unknown translation of Ex. 20:5. The problem is that no other suggestion has produced a quotation close enough to be convincing. Second, the author may be quoting some apocryphal work (unknown—Dibelius, 222; Michl, 174; Mussner, 184; Schrage, 44–45; Christian prophecy—Schlatter, 248; Book of Eldad and Modad—Spitta, 121; Moffatt, 60; Sidebottom, 52–53; cf. Nu. 11:29; Hermas *Vis.* 2.3.4; 1 Clem. 23:2–3; 2 Clem. 11:2–3). Since there is no evidence in the NT of the use of a wider canon (cf. Jude 14), there is no problem with this suggestion. Naturally, such a hypothesis can hardly be proved since the text is unknown, yet it is probably the best suggestion to date in that (1) no more concrete suggestion has proved acceptable, (2) James does appear to be quoting something, and (3) the apocalyptic imagery in James fits with the Christian and Jewish apocalyptic books known so far (Revelation, Jude, 2 Peter, Eth. Enoch, Jub., etc.).

A. Oepke, *TDNT* III, 991, suggests along with Ropes, 262, and Windisch, 27, that this verse is a hexameter, a poem from scripture cited as scripture, but to this BDF, § 487 appropriately comments, "The search for verses and fragments of verses . . . is a needless waste of time and those that are found are of such quality that they are better left unmentioned. . . ." Such a flawed hexameter might just as well be chance, if a writer has any rhythmic sense.

Yet the problems of the verse only begin with those of its origin, for lacking the context from which it was drawn (which the author must have expected his readers to know), the meaning of the verse is highly debatable. With most scholars we agree (*contra* Spitta, 118, 120, and *Zürcher*) that πρὸς φθόνον begins the citation because it comes after λέγει and fits well with ἐπιποθεῖ, and that μείζονα begins the next clause because of the following δέ, but the subject of the quoted clause remains in doubt: (1) God, (2) πνεῦμα meaning Holy Spirit, or (3) πνεῦμα meaning human spirit. One must work toward a conclusion.

God is undoubtedly the subject of κατῴκισεν (an NT *hapax legomenon* which produced the more common κατῴκησεν as a scribal error in K P L it. Vg Byz. Lect.), for whether one thinks of the human spirit (Gn. 2:7) or the Holy Spirit it is the universal theme of scripture that God causes it to dwell within. This conclusion and that God is the subject of δίδωσιν and λέγει make it antecedently probable that God is also the subject of the main clause (unless one emends it as Findlay does), but the question to be raised is whether God could be the subject of a clause with πρὸς φθόνον (=φθονερῶς: Mayor, 141; Robertson, 626; MHT I, 250; BAG, 865).

Michl (170–171 and "Spruch") and Mitton, 155–156, point out that φθόνος and its cognates are never used positively in the NT, rarely so in secular Greek (LSJ, 1929, cites one positive example), and equally rarely in patristic Greek (normally denied to God; *LPGL,* 1474, points to three applications to God in Alexandria). Nor does the root ever translate the Hebrew *qn'*, indicating God's jealousy, in the LXX. Since neither God nor the Holy Spirit can be the subject, the subject must be the human spirit—"the spirit which God implanted in man turns towards envious desires" (*NEB*), which term "spirit" may designate the soul or the evil impulse (*yēṣer*). The background is the well-known teaching of the corruption of humanity, perhaps including the idea that God creates the evil impulse (so 1QS 3:13ff. and some rabbinic sources). The grace of 4:6, then, is the good impulse or the Holy Spirit which counters the evil impulse in those who submit to God.

Attractive as this interpretation is, it has its problems. First, this translation does not fit well in context, for although the structure is parallel to 4:4, this translation ignores 4:4 and jumps back to 4:1–3. The citation, then, does not support the parenesis of 4:4. Second, as 1 Macc. 8:16; 1 Clem. 3:2; 4:7; 5:2; and Test. Sim. 4:5 show, ζῆλος and φθόνος are parallel terms. Since James has already used ζῆλος so negatively, he may deliberately select φθόνος as a synonym not yet used. Third, the alternative interpretation fits well with 4:4, giving a basis for the statement.

Most commentators, then, do see God as the subject (Hort, 93-94; Ropes, 263; Dibelius, 223-224; Mayor, 144-145; Mussner, 182-183). That God longs for his creation is a theme found in the OT (e.g. God is the subject of ἐπιποθεῖν in Theodotion's version of Jb. 14:15b; cf. *Frg. Tg.* on Gn. 2:2, "On the seventh day Yahweh's *Memra* longed for the work which he had made"; cf. Jeremias; Apoc. Mos. 31:2). That God is jealous is also a well-known theme (Ex. 20:5; 34:14; Dt. 4:24; etc.), which could logically be translated by either ζῆλος or φθόνος. That God put the spirit in man is also well established (Gn. 6:3 LXX; 6:17; 7:15; Ps. 104:29-30; Ezekiel 37; Wis. 12:1). What is more, several passages refer to the need to keep this spirit pure (Test. Naph. 10:9 [Hebrew]; b. Shab. 152b; Test. Jud. 20:1; 1QH 1:15; 12:12; CD 5:11; 7:5). Thus if the spirit turned toward the world, God's jealousy would be aroused. Such a threat clearly supports Jas. 4:4.

A key parallel text is Hermas *Man.* 3.1-2; cf. *Man.* 5.2.5; 10.2.6; 10.3.2; cited by Dibelius, 223-224; Cirillo; and Seitz, "Spirits," although rejected by Laws, 176-177. The passage speaks of a spirit "which God has made to dwell [κατῴκισεν] in this flesh," a spirit which may be corrupted and returned a lying spirit. Dibelius reads this as a "demonological ethic," but in the light of Jewish *yēṣer* theology and the two-spirit doctrine of Qumran such a supposition is not needed, although the Hermas passages are not totally clear. For the purposes of this discussion the important point is that an originally good spirit (soul? or inclination?) may go astray and turn evil (into the evil *yēṣer* or be inspired by an evil spirit). This teaching is a warning and thus similar to James, either as an interpretation of this passage in James or as dependent upon a similar tradition. See further Davids, 388-389.

(6) God is a jealous creator. He created the human spirit for fellowship with himself, so one should beware when one seeks the world instead. Yet in that situation God does not reject the person, but gives (the present tense of δίδωσιν indicates something presently being given, not the "givens" of creation) a greater gift (χάριν). While the gift has been interpreted as the Holy Spirit (Schlatter, 252), help in giving God one's undivided allegiance (and so tantamount to the Spirit, Ropes, 265; Hort, 95-96), or eschatological exaltation (Mussner, 184), it may simply be forgiveness, the chance to repent. The quotation from Pr. 3:34 (LXX as in 1 Pet. 5:5-6; 1 Clem. 30:2; all of which use ὁ θεός for ὁ κύριος of the LXX) states that God resists the proud (which idea may be picked up in 5:6; cf. Schökel) but gives grace to the humble (cf. 1:9). The call, then, is to submit to God. If one remains proud and continues to seek the world, God's jealousy, God's resistance will surely fall. But all is not lost. There is still an even greater graciousness to God. If one will simply humble

oneself, God will extend his grace and mercy. This verse, then, is a solid basis on which to build an emphatic call to repentance, which James proceeds to do.

See further Brushton; Coppieters; Findlay; Jeremias; Laws, "Scripture"; Michl, "Spruch"; Schökel.

c. Call to Repentance 4:7–10

(7) The οὖν clearly shows that these imperatives (10 in all in 4:7–10) are an expansion of the Pr. 3:34 quotation and the previous parenesis (although Laws, 180–181, rejects this idea and makes the relationship tangential). Such a use of Pr. 3:34 must have been common in the early church, for, as Dibelius, 225–226, points out, 1 Pet. 5:5–9 has a similar set of ideas, i.e. submission to God (ταπεινώθητε as in 4:10) and resistance to the devil (ἀντίστητε), as does 1 Clem. 30, although with a different application. The structure was hardly a fixed one, even if the 1 Peter passage suggests that in at least some areas of the church resistance to the devil was joined to submission to God.

The structure of the imperatival section is clearly a series of couplets (cf. Hill, 12; Ekstrom, 26–27):

ὑποτάγητε . . . (topic)

{ ἀντίστητε . . . καὶ φεύξεται . . .
{ ἐγγίσατε . . . καὶ ἐγγιεῖ . . .

{ καθαρίσατε . . .
{ ἁγνίσατε . . .

{ ταλαιπωρήσατε . . .
{ ὁ γέλως . . . μετατραπήτω . . .

ταπεινώθητε . . . ὑψώσει . . . (conclusion)

The first and last imperatives are virtual synonyms and thus form an *inclusio*. Verse 9 may be a parallel couplet in concept only or perhaps two units. The final imperative clause structurally resembles the first couplet and thus underlines the first imperative as the topic of the whole.

While Schökel's idea of "thematic announcement" in 4:6 expanded in 4:7–5:6 is creative, only his section on 4:7–10 is convincing. He just does not fit 4:11–12 into his formula.

God, according to James, will grant his grace (forgiveness?) to the humble. Therefore the readers must submit to God. The rest of the section will explain how this is to be accomplished. Not only does Ps. 37(36):7–9 have such a command (Hort, 97), but the idea is common in the NT with reference to Ps. 8:6(7) (Heb. 8:1; 1 Cor. 15:27–28; Eph. 1:22) and is also common in parenetic literature, although only 1 Pet. 5:6 uses it with reference to God (see below on 4:10). James, of course, has already used the idea in 1:9–11, for the verb indicates the process of becoming ταπεινοί (Ropes, 268).

This submission is accomplished first by resisting (i.e. *not* submitting to) the devil, which is precisely what God does to the proud, whom James probably views as acting like the devil (4:6). The idea of resisting the devil occurs not only elsewhere in the NT (1 Pet. 5:8–9; Eph. 6:13), but also in Test. XII (Test. Sim. 3:3; Test. Iss. 7:7; Test. Dan 5:1; Test. Naph. 8:4; cf. Test. Ash. 3:3, which indicates that the double-minded serve Beliar) and Hermas (*Man.* 12.5.2). In most of these passages the flight of the devil is explicitly mentioned. The means of resistance is either good works (Test. XII) or total commitment to God. For James there would be little difference between these two, although his emphasis here is on total commitment.

This verse, however, has unveiled James's underlying theology. His previous statement that testing arose from the evil impulse (1:13–15) served a parenetic purpose in context and emphatically denied that God was the source. Now he reveals (as in 3:3, 15) that behind the evil impulse lies the devil: suprapersonal forces of evil are behind personal evil. Here James agrees not only with Paul (e.g. his ideas on the devil and "the principalities and powers"), but also with the gospel tradition (Mt. 4:1–11 par.; Mt. 8:28–34 par.; Lk. 22:31; Jn. 13:2, 27).

See further Gerhardsson.

(8) The second half of the couplet, "draw near to God . . . ," gives the positive aspect of the first. To resist the devil is to commit oneself to follow God or to draw near. God will not be unresponsive. On the one hand, this clause recalls many prophetic promises (2 Ch. 15:2–4; La. 3:57; Ho. 12:6–7; Zc. 1:3; 2:3; Mal. 3:7) indicating the conversion of the people; on the other hand, the act of drawing near is a cultic technical expression (Ex. 19:22; 24:2; Dt. 16:16; Psalms 122, 145) also used in other works with cultic imagery (Heb. 4:16; 7:19; Test. Dan 6:2). While James probably has no concrete idea in mind (e.g. the priesthood of all believers; cf. Mitton, 159; Cantinat, 209), the cultic imagery was part of his heritage and bridges between the military metaphor of 4:7b and the cultic metaphor of 4:8b.

The next couplet shifts the structure from an imperative used as a conditional clause (imperative + καί + future = a conditional sentence, probably due to Semitic influence) to a strong imperatival call to purity. The handwashing imagery was originally purely cultic (Ex. 30:19–21; R. Meyer, *TDNT* III, 421–422; F. Hauck, *TDNT* III, 424), but even in the OT a moral sense quickly arose and a transfer to the inner self, the heart, was frequently made (Is. 1:16; Je. 4:14; Jb. 22:30; Ps. 26:6). The junction of hand with heart, of outward deed with inward disposition was also pre-Christian (Pss. 24:4; 73:13; Sir. 38:10). The term "purify" is likewise a term for fitness for cultic participation (e.g. Ex. 19:10; Nu. 8:21; Jos. 3:5; 1 Ch. 15:12; Jn. 11:55; Acts 21:24, 26) which has taken on an ethical meaning (1 Pet. 1:22; 1 Jn. 3:3; Barn. 5:1; 8:3; cf. H. Baltensweiler, *DNTT* III, 101–102). Thus in the NT one finds the moral call to purity (Mt. 5:8; Mk. 7:21–23 par.), a call that John, Hebrews, 1 Peter, and the Pastorals take up. The call is for right deed and right commitment: pure hands would do good works and pure hearts would be totally committed.

This sense is underlined by the two vocatives. The ἁμαρτωλοί (cf. 5:20) are those who act contrary to the law of God (Pss. 1:1–5; 51:15 [50:13]; cf. Cantinat, 209); they disobey God in their actions. The δίψυχοι (cf. the longer discussion on 1:8) as in Test. Ben. 6 and Test. Ash. 3:1–2 (cf. Sir. 2:12; Hermas *Man.* 9.7; *Vis.* 3.2.2) are those who try to be committed to both good and evil, God and the world. They lack the virtue of ἁπλότης and thus must indeed purify their hearts.

See further Wolverton, 172; Edlund, 62–69; Marshall, "Δίψυχος"; Daniélou, 362–365.

(9) The purification demanded should take the form of repentance, a repentance the aorist imperatives imply needs to begin (MHT I, 76; BDF, § 337). Ταλαιπωρήσατε, an NT *hapax legomenon,* indicates neither voluntary asceticism (Mayor, 147) nor an eschatological judgment (Dibelius, 227–228), but the inner sorrow and wretchedness one experiences when one realizes that he is in a sad condition (BAG, 810; cf. ταλαιπωρία: Rom. 3:16; 1 Clem. 15:6; Ps. 12:5 [11:6]; ταλαίπωρος: Rom. 7:24; Rev. 3:17; Epict. 1.3.5; Hermas *Sim.* 1.3, where this term describes the δίψυχος). The inner attitude is to be matched by outward expression, i.e. mourning and weeping, which was on the one hand the proper response to outward danger and distress (Ps. 69:10–11; Is. 32:11; Je. 4:8; 9:2; Am. 5:16; Mal. 3:14) and on the other became the response to fear of God's judgment, i.e. the response of the repentant heart (2 Sa. 19:1; Ne. 8:9; Lk. 6:25; Acts 18:11, 15, 19, which all associate the two terms). The terms are in fact interchangeable (Mt. 5:5 par. Lk. 6:21; in both cases sin is the probable cause). This is the language of the preacher of repentance: judgment is coming; therefore mourn now (repent) so that you do not mourn then.

The parallel line of the couplet expands upon the first. Perhaps remembering the words of Christ (Lk. 6:21, 25: οὐαί, οἱ γελῶντες νῦν, ὅτι πενθήσετε καὶ κλαύσετε) and in tune with the OT (Am. 8:10; Pr. 14:13; 1 Macc. 9:41; Tob. 2:6) the author commands an end to feasting (the opposite of πένθος according to Philo *Exsec.* 171, and Amos) with its associated laughter (cf. K. H. Rengstorff, *TDNT* I, 658–661, who shows that laughter is associated with fools [Pr. 10:23; Sir. 21:20; 27:13] and with people who have declared their independence of God) and joy, both of which characterize a life devoid of tension with the world, thus a profane life (Jn. 16:20; Marty, 164). Instead, one should have mourning and dejection (κατήφειαν, a biblical *hapax legomenon*; Plut. *Mor.* 528; Philo *Spec. Leg.* 3.193), for in the light of the coming judgment or a present realization of sin this response is only reasonable—they are, after all, sinners (4:8). The turning from one state to another is a sign of true repentance, for mourning is appropriate once the enormity of sin really crashes in upon one's world view.

Μετατραπήτω, an NT *hapax legomenon* and a poetic term found in B P 1739 etc., has been replaced by the more common μεταστραφήτω in ℵ A and the Byzantine tradition. The number of *hapax legomena* in this passage has led Seitz, "Relationship," to posit that this passage depends upon a lost apocryphon quoted in 1 Clem. 23:3–4 and 2 Clem. 11:2–3; cf. Hermas *Sim.* 1.3; *Vis.* 3.7.1. This supposition must remain unproved because the focus of the quotation in the passages cited is different from that in James, and the original context of the quotation is apparently nonexistent; cf. Laws, 185.

(10) Such true repentance will not be without results; God will give grace to the humble. The terminology deliberately calls one back to the quotation upon which this segment is a midrash and to 4:8a, where structurally similar Semitizing syntax first promises God's reception of the penitent. The theme here is well known in the OT (Jb. 5:11; 22:29; Ps. 149:4; Pr. 3:34; 29:25; Ezk. 17:24; 21:31), the intertestamental literature (Sir. 2:17, οἱ φοβούμενοι κύριον . . . ἐνώπιον αὐτοῦ ταπεινώσουσιν τὰς ψυχὰς αὐτῶν; 3:18; Test. Jos. 10:3; 18:1; 1QH 3:20; 15:16), and the NT (Mt. 23:12; Lk. 14:11; 18:14); this NT literature (all Jesus logia) probably forms the immediate background for James (cf. the verbal similarity; cf. also 1 Pet. 5:6). The point is clear: all is not lost; only self-abasement and repentance is needed to gain the true exaltation which comes not from the world, but from God (cf. 1:9–11).

4. PURE SPEECH IS UNCONDEMNING 4:11–12

The relationship of these next two verses (which obviously form a unit themselves) to the rest of the chapter is difficult to discern. The familiar theme and traditional handling make it possible that on one level Cantinat, 212, is correct: they are simply a free-floating admonition. The address differs from 4:1–10 as μοιχαλίδες and ἁμαρτωλοί give way to ἀδελφοί. There is an imperative, but it is negative, unlike those in 4:7–10. Structurally the imperative plus vocative construction begins new segments in James (1:2, 16; 2:1; 3:1; etc.). Likewise 4:10 clearly rounds off a section.

Neither Mitton's suggestion, 165, that these verses form a contrast with 4:10, not Moffatt's, 37, that they belong after 2:13, has proved convincing. Ropes, 273, argues that they are an appendix but never proves how they fit. Structurally we have what must have originally been a free parenetic exhortation.

On the other hand, as part of the total context here these verses are hardly inappropriate: they serve a redactional function. Most of the themes mentioned in them are picked up from previous sections (1:19–26; 2:8; 3:1–18). The author is ending a larger segment on the problem of community conflict. He has first traced this to worldliness (discussed again in a new way in 4:13–5:6), which earned the hearers a strong prophetic rebuke, but he has not forgotten that the divided heart expresses itself in inner community strife (4:1), including the putting down of others (3:9–12). One does not have to agree with Schlatter, 257–260, that it was Judaizers rejecting other Christians as lawless, or with Schammberger, 71, that it was Gnostic teachers rejecting the unenlightened, to see that such a situation would as likely be a problem in James's community as it is today and that one as full of concern for communal unity as James must speak to it.

One must not speak against or criticize one's fellow community neighbor, for to do so is to put oneself above the human situation and take the place of God. Such criticism also violates the law of love of neighbor, and thus is self-condemning behavior.

(11) The command not to slander another person (καταλαλέω) is well known in the OT (Lv. 19:16; Pss. 50:20; 101:5; Pr. 20:13; Wis. 1:11). Slander was likewise attacked in Jewish communities of the NT period and later (Test. Iss. 3:4, where it is contrasted to simplicity, ἁπλότης; Test. Gad 3:3; 5:4; 1QS 4:9, 11; 5:25–26; 6:26; 7:2–9; *Midr. Ps.* on Ps. 12:3; *Mek.* on Ex. 14:31; *Dt. Rab.* 6 on Dt. 24:9). The Christian community also needed the unity which slander destroyed, so among Christians it also comes up frequently in vice lists (Rom. 1:30; 2 Cor. 12:20; 1 Pet. 2:1; 2 Pet. 2:12; 3:16; 1 Clem. 30:1–3, which uses Pr. 3:34 in the context; Hermas *Man.* 2.2–3, with ἁπλότης; 8.3; *Sim.* 8.7.2, with δίψυχος; 9.23.2–3). One notes in reading these passages that many of the themes of 4:1–10 reappear, and this reappearance argues that these verses are not placed here accidentally.

The reason not to slander is that by attacking or setting oneself as a judge over a community member (ἀδελφόν) one is actually breaking the law which one claims to be upholding (the use of καταλαλεῖ and κρίνει is to show that the one action does both acts, not that the person directly or consciously slanders the law). If one can judge with respect to the law (here εἰ δὲ νόμον κρίνεις is using νόμον as an accusative of respect as it slips toward the end of the clause), one is no longer under the law (ποιητὴς νόμου) but a judge (the absolute sense of κριτής already anticipates 4:12). The command not to judge is found elsewhere (Mt. 7:1–5; Lk. 6:37–42; Rom. 2:1; 14:4; 1 Cor. 4:5; 5:12; cf. Jn. 7:24; 8:15–16), but the reason given here, that such judging breaks the law, is unique. While James may well be dependent on the Jesus logia cited above, Lv. 19:18, previously cited in 2:8–9, is probably foremost in his mind (cf. the use of πλήσιον in 4:12 and the similar argument in Test. Gad 4:1–2).

(12) The law is broken in another sense as well as that in 4:11, for in setting oneself up as judge, one has usurped the role of God. That God is the lawgiver is explicit in the OT (cf. νομοθέτης in Ps. 9:21 LXX) and in later works (cf. νομοθετέω in 2 Macc. 3:15; Heb. 7:11; 8:6). His sole right to judge forms a theme in John and Paul (John 5; Rom. 14:4). This is because only God has authority over life and death (Gn. 18:25; Dt. 33:39; 1 Sa. 2:6; 2 Ki. 5:7; Ps. 75:7; Is. 33:22; Mt. 10:28; Heb. 5:7; 2 Tim. 4:8; 1QS 10:18; m. Ab. 4:8; Hermas *Man.* 12.6.3, which also uses δυνάμενον σῶσαι καὶ ἀπολέσαι; *Sim.* 9.23.4; *Mek. Amalek* 1 on Ex. 17:9; 1 Clem. 59:3); thus usurping his judging authority by judging a person is really a blaspheming of God (so also Test. Gad 4:1–2). It is indeed a breaking of the law and rightly introduces the rhetorical question, "and who are you, you who judge your neighbor?" Who indeed do humans think they are?

Influenced by Rom. 14:4 the Byzantine text has several minor variants, e.g. ὅς κρίνεις for ὁ κρίνων and ἕτερον for πλησίον. The ease of such errors is clear, especially if one does not realize the point James is making with πλησίον.
    See further Delling, 26–27.

TESTING THROUGH WEALTH 4:13–5:6

THE preceding section has dealt with the love of the world, the divided heart, and its results in the community. Now James moves to another major theme of the work, the rich and their sins, i.e. the results of the love of the world.

This section is not directly connected to 4:1–12, although the flow of thought moves smoothly enough, but forms a separate unit addressed to two distinct classes: merchants and landlords. As such it picks up on the themes of 1:9–11, 27; 2:5–7. The groups are addressed in the style of prophetic denunciation. That James intends the two paragraphs to be read as a single unit is clear from the repeated ἄγε νῦν (4:13; 5:1), the unity of the topic, and the address to the ἀδελφοί in 5:7 that closes off the segment.

The merchant class in the church stands self-condemned, for they plan and think only in terms of worldly gain rather than in terms of God's will and ultimate realities. They ought instead to be humble; their sin appears in their failure to share with the poor. The landlord class, on the other hand, are the rich who stand under divine judgment. Their fleeting wealth will condemn them to hell, for they have withheld from the poor their due. The cry of the poor will be their undoing.

See further Noack, "Jakobus."

1. THE TEST OF WEALTH 4:13–17

(13) "Come now!" James exhorts the merchants, using a type of vernacular address found only here in the NT (4:13; 5:1), but common in similar conversational works (Epict. 1.2.20, 25; 1.6.37; 3.1.37; Xen. *Ap.* cf. BDF, § 144, which describes this particle as a frozen imperative). The merchants are not named οἱ πλούσιοι (cf. 5:1), but οἱ λέγοντες, which means James sees them as within the community rather than as outsiders (cf. comment on 1:9–11 but cf. Laws, 190, who sees in the lack of ἀδελφοί the reference to unbelievers). The circumlocution may also indicate that the merchants were not wealthy yet, for in Palestine trade was seen as a way to obtain the fortune needed to purchase the estates on which the

171

"good life" might be lived (Grant, 72–76; Heichelheim, 150; Baron I, 255–259; Jeremias, *Jerusalem*, 30–57, 195).

These merchants are making typical plans: setting the time of departure (the ἤ is better attested than the Byzantine καί), selecting "such and such a city" (on the vernacular but technically improper use of ὅδε cf. BDF, § 289), determining the length of stay (ἐνιαυτόν: the ἕνα of A and the Byzantine tradition attempts to make this length more specific), and projecting the profit from the venture. Their plans are firm and expectations certain in their own eyes (the future in all four verbs is more likely than the aorist subjunctive found in the Byzantine text; thus B P ff Vg etc. have preserved the correct reading; cf. 4:15). There is nothing unusual about the situation, for merchants did this daily all over the Greco-Roman world, nor is anything apparently unethical. What bothers James is simply the presumption that one could so determine his future and the fact that these plans move on an entirely worldly plane in which the chief value is financial profit.

(14) With the anacolouthon of a relative clause James points out their foolishness: "Come now, you who make plans—you don't even understand how little control you have over life itself." These people are those (οἵτινες rather than the classical οἵ) who do not understand concerning the future (αὔριον, "tomorrow," whether τὸ τῆς αὔριον ℵ K L Vg; τά A P 33; or simply τῆς αὔριον, "the life of tomorrow," p⁷⁴ B, is the correct reading is hard to determine, although one suspects the endings of αὔριον and ποία may have given rise to the first two readings; cf. Schlatter, 262–263) or even what sort of a life they might have (ποία ἡ ζωὴ ὑμῶν: the readings ποία γάρ A K L P and ποία δέ are surely secondary attempts to smooth out the clause). The truth is that their life is a vapor or smoke, which appears briefly and then disappears. The concept is well known in Jewish (Pr. 27:1; Sir. 11:18–19; Jb. 7:7, 9, 16; Ps. 39:5–6; Wis. 2:1–2, 15; 3:14; 2 Esd. 4:24; Philo *Leg. All.* 3.226; Eth. Enoch 97:8; 1QMyst 1:6 = 1Q27; 1QM 15:10), Hellenistic (Ps.-Phocyl. 116; Seneca *Ep.* 101.4; cf. Dibelius, 233), and Christian works (Lk. 12:16–20, which may be the basis of this discussion; 1 Clem. 17:6; cf. Jas. 1:9–11, where another metaphor with the same meaning appears). Life appears and disappears (φαινομένη . . . ἀφανιζομένη — the similarity in sound is likely deliberate); one who really understands this fact would not make plans as if it were not true, but would look to him who truly does have control over life.

(15) In giving the correct viewpoint James again makes an anacolouthon, for while ἀντὶ τοῦ λέγειν is good Greek, it presumes that οἱ λέγοντες in 4:13 is a conjugated verb: "You say . . . instead of saying. . . ." What ought to be said would recognize that God has full control over all

of life: "If the Lord wills. . . ." This idea is not exclusively Christian, for as Dibelius, 233–234, has fully demonstrated, many classical writers said the same (e.g. Plato *Alc.* 1.31.135d; *Phdr.* 80d; Epict. 1.1.17; 3.21.12; 3.22.2; cf. G. Schrenk, *TDNT* III, 47). Jewish and Christian authors also made similar statements (1QS 11:10–11; m. Ab. 2:12; 1 Cor. 4:19; 16:7; Heb. 6:3; Acts 18:21; Rom. 1:10; Phil. 2:19, 24; Ign. *Eph.* 20:1). There is no great originality here except that for James and his Christian tradition it is the risen Christ and the one God who control all of history and who therefore must be taken into account, rather than simply the gods in general.

The fact that this first clause is a common expression clarifies the rest of the sentence: "we will both live and do this or that." The Byzantine text (K L 35 etc.) reads ζήσωμεν, ποιήσωμεν, which would then be, "If the Lord wills and we live . . ." (the second καί is omitted), a marked contrast to the normal form of the saying, stemming from the confusion of o and ω and a misunderstanding of the conditional structure. The text in James either intends the καί . . . καί structure to be read "both . . . and," or the first καί to be a translation of the Semitic *waw* of the apodosis; the former explanation is the more likely.

Thus the proper attitude does not exclude plans: "we will live and do this or that" assumes planning is proper. But this attitude conditions plans by the will of God, recognizing both human finiteness and divine sovereignty. This naturally means that divine moral guidelines will be followed and divine goals sought as one plans conscious of the divine will.

(16) The case of these merchants, however, is far from the proper attitude, for in contrast to it (δέ strengthened by νῦν) they boast in their arrogance, a term significantly linked to the world and specifically to possessions in its only other NT use (1 Jn. 2:16; cf. Test. Jos. 17:8; 1 Clem. 21:5, where ἐγκαυχώμενος ἐν ἀλαζονείᾳ is contrasted to boasting in God, and ἀλαζών in Pr. 21:24; Jb. 28:2; 2 Macc. 9:8; Rom. 1:30; and 2 Tim. 3:2, where it appears in a vice list). This attitude which plans and acts as if God did not exist and as if they instead of God controlled life is evil: "all such boasting is evil." Boasting (καύχησις) is rarely anything but evil in scripture (1 Cor. 1:29; 5:6; Gal. 6:13; Rom. 3:27; 4:2), unless it is a boast in suffering, service for Christ, or God (Jas. 1:9; Rom. 5:2–3; 1 Thes. 2:9; Phil. 2:16). This boasting does not fit those categories, for these are people who have shut God out of their commercial lives, although they may be pious enough in church and at home. This whole category of confident, not to say arrogant, planning is evil (πᾶσα . . . τοιαύτη), declares James: no part of life is outside the rule of God. Here James looks down the road of commercial independence and sees the

dangers Hermas would later rebuke as already fully actualized (Hermas *Vis.* 2.3.1; *Man.* 3.3; *Sim.* 6.3.5).

(17) The author concludes his teaching with a maxim. The change to third person singular from second plural and the impersonal tone indicate that this is a proverb known to the author that he uses as he previously used proverbs in 3:18 and 2:13. The source of the saying cannot be determined, although some have speculated that this could be a saying of Jesus (cf. Adamson, 181) and Laws, 194, argues it is an exposition of Pr. 3:27–28. There are, nevertheless, some indications of a Semitic origin: (1) in the paratactic construction (καί) instead of a hypotactic "if . . . then" clause, (2) in the pleonastic, but rhetorically emphatic, αὐτῷ (BDF, § 446), and (3) in the similarity to ἔστιν ἐν σοὶ ἁμαρτία of Deuteronomy (15:9; 23:21; 24:15 LXX).

This maxim, however, is not without a context, for the οὖν indicates that the author understands it as a summary of the preceding section. Yet if this is so, in what way is it a summary? First, it is not speaking of sins of omission per se, but of acts which one knows one ought to do (εἰδότι . . . ποιεῖν) and does not do (e.g. Jb. 31:16–18; Lk. 12:47–48). Second, it is clear that the surface good one ought to do is to plan with a consciousness of God: the failure to do this is not just foolish or bad (πονηρά), but sin (ἁμαρτία). Third, the context is that of merchants whose business interests lead them to forget God (cf. Sir. 11:10; 31:5) and thus of Christian warnings against greed and hoarding (e.g. Lk. 12:13–21). Because of the context the use of καλόν (the anarthrous construction is not remarkable, BDF, § 264) instead of καλῶς (cf. 2:8) is interesting, for it parallels the doing of the word/law of 1:21–25 (cf. Cantinat, 219) and the doing of charitable deeds (τὸ δὲ καλὸν ποιοῦντες) in Gal. 6:9. Thus it may well be that while on one level James is warning merchants about forgetting God in their business, on a deeper level he is reflecting on ideas such as those in Lk. 12:13–21 and viewing the whole motive of gathering wealth rather than doing good with it (i.e. sharing it with the poor) as a failure to follow known standards of Christian guidance, i.e. the total tradition about sharing with others (e.g. Luke 12; cf. Noack, "Jakobus," 19; Reicke, *Diakonie*, 37–38; Laws, 193). Whatever his intention, such an interpretation bridges well to the next subsection.

2. THE TEST BY THE WEALTHY 5:1–6

James moves from addressing the merchant class within his community to castigating the landholding class which is clearly outside the community. The connection is the internal one that both classes are led astray by the desire for wealth and perhaps also the external one of a traditional link (e.g. Eth. Enoch 97:8–10). While the section has similarities to the warnings to the rich in Wis. 2; Hermas *Vis*. 3.9.3–6; and elsewhere (Dibelius, 235), the tone is quite different, for now it is not a parenetic tone, an expostulating tone, or even a warning tone (e.g. the vernacular exhortation in 4:13–17), but a sharp, cutting cry of prophetic denouncement. Their doom is coming; woe to them! Only two pre-Jacobean traditions have this tone in their treatment of the rich: the apocalyptic tradition of Eth. Enoch 94–97 and the sayings tradition in its Lucan form, i.e. Lk. 6:20–26.

See further Grill; Riesenfeld, 47–58.

(1) "Come now!" cries James, not as a summons to see the foolishness of their position (4:13), but as a cry to bewail the punishment coming upon them. The landlords believe themselves to be wealthy, possessing the best that life has to offer, including religious and civil preferment. James calls them to weep (κλαύσατε), the proper response to disaster (La. 1:1–2; Is. 15:2, 5; Je. 9:1; 13:17), for disaster is what is overtaking them. The weeping is defined as "crying out" (ὀλολύζοντες, an onomatopoetic word used only here in the NT; cf. BAG, 567), which sweeps along with it the prophetic exhortations to cry out over divine judgment; all 21 uses in the LXX are in the prophets (Is. 10:1; 13:6, ὀλολύζετε ἐγγὺς γὰρ ἡμέρα κυρίου; 14:31; 15:2–3; Je. 31:20, 31; Ezk. 21:12; Ho. 7:14; Am. 8:3; cf. H. W. Heidland, *TDNT* V, 173–174). They are in fact to cry out over the misery (ταλαιπωρίαις, another prophetic term, used elsewhere in the NT only in Rom. 3:16=Is. 59:7; cf. Is. 47:11; Je. 6:7, 26; Jas. 4:9) which is coming upon them. The concept here is that of the late Jewish denunciation of the rich built upon the prophetic condemnation of the wicked who were rich (e.g. Am. 6:1–9; cf. Davids, 184–221, 232–266; Introduction, 41–47; Dibelius, 39–45; Mussner, 76–84). They appear to be living well, but they ought to weep because misery is coming upon them: the eschatological hour (whether or not thought of in the sense of the imminent parousia of Christ; cf. Feuillet, "sens," 278) is so vividly and surely present in the prophet's sight that the appropriate weeping may begin immediately (cf. Lk. 6:24; Mt. 8:12; 13:42; 19:24), as anticipatory joy was appropriate in Jas. 1:2, 12.

(2–3a) This anticipatory sense is maintained as the author brings out the first reason for weeping: "your wealth is temporal" (using a perfect in all three verbs as a prophetic anticipation of the event; cf. Is. 44:23; 53:5–10; 60:1). The temporality is underlined by each of the three descriptions. (1) Their wealth (πλοῦτος, the general descriptive term picking up πλούσιοι) is spoiled. Σήπω is a *hapax legomenon* in the NT which properly means "to rot" but expands to indicate general decay (Sir. 14:19; Bar. 6:72; cf. LSJ, 1594). (2) Their garments are moth-eaten; σητόβρωτος is an NT *hapax legomenon* used in the LXX only in Jb. 13:28, but the image is traditional (Pr. 25:20; Sir. 42:13; Is. 33:1; 50:9; 51:8). (3) Their gold and silver are rusted; κατιόω, an NT *hapax legomenon,* is used once in the LXX (Sir. 12:11; cf. Epict. 4.6.14). It is likely that the last two terms make specific the more general first term, for money and garments are the traditional forms of wealth other than land. The traditional nature of the terms and particularly the scientifically strange nature of the last term give a clue to what is intended in the cultural context (*contra* Windisch, 31, who believes it indicates the class origins of the author). The rust or tarnish of precious metals was proverbial (e.g. Bar. 6:12, 24; Sir. 29:10) and the proverbial sense indicated not only temporality, but also uselessness: "Help the poor man for the commandment's sake, and grieve not for the loss. Lose money for the sake of a brother or a friend, and let it not rust under a stone or a wall. . . . Store up almsgiving in thy treasuries, and it shall deliver thee from all evil" (Sir. 29:9–12, *APOT*). The garments which are food for moths and the money which is tarnishing are not being used by their owner, and yet they could have been used by the poor. Thus this passage comments upon Mt. 6:20, where Jesus contrasts the stored rusty and moth-eaten treasure with the lasting treasure which is in heaven when the goods are given in charity (cf. Riesenfeld, 54–55). Temporality is one side of the coin, but the very temporality of goods points to their being withheld from the service for which God intended them.

(3b) The second and more important reason for weeping has already been suggested by the first: they will be judged and condemned for their selfish use of temporal goods. The rust (which naturally includes their waste of garments and other goods as well) will be a testimony against them (ὑμῖν is a dative of disadvantage; Cantinat, 223, discusses the dative of advantage, but "against" is clearly the sense of the passage; on εἰς μαρτύριον see Mt. 8:4; 10:18; 24:14). Thus their very hoard of goods and its decay will witness in the last judgment (therefore the future ἔσται) that they failed to share with the poor (cf. Eth. Enoch 96:7). Their guilt will be apparent (cf. Laws, 198–199).

Not only guilt but also judgment will result, for the rust will eat (cf. BDF, § 74 on the form of the future) their flesh like fire (in an attempt to clarify the jumbled images A P 614 etc. have repeated ὁ ἰός before ὡς; Ropes, 287, tries to join ὡς πῦρ to the following clause; cf. Dibelius, 237, for further emendations). The image of the last judgment as fire eating one's flesh is explicit in Jud. 16:17, but similar images are frequent in prophetic and other literature (Nu. 12:12; Is. 30:27; Ezk. 7:19; 15:7; Am. 1:12, 14; 5:6; 7:4; Ps. 21:9 [20:10]; Wis. 1:18; Acts 11:5; 1QH 3:29; 6:18–19; 8:30–31). The picture is terrifyingly clear: the testimony of wealth will be so damning, it will be as if it were fire burning them, σάρξ being the

metaphor for the person (as in Lv. 26:29; Jb. 4:15), for they will receive
the fire of hell (Mt. 25:41; 2 Pet. 3:7; Jude 23; Rev. 11:5; 20:9).

To this prediction of damnation the author adds a final ironic threat.
"You have treasured up," he states: that they knew well enough. But it
is "in the last days" and so is not for their good, but their damnation.
Many interpreters have used the analogy of Rom. 2:5 to suggest that while
the people see piles of wealth, James believes they have treasured up
wrath against future judgment (cf. Adamson, 185), but such an interpretation, though not far wrong, does miss the eschatological tension in the
passage. The phrase "last days" refers to the NT conviction that the end
times, the age of the consummation, had already broken in upon the world
in Jesus (e.g. Ho. 3:5; Is. 2:2; Je. 23:20; Ezk. 38:16; Da. 2:28; "the kingdom
of God is near" in the synoptics; Acts 2:17; Heb. 1:2; 2 Tim. 3:1; cf.
Cullmann). *These* people had treasured up as if they would live and the
world would go on forever, but the end times, in which they have a last
chance to repent and put their goods to righteous uses, are already upon
them. The irony is not just that of Mt. 6:19–21, but also that of the rich
fool (Lk. 12:15–21; cf. Percy, 70–71; Laws, 200).

(4) "Behold," cries James, using a rhetorical interjection which for
him functions within paragraphs to call attention to important images and
examples (3:4, 5; 5:4, 7, 9, 11), "the wages of those you wronged cry out
against you." The imagery of the hired laborer (ἐργατής, Mt. 9:37; 10:10;
Lk. 10:2, 7; or μίσθιος, Lk. 15:17, 19, 21; μισθωτός, Mk. 1:20; Jn. 10:12)
who mows (ἀμάω, NT *hapax legomenon*) the fields (χώρας, as in Lk.
12:16; 21:21; Jn. 4:35) of an absentee or rich landowner was common in
the history of Israel from monarchial times onward (cf. de Vaux, 167).
Likewise the practice of paying wages late or legally bilking the worker
of his wages is ancient, as a host of laws and prophetic threats demonstrate (Lv. 19:13; Dt. 24:14–15; Jb. 7:1–2; 24:10; 31:13, 38–40; Je. 22:13;
Mal. 3:5; Sir. 7:20; 31:4; 34:21ff.; Tob. 4:14; Mt. 20:8; Test. Job 12:4; Ps.-
Phocyl. 19).

It is hard to decide whether one should read ἀφυστερημένος, "withhold,"
an NT *hapax legomenon* found in א B, or ἀπεστερημένος, "rob," "defraud,"
found in A P Byzantine text (cf. 1 Cor. 6:8; 7:5), which is found in a similar
context in Mal. 3:5 (cf. Sir. 34:22). The former term is more difficult and the latter
more traditional, yet precisely here James calls on traditional language in its
strongest forms.

The cry of the laborer, who would likely be hungry from lack of
money for food, is pictured as the cry of the wrongfully imprisoned wage,
a cry for vengeance (Gn. 4:10; 18:20; 19:13; Ex. 2:23; 1 Sa. 9:16; Ps. 12:5
[11:6]; Sir. 21:5; 35:21; Lk. 18:17; Rev. 6:9–10; Eth. Enoch 47:1; 97:5).
To say that the cry (βοή, NT *hapax legomenon*) of those reapers has

entered the ears of the Lord Sabaoth, a phrase duplicated in Is. 5:9 LXX, where woe is pronounced on those acquiring large estates (cf. the other 60 times σαβαώθ is used in Isaiah as opposed to 9 times in the rest of the LXX; cf also Marshall, 31; Laws, 202–203), means that doom is imminent. For God to hear the cry of the poor is for him to bring judgment on their oppressors (cf. Pss. 17:1–6; 18:6; 31:2; Hermas *Vis.* 3.9.6). The term "Lord Sabaoth" used here can only heighten this sense by referring to the majestic power of the prophetic God of Isaiah and the judgment which did follow his prophecy. James is using traditional material to attack a traditional class of oppressors; whether specific practices which withheld wages or the possession of large estates per se is in mind (cf. Is. 5:7–9; Mk. 12:40; Lk. 20:47) one cannot determine. James sees injustice as part and parcel of why the landowners have their wealth to treasure up: he knows that in these last days the injustice is about to reap its doom.

(5) James now joins the theme of 5:3 to the accusation of injustice in 5:4. The wealthy have lived a life of luxury on the earth (ἐτρυφήσατε, an NT *hapax legomenon* used neutrally in the OT: Ne. 9:25; Is. 66:11; Sir. 14:4), in contrast perhaps to what they will receive later, and they have lived in indulgence (ἐσπαταλήσατε; note the pejorative tone in 1 Tim. 5:6; Ezk. 16:49; Sir. 21:15; cf. Sir. 27:13; Hermas *Man.* 6.1.6; 6.2.6; Barn. 10:3). This is precisely the life-style of the rich man in the parable of the rich man and Lazarus (Lk. 16:19–31), a life-style also condemned in other Jewish writings (Am. 2:6–8; 8:4–6; Is. 1:11–17; Eth. Enoch 98:11; 102:9–10), for it is self-indulgence in the face of the poverty of others. Whether or not James knew Luke's parable, he has painted its setting beautifully.

But this temporal existence is absurd, for it is a nourishing of one's heart (i.e. indulging one's passions or inclinations; cf. Is. 6:10; Ps. 104:15; Mk. 7:21; Lk. 21:34; and Davids, 1–79; T. Sorg, *DNTT* II, 182) in the day of slaughter. The "day of slaughter" has been a difficult term which has been emended (by adding ὡς before ἐν as in the Byzantine text tradition), shifted to the future by making ἐν equivalent to εἰς (Chaine, 118), or made an event of the past with respect to the death of the poor (Dibelius, 239; Windisch, 31). For the latter interpretation it is the day when the righteous suffer and die (Eth. Enoch 100:7; Sir. 34:22) while the wealthy feast, perhaps with specific reference to the crucifixion of Jesus (Aland, 103). However, these interpretations ignore the background of the term and the tone of the passage. While the term never appears literally in the LXX (Je. 12:3 is the closest), its equivalent does in the MT (Is. 30:24) — it is part of a long tradition of the day of God's judgment as a day of the slaughter of his enemies (Is. 30:33; 34:5–8; Je. 46:10; 50:26–27; Ezk. 39:17; Pss. 22:29; 37:20; 49:14; La. 2:21–22; Wis. 1:7; Rev. 19:17–21; cf. Grill and Is. 63:1–6; Je. 12:3; 25:34; Ezk. 21:15). More importantly, Enoch explicitly connects the judgment of the rich to such an apocalyptic day: "Ye . . . have become ready for the day of slaughter, and the day of darkness and the day of the great judgement" (Eth. Enoch 94:9, *APOT*; cf. Eth. Enoch 97:8–10; 99:15; Jub. 36:9–10; Sl. Enoch 50:5). Furthermore, the expression appears for the apocalyptic day in 1QH 15:17–18: "But the wicked thou didst create . . . to the Day of Massacre . . ." (*lywm hrgh*; Vermes's translation), and its sense occurs elsewhere in the DSS (e.g. 1QS 10:19; CD 19:15, 19; 1QM 1:9–12; 13:14). In other words, given this tradition and the apocalyptic tone of the rest of the passage, one can hardly doubt that the eschatological day of judgment is intended (so Laws, 203–204; Spitta, 134; Ropes, 290; Marty, 188; Cantinat, 228; Mussner, 197–198 — some go further to specify it as the time of Jerusalem's destruction but this is unlikely, Schlatter, 270; Feuillet, "sens," 273–279).

Here, then, is a combination of the teaching of the parable of the rich man and Lazarus with that of the rich fool. The wealthy live luxuriously, heedless of the poor, as if this is what life were for; indeed, they live as in a day of slaughter (there is perhaps some irony intended as they slaughter animals for their feasts). But the day of slaughter has arrived — their slaughter, for they are the "fatted calves," the enemies of God whom he will slaughter when he appears. The eschatological day which arrived in Jesus is moving toward its conclusion so surely that it is already here. Yet they live as if it did not exist!

(6) James adds one final, conclusive charge which rounds off the passage and bridges toward the next section of the book. "You have condemned and killed the righteous!" The sense is clearly that of judicial "murder." The term καταδικάζω is forensic enough to be parallel to the similar charge in 2:6 (ἕλκω εἰς κριτήρια; cf. LSJ, 889). The use of φονεύω gives the author's moral estimate of the result of the judicial process, an evaluation made repeatedly of the legal assaults of the rich on the poor in the Jewish piety-poverty tradition (Pss. 9:18; 10:8–9; 37:14, 32, 35; Pr. 1:11; Is. 3:10, 14; 57:1; Am. 2:6; 5:12; Pss. Sol. 3; Eth. Enoch 96:5, 8; 98:12; 99:15; 103:15; 1QH 2:21; 5:17; 15:15–17; 4QpPs37 2:7; Wis. 2:10–20). The claim of Spitta, 135, and Reicke, *Diakonie*, 51, that James depends upon the Wis. 2:20 passage remains unestablished because of a lack of verbal parallels. That legal confiscation of the property of the poor might be seen as murder appears in Sir. 34:22.

The "just one" whom the rich murder might be a particular person, either Christ (as in Acts 3:14; 7:52; 22:14; 1 Pet. 3:18; 1 Jn. 2:1, 29; 3:7; cf. Is. 53:11: only the first three passages have a titular use of the term; cf. older commentators; Feuillet, "sens"; Longenecker, 46–47) or James himself (Rustler, 59; H. Greeven in Dibelius, 240 n. 58; and Euseb. *HE* 2.23). Alternatively one has a generic collective term as one would frequently observe in the passages cited (e.g. Wis. 2:20; Psalm 37; 4QpPs37). The latter appears more likely, for there is no tradition that the rich in particular killed either Jesus or James, although the author would surely include Jesus under this general category of righteous sufferer (cf. Mussner, 199; Laws, 204–206; Cantinat, 229–230).

The οὐκ ἀντιτάσσεται ὑμῖν is normally read as a statement referring to the nonresistance of the righteous in the tradition of the gospel (Is. 53:7; Mt. 5:39; Rom. 12:19; 1 Pet. 2:23; Hermas *Man.* 8.10; Cantinat, 229; Laws, 206–207; Windisch, 31), and one cannot rule out this option. But we note that ἀντιτάσσεται is present tense, unlike the preceding verbs. This could just be a vivid present in the middle of a series of aorists, as in Is. 53:5–7 LXX, but the emphatic position of the verb makes this interpretation unlikely (cf. Ropes, 292). Since the verb can mean either legal or military resistance (LSJ, 164; MM, 49), it seems more likely in the light of its climactic position and passages such as Rev. 6:9–11 that one should read this as a question, as Hort did in the WH text: "Does he not resist you?" Yes, he does; by calling for justice before God's throne. The just one died quietly (from starvation or outright murder), but he still speaks. They have killed the poor righteous Christians, *but* their voice is now still resisting them (the language may recall God's act in 4:6), like the wages still crying out. The eschatological day is here. This cry of doom prepares one for the following comfort addressed to the suffering Christians.

This interpretation, of course, rejects Feuillet's claim ("sens") that Christ is the Righteous One who resists the rich now in heaven (or is about to in eschatological judgment), or Ropes's claim that the righteous Christians resist their persecutors in this present world by testifying against them. This basis for the interpretation of heavenly accusation is that the passage has an eschatological tone and that parallels to such accusations exist (e.g. Revelation 6).

See further Aland; Longenecker, 46–47.

CLOSING STATEMENT 5:7–20

THE concluding major segment of the epistle flows out of the preceding one; there is little break in thought, although the addressees change. Yet one finds within this section a complex of four major paragraphs which round off the letter: 5:7–11, 12, 13–18, 19–20. The second, third, and fourth are dictated by the epistolary form and thus respectively speak of oaths, a health wish, and the purpose for writing, all of which one would expect in the literary epistle and which are also found in the endings of 1 John and Hebrews (cf. Francis). The first paragraph summarizes the theme of rich and poor (*Armenfrömmigkeit*) by combining the response of the poor (ἀδελφοί) with the call to patient endurance and community harmony, while the next three paragraphs have to do with the use of the tongue and resistance to sin. Thus there is a merging of themes in this summary section and some disjointedness as the redactor pulls materials together, yet there is a real sense of unity with the rest of the book as themes are resumed and brought into dynamic relationship with one another.

1. ENDURANCE IN THE TEST 5:7–11

The first closing paragraph (5:7–11) calls upon the readers to exercise patience (μακροθυμέω, the root appears 4 times in the 5 verses, or ὑπομονή, the root appears twice), resuming the theme first appearing in 1:2–4, 12. Patience, not resistance, is the virtue of the poor, for their hope is the parousia. While waiting they must preserve community harmony (cf. 4:11–12; 3:1–18; 1:19–21), for the same one who will destroy the rich will also judge them. They can take courage, however, from the stories they have learned about the suffering of the prophets (e.g. Hebrews 11) and particularly Job, that generous succorer of the poor whose tale speaks of consummate patience. God loves them and has not forgotten them.

(7) The response of the suffering Christians (ἀδελφοί) is given in the light of the sure and present judgment of the rich (οὖν); one cannot read 5:7–11 separately from 5:1–6. The members of the Christian community

181

are to be patient (μακροθυμήσατε; the verb is used here in 3 of its 10 occurrences in the NT). Patience has already been indicated as a cardinal virtue produced by testing (1:2–4, 12), although in that case a synonym, ὑπομονή, was used; Col. 1:11 places the two terms in parallel. As in 4:1–3, the author shifts vocabulary for stylistic reasons (variety) or theological reasons or redactional reasons (use of a new source), but does not shift his basic theme. Here the latter two reasons may come into play, for the passages do not have the same style as chap. 1, and the element of suffering due to other people may make μακροθυμία the preferred term. What is clear is that the author is calling on Christians not to take the judgment of the wicked into their own hands, but to wait for God to avenge them; at the same time they are called not to compromise the faith; both giving in to the world and attacking the world are wrong (e.g. Heb. 6:12, 15; 10:32–39; 12:1ff.; 1 Pet. 4:12–19; Rom. 12:9–21; Rev. 13:10; 14:12; even in Revelation the ἅγιοι never strike back, but Christ avenges them; cf. F. Horst, *TDNT* IV, 374–387; F. Hauck, *TDNT* IV, 581–588; U. Falkenroth and C. Brown, *DNTT* II, 768–776).

They are to be patient, enduring "until the parousia of the Lord." Two basic interpretations of this phrase have been offered. One group, noting that in chap. 4 and 5:1–6 it is God who will judge and that this theme is common in the OT and apocalyptic presentations of the final judgment, argues that it is *not* the coming of Christ but the coming of God in judgment that is intended.

Cf. Test. Jud. 22:2; Test. Lev. 8:11; Ass. Mos. 10:12; Eth. Enoch 92–105; Test. Abr. 13; Syr. Bar. 55:6; Hermas *Sim.* 5.5.3; 2 Clem. 7:1; some of these passages use παρουσία, but as Dibelius, 243, notes, there are textual problems in each case; Spitta, 136–137; Meyer, 121; Bousset, 291; Easton, 66; Cantinat, 232; Feuillet, "sens," 261–280. Feuillet's arguments founder on the fact that he must interpret all of Matthew in this sense, as well as reinterpret Jas. 5:1–6; he does not succeed; cf. criticisms in Dibelius, 243; Mussner, 201. The other arguments depend upon reading the epistle as basically a Jewish document.

The majority of commentators note the strongly Christian tone throughout James, the doubtfulness of references to the parousia of God, and the common technical sense of parousia in the NT, and therefore argue that the event referred to here is the coming of Christ (1 Cor. 15:23; 1 Thes. 2:19; 4:15; 5:23; 2 Thes. 2:1; 2 Pet. 1:16; 3:4; 1 Jn. 2:28; Mt. 24:3, 27, 37, 39; cf. A. Oepke, *TDNT* V, 865–871; G. Braumann, *DNTT* II, 898–901; Dibelius, 242–243; Mussner, 201; Laws, 208–209). This seems to be the most reasonable position, for James is not a thinly Christianized Jewish document, but a thoroughly Christian one; it is hard to see how a Christian writer could mean anything else by this term, and it is easy to understand how James, like most NT writers, could refer to God as judge in one breath and Christ in the next (e.g. Revelation). The Christian hope, then, is the coming of Christ when all the wrongs suffered will be set right.

But waiting for God to act is a long process (cf. 2 Peter 3!), so James gives his readers an example of such patience from everyday life. "Behold," he says, using a strong introduction to his example, the second of four uses of ἰδού in this chapter (it appears only in chaps. 3 and 5), "the farmer." The picture is that of the small farmer in Palestine, not the hired laborers of 5:4 (ἐργατής), who were often once small farmers and dreamed of yet owning land, but who were either not the firstborn or had lost their land to large landholders due to hard times. The small farmer plants his carefully saved seed and hopes for a harvest, living on short rations and suffering hunger during the last weeks. The whole livelihood, indeed the life itself, of the family depends on a good harvest: the loss of the farm, semistarvation, or death could result from a bad year. So the farmer waits for an expected future event (ἐκδέχεται); no one but he could know how precious the grain really is (τὸν τίμιον καρπὸν τῆς γῆς is one indication that the author has a small farmer in view; cf. Mussner, 202). He must exercise patience no matter how hungry he is (μακροθυμῶν), for he waits with a view toward the coming harvest (ἐπ' αὐτῷ). This patience must last "until he receives the early and late rain."

A P 33 have tried to clarify by adding ἄν after ἕως; more importantly ὑετὸν has been added as an interpretation in A P and the Byzantine tradition and καρπὸν in ℵ 398 etc., apparently by someone ignorant of Palestine and the LXX, while p⁷⁴ B it. Vg have preserved the shorter reading of the text that explains both the others.

The thing which receives the rain is probably the fruit (i.e. αὐτῷ), not the farmer, but the reference to the early and latter rains has caused a lot of discussion. First, the expression occurs elsewhere only in the LXX (Dt. 11:14; Je. 5:24; Ho. 6:3; Joel 2:24; Zc. 10:1). Second, the phenomenon of early rain (October-November or December-January) and latter rain (March-April), both of which are utterly necessary for proper growth, is limited to the east end of the Mediterranean (i.e. from the Taurus Mountains south to the Judean Negeb; Baly, 47–52; Dalman, I, 115ff., 172ff., 291ff.). On the one hand, Dibelius, 243–244, Marshall, 106, and Laws, 212, claim that this was simply a traditional image noted by the author in passing, especially since Dt. 11:14 is part of the *Shema'* and thus recited daily (cf. Mussner, 202). On the other hand, Hadidian, 228; Kittel, 81; Mayor, 162; Adamson, 191; and Oesterley, 392ff., 401, all argue that this reference points to a Palestinian provenance. Several reasons may be given: (1) the ellipsis of ὑετὸν is more likely as part of James's habitual vernacular style (e.g. 3:11) than as part of a reference to scripture; (2) there is no evidence in rabbinic literature, other Jewish materials,

the Apostolic Fathers, or early apologists (Ropes, 297) that this image
was used outside Palestine or in Christian tradition; (3) the themes of the
passages cited do not match the theme of patience in James, so at least
the application is novel; and (4) the whole context both here and in 5:1-6
fits the agricultural situation in Palestine before AD 70. Thus it is best to
view this as a natural image from an author familiar with the climate who
pictures vividly the farmer watching anxiously but patiently until the rains
which his crop needs come.

(8) The example being finished, James draws the conclusion by repeating the imperative from 5:7: "*you* be patient as well" (the οὖν found
in p⁷⁴ ℵ L is correct in intention, but is an addition to smooth James's
grammar). The point is not the length of time one must wait (i.e. parousia
delay), but whether one will endure the period of waiting, for James explains the first imperative by a second one: "establish your hearts," meaning to stand firmly in the faith, not to give way to doubt (Jdg. 15:5-8; Pss.
57:7; 90:17; Sir. 6:37; 22:16-17; 1QH 2:7; 7:6; Rom. 1:11; 1 Thes. 3:13;
2 Thes. 2:17; Heb. 13:9; cf. G. Harder, *TDNT* VII, 655-657). The point
is not the length of the waiting, but the need to remain firm during the
interim period "before the harvest." That James does not expect the
period to be long is clear when he says the parousia of the Lord (cf. 5:7)
is near (ἤγγικεν). While famous for its use with the kingdom of God in
the synoptics, e.g. Mk. 1:15, ἤγγικεν is used several times of the parousia
(Rom. 13:12; Heb. 10:25; 1 Pet. 4:7). The tension of 5:1-6 is taken up
again; the day is virtually upon them; the finish line is just ahead: the
important point is not to give up now and lose all that for which one has
already suffered.

See further A. Moore, 149-151.

(9) In the context of a community under pressure and the impulses
of ἐπιθυμία/ἡδονή as they wait for the parousia, it is not surprising that
James finds it necessary to warn against disunity in the community. While
Dibelius, 244, feels this verse is totally separate from its context which
the new address, ἀδελφοί, *may* indicate, surely the redactor put it here
precisely because he felt it interpreted this context. One side of μακροθυμία is μὴ στενάζετε κατ' ἀλλήλων, "do not moan about one another." The important functional term here is κατ' ἀλλήλων, for generally
the idea of groaning or moaning is a proper response to painful external
circumstances (Mk. 7:34 — Jesus; Rom. 8:23; 2 Cor. 5:2, 4; in the LXX
the term is a frequent expression of Job, Isaiah, and Ezekiel, but Heb.
13:17 says one should not make others groan; cf. LSJ, 1638; BAG, 773,
for further examples). The problem arises when one groans, moans, or,
in other words, complains about (in the negative sense of "against,"

κατά) someone else, particularly if that person is within the community (for *communal* harmony is James's concern; presumably some moaning on account of the rich would be justified in the light of 5:1–6!). Such groaning is another way of expressing the μὴ καταλαλεῖτε ἀλλήλων (4:11); indeed, the sigh at the mention of a name may be eloquent itself or invite a question which in turn will produce a "reluctant" criticism, "Since you asked. . . ." This complaining, James claims, will produce judgment, i.e. will produce guilt with which God will deal severely, and thus must be avoided (ἵνα μὴ κριθῆτε).

This passage forms a commentary on the type of reciprocity expressed in Mt. 7:1, μὴ κρίνετε, ἵνα μὴ κριθῆτε, *contra* Dibelius, 244, who feels that since James expresses no *jus talionis* he cannot be either assuming it or applying the first saying in Mt. 7:1–5 in a way different from Matthew: even the least criticism renders one liable to judgment. Such attacks on disturbances of community harmony were also necessary elsewhere, e.g. Qumran (see the references on 4:11–12; cf. Mussner, 204–205, who cites the attack on the "princes of Judah" for their complaining and hatred in CD 19:15–26, especially line 18).

The reason why such a command is especially important is that "the judge stands before the door." This idea is introduced by ἰδού, a stronger particle than γάρ in calling attention to the reason (BAG, 371), although its frequency in this chapter where γάρ is never used may make it more a stylistic preference. That the judge, probably Christ in the context of the parousia of 5:7, 8 (*contra* Laws, 213), who alone has the right to criticize the Christians (4:11–12) and who will judge the complaining Christian (e.g. 1 Cor. 3:10–17; 2 Cor. 5:10), stands before the door is an image, not of the place of judgment (i.e. the city gate, as Cantinat believes, 237), but of its imminence (Mk. 13:29 par. Mt. 24:33; Rev. 3:3, 20; cf. the sense of the parable in Mt. 24:45–51 par. Lk. 12:42–46; Mk. 13:34–37). The nearness of the eschatological day is not just an impetus to look forward to the judgment of "sinners" and so stand fast in the faith oneself (μακροθυμέω), but it is also a warning to examine one's behavior so that when the one whose footsteps are nearing finally knocks on the door, one may be prepared to open, for open one must, either for blessing or for judgment. The coming Lord is also the judge of the Christian.

(10) To strengthen the community is to stand fast under the pressure of suffering (and thus more in relation to 5:7–8 than 5:9). James refers to two examples of others who have stood firm, one general and the other specific. They are to "receive an example" (ὑπόδειγμα: positive example, Sir. 44:16; 2 Macc. 6:28, 31; 4 Macc. 17:23; Jn. 13:15; 1 Clem. 5:1; 6:1; 46:1; 63:1; Jos. *War* 6:103; Philo *Rer. Div. Her.* 256; negative example, Heb. 4:11; 2 Pet. 2:6) from the suffering (κακοπάθεια, NT *hapax legomenon,* but in LXX Mal. 1:13; 2 Macc. 2:26, 27; 4 Macc. 9:8 with ὑπομονή;

cf. κακοποθέω, 2 Tim. 2:9; 4:5) and the endurance of the prophets. The first term is more passive; namely the prophets did in fact suffer, while the second is more active; i.e. in the situation of suffering they endured. Together the words form a hendiadys (examples in BDF, § 442 [16]; cf. Björck, 1–4), i.e. the endurance of the prophets under suffering or "patience in the midst of affliction" (Björck), for it is not the suffering which forms the example but the fact that those who suffered did in fact endure patiently. In giving such an example the author is referring to well-known stories of the worthies of the OT and Hasmonean periods that his readers had probably heard from childhood (cf. ἠκούσατε in 5:11). Such narratives were frequently used to exemplify both virtues and vices and their results. A little reflection would show them they were following in great footsteps.

Besides the examples given above with ὑπόδειγμα see Ezk. 20:4–5; Sir. 44–50; 1 Macc. 2:49–64; Hebrews 11; Jub.; Test. XII; the cult of the prophets in Mt. 23:29–31; and the recalling of misdeeds against the prophets in Dn. 9:6; Test. Lev. 16; Mt. 23:29–39; Mk. 12:1–12; cf. Mussner, 205–206, who cites a large number of works on the theology of suffering and the prophet-martyr tradition.

In calling them "prophets who spoke in the name of the Lord," James is indicating that their suffering came from their service to God; he is not limiting his list to exclude nonprophets, for the rubric would include all those who confessed their faith, from Abraham through David to the Maccabean martyrs; cf. Heb. 11:32–38, which lumps such a group together, and the explicit use of κακοπάθεια in 4 Macc. 9:8. The company of those who suffered is blessed and forms the example for later Christian martyrs. The significant fact is the lack of Christian martyrs, indicating either an early date or the lack of circulation of such stories, and the lack of mention of Christ, probably because the author hesitated to group him with others (cf. Cantinat, 238, who points out that Christian literature normally mentions either Christ *or* other people as examples rather than both; when Christ is cited he is always either given as the sole example or else put in a clearly separate category).

ℵ has substituted the more Hellenistic virtue καλοκαγαθία (cf. 4 Macc. 1:10; Ign. *Eph.* 14:1) for κακοπαθία. A K L have omitted the ἐν.
See further Björck.

(11) Having cited the suffering of the "prophets," the author uses ἰδού to drive the point home: "we count those who endured blessed." The implication is clear: you will also be blessed if you remain firm. The concept of blessedness has already been mentioned in 1:12; here again and even more clearly sayings such as Mt. 5:11–12 are in mind, as well as the eulogies of the heroes of the past (cf. U. Becker, *DNTT* I, 215–218). The necessary quality for receiving this blessing is not great deeds or

ringing sermons, but patient endurance whatever the situation. The one who endures to the end will truly be saved (Mt. 10:22; 24:13; Lk. 21:19; on the eschatological tone of ὑπομένω, cf. comments on 1:3, 4, 12, and F. Hauck, *TDNT* IV, 585–588). This connection of blessing with enduring is not original in James (e.g. Theod. of Dn. 12:12; 4 Macc. 7:22), but James has certainly brought it forcefully to the attention of the Christian tradition.

In the passage in James cited above some texts substitute the present for the aorist, misunderstanding that the reference is to past worthies, for those in the present have yet to earn this blessedness.

Connecting onto the term ὑπομείναντας (and thus taking its force from the ἰδού) by using a prominent ὑπομονήν, James cites a concrete example, Job. The story of Job was a favorite in Jewish and Christian circles, so it is not in the least surprising that Job was often used as an example (e.g. Ezk. 14:14, 20; Test. Abr. 15:10; 1 Clem. 17; Clem. Alex. *Strom.* 2.103–104). More important for James's purpose is the fact that Job was a prime example of enduring under testing (cf. Korn, 68–70). More than one person has noted that Job appears less than patient in the canonical book; e.g. Cantinat, 239, cites Jb. 7:11–16; 10:18; 23:2; 30:20–23 as examples. It appears certain, therefore, that James is citing Job, not from the canonical record, but from the expanded traditions which the community had heard, such as the one which is recorded in Test. Job. When this work is examined several reasons for James's reference to Job are apparent: (1) the term ὑπομονή and its cognates are frequent (Test. Job 1.2; 4.5–4.6; 27.3–27.10; 39.11–39.13), (2) the complaints of Job so prominent in the canonical book are totally absent except in the mouth of his wife, (3) the testing is clearly cast in the form of the testing of Abraham, a testing from Satan (i.e. πειρασμός), and (4) the charity of Job is underlined (Test. Job 9–15; also in canonical Job 29:12–17; 31:16–23). Thus the example in Test. Job is one of a man who shared his goods freely but nevertheless suffered because his witness to God angered Satan. During his suffering he demonstrated consummate patient endurance and so justly received God's praise in the end. While it is unlikely that James had read the extant Greek Test. Job, it is certain that such narratives were common in his period.

See further Davids, "Tradition," 117–119; Spitta, "Testaments," 170–177.

Having cited the patience of Job, James adds καὶ τὸ τέλος κυρίου εἴδετε. (The reading ἔλεος in 1739 is secondary, perhaps coming from the last clause of the verse; the reading ἴδετε A B² L P Ψ 33 [text = ℵ B* K etc.] is also secondary despite Dibelius's doubts, 247–248, for [1] James never uses the imperative of οἶδα, [2] the sentence structure with ἴδετε would be very awkward [κυρίου. ἴδετε ὅτι . . .], [3] the reading accepted forms a parallel between ἠκούσατε and εἴδετε, a common construction in James, and [4] the earlier witnesses do appear on the side of the text as is.) But what "end of the Lord" do they know? While some have resorted to emendation (e.g. Preuschen, 79, removes κυρίου and adds a verb like θεωροῦντες), and others have referred τὸ τέλος to the parousia (Strobel, 259, although the aorist tense of εἴδετε rules this out), many have tried to see this phrase as expressing the results of Christ's (i.e. κυρίου) sufferings and death (i.e. his exaltation; Augustine; Bede; Bischoff, 274–279). Such a dual meaning of κύριος in the passage is unlikely (in the previous phrase it must mean God), and particularly since analogous examples of τέλος κυρίου are available which clearly mean "the result the Lord produced" or "the result of the life of the person" (Test. Gad 7:4; Test. Ben. 4:1; Test. Ash. 6:4; 4 Macc. 12:3; Wis. 2:16–17; 3:19; m. Ab. 1:5, sôp = τέλος; cf. Heb. 13:7; the construction itself is surely a Semitism). The sense of the phrase is not that of teleological end, i.e. God's purpose ("the purpose of the Lord," *RSV*; cf. Mitton, 189–190) but the result God brought about as known from the story of Job, i.e. blessing. As in the case of Job, the Christian can expect ultimate good.

The reason for this hope is clear: God is not vicious; he does not love watching people suffer. Rather he is compassionate. Πολυσπλαγχνός is a biblical *hapax legomenon* which occurs later in Hermas (*Man.* 4.3.5; *Sim.* 5.7.4, also used of κύριος = God), then still later in Clem. Alex. *Quis Dives Salvatur* 39.6; Act. Thom. 119 (cf. πολυσπλαγχνία, appearing as a divine attribute in Hermas *Vis.* 1.3.2; 2.2.8; 4.2.3; *Man.* 9.2); the term is an intensive one apparently created in the church, perhaps by James. God is also merciful (οἰκτίρμων). This is the teaching of the Psalms (Pss. 103[102]:8; 112[111]:4 [in LXX ἐλεήμων καὶ οἰκτίρμων ὁ κύριος]; cf. Sir. 2:11) and of the general tone of scripture. God cares for those who suffer; he will bring a good end out of it all (Rom. 8:28ff.). Thus, as the example of Job shows, if one is patient enough the time will come (i.e. in the parousia) when the good end of the Lord will appear.

See further Bischoff; Gordon; Preuschen; Strobel, 255ff., 259.

2. REJECTION OF OATHS 5:12

(12) The next topic which the author takes up is that of oaths. There is certainly a continuity here with his general concern over the use of the tongue (1:26; 3:1–17; perhaps 4:1–3; 5:9), but a specific connection to anything which precedes is unlikely, although the threat of impending judgment (ὑπὸ κρίσιν πέσητε) may have made its position here logical (cf. παρουσία in 5:7, 8; ὁ κριτής in 5:9). The δέ shows a disjunction in thought,

as does the return to the introductory formula ἀδελφοί μου, and the πρὸ πάντων should be viewed as an emphatic epistolary introduction (e.g. 1 Pet. 4:8; 3 Jn. 2; and the papyri cited in Cantinat, 241; Mitton, 191; Mussner, 211), not as referring to the preceding and making 5:12 more important (Reicke, 56). Here one has what could be an "asterisk" or similar mark in the margin in modern printing, for it calls attention to the next issue to be discussed. The placing of this command in the closing of the epistle has to do with the normal use of an oath in the conclusion of such a letter (see above, pp. 26, 181).

The swearing of oaths was limited in the OT to those which one would fulfil (Ex. 20:7; Lv. 19:12; Nu. 30:3). In some cases the swearing of oaths was commanded (Ex. 22:10–11) or indeed done by God (Nu. 14:21; Dt. 4:31; 7:8). In the NT one can also find examples of oaths used or responded to by Jesus (Mt. 26:63) and by Paul (Rom. 1:9; Gal. 1:20; 2 Cor. 1:23; 11:11; 1 Thes. 2:5, 10; Phil. 1:8). In the OT there is already a problem with using oaths too lightly (Je. 5:2; 7:9; Ho. 4:2; Zc. 5:3–4; Mal. 3:5), and the warnings against oaths were later expanded into a counsel to avoid oaths whenever possible so as to prevent their frivolous use (Sir. 23:9, 11; Philo *Decal.* 84–95; *Spec. Leg.* 2.2–38; cf. J. Schneider, *TDNT* V, 459–461; Laws, 221–222), which was similar to the counsel of Epictetus and other Greeks, although on different grounds (Epict. *Ench.* 33.5; cf. Bonhöffer, 30–31, and the literature cited by Dibelius, 248–249). Some Jewish groups, notably the Essenes, totally prohibited oaths except those of their initiation into the group or of properly constituted court procedures (Jos. *War* 2:135, 139–143; *Ant.* 15:370–372; CD 9:9–10; 15:1–2, 8–10; 16:8–9; 1QS 2:1–18; 5:8–11; cf. Sl. Enoch 49:1; b. B. M. 49a). It is such groups which form the closest parallel to the total rejection of oaths in the NT, for the reasons given include not just the prohibition of the use of the divine name, but also the need for simple, honest speech at all times.

The prohibition in James is obviously a variant of the Jesus logion in Mt. 5:33–37 (cf. Mt. 23:16–22):

Mt. 5:34–37	*Jas. 5:12*
μὴ ὀμόσαι ὅλως	μὴ ὀμνύετε
μήτε ἐν τῷ οὐρανῷ . . .	μήτε τὸν οὐρανὸν
μήτε ἐν τῇ γῇ . . .	μήτε τὴν γῆν
μήτε εἰς Ἱεροσόλυμα . . .	
μήτε ἐν τῇ κεφαλῇ σου . . .	
	μήτε ἄλλον τινὰ ὅρκον
ἔστω δὲ ὁ λόγος ὑμῶν	ἤτω δὲ ὑμῶν
ναὶ ναί, οὒ οὔ	τὸ ναὶ ναὶ καὶ τὸ οὒ οὔ
τὸ δὲ περισσὸν τούτων	ἵνα μὴ ὑπὸ κρίσιν πέσητε
ἐκ τοῦ πονηροῦ ἐστιν	

Several points can be raised about their relationship. First, James does not cite this as from Jesus, but then he never cites anything as being from Jesus, despite his obvious closeness to the tradition. The readers may well have been expected to know the source. Second, the tradition in Matthew is fuller, with more examples and explanations of the examples than in James (the examples do in fact conform to known oath formulae and circumlocutions of later Judaism, e.g. Philo *Spec. Leg.* 2.2; b. Shebu. 35b; Str-B I, 330–336). Third, the grammar of the tradition in James, using the accusative after ὀμνύω, is more classical, while Matthew's ἐν plus dative is a typical NT structure (cf. Mt. 23:16–22), which conforms to Semitic usage (Robertson, 471; the present tense in James implies the prohibition of an existing practice, while the aorist in Matthew does not, MHT III, 75–77). Fourth, later Christian tradition knows a mixed saying-form which fits James's meaning (Justin *Apol.* 1.16.5; Clem. Alex. *Strom.* 5.99.1; 7.50.5; 7.67.5; Clem. *Hom.* 19.2.4; cf. Dibelius, 250). Fifth, Matthew's ending points to the demonic as the source of oaths, while James threatens judgment (the εἰς ὑπόκρισιν instead of ὑπὸ κρίσιν in P and the Byzantine text tradition is an obvious misreading and weakening; other textual variants are harmonizations), but the sense of the two prohibitions is obviously the same.

The real question, then, is whether Matthew is something of a nomistic expansion of the core tradition. Those who hold to the exclusive originality of James argue that Matthew has taken the prohibition against oaths and made it into a substitute oath, i.e. your strongest affirmation or negation should be the doubled yes or no (as in *Mek. Yitro* [*Bahodesh*] 5 [66b]; Sl. Enoch 49:1; 42:9; cf. Dibelius, 249–251; Meyer, 162–163; Marty, 202; Minear; Cantinat, 243–244). This explanation is not necessary, for there is Semitic evidence that the yes-yes, no-no formula means "let your word be (an outer) yes (which is truly an inner) yes, etc." (e.g. *Sipre* Lv. 91b on Lv. 19:36; b. B. M. 49a; cf. Kutsch, 206–218; Stählin, 119–120; Mussner, 215–216). If this evidence is accepted there is no essential difference between Matthew and James, who states "let your yes be (a true) yes and your no (a true) no." The structural variety would indicate that the saying circulated in more than one form in the church with James having a shorter, more classical form and Matthew a longer, more Semitic one. Priority cannot be established, especially since mixed forms were also known.

James, then, prohibits not official oaths, such as in courts (for none of the sayings in Jewish or Christian sources touches on these; cf. Windisch, 32–33), but the use of oaths in everyday discourse to prove integrity. The community member ought not to use oaths, for his yes or no should be totally honest, making oaths unnecessary; truthfulness is the issue. Since God holds one to this standard, oaths are dangerous, for they make some speech more honest than other speech. Thus they must be avoided to keep this deceptive idea from bringing God's judgment (in the final judgment, as the context shows) upon one when he is less than truthful. The demand of the church was for absolute truthfulness in all speech, nothing more and nothing less (cf. 2 Cor. 1:15–2:4, where Paul defends himself against the charge of being less than truthful).

See further Kutsch; Laws, 219–224; Minear; Stählin.

3. HELPING ONE ANOTHER THROUGH PRAYER/FORGIVENESS 5:13–18 (HEALTH)

(13) In this third segment of the concluding section (cf. above, p. 181) James returns to the theme of prayer, partly in summary, partly because health wishes were customary in the endings of epistles, and partly because it prepares for a final exhortation to repentance. The section begins with three paratactic units which each consist of two clauses in a rhetorical asyndeton (Smyth, 484–486; Robertson, 1023, 430; BDF, § 494). Structurally this verse is similar to 1 Cor. 7:18, 21, 27. Dibelius, 252, and Mussner, 217, following Bultmann, 15 (cf. Thyen, 40–63), argue that this structure is a declarative sentence followed by an imperative: "Someone among you suffers. Let him pray!" Yet the rhetorical force is just as strong if this construction is considered as in the Nestle and UBS texts, as well as in most translations (although *Zürcher* and *JB* restructure the two clauses into the "if . . . then" form), a question followed by an imperative: "Does someone among you suffer? Let him pray!" James uses questions frequently (22 in all); 3:13 is a parallel type of construction where the τίς is clearly interrogative, and the examples given for the declarative structure are either not that close to James (Philo *Jos.*144; M. Ant. 8.50.1; Teles 6.14; Dem. *De Cor.* 18.274 all lack the τίς, the indicative verb, particularly in first place in the clause, or the imperative) or are best understood as questions plus imperative (1 Cor. 7:18). Thus the style is the lively discourse of oral style, but the conditional nature of the constructions appears clearly in the interrogative first clause (Cantinat, 245).

In this paragraph James turns from suffering to joy and back to suffering. The person who is suffering misfortune is to pray. The misfortune expressed in κακοπαθεῖ is not illness, but physical circumstances or personal situations that cause the person distress. In other words, the inner experience of having to endure misfortune is indicated more than a specific form of misfortune (BAG, 398; W. Michaelis, *TDNT* V, 936–937, who cites Josephus's using the term especially for military misfortune; cf. 2 Tim. 2:9; 4:5). In the context (although perhaps not as originally formulated) persecutions like those of the prophets (5:10), the suffering at the hands of the wealthy, and similar personally distressing situations should be included. The point James makes is that one ought not to complain or strike out, one ought not even to bear it with quiet resignation as the Stoics advised, but rather one should pray, i.e. act as the pious Hebrew did in the Psalms (e.g. Pss. 30; 50:15; 91:15; Pss. Sol. 15:1); one should cry out to God and trust in him to redress the wrong and correct the evil. God is one who can be trusted "in the dark."

On the other hand, if one is in good spirits, i.e. joyful or of good courage even if the external situation looks poor (cf. Acts 27:22, 25; Symmachus Ps. 32:11; Pr. 15:15), one should also not forget God. Rather, one should sing and praise God. Ψάλλω appears 56 times in the LXX; originally indicating a song with string accompaniment (Pss. 33[32]:2, 3; 98[97]:4, 5; 147[146]:7; 149:3), it generalized to indicate any song of praise (Pss. 7:17[18]; 9:2, 11[3, 12]; etc.). This instruction fits with the NT theme of private and public praise (1 Cor. 14:15; Eph. 5:19; cf. Col. 3:16), which was expressed in either rational forms or "spiritual" forms. James, then, wants God remembered in all situations, good as well as bad. Turning to God in need is half the truth; turning to him in praise either in the church or alone when one is cheerful (whatever the situation) is the other half. God is not just an errand boy to help human need, but one who deserves worship and praise at all times (Phil. 4:4, 6; Eph. 5:20; 1 Thes. 5:16–18) and a person to whom one may relate no matter what the circumstance.

(14) Finally, one might find himself in a third condition which was neither external suffering nor inner cheerfulness, namely, ill. It is true that ἀσθενέω may indicate weakness of any form (e.g. Rom. 4:19; 1 Cor. 8:9; 2 Cor. 11:29; cf. BAG, 114, for other meanings), but the contrast with κακοπαθεῖ, the need to call the elders to him, the use of oil, and the two terms σώσει and κάμνοντα indicate that illness is intended. Here there is no question of outward reverses through the evil in others, suffering for the faith, or similar sources of internal distress (i.e. 5:13); the person is sick, which means that the cause lies outside the human sphere: either God or evil powers must be involved.

In this circumstance the person is directed to "call the elders of the church." This at once indicates that the person is very ill (i.e. too ill to go to the elders so presumably he sends friends or relatives for the elders) and that the office of elder was already established in the church. The attempt of Spitta, 144, to read ἐκκλησίας as if it were συναγωγή or qāhāl, for which the LXX does use ἐκκλησία, e.g. Sir. 30:27, and thereby see these people as Jewish elders analogous to the rabbis of b. B. B. 116a; b. Hag. 3a; and similar narratives, is surely wrong in terms of early Christian use of ἐκκλησία and the role of Jewish elders (cf. even Meyer, 163–167). Nor is K. L. Schmidt, TDNT III, 513, correct to refer the elders to the church "as a whole." When the office was established is hard to determine, for while there were Jewish antecedents (Ex. 3:16; 24:1, 9; Numbers 11; Dt. 5:23; 19:12; Ezr. 10:14; Sus. 5, 29, 34; Mt. 26:3), as one would expect in a patriarchal society, the term is never used of a Christian office in the gospels, but it suddenly appears in the early narratives of Acts (11:30; 14:23; 15:2; 20:17) and the epistles (1 Tim. 3; 5:17; Tit. 1:5; 1 Pet. 5:1; 2 Jn. 1; cf. Phil. 1:1). There is never any discussion of the propriety of the office, so it is reasonable to conclude that it was absorbed from the synagogue, although given a distinctly Christian character (G. Bornkamm, *TDNT* VI, 651–683; cf. the literature cited by Mussner, 219, and L. Coenen, *DNTT* I, 192–201). One notices that in James it is not just any older person who is called, but officials, the elders of the church, which in this case is surely the local congregation (Rom. 1:7; 1 Cor. 1:2; 4:17; 11:16; 1 Thes. 2:14; although in the cases of Rome and Corinth the church in the locality surely included more than one congregation; cf. Stuhlmacher, 70–75). The call is a general call; whether one or many or all the elders respond is not mentioned, although the plural verb indicates James expects several to come.

The actions of the elders indicates their specific Christian function. They pray over (ἐπ') the person (the preposition gives the picture of the prayer directed toward the person or perhaps of hands laid upon the person in prayer and anointing), which was well known among Jews (Pss. 35:13; 41:4; Jb. 2:11; Tob. 1:19; Sir. 7:35; 31:9–15; b. B. B. 116a; b. Ber. 34b (Bar.); b. Sanh. 101; *Abot R. Nat.* 41; 1QapGen 20:21–22, 29), anointing the person with oil simultaneously (while the participle indicates that the prayer rather than the oil is the primary act, the construction reads naturally with the anointing being part of the prayer act). The use of oil in healing was not uncommon in the ancient world (Is. 1:6; Je. 8:22; Mk. 6:13; Lk. 10:34; Jos. *Ant.* 17:172; *War* 1:657; Life Adam 36; Apoc. Mos. 9:3; Sl. Enoch 22:8–9; 8:35; Philo *Som.* 2.58; Plato *Menex.* 238; Pliny *Nat. Hist.* 23.39–40; Galen 2.10; cf. H. Schlier, *TDNT* I, 230–232). But the function of the oil in James is not medicinal except insofar as it partakes of the eschatological oils (see Life Adam 36; Apoc. Mos. 9:3; Is. 61:3). Thus it is either the outward sign of the inward power of prayer or, more likely, a sacramental vehicle of divine power (Dibelius, 252), as in Mk. 6:13.

The anointing is "in the name of the Lord" (the omission of this in B and of τοῦ in A 33 is surely an error; cf. Daube, 236). The calling out of Christ's name in baptism (Acts 2:38; 8:16; 10:48; 19:5; Mt. 28:19, two of which use ἐν; cf. Jas. 2:7) and in the rites of healing and exorcism was normal in the early church (Mk. 9:38; Lk. 10:17; Acts 3:6, 16; 4:7, 10; 9:34); this practice indicates that in calling out the name the baptizer/healer/exorcist was acting as the representative of God calling upon the power of God (cf. H. Bietenhard, *TDNT* V, 277, who also gives background). It is God's power (i.e. ὁ κύριος in 5:15) which will heal the person. Thus one finds three actions in the healing rite: prayer, anointing, and the calling out of the name of Jesus. This is not a magical rite, nor an exorcism (cf. Dibelius, 252), but an opening to the power of God for him to intervene whether or not the demonic is involved. It is also interesting to note that this is not the special gift of an individual, unlike 1 Cor. 12:9, 28, 30, but the power of a certain office in the church (for which no NT passage suggests gifts of healing were a qualification). This exercise of eschatological power as a duty of office is something not present in the synagogue elders. Yet it was a power regularly exercised in the church during the first centuries of its existence (cf. Kelsey, 104–199).

See further Bord; Friesenhahn; Laws, 225–232; Luff; Lys; Meinertz, "Krankensalbung"; Michaelis, 130–140; Pichar; Vermes, 61–63, 72–78.

(15) The prayer of faith (εὐχή, used in the NT twice of vows, Acts 18:18; 21:23, but frequently used in Hellenistic literature of prayer, unlike the LXX; cf. BAG, 329) will save the sick person (τὸν κάμνοντα, an NT *hapax legomenon* meaning to be weary, hard pressed, or ill; LSJ, 872–873; *LPGL,* 700; no sense of being near death is indicated, simply severe illness). The term "prayer" naturally sums up the whole action of 5:14, keeping the stress of the verse on prayer. It is a prayer of faith, i.e. the prayer which expresses trust in God and flows out of commitment to him, for only such prayers are effective (cf. Jas. 1:5–8; 4:3; Mk. 2:5; 5:34; 10:52; 6:6; Acts 14:9, where faith or lack of it is the condition for healing). The faith is that of the one who prays, i.e. of the elders who have *ex officio* healing power, not that of the sick person (who may or may not be in a condition to exercise much of anything). The promised result, which must have been normally the case (*contra* Dibelius, 255; the use of officers rather than pneumatics per se does not exclude either effectiveness or the possibility that some pneumatic gifts were part of the reason the person was selected for office), is that the power in the prayer will heal (σώσει as in Mk. 5:23, 28, 34; 10:52; Jn. 11:12, meaning heal, rather than its eschatological sense in Jas. 1:21; 2:14; 4:12; 5:20[?]). That this power is God's power comes in the parallel statement, "the Lord will raise him up" (Mk. 1:31; 2:9–12; 9:27; Mt. 9:5–7; Acts 3:7; Jos. *Ant.* 19:294); ἐγείρω thus indicates that σώζω does mean physically heal; standing up or rolling up one's bed was the natural consequence of healing. The promise was one trusted in James's church.

The rest of the verse connects the possibility of sin to the illness. Such a concept is not unknown in the NT (Mk. 2:5; Jn. 5:14; 9:2–3; 1 Cor. 11:30) and it was well known in Judaism (Job; 2 Ki. 20:3; 19:15–19; Tob. 1:18; Sir. 3:26–27; m. Shab. 2:6; b. Shab. 32a–33a; b. Ned. 41a; b. Ber. 5a; cf. Scharbert; Peake; Davids, 94–150). In James it is clear that sin is not necessarily, though it may be, the cause of illness; κἄν, "and if" (BDF, § 374), plus ᾖ πεποιηκώς, the perfect subjunctive, indicate possibility, the perfect perhaps showing that the person has not been forgiven and so is in a state of guilt. The person would do well to follow the rabbinic advice (b. Ber. 5a) and examine himself. Should sin be the cause, the healing for which the elders pray will not end with the body. It will be a total healing and include the soul, the forgiveness of sins (as in Mk. 2:5; cf. Mt. 12:32; Lk. 12:10). The statement is simple and straightforward: two promises, one for the body (the obvious, pressing need), the other for the soul. The person will be healed totally.

(16) Since healing is connected with the forgiveness of sin, one is not surprised to see the author discuss that topic next. After all, the book is moving in that direction, for 5:19–20 will continue the topic. Thus 5:16–18 are in fact a transitional section. Yet this transitional character makes 5:16 problematic, for its first segment appears to be a saying unrelated to the previous verse, yet joined to it by the οὖν (omitted in the Byzantine text) and the ἰαθῆτε. Here Cantinat, 254, and Mussner, 227, are incorrect in referring to Is. 6:10 LXX and its citations in the NT, and to Dt. 30:3; Ps. 30:2–3 [29:3–4]; 1 Pet. 2:24 (Is. 53:6); and other texts in the LXX where healing is spiritual; rather, Dibelius, 255, is surely correct when he notes that in the context the redactor must be thinking of the physical healing of 5:14–15, for except in quotations ἰάομαι always refers to physical healing in the NT. The solution to the problem appears to be that James, perhaps using a familiar saying, does move toward 5:19–20, but at the same time he consciously generalizes, making the specific case of 5:14–15 into a general principle of preventive medicine; thus the healing is general rather than referring to the specific case or, as Mussner, 227, argues, an epidemic. This interpretation avoids the problem of having to find parts for the sick person and the elders in the verse (as Ropes, 309) and takes the plurals seriously (ἐξομολογεῖσθε), while it accepts a real connection with the context as indicated by the vocabulary and grammar (cf. Laws, 232).

Christians, then, are to confess their sins to one another. The act of confession was important in Hebrew religion for individuals (Lv. 5:5; Nu. 5:7; Pss. 32:5; 38:3–4; 40:12; 51:3–5; Pr. 20:9; 28:13; Jb. 33:26–28; Pss. Sol. 9:6; 1QS 1:23–2:1; CD 20:28) as well as for the community (Lv. 16:21; 26:40; Dn. 9:4–10; Ezk. 10:1; Bar. 1:15–2:10; Jud. 9:1–14; Tob. 3:1–6; 3 Macc. 2:2–20; 6:2–15). Most of these passages are connected with healing from illness or salvation from some other distress which God has brought upon the community or person. Likewise the NT (Mk. 1:5; Mt. 3:6; Acts 19:18; 1 Jn. 1:9) and the early church knew of confession of sin (1 Clem. 51:3; 52:1; Did. 4:14; 14:1; Barn. 19:12; Hermas Vis. 1.1.3; 3.1.5–6; Sim. 9.23.4). In all of these cases (with the possible exception of 1 Jn. 1:9) there is an open and public acknowledgment of guilt, usually in the church (or community gathering in Judaism; cf. O Michel, *TDNT*

V, 202–220). The Psalms were at times a public announcement of a pre-healing private confession, while many of the passages cited picture an action which normally took place openly in preparation for healing (even John the Baptist looks to national healing) or prayer (Hermas). James, then, is speaking of confession in the community meetings (although he certainly does not exclude more detailed and private confession to another person), to one another (ἀλλήλοις). The role of the elders is not mentioned (although in 5:15 they surely listen to a confession); one can assume that they guide the process.

The confession purifies the community from sin (the reading τὰ πα-ραπτώματα in the Byzantine text is probably wrong in terms of James's 8 other uses of ἁμαρτία and its cognates, but would not change the sense), which purification prepares the members of the community to pray for one another. While the prayers might include those for forgiveness, it is more likely that they intend the healing of sick members of the community by the forgiving of the sins (the reciprocal nature of ἀλλήλων as well as the plural of εὔχεσθε, προσεύχεσθε in B A, a conformity to normal NT vocabulary, points to communal prayer). Thus the conclusion is healing, ὅπως ἰαθῆτε, whether of actual acute disease or potential disease; such prayer will lead to health in the community. Without confession and forgiveness there will be no healing (cf. 1 Cor. 11:30–32; 1 Jn. 5:16–17, which, while difficult, appear in the same relative position in their epistles).

Yet the community may well have had some question about prayer. How could it heal? Were there not unanswered prayers? How dare one pray for forgiveness? James encourages their prayers with a statement of its effectiveness. The prayer of a righteous person does have great power (πολὺ ἰσχύει). The righteous person is certainly not Elijah in heaven (Spitta, 149), nor necessarily a prophet or specially holy person in the community, although their examples were important (Gn. 18:16–33; 20:7, 17; Nu. 21:7; 11:2; 14:13–19; Jb. 42:8; Je. 15:1; Amos 7; Sir. 45:23; cf. Eichrodt, II, 443–453, 462–463; Mussner, 228); the righteous person is the community member, the person who confesses his sins and adheres to community standards (Mt. 1:19; Heb. 12:23; Jas. 5:6; 1 Pet. 4:18; 1 Jn. 3:7; Rev. 22:11; cf. H. Seebass and C. Brown, *DNTT* III, 358–377; like the Qumran covenanters, the early Christians knew themselves both sinners [1QH 4:30; 1QS 11] and righteous [1QS 9:14; 1QH 2:13]). It is the *ordinary* member in good standing, not just the elders or prophets, whose prayer is powerful, as the following example shows.

The participle ἐνεργουμένη cannot be translated with certainty. Dibelius, 256, takes it as an adjective, "the energetic prayer" (as in Wis. 15:11; 2 Cor. 4:12); Cantinat, 256, and Laws, 234, do as well; Mussner, 228, takes it as a modal or temporal participle, "when it is effective" (i.e. when it reaches God and he hears it); Ropes, 309, as a passive participle, "when it is exercised"; Mayor, 177–179, "when it is actualized (by the

Spirit)" (Rom. 8:26); and Adamson, 199, and many older English commentators as a mode of the main verb, "in its working." Certainly it does not mean that the harder one prays the more likely the prayer is to be answered. Mussner and Mayor are probably correct that this participle points to God as the active agent: prayer is strong, not the prayer itself, but God's response to it. Thus as in 5:15, "the Lord will raise . . . ," James makes the difference between prayer and magic clear. God hears prayer; thus the Christian with a clear conscience (cf. 4:3!) should pray boldly (Pss. 145:18; 34:15, 17; Pr. 15:29).

See further Althaus; Clark.

(17–18) Having encouraged the Christians to pray, James produces a powerful example to back up his assertion of the effectiveness of prayer — Elijah. Elijah was simply another human being like all those in the congregation reading the epistle (ὁμοιοπαθής, as in Acts 14:15; cf. Wis. 7:3; 4 Macc. 12:13), not a heavenly being or a specially perfect person, despite the many legends circulating about him and the story of his ascension into heaven (cf. J. Jeremias, *TDNT* II, 929–930; Str-B IV, 769; Schechter, 52–53; Molin; Mussner, 229). The example was probably selected because Elijah in legend (not in the OT) was a well-known personage with a reputation for prayer. 1 Ki. 17:1 and 18:42 never mention prayer, nor does Sir. 48:3, although 1 Ki. 17:20–22 does, so his reputation does not come from the OT. But in later tradition, e.g. 2 Esd. 7:109, he is very powerful in prayer (cf. m. Taan. 2:4; b. Sanh. 113a; j. Sanh. 10, 28b; j. Ber. 5, 9b; j. Taan. 1, 63d: the talmudic passages are elaborations of popular traditions of an earlier period; cf. Davids, "Tradition," 119–121). He was also seen as a helper of the oppressed (b. Kidd. 40a; b. Ned. 50a; b. Sanh. 109a; cf. Mk. 15:34–36).

Elijah prays and it does not rain three years and six months. The length of time itself comes from legend (as in Lk. 4:25) and is probably a symbolic round figure, half of 7, for a period of judgment (Dn. 7:25; 12:7; Rev. 11:2; 12:14; cf. Dibelius, 256–257, Mussner, 229). Again Elijah prays, and heaven gives rain and the earth sprouts her fruit. The example is constructed to underline the point of comparison. The earth receives no rain; the readers would certainly picture it as dry and dead, as the Christian might feel when ill. The prayer ascends and heaven, i.e. God (1 Ki. 8:1; 1 Sa. 12:17; Jos. *Ant.* 14:22), gives rain with the result of new life and fruitfulness, much as the person would feel when prayer was answered by healing. The example of Elijah encourages one to prayer, while the picturesque presentation would appeal to those in need at a very deep level, whether or not James is conscious of this psychological power. Prayer, then, *is* effective. The righteous members of the community dare release the power of great Elijah, for God will hear them as well.

The use of paratactic structure instead of subordinating conjunctions, the fact that καί connects all six clauses, the προσευχῇ προσηύξατο construction (as in Gn. 2:17; 31:30; Is. 30:19; Jn. 3:29; Lk. 22:15; cf. BDF, § 198; MHT I, 75–76; Plato *Symp.* 195), and the unusual τοῦ μὴ βρέξαι (as in 1 Ki. 1:35; Is. 5:6; Acts 3:12; 15:20) instead of ἵνα μὴ βρέξαι, all indicate strong Semitic background, perhaps borrowing from a Semitic source.

4. CLOSING ENCOURAGEMENT 5:19–20

James concludes with a final exhortation which on the one hand flows out of the theme of confession and forgiveness of the preceding section (5:13–18) and on the other gives what must have been the author's purpose in publishing the epistle, i.e. turning or preserving people from error (cf. the similarity in 1 Jn. 5:21). The address ἀδελφοί μου indicates that these verses are a separate unit, but one cannot look at the formal separation and juxtaposition of traditional themes beside one another without remembering that there is often an internal thematic connection, a reason why the segments are placed where they are, whatever the source, as is apparent in this case.

(19) "If someone among you," begins James (ἐν ὑμῖν, which, as in 5:13, 14, could be a Semitizing construction, although there are classical parallels; MHT III, 210), indicating that, as in 5:15, 16 or in the whole of the epistle for that matter, he is thinking of the community member who apostatizes, not about missionary involvement among either Jews or gentiles (although that would be a logical extension of the passage for the modern interpreter). The possibility that this community member might "wander from the truth" forms the situation under consideration. To wander (πλανηθῇ) is to apostatize, i.e. to reject the revealed will of God and to act contrary to it, either through willfulness or the deceit of others (including demonic powers). The term is used in the LXX for transgression of the law, especially idolatry (Is. 9:15; Je. 23:17; Ezk. 33:10; cf. Ezk. 34:4; Pr. 14:8; Wis. 5:6; 12:24; Sir. 11:16). In the apocalyptic literature of later Judaism it takes on the ethical dualistic sense which it also has in Qumran (Test. Jud. 14:1, 8; 19:4; 23:1; Test. Gad 3:1; Test. Lev. 3:3; 16:1; Test. Dan 2:4; Test. Sim. 2:7; etc.; 1QS 3:1; 5:4; CD 3:1; 4:14; 5:20; Satanic influence is generally seen behind these actions; cf. H. Braun, *TDNT* VI, 233–253, who unfortunately connects the data too closely to Gnosticism). This same sense of the rejection of the right way and wandering into moral corruption (often due to the devil) appears in the NT: Mt. 18:12–13; 24:4–5, 11; Mk. 12:24, 27; 13:5–6; Rom. 1:27; Eph. 4:14; 2 Thes. 2:11; 2 Tim. 3:13; Tit. 3:3; 1 Pet. 2:25; 2 Pet. 2:15, 18; 1 Jn. 2:26; 4:6; Rev. 2:20. Thus the seriousness of the problem appears from the first, particularly since morally corrupt behavior was neither accepted nor glossed over in the early church, but exposed and rejected.

The wandering is "from the truth" (the substitution of ὁδοῦ or addition of τῆς ὁδοῦ in p⁷⁴ ℵ 33 81 is clearly an alteration motivated by traditional phraseology, i.e. "the way of truth," and the terminology in 5:20). This fact does not make it in any sense intellectual and less practical. Truth is a way to go, a way of life in Judaism (Pss. 25:4-5; 26:3; 86:11; Tob. 3:5; 1QS 1:12, 26; 3:19; 4:17; etc.) as in the NT (Mt. 22:16; Jn. 3:21; 14:6; Rom. 1:18; Eph. 6:14; 1 Pet. 1:22; 1 Jn. 1:6). That it is this sense of truth which is intended becomes clear in the next verse where the way (ἐκ πλάνης ὁδοῦ αὐτοῦ) becomes the parallel idea, for the "way" of a person is not simply his thoughts, but his life-style (cf. Jas. 1:8; Dt. 11:28; 30:19; Pss. 1:1; 101:2; 139:24; Pr. 2:19; Sir. 21:10; Mt. 7:13-14; 21:32; 22:6 par. Mk. 12:14; Lk. 1:79; Acts 9:2; 13:10; 19:20; 24:22; 1 Cor. 4:17; 12:31; Jude 11). Thus to be turned ἐκ πλάνης ὁδοῦ (there is Semitic coloring in the expression in the lack of the article, BDF, § 259) is to be turned from a wrong way of life, an error of life-style (Wis. 12:24; Pr. 2:15; cf. Is. 9:15; Ezk. 34:4; Wis. 5:6). The person must be turned from the wrong way to the right one (cf. Did. 1), from falsehood to truth.

Those in the community who have erred from the truth or are in error with respect to their life-style are those disregarding some of the moral norms of the community and thus are in need of someone to bring them back, to turn them (ἐπιστρέψῃ τις αὐτόν). This "about-face" is well known in the OT and NT (Is. 6:10; Ezk. 33:11; Sir. 18:12; Wis. 16:7; Acts 3:19; 9:35; 2 Cor. 3:16), as is the desire (or even command) to motivate others to turn (Lv. 19:17; Ps. 51:13; Ezk. 3:17-21; 33:7-9; Sir. 28:2-3; Test. Ben. 4:5; b. Shab. 54b; 1QS 10:26-11:1; CD 13:9-10; Mt. 18:12-15; Gal. 6:1; 1 Thes. 5:14; 2 Thes. 3:15; 2 Tim. 2:25; 1 Jn. 5:16; Jude 23; Polycarp 6:1). The promise James is making is to those in the community who see the person in error and in proper meekness and humility (cf. 3:17!) attempt to turn him back to the narrow way, the true way of the community.

(20) Such a Christian should remember or become aware of the teaching of the church on such matters (the γινωσκέτω ὅτι read in ℵ A K P Vg etc. is omitted in p⁷⁴ and read as γινώσκετε ὅτι in B 69 etc.; the latter reading is probably a scribal error or an attempt to bring the verb into line with the previous plural imperatives; it could indicate a new teaching to be given or, more likely, an exhortation to be fully aware and act on what one has already heard; cf. Metzger, 685-686). This teaching is that such an action of bringing another to repentance, i.e. restoring him to the community, "will save his soul from death and cover a multitude of sins." The concept of saving a soul from death is clear enough, for death is plainly the final result of sin, usually thought of as eternal death or the last judgment (Dt. 30:19; Jb. 8:13; Pss. 1:6; 2:12; Pr. 2:18; 12:28; 14:12; Je. 23:12; Jude 23; 2 Esd. 7:48; Syr. Bar. 85:13; Did. 1; Test. Abr.

10; cf. W. Schmithals, *DNTT* I, 430–441). That sin can result in physical death is also clear (1 Cor. 15:30, as well as many of the above OT examples) and this may be part of James's meaning (as in 5:14–16), but the tone appears to go beyond physical death and recognize death as an eschatological entity, at least where one dies in sin (cf. 1:15). It is the soul, i.e. the whole person (cf. comment on 1:21; Moule, 185; C. Brown, *DNTT* III, 676–689), which is liable to death. It is probable that one should read "his soul" (ψυχὴν αὐτοῦ with א A P 33 it. Vg), not simply "a soul" (ψυχήν with K Ψ) or "a soul from death itself" (ψυχὴν ἐκ θανάτου αὐτοῦ with p⁷⁴ B), partly because of the weight of the witnesses and partly because it explains both the other variants.

Parallel to saving the person from death is the idea of covering a multitude of sins. To cover sin is normally to procure forgiveness (Pss. 32:1; 85:2; Dn. 4:24; Sir. 5:6; Tob. 4:10; Rom. 4:7). This idea of "a multitude of sins," which here serves to describe not the state of the sinner but the extent of the forgiveness, also has biblical precedents (Pss. 5:10; 85:2; Ezk. 28:17; Sir. 5:6; 1QH 4:19). The expression "covers a multitude of sins" is found in Pr. 10:12 ("love covers a multitude of sins") and is quoted in 1 Pet. 4:8; 1 Clem. 49:5; 2 Clem. 16:4 (cf. 1 Cor. 13:4–7). It is possible that James is dependent for his expression on the Jewish Christian tradition which contained that phrase (not on the LXX, for it is not similar at all; cf. Ropes, 316); in later Christian tradition this was considered a dominical saying (Clem. Alex. *Paed.* 3.91.3; *Didascalia* 4; cf. Dibelius, 258). Spitta, 152, may well be correct in asserting that the idea by Christian times was the erasing of the sins from the record on the heavenly tablets (cf. Sir. 3:30; Tob. 4:40; Eth. Enoch 98:7; 100:10; Test. Abr. 12:13), but while in harmony with the apocalyptic vision of James, his hypothesis goes beyond the evidence. One must conclude, then, that the image is one of forgiving sins, of making atonement for sins.

Whose soul is saved? whose sin is covered? It is at this point that there is disagreement. There is certainly evidence that turning others to repentance would procure salvation or forgiveness or reward for the "preacher," not only in postbiblical texts (m. Ab. 5:18; b. Yom. 87a; Barn. 19:10; 2 Clem. 15:1; 17:2; Epistola Apostolarum 39; Pistis Sophia 104; cf. Dibelius, 259–260), but also in some biblical texts (Ezk. 3:18–21; 33:9; 1 Tim. 4:16). Thus one could interpret this passage to say that the "Christian" who knows of another's sin is responsible, that when he turns the other he fulfils the responsibility, and that he thus saves his own soul, covering the sins of himself or of the person caught in sin (cf. Cantinat, 262). The majority of commentators, however, believe that the soul saved is that of the sinner, while the sins covered are those of the converter, or both the converter and the sinner (Dibelius, 258–260; Mussner, 253; Laws, 240–241; Ropes, 315–316). This interpretation is possible, although the need to assign the one promise to one party and the other to another appears illogical; James is quite able to express parallel ideas in parallel phrases (cf. 4:7–9!). More than likely they both refer to the same person and Dibelius has simply read later doctrine into an early phrase which would not have appeared to express it without the later parallels. The most likely antecedent, αὐτοῦ, is the sinner (the αὐτοῦ with ψυχήν referring to the αὐτοῦ with ὁδοῦ) and thus both phrases probably refer to his forgiveness: he is saved from destruction and freed of his sins through repentance. One cannot, however, rule out the other interpretation which stresses responsibility for the brother.

James, then, concludes with the purpose of his work. He does not discuss sins simply to moralize or condemn. He discusses sin to point out to erring community members the results of their behavior and to bring them to repentance. He hopes to save them from damnation and procure forgiveness for their sins. It is this apostolic goal he urges on his readers, and having encouraged them to follow in his steps and take up where he ends, he concludes the epistle (cf. 1 Jn. 5:21).

INDEX OF AUTHORS

INDEX OF SUBJECTS

206

INDEX OF GREEK WORDS DISCUSSED

INDEX OF ARAMAIC – HEBREW
WORDS AND PHRASES

INDEX OF WORKS CITED

4. DEAD SEA SCROLLS

5. RABBINIC WRITINGS